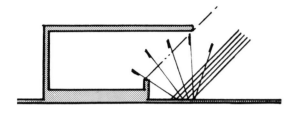

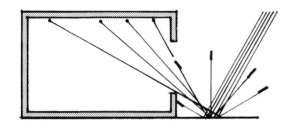

WILLIAM M. C. LAM

SUNLIGHTING

AS FORMGIVER FOR ARCHITECTURE

VNR VAN NOSTRAND REINHOLD COMPANY
_____ NEW YORK

Printed in the United States of America

Designed by Ernie Haim

Van Nostrand Reinhold Company Inc.
115 Fifth Avenue
New York, New York 10003

Van Nostrand Reinhold Company Limited
Molly Millars Lane
Wokingham, Berkshire RG11, 2PY, England

Van Nostrand Reinhold
480 La Trobe Street
Melbourne, Victoria 3000, Australia

Macmillan of Canada
Division of Canada Publishing Corporation
164 Commander Boulevard
Agincourt, Ontario M1S 3C7, Canada

16 15 14 13 12 11 10 9 8 7 6 5 4 3 2

Library of Congress Cataloging-in-Publication Data

Lam, William M. C.
   Sunlighting as formgiver for architecture.

   Bibliography: p.
   Includes index.
   1. Architecture and solar radiation. 2. Daylighting.
I. Title.
NA2542.S6L35 1986   720'.47   85-11169
ISBN 0-442-25941-7

Contents

Preface

At the beginning of my career as an architectural lighting consultant, I wrote a series of articles in *Architectural Record*, "Lighting for Architecture" (1959-60), to remind architects that the uncomfortable, unpleasant, unattractive luminous environments characteristic of most of their new buildings were the result of their abdication of lighting design to engineers untrained in design. I tried to describe some basic rules and elements with which to order the design of lighting for buildings. I stressed the need to develop a lighting "program" that addressed and expressed the specific and complex uses of a building, rather than relying on simplistic numerical criteria.

In *Perception and Lighting as Formgivers for Architecture* (McGraw-Hill, 1977), I was able to articulate more precisely the nature of human needs and environmental objectives as a result of many years of observation, the testing of concepts with students, and interaction with clients on over 600 projects. Case studies of my projects illustrated the applications of my principles of perception and my definition of what makes a good luminous environment in "ordinary," functional working buildings such as schools, offices, hospitals, and factories, as well as buildings deemed special enough to warrant attention to aesthetics—museums, concert halls, hotels, and libraries.

My focus was thus on integrating artificial lighting to reinforce rather than distract from the architectural concepts. An important stimulus to my thinking in this period was my involvement on teams that were developing integrated systems (architectural, lighting, HVAC, structural). On these projects lighting clearly took its place along with structure as a potential "formgiver" for architecture. I suggested that the most important role of natural lighting was that of adding visual "sparkle" and excitement to the interior environment. For this attitude I was taken to task by a professor from England who wrote, "Your book is what I have been waiting for in twenty years of teaching, but I disagree on one point. You describe the use of daylight primarily for its amenity; on this side of the ocean we consider it the primary source." By that time, I had already come to agree with the criticism and wrote back saying so. This book, then, is both a correction and a continuation of my earlier book.

Specific impetus for *Sunlighting as Formgiver for Architecture* came from the energy crisis of the '70s and programs sponsored by the U.S. Department of Energy. I was challenged and stimulated by my involvement, along with other energy-conscious designers/specialists, in the AIA Energy Inform and SERI Passive Solar Commercial Building programs. These programs offered architects the opportunity to participate in workshops, have energy-focused critiques, and redesign (on paper) existing buildings or actually revise buildings in the design phase. I was invited to participate as a workshop leader and design critic in these programs. Materials that my staff and I prepared for these workshops were the beginnings of this book. The interactions I had with the other members of the consulting/critic team and many excellent design groups at these programs were helpful in further reinforcing and refining my original ideas about sunlighting's potential.

The attention attracted, interest generated, and contacts made by these DOE-sponsored programs created immediate opportunities for realizing and evaluating sunlighting concepts that had begun to crystallize during these workshops. Among the very large projects that ensued almost immediately was the TVA Chattanooga Office Complex, followed by a project with some of the TAC members of the TVA design team, GSIS, Manila. These buildings and almost all the other case studies in this book represent a single generation of sunlighting design because they were designed almost simultaneously. Only a few, such as the Missouri Medical Library, benefited from my being able to evaluate previously completed projects, including one from the SERI program, Johnson Controls.

The Federal Government-sponsored programs of the late '70s created an unusual amount of exploration of energy-conscious design, including sunlighting. I am grateful for the opportunities that arose from this impetus and hope that this book will help extend the influence of this short but crucial period, which brought together so many outstanding individuals committed to a common cause—among them Larry Bickel, Mike Sizemore, Si Daryanani, Sarah Harkness, Don Watson, Ed Mazria, Bill Caudill, Richard Stein, Tom Vonier, Margo Villecco, Peter Calthorpe, Scott Matthews, Bill Higgins, John Eberhard, Ralph Knowles, Sym Van-Der Ryn, Doug Kelbaugh, J. W. Griffith, George Way, Stuart White, Brandt Anderson, Timothy Johnson, Douglas Mahone, Ian McHarg, Stephen Selkowitz, Benjamin Evans, and Harrison Fraker.

Acknowledgments

Even though this book is about the qualitative and design aspects of sunlighting more than about energy conservation, I must begin by thanking the Department of Energy for sponsoring the Energy Inform and SERI Passive Solar Demonstration programs, and the managers and consultants who invited my participation in these programs, which broadened my interest and redirected my consulting practice to include sunlighting.

I am thankful for the opportunities to teach sunlighting at the Harvard Graduate School of Design, MIT, and at a number of lectures, workshops, and conferences (many of them with DOE support).

Essential to my practical knowledge and to the very existence of the case studies were my clients—the building owners and architects who invited me to join their design teams, with whom the concepts were developed, and who were generous in furnishing information and graphic materials.

In addition to the other members of the design teams credited in the case studies, the editorial "we" almost always included past and current associates and staff in my own office in Cambridge, William Lam Associates, Inc. (i.e., John Powell on TVA, Jeffrey Berg on GSIS and Soddy Daisy High School, Peter Coxe on Carrier, Bob Osten on Missouri Medical Library, and David Laffitte on the University in the Middle East.) It was through their work on the projects that concepts were challenged and details were developed, along with procedures for model testing and data presentation.

The computerized model-testing equipment package used on later projects and for creating generic data for sidelighting and toplighting benefited from Bob Osten's knowledge of mathematics and lighting, together with the electrical engineering and computer programming skills of my son Tom, who happened to be passing through Cambridge when we needed him most.

In the actual preparation of this book, my sporadic efforts were reinforced with the full-time participation of a former student, Victor Olgyay, who for several months, with unfailing good humor, worked hard with me in developing the first draft. In addition, he provided invaluable logistical support in assembling data and graphic materials.

Upon Victor's return to MIT, my son John took over logistical and technical support on the final manuscript. He turned out to be a tough critic and subsequently edited and rewrote substantial portions of the book, with periodic consultation and help from his brother Tom.

David Laffitte's sketches established the graphic style used. I thank Susan Gebhardt for endless word processing and equally endless moral support. Paul Zaferiou, Jennifer Pieszak, Keith Yancy, and Margaret Young contributed in a variety of ways.

I am indebted to Professor Edward Sekler for reviewing the manuscript for historical references, and for criticism from Professor Lawrence B. Anderson.

I am appreciative of the patience and efforts of Emily Pearl, my editor at Van Nostrand Reinhold, who turned my piles of material into a book.

Finally, I would have faltered long before the end without the encouragement and advice of my wife Dianne, to whom this work is dedicated.

Introduction

THE SUN: PROBLEM OR OPPORTUNITY?

Throughout history, throughout the world, the sun has been worshipped by mankind. Its benefits have been recognized, praised, and prayed for and the potential problems of its presence adapted to.

In former times, the predictability of sunlight and its modification by weather formed the basis of seasonal and daily work, play, and rest schedules and the forms and materials of clothing, portable shelter, and buildings. The constant, regular movement of the sun was recognized in sundials, ceremonial monuments, and everyday structures, which were designed to relate very specifically to those movements and the resulting local climates (fig. I-1).

Sunlighting is the conscious design of a building form to use direct sunlight for illumination and thermal benefit. It has evolved slowly over generations to suit visual and thermal needs, within the restrictions of available construction materials and skills. Buildings so designed respond both to direct sunlight and to sunlight modified through diffusion or reflection by the sky vault, clouds, natural or man-made elements of the landscape, and the buildings themselves. The architecture shaped by sunlighting is positive and selective in the admission and redirection of direct sunlight.

The indigenous architectures of the world are the primary examples of sunlighting. Upon analysis there is inherent logic in their forms, orientation, penetrations, overhangs, and colors. Ideal solutions have been modified as necessary to accommodate conflicting planning and design decisions.

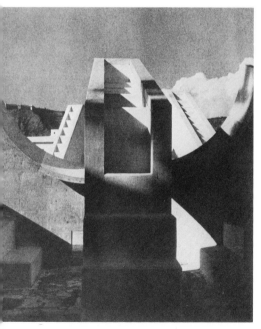

I-1. One of the sundials at Jaipur, India constructed about 1724. (Reprinted, by permission, from Olgyay and Olgyay, *Solar Control and Shading Devices*, p. 25)

Design evolution usually eliminates the illogical when there is no rush to document or standardize; thus, those concepts that become standardized through repetition are generally the more "natural" solutions to sunlighting problems. For example, the sunlighting of traditional public spaces in humid, tropical Java took the form of ground-reflected light from wide, open walls covered by widely overhanging roofs. In the hot, dry deserts of Iran, where nights can be very cold, sunlighting gave form to massive walls and roofs. In the temperate climate of Peking, China, the most important spaces were oriented toward the south.

One would expect that advancing technology should have led to even more intelligent use of sunlight. But a glance at most of the commercial and institutional buildings around us indicates otherwise. A few examples of the influence of sunlight on building form during the last century merit mentioning.

In the late 1920s, the *Zeilenbau* (row house) plan came into vogue in postwar Germany. It advocated the construction of long, parallel, north/south rows of narrow buildings with fenestration oriented east and west (figs. I–2, I–3). It was hoped that this would distribute sunlight equally through the buildings. However, after several of these buildings were constructed, it became evident that almost no sunlight entered during the winter, when the light was most desirable; during the summer the buildings became uncomfortably hot. By the early 1930s, the preferred orientation was again to the south.

I–2. With the Weimar Republic in postwar Germany came the Zeilenbau plan, with long, narrow apartment buildings oriented on a north/south axis.

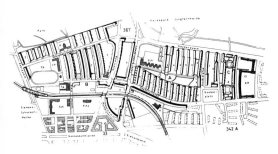

I–3. Plan of the apartment complex of Siemensstadt, built in 1929 near Berlin. Most apartment buildings in this workers' community faced east and west.

Unfortunately, in the following turbulent years, aesthetics rather than environment prevailed as the dominant architectural influence, and the lessons concerning the orientation of buildings were all but forgotten. In the post–World War II United States, concern with natural lighting experienced a brief renaissance. Concurrent with the baby boom of the 1950s was a renewed interest in the use of daylight in the design of schools, which were being constructed by the dozen. Artificial skies, directional glass blocks, and studies in perception and visibility flourished until the introduction of the fluorescent lamp and mechanical HVAC systems in the late 1950s. Since then, sunlight in architecture has generally been ignored or treated as a problem rather than as an opportunity, rejected as undesirable instead of directed and employed for benefit.

Architect Raymond Steinback of Atlanta, recalling his days at MIT in the early '50s, has suggested that orientation and shading started to decline as major design concerns in the architectural profession with the Weathermaster House Design Competition. This national competition, sponsored by Westinghouse, was based on the premise that by designing around air conditioning, the same house could be built anywhere, with any orientation.

Theoretically, the riches of advancing technology should have provided unlimited opportunities to optimize design solutions for using the sun, creating comfortable visual and thermal environments with minimal use of other energy sources. But the availability of modern techniques and options such as skeletal structures, majestic expanses of glass, high-performance glazing, precast concrete, complex poured-in-place concrete forms, and other advanced construction materials and processes, along with revolutionary analytical tools such as computer calculations, simulation, and graphics, have perhaps become problems in themselves because they create virtually unlimited choices in building design. In employing a myriad of solutions, significant problems remained unidentified and unresolved.

Unlimited choices require careful judgment in selecting the appropriate response to objectives; problems must first be correctly defined— a process that has been largely misguided. In response to the number of choices, the era of the all-knowing master builder has been superseded by input from a range of specialists. The matrix of responses to different yet interrelated design issues must be coordinated to produce an integrated instead of layered result. In addition, problems cannot be resolved without accurate assessments of past solutions. What were the difficult circumstances and incorrect assumptions? Why were they made and what are their consequences?

A number of factors have resulted in poor utilization of sunlight, particularly in North American buildings constructed since the 50s. Instead of interacting with the environment, these windowless or effectively windowless buildings shut out the sunlight. Technological advances have produced buildings that are remarkably poor in providing good luminous and thermal environments for people as well as being cost-ineffective in the use of energy. Technology has been used not to create wise strategies, but to overcome the self-created handicaps of "unnatural" architectural concepts. Let us examine some of the forces that have misguided our logic.

Cheap Energy

Because government regulation controlled return on investment, the road to success for utilities management was to maximize the investment in power plants. To do this, they created decreasing rate structures that encouraged waste by the largest users, whose very low rates were being subsidized by smaller users (whose rates were sometimes more than ten times as much). Much of the ever-increasing demand for more and more electricity and power plants was created not by public need but by the profit motives of privately owned utilities in the United States.

High-Illumination Requirements

To increase the "demand" for more power plants, the power and lighting industries were very effective in promoting ever-increasing illumination levels and incorporating them into codes. In some cases "required" light levels were so high that artificial lights had to be used all the time, regardless of the external climate and availability of natural light. Such lights often heated buildings to the extent that air conditioning was needed year-round (figs. I–4, I–5, I–6).

I–5. Growth of illumination levels for general interior lighting

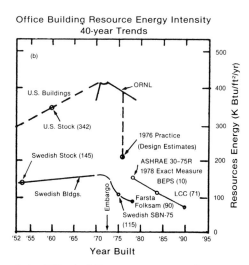

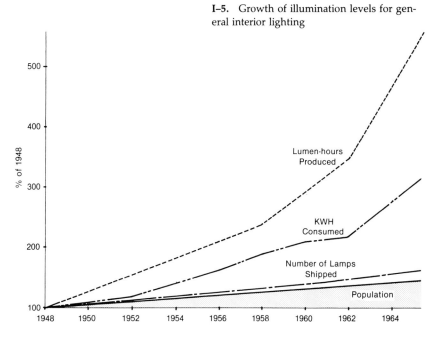

I–4. Office building resource energy intensity—40-year trends. (Reprinted, by permission, from SERI, *A New Prosperity—Building a Sustainable Energy Future*)

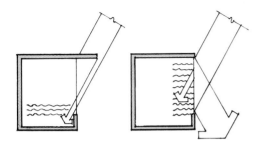

I–6. Shading (left) vs. low-transmission glass (right).

I–7. The John Hancock building in Boston, Massachusetts–a significant corporate image and winner of many design awards. (Photograph courtesy of John Lam)

Increased lighting requirements were also fostered by an unconscious conspiracy of building professionals. Electrical and mechanical engineers, being paid percentage fees, were happy to have their portions of building budgets increase dramatically. No more effort was required to specify more fixtures or larger lamps and air-conditioning units. It was much easier to design for quantitative goals than to address qualitative needs.

Electrical engineers, untrained in the principles of perception or space design but given the design responsibility, were happy to have the crutch of simplistic numerical standards as the principal design criteria.

Too many architects abdicated much of the responsibility for the design of a building's interior environment to engineers in exchange for the freedom of designing any glass box that met their fancy, regardless of its functional implications. Separating skin from structure, they maintained the myth that nothing had been compromised. Extolling the exterior forms of Mies-like curtain-wall buildings, without reference to their well-known environmental discomforts (glare, overheating on the sunny side, underheating on the shady side), encouraged more and more such buildings to be built.

In addition, architectural reviews favor exterior features; interior coverage is usually limited to lobbies and public spaces. Scan the articles and you will find scarcely a single photograph of the interior working spaces for which the buildings were presumably built. When interiors are shown, the unattractive glaring ceilings full of fluorescent lights are usually cropped out of the photograph, and the furnishings are featured instead.

To reduce the problems of excessive glare and local overheating (simultaneous with cold drafts) caused by ignoring orientation and shading, high-tech materials such as mirror glass were developed and used rather than revising the overall concept. Thus, behind acres of mirror-glass walls hung venetian blinds to control the glare, and glaring fluorescent lights burned all day long from window to window (figs. I–7, I–8). Having thrown away several feet of ceiling cavity to HVAC, these low-ceilinged spaces were gloomy, reflecting the occupants' image in the mirrored, low-transmission glass even on clear days. If heat-absorbing glass was used instead, occupants also suffered from the radiant heat emitted from the glazing.

Many architects liked to design such curtain-wall office buildings because the process was easy and profitable. Little more was required than deciding on a building shape and selecting materials—a curtain-wall system and color, an acoustic ceiling system, and a recessed light fixture. Beyond that, the only design effort expended often appeared to be in the main lobby.

Obviously, these buildings would not have been built had they not been accepted by developers, who liked the low first cost and rapid construction, which maximized the leverage of their capital. Such buildings will continue to be constructed as long as the high operating costs can be passed on without complaint to clients who are more interested in the corporate image of dramatic exterior forms than in the quality of the interior working environment or operating economy (figs. I–9, I–10).

Office buildings were not the only types designed without regard to the environment. Architects also applied abstract form rather than logic in museums (Kevin Roche's Lehman Wing of the Metropolitan Museum, for example), in university libraries (such as James Stirling's Cambridge University History Faculty Building), and virtually every other building type.

Design awards from the profession itself also tend to recognize form rather than performance, a notable exception being the Agha Khan awards for Islamic architecture. The jurors generally judge primarily by graphic presentation and ignore other factors, even if problems are well known. The Agha Khan awards are based on site visits that assess the quality of the environment and the response of the users and owners.

Now that the idea of limitless cheap energy has been recognized as a myth, users are beginning to question the qualities of the totally artificial environment produced by the architecture of technology. It is time to reexamine the traditions of the world's indigenous architectures, which evolved around climate and human needs. Former sunlighting practices in the United States and present practices in less wasteful countries need merely be further developed for today's more stringent context of programmatic needs, user expectations, and advanced building materials and processes.

I–8. The interior of the John Hancock office building—gloomy and depressing.

TRADITIONAL FORMS AND TODAY'S CONTEXT

What are the forms of indigenous *sunlighting* and how do they differ from those of *daylighting*? How does today's context differ from that of the past, and how do the differences change the design objectives that should shape the resulting architectural forms?

Indigenous *daylit* buildings occur in the predominantly cloudy countries of northern Europe. Large, high, unshaded windows located near the ceilings use diffuse light from the sky directly as the dominant light source (fig. I–11). In contrast, the indigenous forms of *sunlit* architecture in sunny dry climates throughout the world—those forms that evolved via the common building experience—use smaller, shaded windows located relatively low in the wall to best control glare and heat and utilize the sunlight indirectly reflected from the ground and building surfaces (fig. I–12). In both circumstances, control of light and heat evolved in the context of the intended activities within the space.

The context of current architectural design can be summarized in the following parameters:

I–9. The south side of the Harvard Graduate School of Design: mirror glass.

☐ Floor plans of buildings used to be restricted by the limits of natural lighting and ventilation requirements. Today, the extent of a building's floor area is often much greater and is determined by organizational needs (for communication, work flow, and the like) and by the need to maximize utilization of expensive real estate.

☐ Because of construction costs and lack of air conditioning prior to the mid-twentieth century, natural lighting was often reduced to the minimum necessary for thermal comfort. Work was adapted to the physical environment, slowed down, stopped, or moved as necessary. Most critical tasks were located near the best light.

I–10. The inside: students attempt to block the glaring sun with partitions and paper pasted over the windows.

Today, in wealthy, industrialized countries like the U.S., we expect to be able to do anything, anytime, anywhere, due to the availability of electric lighting and air conditioning. We expect to have both the desired light *and* heat in any size or shape of building.

☐ Because open windows used to be the principal source of ventilation, there was little difference between similar shading devices placed on the interior or exterior of the glazing plane. This factor is much more important in today's sealed, air-conditioned buildings.

☐ Building occupants used to control their own environment, by opening and closing blinds as necessary. Today, the notion of control of and responsibility for our environment is often relegated to an afterthought. In large common spaces trafficked by many people, the occupants are likely to take the most convenient rather than the best, most obvious course of action (i.e., do nothing rather than adjust the blinds). The centralized, automated control system must therefore be relied on. Better yet, an optimum design should be comfortable and economical without any local adjustment.

☐ When natural light was the only alternative, building occupants accepted the glare and heat of sunlight or adjusted the situation. Today, adequate glare-free artificial lighting is available. Sunlighting must therefore achieve control of quality as well as quantity or it will be shut out and not utilized. The increasing use of video display terminals makes exacting control of light distribution and glare even more important. However, this factor is likely to change with advances in display technology.

☐ Technology has brought us sophisticated automatic controls that can make louvers track the sun to shade or reflect according to multifaceted programs that were not possible before.

☐ In the more recent past, architects and their clients did not consider energy costs important. Today, the use of energy in buildings is for many a legitimate programmatic concern.

☐ Today we have sophisticated instrumentation for predicting the lighting performance of sunlighting and for analyzing its benefits in terms of energy and cost. This is a mixed blessing. People used to make good value judgments with less quantitative information. We must reassert the importance of the qualitative and consider all the factors involved rather than only those that are most easily quantifiable.

☐ Many design solutions were formerly limited by technical means. There were more stringent limits to dimensions of clear window openings, sizes of glass, sizes of economically attainable mirrored surfaces, trellis members, and so forth. The limits now are those of trade-off decisions rather than of technical feasibility. It is important to make these decisions on the basis of value (cost and benefit) rather than cost alone.

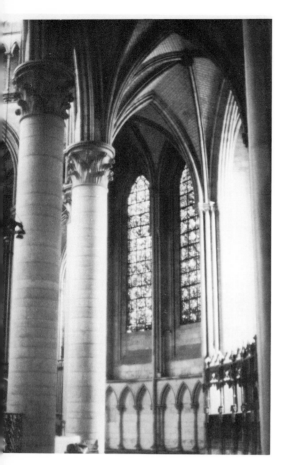

I–11. Daylighting in overcast climates often included stained glass placed as high as possible in the space.

I–12. Sunny climates encourage small, shaded windows located relatively low in the space. (Photograph courtesy of Norman Carver)

☐ What is unchanged is that people have always enjoyed seeing sunlight and always will, as long as they are thermally comfortable. In the past, the small scale of buildings ensured that the occupants were always oriented to the outdoor scene, to the time and weather. In today's scale of building, where occupants may be distant from the exterior wall, or at the bottom of a fifty-story atrium throughout their working days, the biological needs for orientation must be consciously provided for.

The challenge and promise of sunlighting today is to use the sun as it was used in the past: to provide economical illumination, comfort, and delight. We must do this in the context of rigid expectations of visual and thermal comfort, large buildings, complex programs, and increasingly expensive energy. We have the analytical tools, materials, and control technologies to meet this challenge. Sunlighting offers the dual potential of buildings that are both comfortable to use and economical to operate.

By presenting the principles, techniques, and design methods involved and projects both planned and completed, I hope this book will help further the evolution of sunlighting as a powerful influence on architecture, improving design and benefiting humanity.

PART I: PRINCIPLES

1 Design Objectives: Sunlighting for Economy and Delight

Sunlighting—designing with instead of defending against the sun's light—is economical. The economies of sunlighting are twofold: more comfortable and productive interior environments for the occupants and lower energy costs for the building.

Sunlighting—the design of spaces that satisfy our needs for biologically important information for orientation and security—is delightful. These needs are fundamental but are often neglected in modern architecture: sunlighting seeks to restore delight to its centrality as a design objective.

The economy of sunlighting fulfills Vitruvius' trinity of commodity, firmness, and delight:

Commodity. Artificial lighting is the major energy user in many of today's buildings, accounting for about 50 percent of the energy consumed in a typical office building. As such, lighting—and its attendant cooling load—represents a large portion of the building's operating budget. Designing with the sun can reduce the total amount of energy used as well as the peak usage. In this age of rising energy costs, sunlighting is therefore a good investment.

Firmness. Sunlighting is not a faddish aesthetic following a trendy concept but the intelligent application of the natural environment to the achievement of programmatic needs. Thus, sunlighting results in buildings whose beauty is not transient or skin deep but firm and enduring. Sunlighting has produced buildings of classic beauty and lasting value the world over.

Delight. Few would deny that the sun can provide especially delightful illumination. More than that, sunlight gives reassuring orientation as to place, time, and weather. When applied with consideration to psychological and physiological needs, sunlighting produces interior environments that are comfortable, delightful, and productive.

DESIGN OBJECTIVES

While Vitruvius' trinity provides a nice set of ideals to strive for, design is never so simple in practice. The purposes, programs, building technologies, and processes of modern design and construction require the collaboration of specialists, the balancing of multiple and interrelated objectives, and the resolution of conflicts. The following five categories of design objectives are better suited to the present day:

1. providing user comfort and delight in the interior environment;

2. satisfying the programmatic needs of the users;

3. minimizing the building energy cost;

4. optimizing the public architectural image; and

5. minimizing the initial building construction cost (fig. 1–1).

In practice, these objectives can be difficult to integrate and balance. The evaluation of architecture according to these categories reveals their synergistic integrations, the trade-offs between them, and the importance attached to each—by intention or by default—during the design process. Many modern buildings reflect almost total adherence to only one or two of these objectives, while ignoring all the others. For example, a building whose goal is solely to create a public image may be expensive to build, waste energy, and be an unpleasant space in which to work. Similarly, a building whose goal is reduced energy use may be ugly within and without (fig. 1–2).

In the struggle to attain these multiple goals, the first category—user comfort and delight—has too often been virtually ignored. In my opinion, user comfort should be the central category to which the other priorities must respond. Although comfort is not the only result desired, it is critical to begin with it as a priority. While the criteria for comfort can easily be integrated with the other concerns, starting with other priorities will often eliminate or severely compromise the potential for achieving interior environmental comfort and delight.

Good design using sunlighting can have an impact on all five goals. Using sunlight in buildings is most important to me because it can improve the quality of life. Building sunlit buildings may entail some increased initial (construction) cost; however, reduced energy consumption during the building's operation can offset this. While it is difficult to quantify with accuracy, a delightful environment can also have a positive economic impact.

Providing User Comfort and Delight

A person's comfort within a built environment has many aspects, including thermal, visual, aural, and psychological comfort. While comfort is not easily quantifiable as a set amount of heat, illumination, window view, and so on, its qualitative parameters can be described. The perceptual processes that underlie comfort are universal, though what individuals find "comfortable" varies according to their expectations and activities. What visual comfort is and how it can be achieved is the focus of this book, although the sun's thermal implications are also discussed.

A comfortable visual environment is one in which the apparent sources of light are surfaces one wants to look at, consciously or unconsciously. It is delightful when the qualitative characteristics of these sights are what one enjoys as appropriate to the moment and activity. To design delightful visual environments, one must first understand vision (how

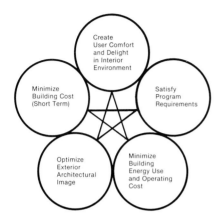

1–1. Balancing the five design objectives creates beautiful architecture.

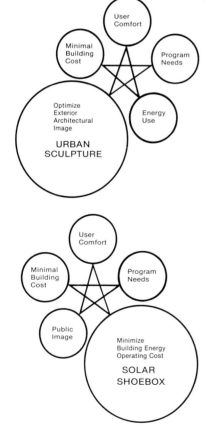

1–2. Architecture suffers when one objective is overemphasized.

we see), perception (what we see), and what we *want* to see in various spaces and for various activities (the nature of a delightful luminous environment). These subjects are discussed in detail in chapter 2. A good luminous environment makes it possible to perform necessary tasks—such as typing or conferring—comfortably. It also helps us on a subconscious level to feel secure in our environment by providing orientation information. The presentation of all the information we need creates a delightful environment.

The inability to create delightful environments can result in direct, measurable economic consequences, such as an inability to draw in customers or lack of improvement in office workers' productivity. These consequences can outweigh the building's initial construction cost. According to studies conducted by the GSA in the 1960s, and more recently by IBM, the total costs of owning and operating an office building over a period of forty years are: 2 percent for the capital costs of site, building, and equipment; 6 percent for operation, maintenance, and reconfiguration of space; and 92 percent (by far the largest) for the salaries of personnel (fig. 1–3). Thus, even a modest productivity increase of 5 percent would have a dollar value equal to twice the initial cost of the building; for an increase of 10 percent the factor would go up to four.

There are a number of studies that show that such a productivity increase may be obtained by improvements in the interior environment. A study by the Buffalo Organization for Social and Technological Innovation (BOSTI) is perhaps the most representative. The BOSTI investigation examined such environmental concerns as: amount of personal space, furniture type and layout, temperature/air quality, lighting, windows, privacy (both speech and visual), and ease of support and communication. With regard to illumination, BOSTI pointed to the importance of intensity, distribution, and control (like control of temperature, control of illumination affects both environmental satisfaction and job satisfaction). BOSTI found that those workers with the most demanding tasks were least satisfied with their lighting, while managers and supervisors were most satisfied. While the predictable effects on ''outcome'' (output) to which environmental factors contribute may seem small, their leverage

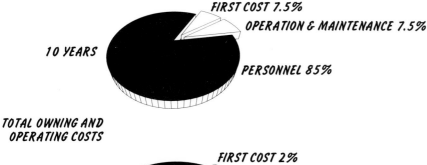

TOTAL OWNING AND OPERATING COSTS

1–3. Typical building operating costs. (Courtesy of Leo Daly)

over the life cycle of a building can be significant. Clearly, the capital costs of the environmental factors inherent in the building's design (and operation) are the least-cost component of the total owning and operating cost.

How Bright Is Best?

It should be noted that "improvement" of lighting does not denote or imply a simple increase in illumination level. Brighter is not necessarily better and can be worse: excessive, not insufficient, light can result in permanent eye damage. The allegation that "more is better" is not substantiated by research. Studies such as that by Butler and Rusmore in 1969 detected "no difference in performance . . . associated with illumination levels above 3.5 footcandles."[1] Further, a 1975 study by the Federal Energy Administration of simulated office tasks concluded:

> For reading comprehension and speed of comprehension, there were no large or important differences in performance as a function of illumination level over the range of 1 to 450 footcandles. This is true for two age groups, one of about 20 years of age and the other ranging from 45 to 62 years. There is a difference in performance between reading good contrast or poor contrast material, and a difference in performance between the age groups; but neither of these differences is related to changes in illumination.[2]

It is my contention that improvements in the morale or sense of well-being on the part of the worker (i.e., how comfortable, pleasant, and delightful an environment is) will inevitably have a greater effect on performance than simple increases in illumination levels.

Satisfying Programmatic Needs

A building does more than provide comfort for humans, and the requirements of what takes place within a building often determine its form. The organization and nature of the client's business often dictate to the designer the building's form and the sunlighting strategies that may be employed. Objects within the building may even have a specific influence on illumination—for example, the preservation requirements for artwork in a museum. Sunlighting must respond to a building's programmatic requirements.

Minimizing Building Energy Cost

Designing without considering energy costs is akin to farming without considering water supply. The issue of using the earth's finite supply of stored energy has been raised above simple economics to become a moral issue. It is almost criminal to waste our energy resources selfishly. We have the means to devise greater efficiencies; we should not wait until the market forces us to practice what we are capable of accomplishing.

Energy costs represent a major portion of a building's operating costs.

[1]P. Butler and J. Rusmore, "Illumination Intensities and Test Performance," Perceptual and Motor Skills 29 (1969): 653–54.
[2]Federal Energy Administration, "Lighting and Thermal Operations Conservation Paper #18," (1975), II–4.

Lighting in turn accounts for a significant portion of the energy used (fig. 1–4). In a typical office building, lighting accounts for 24 percent of the BTUs used annually. Because lighting uses electricity, which is the most expensive form of energy, it accounts for 63 percent of the *dollar cost* of energy. Excessive artificial lighting or inadequate shading of the sun also result in increased demand for air conditioning. Sunlighting can reduce the amount of electricity used.

Sunlighting is a particularly advantageous way to save energy because its potential coincides with the peak electrical demand period—hot, sunny summer days (fig. 1–5). This has increasingly greater economic significance as utilities change their rate structures to reflect more accurately the true costs of generating power. The cost of power reflects the cost of fuel and the cost of generating capacity. Reducing the peak load requirements reduces the need for new power plants. Because the cost of new power plants has risen, utilities are becoming more interested in conservation as an alternative and are moving to penalize peak-time electrical use by means of "ratchet clauses" and higher rates. (A ratchet clause requires that a percentage—often at levels as high as 80 percent—of the year's maximum demand be extended as a fixed demand charge throughout the remaining eleven billing periods. Thus, a building owner must pay an enormous penalty for just one fifteen-minute surge in demand (fig. 1–6).

The built-in cost of peak demand makes it much easier to calculate the dollar benefits of sunlighting. It is also much easier to evaluate a number of buildings along one parameter—for instance, the energy demands (use) of various designs at peak demand time, than it is to calculate a given building's energy savings in many different situations throughout the year. While taking advantage of current energy price structures may save money, it is better to minimize the actual energy consumption. Conservation offers both long-range economic protection for the owner—independent of future pricing practices—and national benefit.

Optimizing Public Architectural Image

Nobody wants an ugly building. Corporate image is often considered to be strongly reflected in the presence and facade of a building that is "different." This superficial "identity" is effective only as long as a building remains alone in its style and place. When similar buildings compete for attention, the result is often rather boring.

Architectural corporate images based on skin-deep styles are apt to be as changeable as styles in clothing fashions, but the nature of the medium consigns them to permanence. A contextual solution based on beauty beyond the facade and universal, everlasting human needs will remain beautiful in its surroundings regardless of its neighbors. Refining our objectives will result in buildings whose identities result from their use, internal organization, and environment, as well as their skins. Such beauty remains even when surrounded by competitors that rival the external presence.

Unfortunately, however, the general public (those who have not lived in the building) and the architectural press seem to recognize only a building's exterior. While the exterior is undoubtedly important, problems occur when this is the designer's dominant concern. A comfortable,

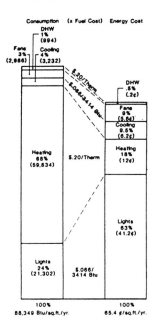

1–4. Typical office-building energy use. (Courtesy of Johnson Controls)

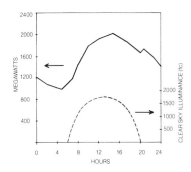

1–5. The coincidence of a typical utility's load curve (solid line) and clear-sky luminance (dashed line) shows how daylighting can aid in load management. Levels of sunlight will coincide similarly. (Reprinted, by permission, from Bryan, "Power Play," *Progressive Architecture*, April 1983)

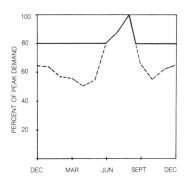

1–6. This seasonal demand curve compares actual demand (dashed line) with the demand that will be charged assuming an 80 percent ratchet clause (solid line) for an all-electric office building. (Reprinted, by permission, from Bryan, "Power Play," *Progressive Architecture*, April 1983)

delightful building concept clothed beautifully will endure, but a building based on a beautiful skin concept is unlikely to be as delightful for the occupants within or retain its external uniqueness over time.

Minimizing Building Cost

A building is most valuable when it provides the maximum satisfaction of the aforementioned concerns at a minimum cost. The initial, short-term costs of construction can be minimized by well-integrated building systems and the use of appropriate materials and methods for a given location. Long-term costs include the operation and maintenance of the building, the cost of money (interest payments), personnel productivity, and the cost of replacing the building. While some of these costs are intrinsic to the building's program, most can be minimized by clever design.

Ideally, these are not conflicting concerns, but synergistic influences that affect each other beneficially. The achievement of this synergism, however, requires the collaboration of specialists—architectural, structural, mechanical, lighting, etc.—for the evolution of concepts and detailed designs. The team design process often proves effective and is detailed below.

CONCLUSION

While I am interested in the use of sunlighting for energy conservation and operating-cost benefits, the greatest challenge in my consulting career is to create buildings that are also delightful environments for working and living.

A windowless office building (or an effectively windowless building in terms of lighting), built of mirror glass to defend against the sun, may be economical to build and operate at today's energy prices. It may also have a conspicuous presence as a unique and beautiful urban sculpture. However, these buildings are often far from delightful environments in which to work.

The best use of sunlighting is not only to save energy and guard against rising energy prices but, more important, to create more pleasant, delightful luminous environments for the occupants. To achieve these objectives, sunlighting must be given the highest priority. To achieve these objectives economically and with elegance in the design of both interior spaces and exterior architectural images requires design teams of the most competent professionals working in a multidisciplinary team process, as described in chapter 10 (and employed in most of the case studies in this book).

To achieve delightful sunlighting more easily, all members of the design team—owners and user's representatives as well as design professionals—should understand the principles of perception and appreciate the subtleties of what makes a comfortable, delightful visual environment. The following chapter should aid that understanding.

2 The Delightful, Healthful, Luminous Environment

Most architects and lighting technicians have very little understanding of the relationships between the *amount* of light and visibility and the *perception* of brightness. Often they do not know the difference between illumination (measured in footcandles or lux) and luminance (measured in footlamberts or candelas)—the basic units in lighting design. They are therefore unable to discern whether a space is insufficiently illuminated or whether it merely *appears* dark because of dark colors on unlit walls. The wrong design process and poor solutions result from accepting single-number footcandle criteria promulgated by the light and power industries (created to sell power).

As a result, lighting is generally designed to produce an exact, measured quantity of illumination at desk level rather than to provide for human perceptual needs. An illuminating engineer can visit a given space and estimate the amount of artificial light by counting the number of fixtures and mentally calculating the number of footcandles present. If that same ''expert'' was asked to estimate the amount of light in a daylit space with his eyes, he would probably be totally confused (having always depended on a light meter) and estimate incorrectly by a factor of ten to one hundred (fig. 2–1). *Because it is difficult to judge the quantity of light, lighting design must be based on what one is able to perceive and what one wants to look at—the quality of the luminous environment.*

Designers must learn to design with concepts that can be judged with their brains and eyes rather than with instruments. This realization is fundamental to taking advantage of the freedom and creative opportunities available in the design of the luminous environment. Other factors that should be considered are the effects of sunlight on the biological health of people and plants and on thermal comfort.

VISIBILITY

As pointed out in chapter 1, humans see well over a wide range of illumination levels. We can see in moonlight as well as in sunlight. An object in direct sunlight may be as much as a million times brighter than the same object illuminated by moonlight, but the human eye can perceive both. The law of diminishing returns operates above very minimum light levels, thereby making additional amounts of illumination increasingly

2–1. Light levels (illuminance) may vary tremendously over small distances with very little perceived difference. Differences are even harder to judge if the surfaces illuminated are of various forms and colors.

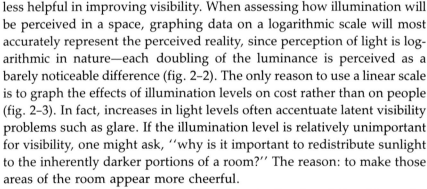

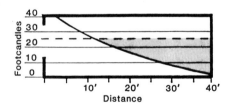

2–3. The economics of natural lighting are best graphed on a linear scale. (Dotted line indicates required illumination level; shaded area represents supplementary "purchased" electric illumination.)

less helpful in improving visibility. When assessing how illumination will be perceived in a space, graphing data on a logarithmic scale will most accurately represent the perceived reality, since perception of light is logarithmic in nature—each doubling of the luminance is perceived as a barely noticeable difference (fig. 2–2). The only reason to use a linear scale is to graph the effects of illumination levels on cost rather than on people (fig. 2–3). In fact, increases in light levels often accentuate latent visibility problems such as glare. If the illumination level is relatively unimportant for visibility, one might ask, "why is it important to redistribute sunlight to the inherently darker portions of a room?" The reason: to make those areas of the room appear more cheerful.

The quality and geometry of the illumination in relationship to the viewer are much more important than the quantity for most tasks. For example, we have all had the experience of tilting a fever thermometer to the "perfect" angle in order to read it or of rearranging ourselves or the television set to eliminate bothersome reflections. Similarly, light coming from the wrong direction can reduce the contrast between ink and paper because of *veiling reflections*. Look at a magazine while facing a window or unshielded light source; compare its visibility when turned away from the light source.

To optimize visibility, the amount of light coming from the trouble-

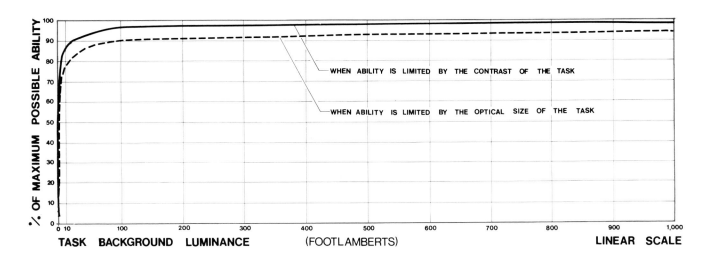

VISUAL ABILITY AS A FUNCTION OF TASK LUMINANCE

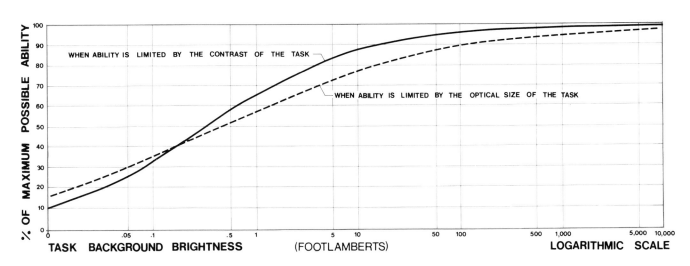

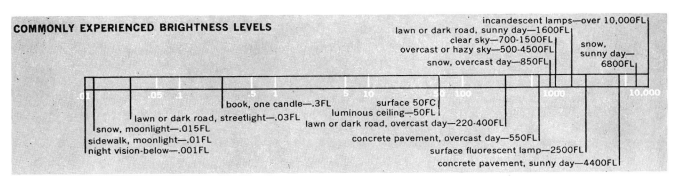

2–2. Commonly experienced brightness levels are best graphed on a logarithmic scale.
(Reprinted, by permission, from Lam, *Perception and Lighting as Formgivers for Architecture*)

some direction (the *mirror angle*) should be minimized relative to that coming from other directions. To know which angles are least desirable, place a mirror at the task location. Since the angle of incidence is equal to the angle of reflectance, the light source, if seen in the mirror, would also be seen as a competing (veiling) reflection on a glossy page. The effect is more subtle on a matte page with glossy ink or pencil writing, where the effect is a reduction in contrast between the dark figures and the light background.

The ideal control over the direction and intensity of light is possible if each task can be provided with its own "task lighting." This is most practical when the activities, furnishings, and equipment can be fixed in location (for example, nurses' stations, hotel registration desks, museum displays). More typically, however, we should provide a general level of illumination suitable for most activities and only provide task lighting to assist with the most demanding tasks, such as drafting. When designing general illumination, the viewing angle and direction cannot be controlled. When desks face in all directions and there are many tasks, the light source should be spread out as much as possible so that only a small portion of the illumination on any task will come from a "troublesome" direction. Examples of "spread-out" sources include the surfaces of light-colored rooms indirectly illuminated by sunlight or electric light sources.

Incidentally, the strategy of providing pleasant general lighting combined with task lighting is far more economical than trying to increase the general level of illumination to that demanded by the most critical task. The comfort of the occupants who are not doing critical tasks will be greater if they are not subjected to excessive levels of light and glaring light sources. Fortunately, the tide is turning against these power-company-inspired "heat-by-light" buildings of the 60s and early 70s.

PERCEPTION

The information sought—what we want to see—should be our focus. Anything that interferes with this is considered visual noise. Therefore, we should illuminate what we want to see, be it a task or a pleasant visual rest area. Conversely, we should not create or accent visual noise!

Brightness

As mentioned above, our perception of brightness is very flat and related more to a logarithmic than a linear scale. We are not aware of large variations of illumination levels within a space or over time. It is difficult to perceive quantitatively the distribution of light in a space (see fig. 2–1). It is easier to perceive a variation in the rate of change in light gradients than the amount of change. It is by such changes of rate that we perceive edges and form.

Since expectation is a large factor in perception, it results in our perceiving wide fluctuations in daylight levels as natural, and thus unnoticeable. The same fluctuations from normally constant artificial light sources would be noticeable and disturbing, or perceived as relevant information—a lamp burning out, or the end of intermission at the theater, for example.

Relative Nature of Brightness

The dominating feature of human vision is adaptation. Everything we see is referred to a reference level, whether of lightness, darkness, or color, and we make our interpretation in terms of this reference level. All visual experience has some basis in past or present knowledge. Brightness, as well as color, is affected by simultaneous contrast, a situation whereby some objects seem brighter than others of equal luminance in a uniformly illuminated space.

In our daily experience, many factors come into play as the eye adapts to each luminous scene. Context, experience, and expectation are all taken into consideration when perceiving whether an object is dark, light, too bright, or dull. For instance, an interior space at night may seem ''brighter'' than a daylight scene even though the exterior luminance is 1,000 times greater. Consider these perceptions in your own experiences:

- [ ] your living room at night versus a dark overcast day outdoors;

- [ ] a bright cafeteria versus a bright cocktail lounge;

- [ ] sunlight on a windowsill versus light fixtures of equal luminance;

- [ ] a bright mural versus a dirty dish cart.

When your mental observations are compared with light-meter readings the results may be surprising!

Aperture Contrast

Similarly, the view out a window may be several hundred times brighter than the interior; however, this difference in brightness will only be disturbing if there is a sharp contrast between the two (worst case: a small opening in the middle of a dark wall). Illuminating the wall area near the window will create a transitional area that will lessen the aperture contrast.

Glare and Sparkle

The lighting industry and electrical engineers try to define glare in terms of luminance and luminance ratios. Webster's dictionary defines glare as an ''interference with visual perception caused by an uncomfortably bright light source or reflection,'' and sparkle as ''an attractive brilliance.'' A sunlit surface of interest is likely to be perceived as pleasant and as ''sparkle,'' whereas a lighting fixture of equal brightness would be considered ''glare.'' While a window view might be momentarily perceived as ''glare'' (e.g., when viewing a face in silhouette to it), it would not be perceived as such if one was looking out the window. To understand what glare is, we must recognize that glare is a perception, and perceptions are interpretations of information, not sensations.

Overcast Sky and Sunlight

One perceives a clear sky as pleasant and a nonuniform, overcast, or partly cloudy sky as interesting, whereas a solid overcast sky is perceived as ''dull.'' Because it is uninteresting, the uniformly overcast sky is likely to be perceived as glaring and "too bright" even when its measured luminance is far less than the sunlit landscape or blue sky.

An object can be regarded as sparkling instead of glaring if it is the desired object of perception, such as a chandelier, a view, or an interesting patch of sunlight. Context—the relevance or irrelevance of a scene—rather than brightness ratios, determines "glare."

Gloom

Gloom is experienced in the following situations:

☐ Conditions for performing an activity are suboptimal: not enough light; focal object obscured by shadows; focal object silhouetted rather than highlighted.

☐ Desired biological facts are:

1. difficult to obtain because observer is excluded from view, sunshine, or feeling of daytime;

2. unclear due to upsetting of constancies such as size, shape, color, or brightness; lack of focal points, visual rest centers, sparkle, or interest; or

3. dominated by unwanted facts: dominance by overly bright ceilings or bright overcast sky; dominance by objects outside the immediate area where privacy is desired.

The view through a bronze or gray heat-reducing glass window usually is not disturbing because the viewer does not "compare" the view with anything. However, the color of the glass will be noticed and will be disturbing if an open or clear window is also in the viewer's field of vision (fig. 2–4). When there is a basis for comparison, the view through such glass appears tinted and gloomy.

Darkness

On an overcast day we will find the ground objects dark in comparison with the overcast sky. (Also, the overcast scene may seem dark, even though luminance levels may be hundreds of times greater than a "bright" interior space.) On a sunny day, when shadows define and emphasize their three-dimensional aspects, these ground objects will appear brighter than the sky. At night, we consider a street "brightly illuminated" when the ground elements are bright, although the sky is always dark and the illumination level may be a thousand times brighter than that on a "dark" overcast day.

Dullness

An object of great interest is seldom described as dull. Conversely, something inherently dull visually cannot be made less dull by greater luminance. It must be changed and given interest by the addition of colors (such as paint in a parking garage), shadows, or the dramatic upsetting of constancies (such as pools of light along paths of circulation). A scene may appear dull because the intended object of attention is dominated

2–4. The view through tinted glass is gloomy when compared with a clear view.

by something dull. Intentional upsetting of constancies can create drama, excitement, or tension. If this upsetting of constancies does not appear to be intentional, the same effects can be gloomy and disturbing. For example, the highlighting of a floor show may make one less conscious of a dining room's features, to positive advantage. Equal highlighting of the kitchen scene viewed through a service door would be unpleasant and make the dining room appear dull.

SUMMARY—VISIBILITY AND PERCEPTION

The quantity of light is only one of many factors that determine how well we see and the overall quality of a luminous space. Each viewer and each space have specific information needs, and each object and task have specific characteristics. Above very minimum illumination levels, relevant lighting *geometry*, rather than *quantity*, is the most effective way to meet these needs and delineate these characteristics. Visibility is also relative to focus, distraction, and context. To increase visibility by brute strength (footcandles) rather than skill (geometry) is wasteful and likely to produce bad side effects in the form of glare.

An understanding of the process of and the components of perception helps to explain why a room interior may appear "too bright" at night but "too dark" during the day (due to the viewer's knowledge of simultaneous exterior conditions). This effect would be increased if there were a black window at night and even a crack of daylight during the day for reference (e.g., around the edge of drawn blackout shades).

Our judgment is altered by what we expect to be bright in a given environment under given conditions for a particular activity. An unlit mural, located as an obvious focal point in a room, would appear dark because we expect it was meant to be featured. A chandelier in a theater always appears too bright if even barely lit during the performance, though not too bright at full intensity during the intermission. Highlighting an empty fireplace or an ugly floor would create a scene described as "too bright" except to the janitor as he was cleaning up. Thus, to produce a predictable, comfortable, brightness perception level, those involved in design must determine what should be perceived, as well as the dimensions of the stimuli (luminance). This most important first step requires that the designer predict the information needs, conscious and unconscious, of the probable users.

THE LUMINOUS ENVIRONMENT

A "good" visual environment is one that satisfies the visual information needs of the occupants. Surfaces of interest are highlighted, surfaces lacking interest are deemphasized. There is a maximum of "signal" (wanted useful visual information) and minimum of "noise" (unwanted, irrelevant visual information). What is lit and how is more important than how much illumination is provided. The best visual environments are those in which the apparent sources of light are those surfaces one enjoys looking at: room surfaces, people, interesting views of nature—information that is subconsciously needed for our activities or for orientation for survival (biological information needs).

Poor, or "noisy" visual environments are dominated by visual information that is irrelevant to the interests or needs of the occupants, is ambiguous or unpleasant, or distracts from desired perceptions. Examples of visual noise indoors include informationless surfaces such as translucent fluorescent light fixtures and luminous ceilings or translucent walls, whose brightness unpleasantly dominates our attention (fig. 2–5).

A typical outdoor example of a poor luminous environment is a totally overcast day. On such a day one's focus is dominated by the bright but uniform, uninteresting sky when one really wants to look at the landscape, buildings, and people to get information relevant to one's activity, interest, or survival. Sunny days are more comfortable because the ground-related objects of interest are relatively bright and most are easy to see.

2–5. Translucent walls are of little interest and compete with both the view outside and objects of interest within the room.

ACTIVITY NEEDS FOR VISUAL INFORMATION

The relationship between what people will be expected to do in a building and where and what kind of light is needed for the various activities imparts the design of any luminous environment. It is important to list and analyze activities that will take place, ranking these actions in terms of priority and frequency.[1]

A look at a programmatic approach to designing space shows that these considerations can be roughly broken down into:

- ☐ activities, which have
- ☐ subactivities, which have
- ☐ visual subactivities, which have
- ☐ various information needs from objects of varying characteristics.

In this process, the designer becomes aware of conflicting demands for optimum performance (fig. 2–6). The following paradigm offers an example:

SPACE: lecture classroom

ACTIVITIES: lecture, discussion, demonstration, audio-visual

SUBACTIVITIES: listening to speaker, music or meaningful nonverbal sounds; taking notes, movement, relaxation

VISUAL SUBACTIVITIES: looking at faces, gestures, clothing, notes, projected images

INFORMATION NEEDS: same as visual subactivities

In order to determine the appropriate characteristics of systems to be employed, each activity must be located in the space and its requirements analyzed along the following parameters:

- ☐ is the object of the activity vertical or horizontal?
- ☐ is the object local or found throughout the space?
- ☐ is the object seen by variation in reflectance, color, texture, shape, or a combination?
- ☐ is the object two- or three-dimensional? Glossy or matte? Light or dark?
- ☐ is there use of CRTs or other special lighting needs?
- ☐ is the activity of long or short duration, or intermittent?
- ☐ are the various activities simultaneous or sequential?

Various types of information needs, object characteristics, and relevant lighting characteristics for activities and subactivities should be sum-

[1]*Lam, Perception and Lighting as Formgivers for Architecture, p. 14.*

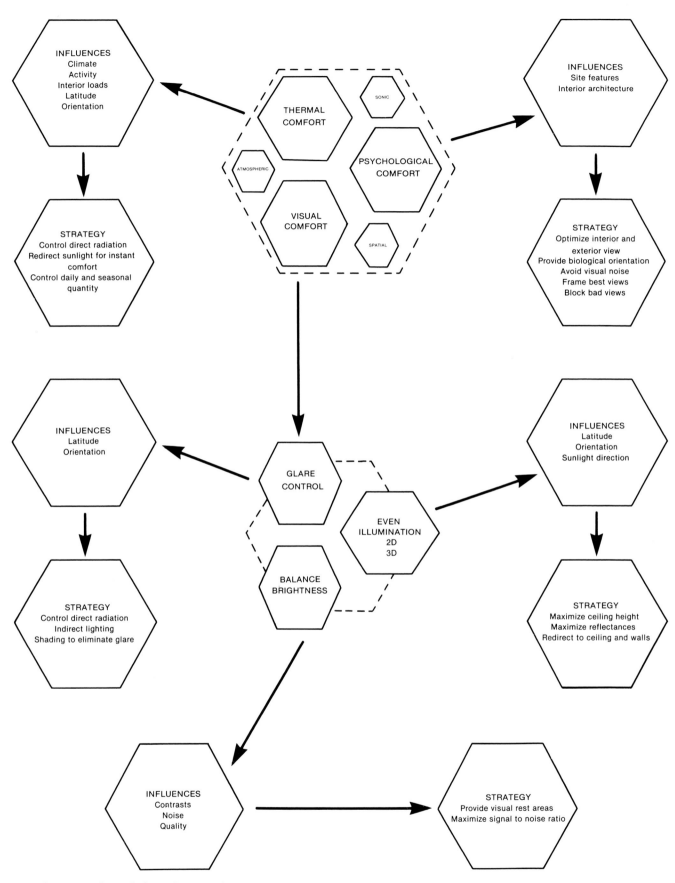

2–6. Competing demands for optimum performance.

SPACE PROGRAM CHART

SPACE _____

BEHAVIORAL OBJECTIVES
1.
2.
3.
4.
5.
6.

WHEN USED:
Day _____ %
Night _____ %

LIGHTING BUDGET
TYPE:

PROJECT _____

BIOLOGICAL AND ACTIVITY NEEDS

a BIOLOGICAL NEEDS

Movement
Relaxation — Stimulation

d PRIORITY

e VISUAL SUBACTIVITIES

Circulation information
Physical Dangers
Orientation in space
  enclosure
  time
  weather
Restful visual activity of interest
  non-activity
No distraction by high signal-noise ratio
  upsetting constancies
  upsetting expectations

b ACTIVITY NEEDS AND SUB-ACTIVITIES

c PARTICIPANTS

f VISUAL OBJECTIVES

Looking at:

g EVENTS

h PRIORITY %

i LOCATION
HOR. | VERT.
Local | General | Local | General

j REMARKS

INFORMATION NEEDS

k INFORMATION NEEDS

Routes, signs, layouts of objects and building elements
Levels, edges, obstacles, people, and other moving objects
Shape of space; relation to exterior
Nature of enclosing structure
Daylight reference
View of sky, winds, rain, sunlight, artwork, and other people
Isolation when desired
No disturbing color
Expected relationship of brightness: interior surfaces to exterior

l OBJECT CHAR.
2D | 3D

m INFORM. NEEDS
Reflectance | Form | Texture | Color (Non disturb'g | Accuracy | Transparency) | Other

n NEG. FACTORS
Context | Cast Shadows

HARDWARE SYSTEM

o CHARACTERISTICS OF VISUAL ENVIRONMENT

Positive, clear articulation of paths, nodes and areas by building elements and graphics
Adequate illumination, shadows, gradients: minimum disability glare, irrelevant disturbing pattern
Spatial and structural articulation
Clear windows, skylights
No glaring light fixtures; relevant order of focus for activity and characteristics of space
No mixed color sources on similar surfaces in similar circumstances
Illuminated wall and ceiling surfaces during the day to balance window brightness and to relate to exterior daytime conditions

p PRIME LIGHT SOURCE CHARACTERISTICS

q POSITION RELATIVE
To surface (Graz'g Angle | Normal Angle) | To viewer (View'g Angle | Mirror Angle)

r SIZE
Max. | Min.

s WAVE CHAR.
Polarized | Full Spectrum | Partial Spectrum

t REMARKS

u NUMERICAL CRITERIA
Unit of Measure | Req. Value

FOOTNOTES

2-7. Space Program Chart. (Reprinted, by permission, from State University Construction Fund, *An Approach to the Design of the Luminous Environment*)

2–8. Visual information is continuously monitored in many activities. The child shown here must pay attention to the ground surfaces to avoid tripping or falling into the water and to the movement of other people to avoid collision.

2–9. Disorientation at the T.W.A. terminal of Kennedy airport. The sloping floors, nonvertical walls, and lack of windows give one no points of reference.

2–10. Gallery of the Guggenheim Museum (Frank Lloyd Wright, Architect). This space is disorienting for similar reasons as the T.W.A. terminal. Here, however, the pictures, which are hung on a true horizontal, do give one a reference level to substitute for a level horizon. (Photograph courtesy of John Lam)

marized for the designer in a Space Program Chart (fig. 2–7). At first glance this chart appears impossibly complicated and formidable. Closer consideration will reveal this chart to simply be an organized format for the ideas any thoughtful and experienced designer unconsciously processes in every design decision.[2]

BIOLOGICAL INFORMATION NEEDS

Survival, protection, and sustenance affect the need to perceive and feel comfortable with the environment. Lighting that provides well for biological needs in most spaces simultaneously takes care of most activity needs.[3]

Inaccurate or inadequate visual information can be distracting and even dangerous. Dissatisfaction or gloom results from any lack deemed unreasonable (i.e., not by choice or in exchange for another advantage). Even during sleep, perception of changes in location, movement, and state is necessary at all times for the protection of the body.

Every activity requires visual contact in order to obtain necessary information. Some examples of activities and their concomitant information needs are:

ACTIVE ACTIVITIES: walking, running, jumping (perception of level, ground surfaces, obstructions, and direction as shown in fig. 2–8), and working (perception of object of focus)

INACTIVE ACTIVITIES: protection from physical attack (from animals, people, machines, weather, fire, and intense sound) and protection of organs (particularly sensory and reproductive) from physical damage

More subtle instances of the need for visual contact can be shown in the need to maintain a sense of equilibrium (fig. 2–9). On a foggy day at the beach, for example, we are uncomfortable because the biological need for a defined horizon is unfulfilled.

Likewise, the effect is uncomfortable in the Guggenheim Museum in New York City (fig. 2–10) where the floors slope but the pictures are hung on a true horizontal.

While these more subtle effects influence perception, there are clear information needs that we monitor continuously and unconsciously in sharply defined areas. These include:

☐ Location, with regard to water, heat, food, sunlight, escape routes, destination, and so on;

☐ Time and other environmental conditions that relate to our external schedules as well as to our innate biological clocks;

☐ Weather, as it relates to the need for clothing and heating or cooling, the need for shelter, opportunities to bask in the beneficial rays of the sun, and so on;

[2]*Dietz, Lam, and Hallenbeck,* An Approach to the Design of the Luminous Environment, *p. 75.*
[3]*Lam,* Perception and Lighting as Formgivers for Architecture, *p. 30.*

☐ Enclosure, the safety of the structure, the location and nature of environmental controls, protection from cold, heat, rain, and other elements;

☐ The presence of other living things—plants, animals, and people—particularly those perceived as dangerous;

☐ Territory, its boundaries and the means available within a given environment for the personalization of space;

☐ Opportunities for relaxation and stimulation of the mind, body, and senses;

☐ Places of refuge, shelter in time of perceived danger.[4]

Once we are aware of this information, we evaluate and reach a qualitative decision. We feel uneasy if information is ambiguous, tense if the facts are bad, disappointing, or signal danger, relaxed if the facts indicate everything is under control, and pleased if control is achieved.

Because of time orientation, during the day we subconsciously expect it to be brighter outside buildings than inside. At night we expect it to be darker outside buildings than inside. We tend to feel "gloomy" when the situation is ambiguous, such as on dark overcast days. The length of the "ambiguous" period is extended by the use of low-transmission glass. It is unexpected, and therefore depressing, to see our reflection when looking out a window at midday when we expect to see the far brighter scene outdoors. Recent studies have indicated that many people suffer from a "short-day syndrome" and are depressed in the winter months. For similar reasons, many, including the author, are less tired flying westward with the day extended than flying eastward with the length of the day sharply reduced.

Because we desire security from a surrounding enclosure, a clear understanding of a building's structure satisfies biological needs (as does a view of sunlight or exterior landscape) and is perceived positively. The ambiguous nature of luminous ceilings or rows of luminous fixtures is likely to be found unpleasant. Although uneven gradients positively defining the shape of solid surfaces seem pleasant and natural, uneven gradients on a uniform flat material seem unnatural and distracting.

For some activities, such as relaxing at poolside, sunlight may be completely positive (fig. 2–11). But, while we all enjoy seeing signs of its presence, being in the sunlight may have definite negative consequences if the light or heat interferes with what we want to see or do (fig. 2–12).

We can, however, welcome feeling and seeing sunlight inside a building, as long as it does not interfere with our activities. Direct sunlight on our desk or work area can be very bothersome—but only if we are unable to move away from it or control it and are exposed to it for a long period of time. In cold climates, we may seek and delight in the radiant warmth of direct sunlight within as well as outside of buildings.

Visual environments are generally most pleasing when the surfaces of interest are the principal apparent sources of light, and the actual sources are concealed from normal view. This is accomplished in indirect lighting of walls and ceilings combined with well-baffled direct lighting of work surfaces.

2–11. Sunlight is completely positive for sunbathing. (Photograph courtesy of Victor Olgyay)

2–12. Sunlight can interfere with such tasks as reading outdoors on a sunny day.

[4]*Lam, Perception and Lighting as Formgivers for Architecture, p. 21.*

Biological Information Needs   21

Sunlight on the walls is welcomed information, not "glare," as would be produced by translucent lighting fixtures of equal luminance. The backlighting produced by the translucent panels in figure 2-5 is not seen as natural sunlight but as informationless unnatural distraction—more frustrating than pleasurable, and therefore "glare."

When we are inside a room at night, looking at a dark window bright with reflections of the room, we perceive the window as "darker" than an interior wall of lower luminance. The wall is nonthreatening, but the window is a source of possible danger since we can be seen through it but cannot see outside. Mirrored or low-transmission glass compounds the difficulty of seeing out at night.

The people on the walkway in figure 2–13 are doubtless very much aware of the water's edge on one side and the wall on the other. Several points are illustrated:

☐ Inherent biological needs—Attention is drawn to the edge as a possible source of danger; there is also an awareness of the location of water.

☐ Object clarity—The edge is emphasized by a change in materials (especially important when illumination is or must be minimal because of conflicting demands, such as experienced in a theater) or where sloping shadows add positive information, supporting one's awareness of stair risers.

Figure 2–14 is a master table of biological needs. It summarizes the visual environment and hardware systems associated with various biological needs. Also included in the table are descriptions of the critical time/situation of each need and the relevant visual information.[5]

Good design must satisfy needs for information and qualitative conditions, rather than only quantitative criteria.

A room that one instinctively finds attractive and appropriate for its purpose is not an aesthetic frill; rather, it is likely to be a more comfortable and productive space. The characteristics of such a space have value, measurable by surveys if not by light meters.

[5]*Dietz, Lam, and Hallenbeck,* An Approach to the Design of the Luminous Environment, *pp. 68–71.*

2–13. Walkway, Venice. (Photograph courtesy of John Lam)

LIGHT AND BIOLOGICAL HEALTH

A variety of physiological mechanisms in man respond either directly or indirectly to the spectral characteristics of sunlight and its artificial equivalents. Most of these responses are indirect, relying on the transmission of light by the photoreceptors in the retina to neural signals, which in turn affect various bodily functions. Although a number of these effects have been identified in animals, for the most part it has yet to be determined to what extent they pertain to and are significant for man.

Most common and perhaps least significant here are the reactions of skin to ultraviolet radiation. While tanning or burning from sustained exposure is now becoming recognized as a source of cancer, the degree of exposure in buildings is of such limited medical importance that it will not be discussed further.

By far the most beneficial function of sunlight to man that we have identified is the production of vitamin D by the absorption of ultraviolet radiation. Vitamin D in turn plays a significant role in the body's absorption of calcium, a deficiency of which can result in rickets in children and osteoporosis in adults. Artificial illumination that simulates the solar spectrum can also induce this metabolic response in humans, but the quantities of ultraviolet radiation available from artificial sources are so low that eight hours of exposure to 100 footcandles is the approximate equivalent of three minutes spent outdoors on a sunny day.

For the aged, institutionalized, or otherwise confined—adults who are getting insufficient vitamin D to meet their biological needs—it may be found desirable or in some cases necessary to provide increased means for ultraviolet exposure. This could have important implications for policy makers, administrators, and building designers. High-level artificial lighting installations could be beneficial, but it is much easier to optimize natural light when possible. Solaria that take maximum advantage of the available sunlight could be required in certain facilities; balconies could be required in homes for the aged; and even normal populations could be encouraged to spend more time outdoors at midday. The Soviet Union is already making significant use of "photaria" (artificially illuminated solaria), particularly for persons living in polar regions or those working underground or in windowless buildings. Whenever sunlight is available at a site, however, solaria would be much more effective and pleasant, by providing several thousand footcandles for those who are unable to get sunlight for much or most of the year. Of course, it would be much easier if one could get a few minutes of sunlight rather than hours of artificial illumination of lower intensities.

LIGHT AND THE EYE

Exposure to light can damage the eye in varying degrees, according to the nature and intensity of the source and the length of exposure. The extent of impairment may range from permanent physiological damage to what is commonly termed "eyestrain." It is certainly clear from a review of the literature that overexposure to light is far more damaging to the eyes than underexposure and that both the ultraviolet and visible

Biological need for visual information	Critical time or situation	Visual information required	Desired qualities	Qualities to be avoided (Implications for the luminous environment and hardware systems)
Physical security	When danger is expected from people or animals	Location of potential threats; the nature of the surrounding enclosure	Eliminate unlighted areas and sources of glare which might conceal danger; clarify the nature of the surrounding enclosure — structure, possible exits, etc.	Avoid flimsy structural forms such as the typical luminous ceiling; avoid obscuring structural elements with unshielded light sources; avoid using sources inconsistently (different sources to light identical surfaces)
	When danger is expected from structural failure	Comprehensible structure with clear continuity and visual logic	Use forms consistent with the expectations of the viewer; use light gradients consistent with the form of the structure which they illuminate	
	When danger is expected from fire	Location of control and prevention equipment; escape routes clearly visible	Use lighting to articulate circulation paths and exits; use color coded fire extinguishers and clear EXIT signs	Avoid unevenly illuminated EXIT signs, EXIT signs which do not dominate their surroundings sufficiently to be clearly visible; eliminate other signs in the vicinity of EXIT signs which would compete for the visual attention; avoid overly bright EXIT signs, on the other hand, in dark environments such as theaters
	When danger may be caused by intense light or glare			Use proper glare shields or other control devices on luminaires so that sources do not achieve an undesired prominence or create disability glare conditions while providing required illumination for tasks or biological needs
	When danger might be anticipated due to unsanitary conditions	Maximum evidence of high sanitation standards	Emphasize clean work areas in kitchens, labs, etc.	Avoid highlighting areas such as dirty dish conveyors or garbage collection areas
Orientation	At all times; maximum when moving	Level horizontal reference clues	Use material joints (e.g. in masonry), moldings, expansion joints, mullions, etc. to establish clear horizontal orientation	Avoid inclined floors without clear visual information defining the nature of the incline; spaces defined by irregular or curvilinear enclosing surfaces without clear horizon clues
		Definition of ground surface contours, enclosing boundaries, obstructions, level changes	Define level changes and edges with highlighting, consistent shadows, changes in material (color, surface, or reflectance)	Avoid distracting elements in the visual field at level changes; avoid confusing elements such as inconsistent shadows or carpet patterns which tend to obscure rather than emphasize level changes
		Location relative to destinations and exits	Articulate the building layout and circulation system by a clear differentiation of circulation nodes and destinations with distinctive patterns of decorative light sources or by selective highlighting of elements such as elevator cores, etc.; corridors should be differentiated from work spaces, and different types of corridor should be treated differently; good graphics should be used, particularly at decision points such as corridors and intersections	Avoid undifferentiated lighting schemes which apply the same design to functionally disparate spaces, providing no visual guidance information. Avoid backlighted signs with opaque lettering, in which the shape of the background typically dominates the intended message

portions of the spectrum are involved. However, the incidence rate of overexposure is so low that it is not of major concern. Normally, we protect ourselves instinctively by squinting or closing our eyes. Exceptions might be the rare individual who views a solar eclipse with the naked eye or does arc welding without protective dark glasses.

Consider the exposure to reflected ultraviolet radiation encountered by the eyes of the average vacationer in a sunny afternoon spent on or near the water. Since millions are exposed to this hazard annually without apparent long-term ill effects, we can conclude that such exposure does not present a significant health hazard.

Despite common public belief, it is clear from the literature that low illumination levels are in no way harmful to the eye. Dr. David Cogan,

Biological need	Condition	Need	Positive response	Negative response
Relaxation of the body and mind	During sleep	Only that required to maintain the sensation of security; uniform conditions of light, sound and temperature desirable	Provide night lights as required for security; switching hardware should be readily accessible	Minimize the number of obtrusive luminous signs visible from sleeping areas; avoid street lighting with poor glare control
	During work	Interesting visual rest centers desirable	Provide visual foci such as views, artwork, positive expression of structural form, decorative or orientation-related patterns of light sources (chandeliers, graphics, illuminated sculpture)	Eliminate competing sources of visual noise such as glaring fixtures
	While awake but waiting or idle	Interesting visual environment	Provide visual foci as above; evidence of sunlight, plants, water elements such as pools or fountains, etc.	Minimize unsightly, unpleasant, or irrelevant elements of the visual environment, since their negative impact will be greatest when the viewer has no conscious preoccupation
Adjustment of the biological clock (time orientation)	Continuous need, particularly strong in unfamiliar situations	Awareness of the state of the diurnal cycle, since luminous conditions in interiors are evaluated with reference to external conditions	Views of exterior conditions should be possible via clear windows or clear skylights	Do not design windowless spaces unless the justification is clear and the omission serves some other need: i.e., in a museum or theater; wherever possible, give a view of more than just sky
Contact with nature, sunlight, and with other living beings	Interior environments	Evidence of sunlight in every space or in nearby and accessible spaces	Visible daylit or sunlit surfaces such as plant material or window reveals; also daylit or sunlit meaningful translucent surfaces such as stained glass or colored glass block	Avoid excessive direct sunlight on work surfaces; avoid informationless distracting surfaces such as translucent windows and skylights; sun control devices if required should create minimum visual noise and figure/background conflict with the view (i.e. large-scale louvers or fine-mesh screening rather than intermediate-scale egg crates or blinds with no inherent visual interest)
Definition of personal territory	Particularly in public or work environments	Visible evidence of personal control and occupation of territory	Provide local lighting which can be controlled by users; provide distinctive or large-scale organization of the visual environment which can be used to locate and identify personal territory from a distance	Avoid public or work environments with no inherent means for personalization of space by the users

2-14. Master table of biological needs. (Reprinted, by permission, from Lam, *Perception and Lighting as Formgivers for Architecture*)

Chief of Ophthalmology at the Massachusetts Eye and Ear Infirmary in Boston, and Professor of Ophthalmology, Harvard Medical School, has been particularly vehement on this subject for many years.

LIGHT FOR PLANT GROWTH

As a by-product of satisfying the user's needs for biologically important information, extensive plantings have been introduced in buildings to make up for their unnaturally large scale and to provide the users with needed contact with nature. In many spaces, particularly atrium spaces, the most stringent lighting is often required for plant material too large to rotate (with greenhouse specimens) and too expensive to replace if unhealthy.

Because the high illumination levels required by some plants used indoors (100–500 footcandles) are many times more than those needed for human activities, plants should be places where sunlight penetration is maximum. In addition, supplementary lighting should be directed specifically to the trees rather than to the overall space (see case studies G1, G2).

Simplistic quantitative criteria for tree lighting are usually incorrect. Horizontal illumination levels measured at the top of a tree do not adequately describe the photons received by the leaves throughout the tree, which are needed for photosynthesis. For example, if four floodlights located directly overhead to illuminate the top of a tree were spread out and directed to illuminate the tree from all sides, the horizontal illumination at the top would be decreased, but the tree would receive an equal amount of illumination with a different distribution. This arrangement of lights would promote a more favorable (rounded, rather than vertical and spiky) tree growth configuration, in the manner of individual trees in open fields rather than trees in the woods.

Criteria

The proper measure of light for tree growth should be the total light (footcandles × hours) received by the tree from all directions, not only on the horizontal plane. Seventy-five footcandles from all directions is generally better than 200 footcandles from a single source. Trees also benefit more from the ultraviolet than the visible spectrum. A few minutes of direct sunlight (approximately 8,000 footcandles) is equivalent to many hours of diffused daylight or artificial light at building interior levels. For example:

8,000 footcandles × .25 hours

= 800 footcandles × 2.5 hours

= 80 footcandles × 25 hours.

SUNLIGHT AND THERMAL COMFORT

The relation between sunlight and thermal comfort in homes is somewhat different than that in offices and other types of buildings that most benefit from sunlighting. In residences, the major effort in solar design is to store heat for use when sunlight is not present. The instantaneous effect of sunlight is less important because homes are generally less occupied during the day than are office buildings. Furthermore, they do not need as much light, and people are free to move about to the most comfortable spots. Residential solar design is primarily that of *solar-thermal-economics*.

The concerns are somewhat different in the sunlighting of offices, where the need for illumination and thermal comfort is simultaneous, and the occupants are less free to move. Here, there should be more concern as to the instantaneous effects of solar radiation on comfort, as well as on energy conservation from good passive solar design.

Redirection of sunlight to illuminate a space more uniformly also has a corresponding effect of redistributing heat, because the indirect light is eventually absorbed by darker colored walls, floors, and furniture surfaces. This slow heat storage minimizes local overheating and reduces heating and cooling energy requirements. As in homes, this contribution has more of an effect on energy cost than on thermal comfort, which can be produced by the HVAC system in any case.

In buildings with sunlighting, the more stringent concern is with solar radiation as it affects comfort. Here people are not free to move at will. A thermostat setting for the room in general will not ensure comfort for those more exposed to the direct rays of the sun. Direct sunlight on the body or clothing may be welcomed when the thermostat is on the low end of the temperature comfort zone (in winter). It will not be wanted when the thermostat is on the high end of the comfort zone (in summer).

Another important radiation effect is that of heat loss or gain to large nearby surfaces that are much colder or warmer than body temperature. This can be a problem with large areas of glass.

I have visited offices on cold days when the curtains or blinds were closed (and desirable light and view shut out) to baffle the radiant heat from hot, heat-absorbing glass. If the thermostat had been lowered, others deeper in the room would have been too cold. Such discomfort would not have occurred if the sunlight had been allowed to pass through clear glass onto the much more massive room surfaces (floors and walls), which would have had little temperature change.

Similarly, if exposed to the cold glass of single-glazed windows, occupants will draw the blinds. This happens when double glazing is not considered to be cost-effective in conserving energy and insufficient value is given to the radiation effects on thermal comfort (see case study C1).

③ Light and its Control

Reducing the importance of high light levels and exact quantities of light as criteria for evaluation requires that designers understand some basic physics of light and its control. This will enable them to best utilize energy to achieve the desired balance of qualitative and quantitative objectives. This chapter will discuss those physical principles most relevant to designers.

LIGHT

In sunlighting, we are concerned with the entire spectrum of solar radiation, including wavelengths of light outside the range of human vision. These include the shorter wavelengths (ultraviolet) that can damage sensitive materials such as those in museums, and the longer wavelengths (infrared) that produce heat (see chart of radiant energy spectrum in chapter 4). While all of the wavelengths in the visible spectrum generally produce similar effects, sunlighting design can, to a degree, modify the balance of the invisible constituent wavelengths (UV and IR) to suit programmatic needs.

Speed of Light

All forms of radiation are transmitted at the same extremely high rate of speed (approximately 186,300 miles per second) and behave alike in many ways. This phenomenon is very important in design. For example, it allows light to be modeled directly at any scale without the need for a scale factor. The modeling of sound is infinitely more complex because, with a speed of 1,100 feet per second, the difference between 1 foot and 100 feet is significant.

There is no loss of light passing through outer space, which appears black because there are no particles to intercept light. Although the level of sunlight is reduced about 30 percent (from 14,000 footcandles to 10,000 footcandles) from the edge of the earth's atmosphere to sea level by the molecular particles of clear air and water vapor, the mass of clear air at building scale absorbs virtually no light.

Light travels in straight lines in a constant medium. When encountering a medium at an angle with a different index of refraction, light will slow down and hence be refracted (fig. 3–1). The speed of light through glass is 30 percent less than it is through air, the phenomenon around which lenses are designed.

TYPES OF LIGHT SOURCES

For designers, the most important considerations about a light source are its size, shape, intensity from various directions, and its location in space.

Depending on its size (relative to its distance from the surface being illuminated), a light source may be a point source, a line source, or an area source. In photometric testing, the measuring distance is more than ten times the maximum dimension of the light source. Thus, a soft white lamp will produce soft shadows and behave like an area source to surfaces a few inches away but act like a point source when at ceiling height. Similarly, a 4′ × 4′ skylight will act like a point source when more than 40 feet away (fig. 3–2).

Point Sources

Illumination from a point source varies inversely with the square of the distance (fig. 3–3). There is no loss of light, only an increase in the area illuminated in each cone of light from a point source. On earth, illuminance from direct sunlight is constant at any height, because the rays are parallel when the light source is an infinite distance away (and changes in distance are insignificant).

Point sources produce sharp shadows.

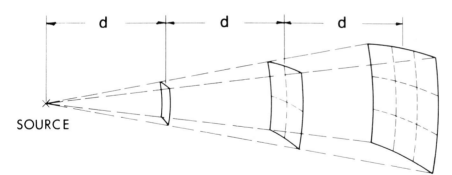

SOURCE

Line Sources

When a light source is a point source on one axis and an extended source on the other, illumination from it varies inversely with distance. Thus, the measured intensity of illumination on a horizontal surface from a continuous narrow skylight or light fixture will be cut in half if the roof is doubled in height (fig. 3–4).

Line sources produce shadows along one axis.

Area Sources

When the light source is extended in both directions, the effect of distance from the light source (ceiling height) is much less. In the case of area sources, the illumination received at any point will vary with the

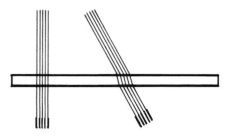

3–1. At angles normal to glass, no refraction occurs. At any other angle, refraction does occur.

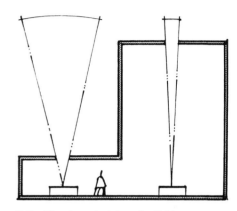

3–2. The characteristics of a light source are relative to its distance from the viewer. At a distance of forty feet, a 4′ × 4′ skylight is a point source; at a few feet, it is an area source.

3–3. The inverse square law. The same quantity of light flux is distributed over an inversely greater area, as the distance from source to receiving surface is increased. (Reprinted, by permission, from IES Lighting Handbook, 1981 Volume)

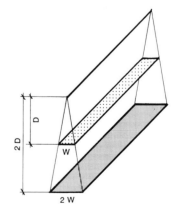

3–4. Line source. Illumination varies inversely with distance.

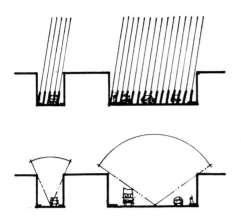

3–5. Top: the sun as a directional point source produces equal illumination on the ground of an alley and a highway. Bottom: the area source of the overcast sky illuminates the highway much more than the alley because it "sees" more sky.

luminance of the source and the solid angle subtended. Thus on an overcast day (sky vault as an area source) a four-lane highway will always receive much more illumination than an alley because the amount of sky "seen" by the alley is much less. On sunny days, the sun as a point source will produce equal illumination on the pavement of both the alley and the highway (fig. 3–5).

In buildings, a large area source of a given luminance (indirectly illuminated or luminous ceiling) produces proportionally higher levels of illumination in a large room than a small one. Conversely, the ceiling of a small room must have a much higher luminance (be much brighter) than the ceiling in a large room to produce the same level of illumination at desk top. This is because the desk in a small room "sees" less ceiling (light source) and more wall area than the same desk in a larger room (fig. 3–6).

The inefficiency of diffused light from the ceiling in small rooms can be greatly diminished by redirecting the light with high-reflectance walls, thereby extending the effective light source. Small rooms are assumed to be inefficient because they often have dark walls. If the walls (or even the top one-third of the walls) as well as the ceiling are white, there will be much less difference in efficiency between large and small rooms.

Although less efficient, the illumination received at desk level throughout a room will be most uniform when the area source is relatively far away (high ceiling), because the differences in solid angle between different points will than be small. Using the entire ceiling and wall surfaces as light sources (via reflected sunlight) will deliver the light with much less glare than would result from the same amount of light from a smaller area source (such as a skylight or a window on an overcast day).

Maximizing the size of area sources produces minimum shadows. Thus, a person casts minimum shadows on his or her work if windows are continuous, and the room (i.e., walls and ceilings) is of high reflectance.

3–6. The ceiling of a small room must have a much higher luminance than that of a large room with wider proportions to produce equal illumination.

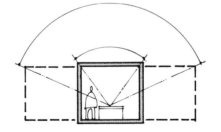 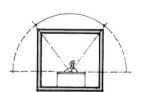

Nondirectional and Directional Sources

Light is almost always nondirectional when generated. Light sources become directional depending on where they are placed relative to other surfaces and the nature of those surfaces. Light from an incandescent bulb hanging in the center of a room is nondirectional. The distribution of this light can be made directional by being blocked off in most directions (placing the bulb in a black can, for instance) or, more efficiently, by being redistributed to a single direction using reflectors or lenses (fig. 3–7).

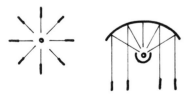

3–7. Nondirectional sources can be made effectively directional.

The distance of the sun from the earth makes sunlight highly directional with virtually parallel rays. This makes diagramming its path in buildings very easy.

CONTROL OF LIGHT

Because of its very high intensity and constant movement, sunlight is difficult to use directly and should be used in a diffused form, ideally as indirect light.

Light can be controlled by taking advantage of a number of phenomena: reflection, refraction, polarization, interference, diffraction, diffusion, absorption, and baffling.

For sunlighting design, control of *reflection* is the most important principle. *Refraction* may be useful for distributing light, and *baffling* can be used to reduce glare when more positive redirection is not possible. The other phenomena listed may be used in developing special materials, but are not of primary significance here.

Reflection and Reflectance

Reflection may be specular, spread, diffuse, or compound depending on the direction of the light reflected. The *amount* of light reflected—*reflectance*—is independent of specularity. The reflectance of a material is the total percentage of light reflected, both diffuse and specular.

Specular Reflection

Specular (mirror) reflections are produced by polished surfaces. The angle of incidence is equal to the angle of reflection and should be diagrammed in that manner (fig. 3–8).

Specular reflectors may reflect very efficiently (mirror glass or special processed aluminum) or inefficiently (polished black marble, black structural glass, or the front surface of clear glass). Do not confuse specularity with efficiency (fig. 3–9). Polished stainless steel reflects light much less efficiently than matte white paint (55–65 percent versus 75–90 percent).

3–8. Specular reflections: the angle of incidence is equal to the angle of reflection.

3–9. Specularity does not imply efficiency (the total amount of light reflected).
(Reprinted by permission, from *IES Lighting Handbook, 1981 Volume*)

Material	Reflectance * or Transmittance† (per cent)	Characteristics
	Reflecting	
Specular		
Mirrored and optical coated glass	80 to 99	Provide directional control of light and brightness at specific viewing angles. Effective as efficient reflectors and for special decorative lighting effects.
Metalized and optical coated plastic	75 to 97	
Processed anodized and optical coated aluminum	75 to 95	
Polished aluminum	60 to 70	
Chromium	60 to 65	
Stainless steel	55 to 65	
Black structural glass	5	
Spread		
Processed aluminum (diffuse)	70 to 80	General diffuse reflection with a high specular surface reflection of from 5 to 10 per cent of the light.
Etched aluminum	70 to 85	
Satin chromium	50 to 55	
Brushed aluminum	55 to 58	
Aluminum paint	60 to 70	
Diffuse		
White plaster	90 to 92	Diffuse reflection results in uniform surface brightness at all viewing angles. Materials of this type are good reflecting backgrounds for coves and luminous forms.
White paint**	75 to 90	
Porcelain enamel**	65 to 90	
White terra-cotta**	65 to 80	
White structural glass	75 to 80	
Limestone	35 to 65	

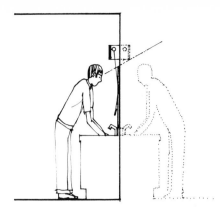

3–10. A simple diagram will show whether a bathroom mirror will reflect a light source into the eyes of the user or only below eye level.

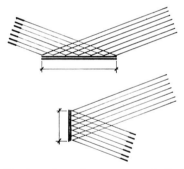

3–11. With a moving light source, specular reflectors must either track the source or be set for a given condition.

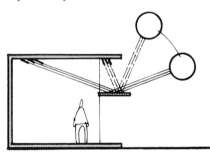

3–12. Specular reflectors are most effective when making large changes of direction.

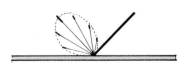

3–13. Spread reflections: a softened reflection at the mirror angle.

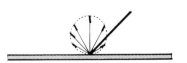

3–14. Diffuse reflections: nondirectional. (Reprinted, by permission, from *IES Lighting Handbook, 1981 Volume*)

When all reflections are perfectly specular, a light source is seen from only one angle. That is why you see your face in the bathroom mirror and not the light overhead (fig. 3–10).

Specular reflections can be useful when perfectly controlled and very detrimental when not controlled. They help control light in well-designed low-brightness fixtures as long as the proper lamp is used, but will produce glare with the wrong lamp or when wall washers are incorrectly aimed. Using specular reflections in sunlighting is even more difficult. With a moving source of light (the sun), specular reflectors must track for maximum effectiveness or settle on a reasonable compromise, such as to optimize one particular condition (fig. 3–11). Care must be taken to ensure that the undiffused sunlight reflects to a building surface and not to eye-level positions.

If the desired reflector geometry of a light fixture or sunlight reflector is not physically possible, it is better to use spread or diffused reflectors than specular ones. In this way, some of the light (rather than none) will go where wanted. Conversely, the light reflected in unwanted directions will be less objectionable. Spread and diffuse reflectors will occur accidentally if mirrors are not kept polished.

Mirrors reflecting direct sunlight must be very flat and free from distortion ("oilcanning"). Otherwise, the patterns of reflected sunlight can be unattractive.

Specular reflectors are used most efficiently when they cause a major redirection of light. In such cases, they intercept the light quite directly and produce a beam of light almost as wide as their surface area. Specular reflectors are less efficient when making small changes of direction, when the light is very oblique to the reflecting surface and requires a proportionately larger surface area (fig. 3–12). For applications of mirror reflectors, refer to chapter 6 (figures 6–72, 6–73), and case studies B7, F1, F2, G1, and G2).

Spread reflections

Spread reflections are softened reflections at the mirror angle created by slight irregularities in the surface due to corrugating, etching, hammering, and so forth. They should be diagrammed accordingly (fig. 3–13).

Spread reflections should be used when a properly controlled direction is possible but a softened image desirable. Some people prefer to see sunlight reflected in that form, but I prefer the sharp edges of untampered sunlight and perfect brightness control at the reflector. However, the softened images from slightly unpolished spread reflectors do have the advantage of hiding imperfect light-receiving surfaces and the distracting images of distorted or dirty reflectors (or filament images in light fixtures).

Diffuse reflections

Matte finishes produce diffuse reflections with no directional control. Regardless of the angle of the light source, matte finishes reflect equally in all directions. In schematic design diagrams, diffuse reflections from matte white ceilings should be diagrammed as nondirectional reflections, not specular (fig. 3–14).

While the luminance (brightness) of a specular reflector will be irregular (different from different directions) and mirror that of the source at one angle, the luminance of a diffuse reflector will depend on the illumination component normal to the surface and the reflectance of the surface (fig. 3–15).

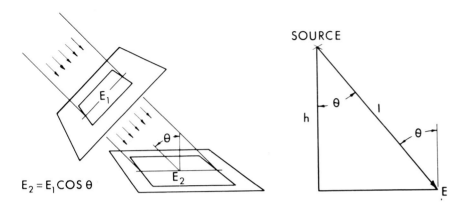

$E_2 = E_1 \cos \theta$

3–15. The Lambert cosine law: light flux striking a surface at angles other than normal is distributed over a greater area. (Reprinted, by permission from *IES Lighting Handbook, 1981 Volume*)

Reflectance of matte materials is dependent on their color and hue. White and yellow have high reflectance; red, blue, and green have low reflectance. Paint charts usually list their respective reflectance values. The reflectances of some common building materials are listed in figure 3–16.

Material	Reflectance (per cent)	Material	Reflectance (per cent)
Bluestone, sandstone	18	Asphalt (free from dirt)	7
Brick			
light buff	48	Earth (moist cultivated)	7
dark buff	40		
dark red glazed	30	Granolite pavement	17
Cement	27	Grass (dark green)	6
Concrete	40	Gravel	13
Marble (white)	45	Macadam	18
Paint (white)		Slate (dark clay)	8
new	75	Snow	
old	55	new	74
Glass		old	64
clear	7	Vegetation (mean)	25
reflective	20–30		
tinted	7		

3–16. The reflectances of common building materials.

Diffuse reflectors reflect light from small particles oriented in all directions. The effective reflectance of a surface is less if that surface is highly configured. For example, if a ceiling is coffered, the illumination it receives will be distributed over a greater surface area, and will be proportionately less efficient in its reflectivity than a flat ceiling of the same material (fig. 3–17). The design implications of ceiling configuration are more important in large rooms than in small rooms, where wall reflec-

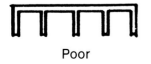 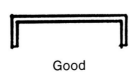 

Poor   Good   Best

3–17. The effective reflectance of ceiling shapes increases with a reduction in surface area.

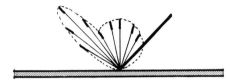

3–18. Combined matte and spread reflections.

tances are more important because they constitute a higher proportion of the room surfaces.

Compound and Semispecular Reflectors

Most materials are compound reflectors. They produce diffuse reflections from the colored base material and some sheen from a shiny transparent surface (fig. 3–18). High-gloss paint and polished white marble give a combination of matte and specular reflections. The effect is quite similar to that of spread reflectors. Shiny fabrics may combine the characteristics of matte and spread reflectors.

As with spread reflections, proper application of compound reflections can be useful. For instance, if a bad geometric relationship between light sources and a polished marble floor or counter is unavoidable, the annoying reflections will be much less noticeable if the marble used is light in color rather than black.

Selective Reflections

Ultraviolet

The color (spectrum) of light reflected will be affected by the color of the reflector. A reflector that reflects all parts of the light spectrum equally is rare, if not nonexistent. Colored reflectors reflect some colors and absorb others. Other reflectors may reflect all visible colors equally but none of those beyond the visible range. Such selective reflectors can be very useful in changing the ratio of visible to ultraviolet light admitted—a phenomenon that is particularly valuable in museums. A zinc-based white paint will reflect only 4 percent of the UV component while reflecting 90 percent of the visible light (fig. 3–19). With multiple reflections the proportion can be improved still further as an alternative to using special UV-filtering plastic glazing.

3–19. Selective reflection in the ultraviolet wavelengths in the region of 253.7 Nanometers. (Reprinted, by permission, from *IES Handbook, 1981 Reference Volume*)

Material	Reflectance (per cent)
Aluminum	
Untreated surface	40–60
Treated surface	60–89
Sputtered on glass	75–85
Paints	55–75
Stainless steel	25–30
Tin plate	25–30
Magnesium oxide	75–88
Calcium carbonate	70–80
New plaster	55–60
White baked enamels	5–10
White oil paints	5–10
White water paints	10–35
Zinc oxide paints	4–5

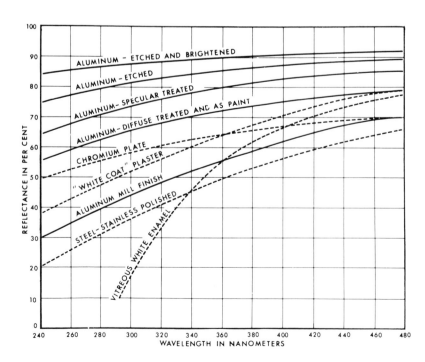

Material	Visible Wavelengths			Near Infrared Wavelengths			Far Infrared Wavelengths			
	400 nm	500 nm	600 nm	1000 nm	2000 nm	4000 nm	7000 nm	10,000 nm	12,000 nm	15,000 nm
	R	R	R	R	R	R	R	R	R	R
Specular aluminum	87	82	86	97	94	88	84	27	16	14
Diffuse aluminum	79	75	84	86	95	88	81	68	49	44
White synthetic enamel	48	85	84	90	45	8	4	4	2	9
White porcelain enamel	56	84	83	76	38	4	2	22	8	9

3–20. Properties of lighting materials showing selective reflection in the infrared wavelengths. (Reprinted, by permission, from *IES Handbook, 1981 Reference Volume*)

Infrared

Infrared radiation is also reflected in different proportions than is visible light, depending on reflector material and color. For example, polished and diffuse aluminum reflectors reflect much more infrared in proportion to visible light than do white enamel reflectors (fig. 3–20). Aluminum reflectors can be used to direct both heat and light into a space or to reject them when they are not wanted through the use of blinds.

Reflecting sunlight into the building from white painted surfaces removes more IR than heat-absorbing glass will, with the additional benefit that the heat-absorbing (and reradiating) surface is located outside of the space. These materials are helpful in increasing the efficacy of sunlight and should be used to get light with a minimum of heat.

Research is needed to determine the IR reflectance of other common materials—such as other types of paint, sand, snow, grass, and concrete—that may be used for sunlight control in buildings.

Refraction of Light

Light is refracted when it passes through materials with different indicies of refraction (general densities). It is much more difficult to make major changes in direction by refraction than by reflection; to do so, the light would have to be bent in several stages. The amount of redirection of light necessary in sunlighting is thus best achieved by other means.

At times, a small change in the direction of light is useful. In such cases, prismatic glass blocks or panels can be used effectively (fig. 3–21).

3–21. Architectural application of a prismatic, directional glass block.

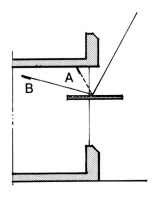

3–22. Very thin refracting sheets may be used to modify the reflecting angle of specular reflecting surfaces (*A* = normal angle; *B* = improved angle).

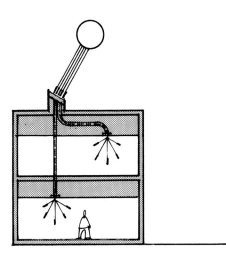

3–23. Piped light.

Unfortunately, a by-product of such refraction is distortion of all views. Therefore, views should be separated from the refracting device, either by providing an additional "view window" or by integrating the device into a reflecting surface (fig. 3–22). Prismatic glass block was used quite extensively in American schools and hospitals in the 40s and 50s, usually in combination with view windows. I always found them most unattractive; perhaps the practice did not continue because others did, too. In recent times there has been some use of clear glass block for interior partitions. It is generally used to borrow light and to provide physical, acoustic, and thermal separation and for decoration, however—*not* for controlled distribution of light.

This limitation may not be important for some applications, such as when permanent privacy is wanted, or when the glazed area is out of normal view. One such application is in glass-block pavements to illuminate spaces below. This was done by John Portman at the Emory University Athletic Center over the gym, pool, and concourses and also at his Marina Center, Singapore, to get light from the plaza to the concourse.

When the scene outside a window is unattractive, a distorted view that presents colors without details may justify the use of refraction for redirecting light to the ceiling. This may be far preferable to the use of a nondirectional diffusing material that is void of inherent interest and appears equally bright from all angles.

Piped Sunlight

Some designers have proposed "piping" sunlight with lenses and tubes, via acrylic rod, or by use of fiber optics, from rooftop to lower level rooms, where the light would then be introduced via light fixtures (fig. 3–23). The cost of such materials on the scale needed and for provision of building volume to be used exclusively for such purposes will always be disproportionate to the possible value in saving energy or providing delight. Why spend so much effort and money to end up with an ordinary light fixture?

This is quite different from using fairly simple devices, such as large one-way tracking mirrors located in multifunctional atria, to redistribute light. This type of device retains the identifying qualities of sunlight and must be integrated into the architecture of a building. Crisp sunlight patterns create views, where delight of the space and associated activities as well as energy savings can be enjoyed.

Transmission and Glazing Materials

Glazing materials vary in their light- and heat-transmitting characteristics. Glazing can transmit, reflect, or absorb solar energy (fig. 3–24). Tinted glazings work by absorbing specific frequencies of light. Low-E glass (e.g., Guardian's *Low-E* or South Wall's *Heat Mirror 88*) is coated with a material that makes it reflect infrared light without altering its transmission of visible light substantially. Heat-absorbing reflective glazings absorb and reflect across the spectrum (fig. 3–25). Remember that the heat is reradiated equally to interior and exterior—hence, it can be very warm near the glazing. The fact that less light is transmitted by reflective glazings often can make interior spaces feel gloomy.

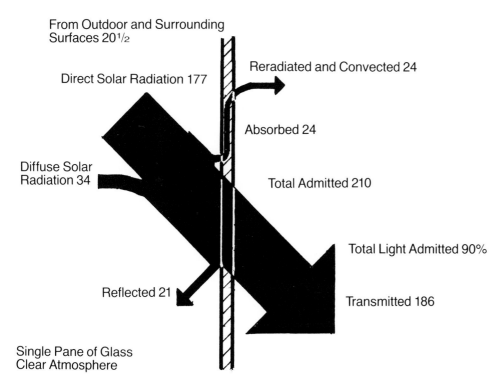

From Outdoor and Surrounding Surfaces 20½

Direct Solar Radiation 177

Reradiated and Convected 24

Absorbed 24

Diffuse Solar Radiation 34

Total Admitted 210

Total Light Admitted 90%

Reflected 21

Transmitted 186

Single Pane of Glass Clear Atmosphere

3–24. Transmission, reflection, and absorption—reradiation of clear single glazing.

Glazing	Transmittances		"R" factor for winter night
	Solar %	Visible %	
Single			
Clear	89	80	.87
Double			
Clear	80	65	2.04
Coated/Tinted			
Clear Low E	52	74	3.13
Green "Solex"	41	68	2.04
Bronze-tinted	41	48	2.04
Reflective			
Grey	6	8	2.27
Gold	9	18	2.94
Silver-Grey	23	29	2.17
Silver-Blue	12	18	2.27
Triple			
Clear	62	75	2.56
Clear Low E	48	70	3.13

3–25. Transmission- and insulation-valued glazings. (Note the *R* value of Low E glazing.)

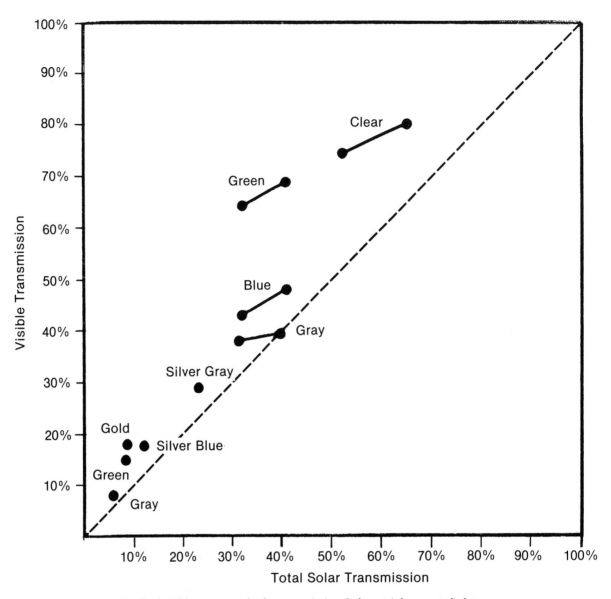

3–26. Graph of visible versus total solar transmission. Leftmost (of connected) dots = double glazing with Low E coating; righmost (of connected) dots = double glazing without Low E coating. Freestanding dots = reflective-coated double glazing.

For the purposes of sunlighting, it is preferable to use a glazing that admits the maximum amount of visible light, while admitting less of the ultraviolet and infrared portions of the spectrum. Green-tinted (*Solex T*) glass has an advantage in this regard (fig. 3–26). Clear double glazing is usually the most cost-effective in temperate climates. Low-E glazing has its advantages but at the present time is at too much of a premium.

The transmittance of glass is affected by the angle from which the light is received. The transmittance from direct sunlight remains fairly steady from normal angle until 50° but diminishes rapidly after 60°. At very oblique angles (80+ degrees), the transmission approaches zero because the light is reflected instead of transmitted.

Data for single glazing with 0.90 transmittance at normal incidence and double glazing with 0.81 are as follows:

angle of incidence	single-glazed window	double-glazed window
0°	0.90	0.81
20°	0.90	0.81
40°	0.89	0.80
50°	0.87	0.77
60°	0.82	0.71
70°	0.77	0.59
80°	0.44	0.29
90°	0.00	0.00

For diffuse radiation, the transmittance for single glazing is 0.82; for double glazing, 0.72.

CONCLUSION

Sunlighting design consists primarily of planning the geometric relationships of architectural elements to the light available in order to direct light where it is wanted. Understanding the nature of light and its control by reflection, refraction, and transmission is necessary to conceive, diagram, and design the architectural forms and details of sunlighting.

4 Sunlight: Source of Light and Heat for Buildings

Very detailed information about sun and sky has been presented in several sources, including Hopkinson's *Daylighting*. Those interested primarily in calculations and the theoretical basis for calculations should consult these sources (See Bibliography). This chapter will only present those facts about the the sun as a source of light that have helped create the architectural forms of sunlighting.

The light of the sun is available on earth in two forms—direct and diffuse. When the sky is clear, buildings receive direct sunlight and sunlight reflected off surrounding surfaces (fig. 4–1). When the sky is overcast, the sun's light is diffused by clouds, and the sky is the apparent source of light (fig. 4–2). Sunlight design applies when sunlight rather than sky light is the predominant condition. Much of the early work applying natural lighting in buildings "scientifically" occurred in northern Europe (especially England) where sky light is the predominant condition. This has sometimes misled designers in other parts of the world, where sunlight is the usual condition. This book is about the sunlighting forms that can be created using natural light.

4–1. Clear blue sky: on a sunny day, the ground is the dominant source of reflected, diffuse sunlight.

4–2. Overcast sky: on an overcast day, the sky is the brightest, dominant source of direct diffuse light.

EXTRATERRESTRIAL SUNLIGHT

In space, just outside earth's atmosphere, sunlight arrives as a pure beam of virtually parallel rays of identical spectral quality. All sunlight falling on a space capsule is received *directly* from the sun. Since there is no substance to intercept the light, the surrounding space is black.

DISTANCE OF THE SUN

Because of the great distance of the sun as a light source (93 million miles), the rays of sunlight falling on the earth are virtually parallel. This fact is very significant. The parallel rays of sunlight have the following effects:

☐ No inverse-square law need be applied to sunlight calculations. With artificial light sources the light rays are divergent and illumination intensity decreases as an inverse square of the distance (see chapter 3). There is no significant diminishing of the sun's illumination with the increases in distance possible within the earth's atmosphere. The light received on the top of a tree is no more intense than that at the bottom, thus generating a uniform growth rate. Similarly, an area of direct sunlight admitted at the top of a fifty-story atrium retains its shape and intensity at the floor.

☐ Simple optical control: the parallel rays of sunlight allow a flat mirror to reflect the exact shape and size of the light beam received.

APPARENT MOVEMENT OF THE SUN

The earth as a whole receives the same amount of sunlight every day and every year. The apparent movement of the sun around the earth is relative and due to the earth's rotation and orbit. The seasonal differences in the daily path of the sun are due to the tilt of the earth's axis (fig. 4-3). At any given moment in time, each portion of the earth receives the sun-

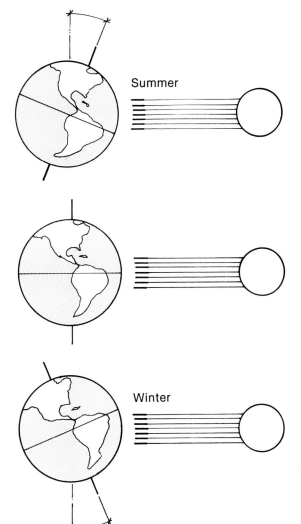

Summer

Winter

23 1/2°

4-3. The tilt of the earth creates the seasons and the altitude of the sun. (After Mazria)

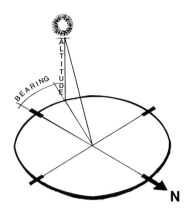

4-4. Bearing and altitude angles of the sun. (After Mazria)

light at a different angle that changes on a daily and annual basis. At any point, the sun is highest at solar noon of each day. The elevation of the noon sun is dependent on the distance from the equator. During equinox noon the solar altitude is equal to 90 degrees minus the latitude. At midsummer noon the altitude is 23.5 degrees higher than the equinox noon, and at midwinter it is 23.5 degrees lower.

Since the sun travels 360 degrees laterally in twenty-four hours, it moves 15 degrees per hour. The design of sundials is based on this fact, as is navigation during sunlight hours. The location of the sun in the sky can thus be described as having two components: its daily movement around the horizon is its bearing angle relative to south. Its height above the horizon, which varies seasonally, is its altitude (fig. 4-4). Sunlighting strategies for various latitudes should be based on the predictable seasonal differences in the sun's altitude as well as other factors such as climate, altitude, proximity of water, vegetation, and buildings (fig. 4-5).

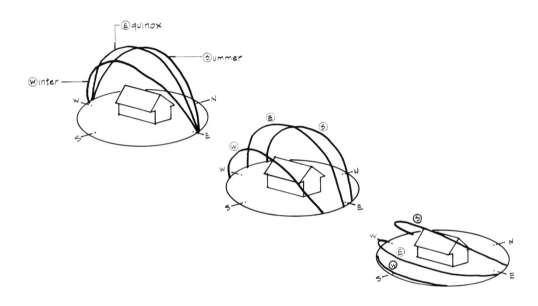

4-5. Designs should be based on the predictable difference in sun angles. The amount of time the sun's altitude angle is below 22.5° and 45° for various latitudes during office hours (8:30 A.M.–5:30 P.M.) suggests where fixed horizontal shading can be most effective.

	0°				40° N				65° N			
BELOW 45°	N	E	S	W	N	E	S	W	N	E	S	W
Dec 21	0	30	75	150	0	110	540	170	0	51	132	51
March 21	0	30	0	150	0	60	0	180	0	117	540	237
June 21	75	30	0	150	0	9	0	129	0	33	0	153
BELOW 22 1/2°												
Dec21	0	0	12	63	0	40	72	160	0	48	132	48
March 21	0	0	0	63	0	0	0	80	0	33	180	153
June 21	12	0	0	63	0	0	0	9	0	0	0	0

POWER OF THE SUN

The sun radiates its energy in all directions. The minute fraction of the sun's energy received by the earth has provided the basis of all life—both the incoming energy used to keep warm and sustain life and the retained fossil energy in the form of coal, petroleum, and other types of fuel. Evolving mankind has become increasingly dependent on using our stored energy reserves to provide the light and heat which in the past were provided exclusively by the sun and renewable energy sources. We have extended the hours of work and play and the level of thermal comfort, independent of geography and climate. However, we have now learned that the supply of nonrenewable energy is not infinite. We have also become aware of the costs in pollution and other negative side effects that can result from the conversion of excessive amounts of energy. We must therefore examine the amount of "free" incoming solar energy we can use to meet our current needs for light and heat and to allow us to extend the use of stored energy for future generations.

At the edge of the earth's atmosphere (normal to the sun), the level of solar illumination is approximately 14,000 footcandles. Even after passing through the atmosphere of a clear sky to sea level, the level can exceed 10,000 footcandles. As a comparison, a brightly lit office might have an average of 30–100 footcandles of electric lighting.

The instantaneous energy of one square foot of sunlight (on a horizontal surface at equinox noon, sea level, 40 degrees north latitude) is equivalent to the visible light of 3.3 40-watt fluorescent lamps, or 6 100-watt incandescent lamps. As heat, this solar energy is equivalent to 88 watts from an electric heater. Even if used inefficiently, there is obviously an abundant amount of radiant energy available from the sun.

ILLUMINATION FROM SUNLIGHT—VECTORS AND SURFACES

Were there no atmosphere surrounding the earth, the intensity of sunlight received at any point (normal to the sun) on the sunny side of the earth would be constant and equal to that at any other point.

Of course, the intensity of light normal to any particular planar surface is dependent on its angular relationship to the direction of the sunlight (fig. 4–6). When the sun is low (and horizontal relative to a point on the earth's surface) the sunlight is received more directly on vertical

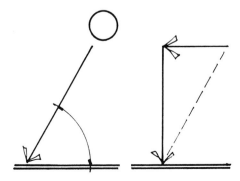

4–6. The directional nature of sunlight allows it to be analyzed by separating it into its constituent vectors.

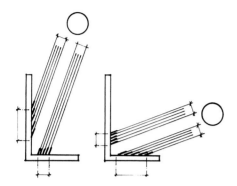

4-7. Sunlight is most concentrated when the receiving surface is normal to the incident angle of sunlight.

surfaces and more obliquely on horizontal surfaces. When the sun is high, any given area of horizontal surface receives more light than a vertical surface of the same area. Thus, while the general illumination in Boston on a clear day differs little from that in Saudi Arabia, because the sun in Boston is lower at winter noon, a north wall will always be brighter in Boston than an equivalent wall in Saudi Arabia. Conversely, horizontal concrete pavement at the equivalent solar time will be brighter in Saudi Arabia than in Boston (fig. 4–7).

TERRESTRIAL SUNLIGHT: MODIFIED SUNLIGHT FOR BUILDINGS

Some designers think of "natural light" as the light from the sky and discount direct sunlight because it is difficult to calculate and control. Proper design of sunlighting requires recognition of the *total* light from the sun after its filtering by sky and clouds and its reflection by ground-level natural and man-made elements (even if difficult to quantify precisely). The composition and the color temperature of sunlight change slightly after it passes through the atmosphere. Figure 4–8 shows the spectral composition of sunlight before and after it passes through the atmosphere.

The relative amounts of light received by a building from sky and ground will vary depending on the position of the sun, sky conditions, and the shapes and reflectances of ground surfaces and objects on the ground.

4-8. Spectral distribution of energy in sunlight above the atmosphere and after passage through one air mass (zenith) containing 20mm precipitable water vapor. (Reprinted, with permission, from Meinel, *Applied Solar Energy*)

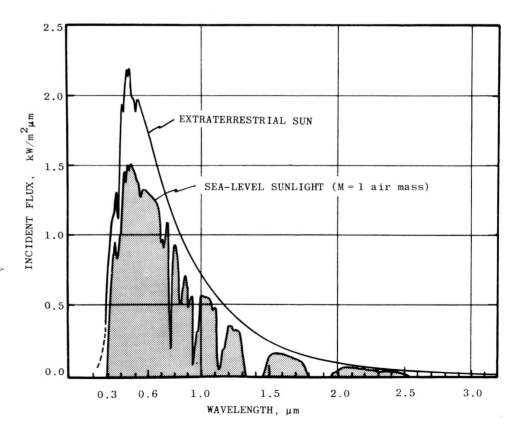

Source	Correlated color temperature (°K)
Sun	4,000
increasing with solar altitude to	5,500
Sky (clear)	10,000–100,000
Sky (overcast)	4,500– 7,000
Global (clear)	5,000– 7,000
Most frequently observed c.c.t.	c6,000
C.I.E. reccs.:	
For photographic purposes—some sunlight present	5,500
North skylight	6,500
(Also B.S.I.)	
Bluer version of north skylight	7,500

4–9. Correlated color temperatures of natural light. (From Hopkinson, *Daylighting;* reprinted by permission of William Heineman Ltd.)

FILTERING BY THE CLEAR SKY

When sunlight passes through the air mass surrounding the earth, some of the light is absorbed and some is scattered by molecules and dust particles. This scattering is more pronounced at the shorter or ''bluer'' wavelengths. Thus, the blackness of space becomes dark blue at the edge of the atmosphere, deep blue in the clear dry air of our highest mountains, light blue at sea level, and almost white when the haze of water vapor and dust is encountered. The sky has a high color temperature, meaning it is ''hotter'' or ''bluer'' than the direct rays of the sun (fig. 4–9).

On a clear day most of the illumination comes directly from the sun, which thus casts sharp shadows. The intensity of illumination from direct sunlight on a clear day varies with the thickness of the air mass it passes through. It is therefore almost entirely dependent on the sun's altitude (fig. 4–10). It is less intense at sunrise and sunset at any latitude; and at noon it is less intense at high latitudes because the sun is lower. Because

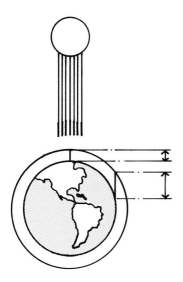

4–10. Intensity of illumination perpendicular to the sun's rays varies with the thickness of the air mass (resulting from solar altitude). (From Hopkinson, *Daylighting;* reprinted by permission of William Heineman Ltd.)

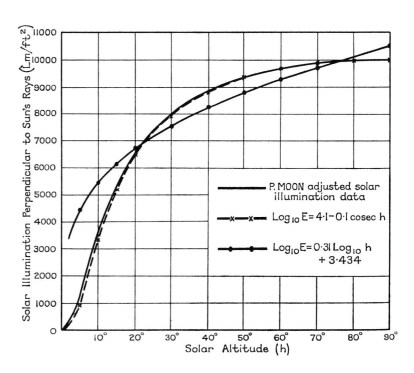

P. MOON adjusted solar illumination data

$Log_{10} E = 4.1 - 0.1\ cosec\ h$

$Log_{10} E = 0.31\ Log_{10}\ h + 3.434$

Solar Illumination Perpendicular to Sun's Rays (Lm/ft²)

Solar Altitude (h)

4–11. Summary of variations in solar illumination perpendicular to sun's rays for sunny and less sunny climates. (From Hopkinson, *Daylighting*; reprinted by permission of William Heineman Ltd.)

Solar altitude (h)	Air mass (m)	Solar illumination perpendicular to sun's rays (lm/ft²)	
		(a) (i) Sunny climates (ii) Less sunny climates (particularly clear skies)	(b) Less sunny climates (average clear skies) (70%)
5°	10·4	1,200	840
10°	5·6	3,560	2,490
15°	3·8	5,280	3,950
20°	2·9	6,520	4,560
30°	2·0	8,000	5,600
40°	1·55	8,850	6,190
50°	1·3	9,360	6,560
60°	1·15	9,670	6,770
70°	1·05	9,870	6,910
80°	1·02	9,960	6,980
90°	1·0	10,000	7,000

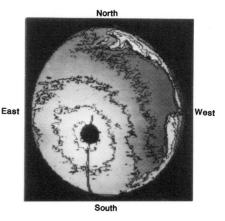

4–12. Luminance distribution of a clear blue sky at Stockholm, October 2, 1953, 14:25–14:50 solar time; 14:00–14:25 Stockholm time. Sun's position is indicated by arrows (From Hopkinson, *Daylighting*; reprinted by permission of William Heineman Ltd.)

the air mass through which the sunlight passes varies little, the sun's intensity (normal to it) changes little from directly overhead until it is below 15 degrees, at which time it is 50 percent of maximum. In figure 4–11, these changes are summarized for totally clear skies and for average clear skies in less sunny climates, such as England. The 30 percent reduction in England implies the presence of haze.

Sunlight intercepted by the clear sky vault becomes a nonuniform luminous source producing about 10 percent of the total clear-day illumination, most of it coming from the brightest area of sky immediately surrounding the sun. While not immediately obvious, this nonuniform distribution can easily be observed by the naked eye if one masks the view of the sun itself.

Note that the darkest part of the blue sky, approximately 90 degrees from the sun, is likely to be quite dim (about 300 footlamberts—equal to clouds on a dark, overcast day). Under hazy conditions, these variations are reduced; the brightest areas become less bright, the darkest less dark (figs. 4–12, 4–13).

The brightness distribution of clear skies suggests that a building design that controls the glare of the direct sun and redistributes direct sunlight effectively will also control the glare and best distribute the light

4–13. SERI sky photograph for a clear sky. Isoluminance contours drawn at 500, 1,000, 2,500, 5,000, and 7,500 footlamberts. (Photograph courtesy of SERI)

```
Location:          Golden, Colorado
Date:              27 June 1981
Time:              11:00 a.m. MST
Solar Altitude:    69°
Solar Azimuth:     -42°
Sky Condition:     Mostly clear with low
                   clouds to NW & SW
Total Horiz. Illum.*: 9184 fc. (sun & sky)
Diffuse Horiz. Illum.*: 1962 fc. (sky only)

Illumination on Vertical Planes
                 Total*    Diffuse**
  North Facing    846 fc    846 fc
  East Facing    3172 fc    596 fc
  South Facing   3205 fc    566 fc
  West Facing    1001 fc   1001 fc
```

from the clear sky because the brightest part of the clear sky is the area immediately surrounding the sun. Except in the area near the sun, the blue sky is less bright than most cloudy or overcast skies.

DIFFUSION AND REFLECTION BY THE CLOUDY SKY

Unlike clear days and totally overcast days, the illumination on cloudy days changes constantly (from 2,000 to 10,000 footcandles) with moments of full sunlight and other moments when the sun is intercepted by clouds. Even when diffused by clouds, there is usually a sufficient concentration of light to cast soft shadows, due to thin areas in the cloud cover (wherever the total illumination is more than 2,000–3,000 footcandles). While the brightest part of the clouds is usually nearest the sun, bright patches may appear opposite the sun when the sunlight reflected off the edges of clouds is visible from the ground below, as it is from an airplane (fig. 4–14).

Because of the rapid and constant fluctuation from direct sunlight to diffused sunlight that occurs on cloudy days, sun-control devices, if they are to control glare completely, should be set in the same way as for clear days at that time (fig. 4–15). Since the brightest clouds are usually near the sun, designing for direct sunlight best controls the glare and redistributes the light from cloudy skies as well.

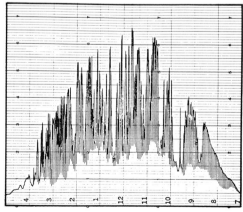

4–14. Clouds are always brighter than the blue sky when seen from above or from the sunlit side. Thin clouds are brighter from below as well. (Photograph courtesy of Tom Lam)

4–15. Continuous recording of exterior horizontal illumination for a clear day (left) shows a smooth curve beginning at dusk and peaking at noon, when the sun is highest. On a cloudy day (right), the jagged lines indicate that illumination fluctuates constantly from clear to cloudy levels. (Courtesy of SERI)

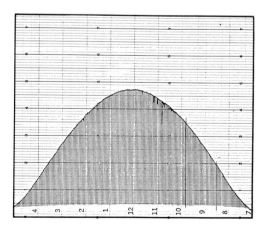

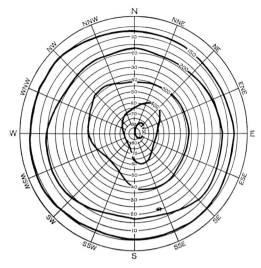

4-16. Luminance distribution of a fully overcast sky at Stockholm, no individual clouds or bright patches visible, October 10, 1953, 09:55–10:15 solar time; 09:30–09:50 Stockholm time. (From Hopkinson, *Daylighting*; reprinted by permission of William Heineman Ltd.)

4-17. SERI sky photograph of an overcast sky. Isoluminance contours are drawn at 140, 500, 1,000, 2,000, and 3,000 footlamberts. (Courtesy of SERI)

DIFFUSION BY TOTAL CLOUD COVER: OVERCAST SKY

Typical overcast skies reduce the sunlight by more than 90 percent. When the cloud cover is so dense that all evidence of the sun is obscured, the luminance distribution is independent of the altitude of the sun. This is the so-called "C.I.E. standard overcast sky," commonly modeled in artificial sky laboratories. In nature, this "totally overcast sky" is rare. The average luminance of the sky is maximum at zenith and decreases to about one-third of maximum value at the horizon (figs. 4–16, 4–17).

In climates that are predominately overcast, it may be important to analyze the luminance distribution more precisely. When designing for sunlighting (where controlling the sun is the most important determinant), knowing the variations in the luminance distribution of overcast skies is irrelevant to the design, as supplemental artificial lighting would be used to balance or raise the illumination level, add highlight and sparkle, and improve (lower) the color temperature. The illumination from an overcast sky varies with the density of cloud cover and the altitude of the sun. When the sun is at 45 degrees, the average illumination should be about 900 footcandles. On a drizzly day, the average illumination is likely to be about 300 footcandles.

```
Date:              27 June 1981
Time:              12:00 Noon MST
Solar Altitude:    73°
Solar Azimuth:     0°
Sky Condition:     Mostly overcast, dark
                   thunderhead to NW & SW
Total Horiz. Illum.*:  1407 fc.
Diffuse Horiz Illum.*:  1407 fc.

Illumination on Vertical Planes*
    North Facing        556 fc
    East Facing         817 fc
    South Facing        829 fc
    West Facing         421 fc
```

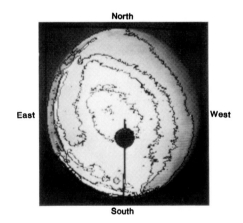

In some cloudy countries such as England, daylighting design was for many decades based on overcast days with average illuminance levels of 500 footcandles, and codes were written to ensure that practice. This practice may have been justified when adequate artificial illumination was not economically possible and buildings were not air-conditioned. By now, many of those countries have abandoned such practices and gotten rid of the excessive, unprotected glazing that resulted in glare and local over-heating when the sun *did* shine.

SUNLIGHT REFLECTED BY NATURAL AND MAN-MADE SURFACES

Because of the generally low brightness of the clear sky in sunny climates, the light reflected from the ground and buildings is often more important than that received directly from the sky. The presence of adjacent buildings may well increase rather than reduce the available light. Even black surfaces in full sunlight can achieve a luminance greater than that of the darkest portions of a blue sky. In designing for sunlighting, one should be aware of potential reflected light from natural and man-made surfaces or better yet plan to shape those elements to take advantage of them when other constraints allow.

Sunny Side (South in the Northern Hemisphere)

In an open space, *ground-reflected light* is of the greatest potential benefit on the sunny side if the immediate foreground is never in shadow (figs. 4–18, 4–19). However, adjacent buildings and trees on the sunny side may place the immediate foreground in shadow, and their shady sides are likely to be the darkest exterior surfaces seen. Keeping adjacent buildings and trees distant will maximize the lighting on the sunny side. Ground-reflected light is greatest when the sun is highest: during summer and at low latitudes. The high solar altitude, together with the reduced degree of foreground and shading required, make ground-reflected light more commonly available near the equator.

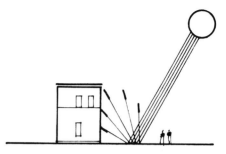

4–18. Ground-reflected light is most available on the sunny side of buildings.

Material	Reflectance	Luminance (Footlamberts)			
		Overcast 1500 Fl	Sunny (Solar Altitude)		
			25° 3970 Fl	45° 7560 Fl	80° 9470 Fl
Green grass	6%	90	238	454	568
Water	7%	105	278	524	663
Asphalt	7%	105	278	524	663
Moist earth	7%	105	278	524	663
Slate (dark clay)	8%	120	318	605	758
Gravel	13%	195	516	983	1,231
Grandolite pavement	17%	255	675	1,285	1,610
Bluestone, Sandstone	18%	270	715	1,360	1,705
Macadam	18%	270	715	1,360	1,705
Vegetation (mean)	25%	375	992	1,890	2,367
Cement	27%	405	1,072	2,041	2,557
Brick—dark red glazed	30%	450	1,190	2,268	2,841
—dark buff	40%	600	1,588	3,024	3,788
—light buff	48%	720	1,906	3,629	4,546
Concrete	40%	600	1,588	3,024	3,788
Marble (white)	45%	675	1,786	3,402	4,261
Paint (white)—old	55%	825	2,183	4,158	5,208
—new	75%	1,125	2,977	5,670	7,102
Snow—old	64%	960	2,540	4,838	6,060
—new	74%	1,110	2,938	5,594	7,008

4–19. Reflectance and luminance of common ground materials under representative sunny and overcast conditions. (Reprinted, by permission, from *IES Lighting Handbook, 1981 Volume*)

Shady Side (North in the Northern Hemisphere)

On the shady side, the quantity of light reflected off adjacent walls and buildings can be very significant. Generally, the benefits of adjacent buildings increase with their height and proximity, unless the reflecting surfaces are excessively shaded (fig. 4–20).

The light reflected onto a building's shady side by sunlit vertical surfaces is maximized when the sun is lowest: during winter and at high latitudes. Thus the view of adjacent buildings from a north-facing win-

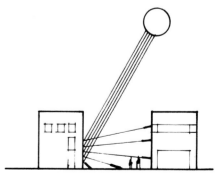

4–20. On the shady side of buildings, the quantity of light reflected off adjacent walls and buildings can be very significant.

dow in Boston is likely to be brighter than that of similar buildings in Singapore or Saudi Arabia. As noted in chapter 2, it can be difficult to realize how bright the view from a north window can be, because the visual interest of an adjacent building will make it appear less glaring than a light fixture or an overcast sky of equal luminance. An unpainted concrete building reflecting 4,000 footlamberts and a brick building reflecting 1,500 footlamberts may not be perceived as being as bright as a 1,000-footlambert overcast sky. This is an important characteristic that makes natural lighting delightful. Since sunlit objects are enjoyable to look at, they will be perceived as pleasurable "signals" rather than visual noise or "glare."

SPECTRAL COMPOSITION OF REFLECTED AND TRANSMITTED LIGHT

Building surfaces and forms affect sunlight in the same way as the natural environment. As light is transmitted, reflected, or scattered, certain wavelengths may be absorbed or redirected more than others, affecting the color and/or efficacy of the light. The luminous efficacy of a light source is defined as the ratio of the total luminous flux (lumens) to the total radiant power (watts). The effect of atmospheric scattering and absorption on the efficacy of sunlight is to increase the ratio from approximately 94 lumens/watt in space to approximately 118 lumens/watt at sea level (at one air mass). The efficacy of sunlight also varies with solar altitude (fig. 4–21).

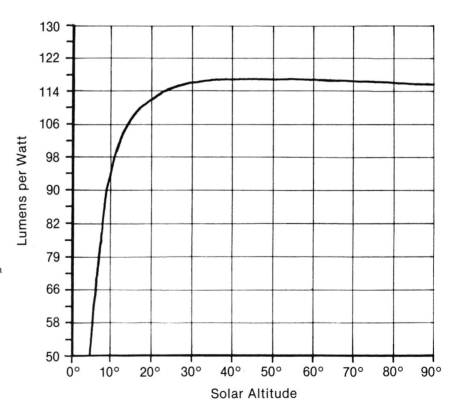

4–21. Luminous efficacy of solar radiation as a function of solar altitude.

This phenomenon may be applied to architecture when choosing the materials and locations for transmitting and reflecting surfaces. In a building in which the cooling load is greater than the heating demand, a greater luminous efficacy is more desirable than in a building with a substantial heating demand.

AVAILABLE WEATHER DATA AND INTERPRETATION

Weather data for determining the sunlight conditions in a given area are available in many forms, none of which is ideal for sunlighting purposes. The National Climatic Center in Asheville, North Carolina, has data from locations throughout the United States, including the National Oceanic and Atmospheric Administration stations. The published monthly summary of local climatological data is also available through local NOAA stations (fig. 4–22).

Perhaps the most commonly used description of available sunlight is known as the "sky cover," which measures tenths of cloudiness, 0 being absolutely clear and 10 being totally overcast. Unfortunately, this measurement is based entirely on visual estimation and is not consistently accurate.

Measurements of total solar radiation in langleys are available in a variety of time intervals, ranging from hourly to annually. Measurements are made using pyrheliometers and/or pyranometers, which are sensitive to a large range of solar flux. Although accurate, these measures are not entirely appropriate for our purposes because the translation from langleys to footcandles of visible illumination is a lengthy task of questionable accuracy. This is, however, the ideal measure for estimating solar gain and sizing HVAC systems.

A third type of data is the "amount of available sunshine." This is recorded in minutes of sunshine and translated into a percentage of possible sunshine. Traditionally (and in some locations currently), a Campbell-Stokes recorder is used. This device employs a lens that burns a piece of paper when direct sunlight is present. Inspection of the paper indicates the duration and intensity of the sunshine.

More accurate measurements are made with a sunshine recorder that uses two detectors, one of which measures global flux and one of which measures scattered flux. When the difference between measurements recorded by the two sensors is greater than a set threshold, the presence of direct sunshine is indicated.

This measurement is interesting because it is a relative comparison between direct sunlight and total light. It is not a reasonable indication of the *intensity* of the direct sun. Rather, it is a measure of whether shadows are cast and when glare from direct sunlight needs to be controlled. At present, solar radiation data are more useful for calculating HVAC loads than for the design of sunlighting (which is more dependent on when and how often glare from direct sunlight needs to be controlled). Combining the data from several methods is best.

JUL 1982 14739
BOSTON, MASSACHUSETTS
GEN LOGAN INTERNATIONAL AP

ISSN 0198-2427

LOCAL CLIMATOLOGICAL DATA
Monthly Summary

NAT WEATHER SERVICE FCST OFC

LATITUDE 42° 22' N   LONGITUDE 71° 02' W   ELEVATION (GROUND) 15 FEET   TIME ZONE EASTERN   WBAN #14739

JUL 1982 — BOSTON, MASSACHUSETTS

WEATHER TYPES: 1 FOG, 2 HEAVY FOG, 3 THUNDERSTORM, 4 ICE PELLETS, 5 HAIL, 6 GLAZE, 7 DUSTSTORM, 8 SMOKE, HAZE, 9 BLOWING SNOW

DATE	TEMPERATURE °F MAXIMUM	MINIMUM	AVERAGE	DEPARTURE FROM NORMAL	AVERAGE DEW POINT	DEGREE DAYS BASE 65°F HEATING (7A)	COOLING (7B)	WEATHER TYPES	SNOW ICE PELLETS/ICE ON GROUND 07AM	PRECIP WATER EQUIV	PRECIP SNOW/ICE PELLETS	AVG STATION PRESSURE	WIND RESULTANT DIR	RESULTANT SPEED	AVERAGE SPEED	FASTEST MILE SPEED	DIRECTION	SUNSHINE MINUTES	% POSSIBLE	SKY COVER SUNRISE TO SUNSET	MIDNIGHT TO MIDNIGHT	DATE
1	75	59	67	-5	40	0	2			0	0	29.87	31	11.5	12.2	19	NW	914	100	0	0	1
2	80	57	69	-3	48	0	4			0	0	29.96	26	12.3	13.2	22	SW	775	85	6	5	2
3	78	65	72	0	53	0	7			0	0	29.76	27	10.1	11.5	14	SW	501	55	8	8	3
4	69	57*	63*	-9	47	2	0			0	0	29.84	08	4.7	10.6	14	SE	911	100	4	3	4
5	77	58	68	-4	50	0	3			0	0	30.10	20	4.7	9.6	17	SE	911	100	4	3	5
6	85	63	74	1	54	0	9			0	0	30.15	23	12.6	12.9	19	SW	906	100	6.	5	6
7	90	62	76	3	60	0	11			0	0	30.03	23	14.0	14.7	20	SW	909	100	0	0	7
8	95	70	83	10	65	0	18			0	0	29.88	25	10.1	10.8	17	W	745	82	5	5	8
9	89	73	81	8	57	0	16			0	0	29.87	28	10.9	11.4	17	SW	771	85	7	6	9
10	84	66	75	2	58	0	10			0	0	29.98	07	3.9	10.1	14	E	895	99	6	5	10
11	80	65	73	0	60	0	8			0	0	30.02	11	7.3	8.3	17	SE	833	92	8	5	11
12	82	62	72	-1	64	0	7	1 8	0	T	0	29.94	12	5.0	6.5	9	SW	136	15	10	8	12
13	92	71	82	9	60	0	17	8	0	0	0	29.99	28	10.0	10.5	16	W	792	88	4	3	13
14	78	68	73	0	58	0	8			0	0	30.14	10	4.7	7.5	12	SE	884	98	9	6	14
15	83	65	74	1	63	0	9	3 8	0	.03	0	30.11	16	4.0	6.6	12	SW	486	54	6	6	15
16	92	70	81	7	65	0	16	8	0	0	0	30.06	19	3.7	8.6	13	SE	820	91	7	6	16
17	97	73	85	11	67	0	20	1 8	0	0	0	30.00	22	7.3	9.5	21	SW	710	79	5	5	17
18	98	75	87	13	69	0	22	8	0	0	0	29.85	25	11.8	12.5	17	SW	643	72	4	5	18
19	98*	75	87*	13	69	0	22	3 8	0	.04	0	29.76	23	10.2	11.8	29	SW	532	60	7	6	19
20	76	67	72	-2	67	0	7	1 3 8	0	1.78	0	29.79	34	5.1	9.4	17	NW	8	1	10	9	20
21	75	66	71	-3	57	0	6	1	0	.06	0	29.89	36	8.2	10.4	16	N	224	25	9	9	21
22	70	61	66	-8	59	0	1	1	0	.89	0	29.82	29	4.9	7.9	16	NW	20	2	10	9	22
23	88	69	79	5	60	0	14			0	.25	0	29.87	30	3.9	8.5	13	SW	453	51	7	6	23
24	80	67	74	0	53	0	9			0	0	30.02	11	1.6	8.9	13	SE	884	100	4	4	24
25	89	65	77	3	57	0	12			0	0	29.96	24	11.7	11.8	17	SW	716	81	4	4	25
26	87	74	81	7	63	0	16			0	.03	0	29.85	27	9.4	10.5	15	W	600	68	6	6	26
27	77	69	73	-1	56	0	8			0	T	0	29.98	10	1.0	10.5	14	SE	760	87	6	5	27
28	74	63	69	-5	63	0	4	1	0	1.14	0	29.81	19	8.0	11.4	17	S	0	0	10	10	28
29	83	66	75	1	57	0	10			0	T	0	29.79	29	13.1	13.4	18	NW	804	92	2	2	29
30	82	66	74	1	58	0	9			0	0	30.06	17	2.9	9.5	17	SE	820	94	8	6	30
31	81	67	74	1	62	0	9			0	0	29.90	16	6.9	9.4	16	SE	574	66	6	4	31

| | SUM 2584 | SUM 2054 | | | | TOTAL 2 | TOTAL 314 | | | TOTAL 4.22 | TOTAL 0 | 29.94 | 25 | 4.1 | 10.3 | 29 | SW | TOTAL 19937 | % FOR MONTH | SUM 182 | SUM 164 | |
| | AVG 83.4 | AVG 66.3 | AVG 74.9 | DEP 1.6 | AVG 59 | DEP 2 | DEP 54 | | | DEP 1.48 | | | DATE: 19 | | | POSSIBLE 27759 | 72 | | | AVG 5.9 | AVG 5.3 | |

PRECIPITATION
> .01 INCH: 8
> 1.0 INCH: 0

NUMBER OF DAYS — MAXIMUM TEMP. ≥ 90°: 7   ≤ 32°: 0
MINIMUM TEMP. ≤ 32°: 0   ≤ 0°: 0

SEASON TO DATE TOTAL 2   TOTAL 396

SNOW, ICE PELLETS > 1.0 INCH: 0

THUNDERSTORMS: 3   HEAVY FOG: 1

CLEAR 4   PARTLY CLOUDY 18   CLOUDY 9

GREATEST IN 24 HOURS AND DATES — PRECIPITATION 1.84 20-21   SNOW, ICE PELLETS 0

GREATEST DEPTH ON GROUND OF SNOW, ICE PELLETS OR ICE AND DATE 0

* EXTREME FOR THE MONTH - LAST OCCURRENCE IF MORE THAN ONE.
T TRACE AMOUNT.
+ ALSO ON EARLIER DATE(S).
HEAVY FOG: VISIBILITY 1/4 MILE OR LESS.
BLANK ENTRIES DENOTE MISSING DATA.

DATA IN COLS 6 AND 12-15 ARE BASED ON 7 OR MORE OBSERVATIONS AT 3-HOUR INTERVALS. RESULTANT WIND IS THE VECTOR SUM OF WIND SPEEDS AND DIRECTIONS DIVIDED BY THE NUMBER OF OBSERVATIONS. ONE OF THREE WIND SPEEDS IS GIVEN UNDER FASTEST MILE: FASTEST MILE - HIGHEST RECORDED SPEED FOR WHICH A MILE OF WIND PASSES STATION (DIRECTION IN COMPASS POINTS). FASTEST OBSERVED ONE MINUTE WIND - HIGHEST ONE MINUTE SPEED (DIRECTION IN TENS OF DEGREES). PEAK GUST - HIGHEST INSTANTANEOUS WIND SPEED (A / APPEARS IN THE DIRECTION COLUMN). ERRORS WILL BE CORRECTED AND CHANGES IN SUMMARY DATA WILL BE ANNOTATED IN THE ANNUAL PUBLICATION.

4–22. Monthly summary of local climatological data as supplied by the National Oceanic and Atmospheric Administration (NOAA). (Courtesy of the National Climatic Center)

SUNLIGHT IN THE UNITED STATES

In the United States, sunshine is plentiful (fig. 4–23). Most areas receive over 50 percent of the possible available sunshine on an annual basis. This does not mean that half the days are 100 percent clear and the other half 100 percent overcast. Actually, there will be substantially more days on which sunshine is present than not. In an area that receives 50 percent of the mean percentage of possible sunshine, it is common that during at least 75 percent of the days, buildings will be subjected to, and require control of, direct solar radiation.

Because the design criteria for clear and partly cloudy days are identical, they should be considered together in contrast to the overcast condition. This is only relevant when using the inferior "sky cover" data since this distinction is inherent in the amount of sunshine data by the method of measurement.

4–23. Top: mean percentage of possible sunshine in the United States (annual); Bottom: total heating degree days.

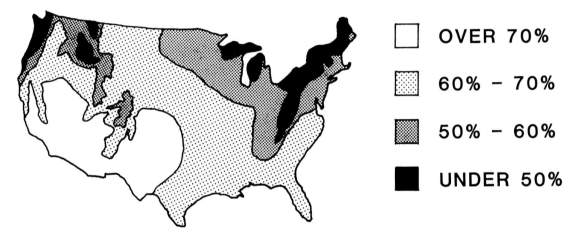

☐ OVER 70%

▒ 60% – 70%

▓ 50% – 60%

■ UNDER 50%

ANNUAL % POSSIBLE SUNSHINE

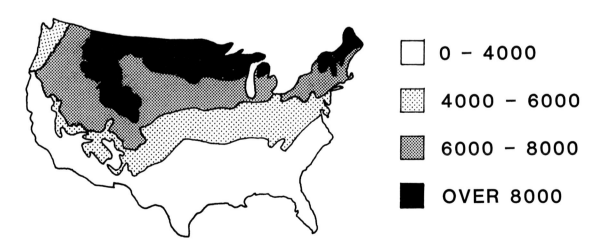

☐ 0 – 4000

▒ 4000 – 6000

▓ 6000 – 8000

■ OVER 8000

ANNUAL HEATING DEGREE DAYS

Inspecting the monthly climatological data summary for Boston, Massachusetts, we can see that during July of 1982 the sun shone 72 percent of the time but on 90.3 percent of the days (fig. 4–24). This breaks down to six absolutely clear days, five days receiving less than 50 percent of the possible sunshine, and twenty days of partly sunny weather. In this month of 72 percent of possible available sunshine weather, 35 percent of the days were less than 72 percent sunny, and 65 percent were 72 percent sunny or better. All days except for three required control of direct solar radiation.

In the December 1982 monthly summary, 39 percent of the total possible sunshine was recorded. More importantly, for eighteen days during that month there was enough direct solar radiation to require control of glare (58 percent of the days were sunny at least 10 percent of the time). Compiling data to reflect these less obvious trends is necessary for design and presentation purposes.

It is also interesting to note that on July 29, 92 percent of possible sunshine was recorded with an observed two-tenths of sky cover. On the following day, July 30, 94 percent of possible sunshine was recorded with an estimated eight-tenths of sky cover. Tenths of sky cover and percentage of possible sunshine are evidently incompatible measurements.

4-24. NOAA monthly climatological data for July, 1982 and December, 1982. (Courtesy of the National Climatic Center)

DEC

SUNSHINE		SKY COVER (TENTHS)		
MINUTES	PERCENT OF TOTAL POSSIBLE	SUNRISE TO SUNSET	MIDNIGHT TO MIDNIGHT	DATE
18	19	20	21	22
249	45	10	9	1
558	100	1	3	2
0	0	10	10	3
310	56	7	7	4
12	2	9	7	5
0	0	10	9	6
517	94	2	4	7
551	100	0	0	8
335	61	5	3	9
30	5	10	8	10
0	0	10	10	11
0	0	10	9	12
537	98	0	0	13
536	98	7	4	14
310	57	7	8	15
0	0	10	9	16
279	51	6	3	17
56	10	9	10	18
0	0	10	10	19
0	0	10	10	20
76	14	10	8	21
529	97	3	3	22
0	0	10	10	23
0	0	10	10	24
247	45	9	9	25
221	41	8	8	26
404	74	7	7	27
0	0	10	10	28
0	0	10	8	29
547	100	0	3	30
360	66	5	8	31
TOTAL 6664	% FOR	SUM 225	SUM 217	
POSSIBLE 17003	MONTH 39	AVG. 7.3	AVG. 7.0	

JUL

SUNSHINE		SKY COVER (TENTHS)		
MINUTES	PERCENT OF TOTAL POSSIBLE	SUNRISE TO SUNSET	MIDNIGHT TO MIDNIGHT	DATE
18	19	20	21	22
914	100	0	0	1
775	85	6	5	2
501	55	8	8	3
911	100	4	3	4
911	100	4	3	5
906	100	6	5	6
909	100	0	0	7
745	82	5	5	8
771	85	7	6	9
895	99	6	5	10
833	92	8	5	11
136	15	10	8	12
792	88	4	3	13
884	98	9	9	14
486	54	6	6	15
820	91	7	6	16
710	79	5	5	17
643	72	4	5	18
532	60	7	6	19
8	1	10	9	20
224	25	9	9	21
20	2	10	9	22
453	51	7	6	23
884	100	0	1	24
716	81	4	4	25
600	68	6	6	26
760	87	4	5	27
0	0	10	10	28
804	92	2	2	29
820	94	8	6	30
574	66	6	4	31
TOTAL 19937	% FOR	SUM 182	SUM 164	
POSSIBLE 27759	MONTH 72	AVG. 5.9	AVG. 5.3	

SUNLIGHT IN THE WORLD

As shown by the global isoflux maps in figure 4–25, most of the world receives abundant solar radiation, more than 5 megajoules per square meter per day. In the northern hemisphere, the quantity of solar flux is generally substantially greater in June than in December, and in the southern hemisphere the reverse is true. Only northern Europe and the less populated areas of North America receive less sunlight than the United States. This climatic difference (of one isoline) represents an increase (in the amount of solar flux) of approximately 25 percent in June, and of approximately 100 percent in December, the time at which it is most desirable.

With sunlight being such a widespread and abundant resource, it is foolish to ignore it in favor of the overcast sky condition on which "daylighting" is based. The glare and heat accompanying sunlight must be controlled regardless, and when sunlight is present the vast majority of the time, it is wise to turn these design problems into assets.

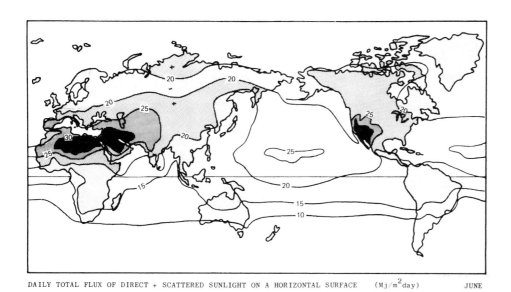

DAILY TOTAL FLUX OF DIRECT + SCATTERED SUNLIGHT ON A HORIZONTAL SURFACE   (Mj/m²day)   JUNE

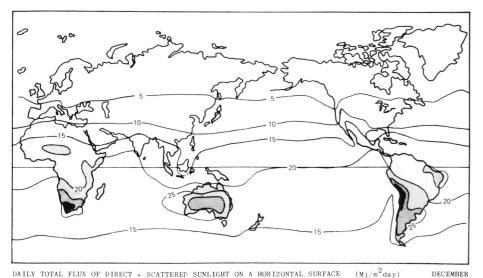

DAILY TOTAL FLUX OF DIRECT + SCATTERED SUNLIGHT ON A HORIZONTAL SURFACE   (Mj/m²day)   DECEMBER

4–25. Global isoflux contours for June and December.

5 Planning for Sunlighting—Concepts

The complexity of satisfying both institutional objectives and human needs makes the development and description of sunlighting concepts difficult.

If the goals were simple, the process might also be simple. If our aim was simply to achieve maximum lighting, or even maximum lighting with minimum energy use, the results could be measured quantitatively and the concepts stated concisely, with procedures and calculations expressed in a linear manner. The success or failure of such straightforward goals could be measured with instruments alone (light meters, watt meters, and the annual power bill). Judging the lowest-cost sunlighting solution would be easy, although considerably more difficult than judging the costs of a windowless building using only artificial lighting.

In the spectrum of design influences, the attempt to fulfill human needs is the complicating factor. People have very real needs and values that are often felt and derived unconsciously and difficult to define precisely.

The multiple design goals discussed in chapter 1 and summarized below suggest a holistic design process. Each strategy and technique must be evaluated by many criteria.

The conventional design of artificial lighting in commercial and institutional buildings has produced disastrous results: unpleasant, uninteresting, and sometimes unbearable visual environments. This can be attributed directly to incorrectly defined goals, resulting in simplistic quantitative criteria and a grossly inadequate design process. The type of multidisciplinary processes required to design electric lighting with humanistic rather than technical goals are applicable to the process of sunlighting design. However, the increase in the number of variables makes the sunlighting design process much more difficult. In aritificial lighting design, one generally starts with a building of a particular shape, plan, and structure. Sunlighting design ideally begins much earlier, with the site planning of streets and buildings and the geometry and form of the buildings. To these variables, add a constantly changing light source with as many potential problems as opportunities, and you can begin to appreciate the complexities.

56

But everything worthwhile in life is complex. It can seem impossibly difficult to get exact answers to such simple, everyday decisions such as what chair to buy, or what to eat. Should we limit the choices only to those that fit within easily defined criteria?

Edward DeBono, in his books on the thought process, makes a distinction between linear and lateral thinking (fig. 5–1). He describes linear thinking as the sequential consideration of factors (typical of Western scientific methods) and lateral thinking as the simultaneous and unstructured consideration of multiple factors (characteristic of Eastern civilizations). He contends that lateral thinking is needed to solve complex problems, particularly in the setting of values and objectives.

This lateral approach is certainly valuable in design, as design objectives are almost never singular and quantitative, but rather overlapping and conflicting, qualitative and quantitative. The process used must therefore be lateral, circular, reiterative. It would be particularly difficult to consider adequately the many simultaneous problems and interactive solutions inherent to sunlighting design without lateral thinking. (The lateral thinking process is reinforced by the use of team design processes recommended in chapter 10.) Concepts must be fully explored, their implications by various criteria weighed, and the results reintegrated into the whole. As DeBono points out, linear thinking is valuable at the end of the process, to carry out the clearly technical objectives and criteria previously defined and put into context by lateral thinking.

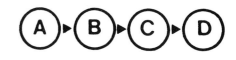

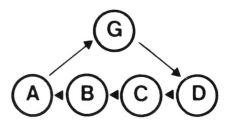

5–1. With lateral thinking (bottom) the steps need not be sequential; one may jump ahead to a new point and then fill in the gap afterwards. Vertical thinking (top) proceeds steadily from *A* to *B* to *C* to *D*. (Reprinted, by permission, from deBono, *Lateral Thinking*)

SUNLIGHTING GOALS: VALUE-IDENTIFICATION PROCESS

The priorities involved in formulating sunlighting design concepts were thoroughly discussed in chapter 1; they are briefly reiterated here to set the tone and context for decision evaluation:

1. User Comfort and Delight in the Interior Environment
   The primary sunlighting goal, user comfort, includes both thermal and visual comfort as well as other biological and programmatic needs.

2. Satisfaction of Other Programmatic Needs
   Satisfaction of structural requirements, circulation, and the like is a necessary factor in the design of functional buildings.

3. Minimum Building Energy Cost
   Energy decisions should reflect the influences of site and program.

4. Optimum Public Architectural Image
   Elegance in the execution of the building is the criterion by which architecture is most often judged.

5. Minimum Building Cost
   If the design is not affordable, it will not get built.

SCALES OF RESPONSE

The ability to achieve the goals of sunlighting listed above is affected by decisions made at six distinct scales. Making the appropriate decision at the larger scale can simplify the detail decisions, or conversely, make sunlighting design very difficult or impossible. To achieve maximum comfort and energy utilization at minimum cost, one should proceed from the largest to the smallest scale. This chapter will discuss the largest two scales in detail: chapters 6, 7, and 8 will discuss the remaining scales in the context of the building form.

1. Urban Design/Master Planning: This is the golden opportunity to make sunlight available throughout the site or development.

2. Site Planning/Building Massing: Carefully shape and locate the building form to get sunlight onto buildings where and when wanted. The form chosen is highly dependent on the site and building program and must be discussed in those terms.

3. Architectural Scale: The configuration of the building's exterior forms and surfaces should arise from the needs and activities of the occupants. This includes locating, shaping, and sizing apertures at the interface of the building's interior and exterior. Shading and redirecting devices are incorporated at this scale to control the quality, direction, and amount of direct reflected sunlight reaching the glazed openings.

4. Hardware: Glazing materials and small-scale supplementary shading, redirecting, and/or blocking devices must be selected to complete the control of the amount and direction of the various components of radiant energy (visible, infrared, and ultraviolet light) entering a given space.

5. Interior Forms and Surfaces: To best utilize the light admitted for both visual and thermal comfort, shape the rooms' interior proportions and surface geometries. Locate surface reflectances to retain and distribute light as desired.

6. Space Use and Furnishings: This includes space planning to best fit the use with the building condition, arrangement of furnishings for visual comfort, selection of materials for their reflectivity or transparency, and user education as to operation of the building.

THE UNIVERSAL DESIGN INFLUENCES: LATITUDE, ORIENTATION, AND CLIMATE.

Each scale has its specific dominating influences, but all reflect the primary influences of latitude, orientation, and climate. The latitude of a site, and the orientation thereof, determine the sun angles relative to a building in the various seasons. Sun angles, in turn, shape the geometric relationships between a building and its environment. Climate influences the degree and manner in which sunlight is used within a building. Climate also determines the relative cost-effectiveness of alternative strategies and devices and the ways in which they may be refined for a specific program. Acknowledging these influences will allow you to take advantage of relationship to the sun at any scale.

URBAN DESIGN/MASTER PLANNING SCALE

Goals

The goal at the urban design scale is to provide access to sunlight throughout the built and natural environment according to the seasonally varying needs for light, heat, and view.

Influences: Scale Specific

In addition to latitude, orientation, and climate, urban design influences include the local topography, microclimate and circulation requirements, and the mix of building uses and required building densities.

Strategies

To maximize the available sunlight, don't block it! Roadway layouts and building uses and heights should be planned and zoned to prevent excessive shading. Major landscaping should be arranged to allow sunlight to reach the various building types according to their need for sunlight, to encourage optimum orientations, and to simplify the achievement of comfortable environments and energy conservation. Ensure maximum sun in winter when the sun is lowest, and expect local control in summer to reduce HVAC load. At this scale expect the building facade to do its own shading, so that it can benefit by redirecting sunlight into the building as desired, and reflecting the remainder onto the shady side of adjacent buildings. Preserve solar access with zoning codes and laws.

Forms

Begin by taking advantage of the topography of the area to create the ideal microclimate. Buildings that step up hillside sites facing the equator receive maximum access to potential winter sunlight. In their book *Site Planning* (M.I.T. Press), Kevin Lynch and Gary Hack state:

> A 10 percent slope to the south receives as much direct radiation (and to that extent has the same climate) as flat land 6 degrees closer to the equator—or the difference in latitude between Portland, Maine, and Richmond, Virginia. Yet at middle latitudes, slope orientation affects radiation rather little in midsummer, when the sun is high. It is far more critical in midwinter, when a moderate north slope may receive only half the radiation of a south-facing one.

The natural overhang at Mesa Verde is an unusual but very effective climate-moderating topography (fig. 5-2). A bowl-shaped topography provides ideal shading of the low summer sun, which is untimely and most difficult to control, particularly for sunlighting (fig. 5-3).

These large-scale natural forms can be emulated by the built environment. Plan height controls to create ideal hills or bowls. Locate the

Rhythm and Ritual

The location and form of buildings at Long-house Pueblo, Mesa Verde, Colorado, provided ancient residents with year-round comfort. The pueblo demonstrates a remarkable ability to mitigate extreme environmental temperature variations by responding to the differential impact of the sun during summer and winter, night and day.

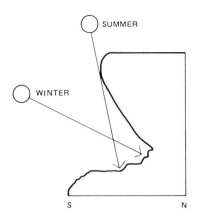

The primary adaptation of the pueblo to the solar dynamic is in its location. The settlement is sited in a large cave that faces south, and the built structures are nestled within. The brow of the cave admits warming rays of the low winter sun but shields the interior of the cave from the rays of the more northern summer sun. Not only the orientation of the cave itself (which measures almost 500 feet across, is 130 feet deep, and arches to 200 feet) but the juxtaposition of the structures within it are responsive to the solar dynamic. The interior structures stay within the summer shadow line, and they are arranged so that one structure steps up from another toward the back of the cave.

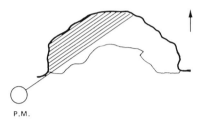

5–2. The climate-moderating form of Mesa Verde. (Reprinted, by permission, from Knowles, *Sun, Rhythm, Form*)

It is thus the location of the cave itself and the siting of structures within the cave that ensured the comfort of the pueblo dwellers. Because of orientation, the irradiation of the cave on a winter day is equivalent to that on a summer day. The performance of buildings within the cave is 56 percent more effective as a solar collector in winter than in summer, providing winter heat and summer coolness with remarkable efficiency.

5–3. Pueblo Bonito. (Reprinted, by permission, from Knowles, *Energy and Form*)

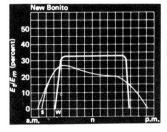

highest buildings further away from the equator to lessen the impact of their shadows and provide sunlighting opportunities for lower buildings (fig. 5–4). Parking and other facilities with less need for sunlight may be arranged on the shady side.

Circulation

Streets are the city's transparent voids, juxtaposed against the opaque solids of buildings, and can be used to get sunlight into densely built areas (figs. 5–5, 5–6). To an extent, the wider the streets, the greater the distance between buildings, and the greater the sunlight penetration and sky view within the urban fabric. Buildings can be taller without shading their neighbors when spaced further apart (fig. 5–7).

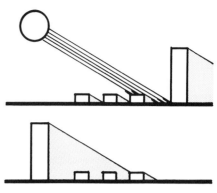

5–4. Locate higher buildings on the polar side of low neighboring buildings to eliminate the impact of their shadows.

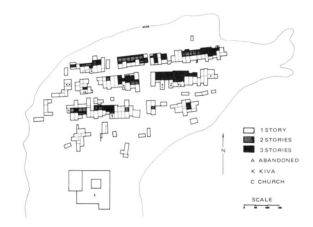

5–5. Acoma Pueblo, New Mexico. Plan shows east/west rows with critical spacing to ensure solar access between the two northernmost rows, based on story height. (Reprinted, by permission, from Knowles, *Energy and Form*)

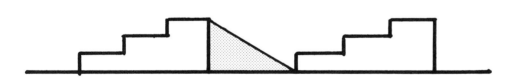

5–6. Top: three-story section; Bottom: two-story section with narrower spacing between rows.

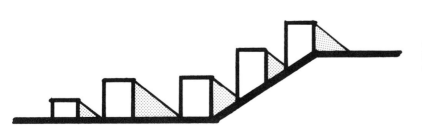

5–7. When farther apart or on a slope, buildings can be taller without shading their neighbors.

The widest streets (avenues) should run east and west to minimize the shading of buildings with equator-facing facades. This will encourage orienting a building's long facades north and south, which in turn allows for the easiest shading and exposure to sunlight to meet sunlighting and seasonal heating and cooling requirements.

In temperate climates, use deciduous trees to allow winter sun to reach south facades. Place them far enough from the building that they shade the sidewalks, but not the buildings, when the leaves are out.

Narrower streets should run north and south to allow winter sun to reach east- and west-facing facades but block extreme low-angle sunlight at the beginning and end of the longer summer days.

Ralph Knowles has written extensively and very well on the subject of planning for solar access by means of what he terms a "solar envelope"—a zoning concept to preserve solar access (fig. 5–8). My few and incomplete recommendations stray from his by emphasizing the relationship of orientation to lighting rather than thermal comfort. In buildings with stringent lighting requirements (where the problems of glare control are particularly important) orienting buildings to allow for simple solar control is more important than maximum access to sunlight.

The above recommendations assume that streets are more or less aligned with the cardinal points (N-E-S-W). This is probably the most common practice throughout the world. Knowles refers to such layouts in the United States as the Jeffersonian grid. However, he suggests that the Spanish grid, used in the older portion of Los Angeles, would be more effective in getting sunlight onto all streets at some time during each day. Although this might be good for the streets and for assuring greater equality of sunlight for housing fronting directly on each street, such an orientation of streets (as exists in Montreal) makes the achievement of comfortable sunlighting of buildings with stringent lighting requirements much more difficult (fig. 5–9).

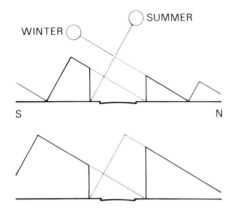

5–8. The solar envelope concept. The solar envelope is a container to regulate development within limits derived from the sun's relative motion. Development within this container will not shadow its surround during critical periods of the day. The envelope is therefore defined by the passage of time as well as by the constraints of property. (After Ralph Knowles, *Sun, Rhythm, Form*)

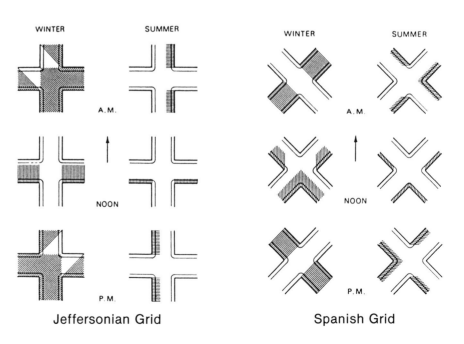

Jeffersonian Grid   Spanish Grid

5–9. Street orientation. (Reprinted by permission, from Knowles, *Sun, Rhythm, Form*)

More often than not, the designer does not have a "clean slate" to work with; planning generally occurs in a developed area. In this instance, analyzing a built environment with the aforementioned recommendations in mind should reveal the appropriate degree and character of response. While the degree of influence is much more limited, several significant areas can be addressed. The implementation of such recommendations often takes the form of zoning codes; an interesting example is that of New York City, which recognizes the reflectivity of buildings as well as their bulk and placement.

When absolute government control prevails, implementation of planning decisions presents no problem, as shown in the plan of Peking's Forbidden City, in which all major buildings face north and south; only service buildings face east and west (fig. 5–10).

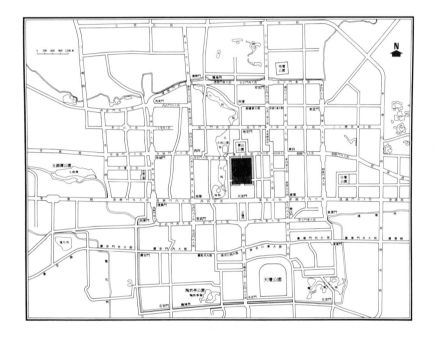

5–10. The Forbidden City, Peking, China. From the master plan of the city, to the site planning and the individual buildings, orientation to the cardinal points is faithfully followed. At the building scale the overhang is equal on all sides, but openings are reduced on the north, and buffer zones are placed on the east and west. (Reprinted, by permission, from Yu Zhuoyun, *Places of the Forbidden City*)

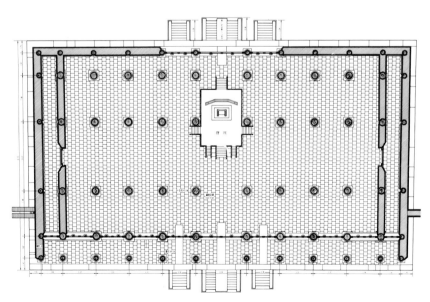

5–11. Energy-conserving plan (top) versus conventional site plan (bottom) for Burke county. (Courtesy of the Urban Land Institute)

SITE PLANNING/BUILDING MASSING

Goals

The goal at the site planning scale is to get sunlight onto buildings where and when wanted, by carefully shaping and locating the building forms.

Influences: Scale Specific

The ever-present influences of latitude, orientation, and climate are here joined by the decisions made at the urban design scale: street orientation, massing of adjacent buildings, and so forth. The local topography and nature of the site (microclimate, bodies of water, and trees) are dominant influences, along with the space needs and other programmatic concerns of the building. These programmatic needs define the visual and thermal comfort criteria. (For example, direct sunlight might be welcomed in a public space but not in an office or library.) Because the nature of the site and the building program have such a direct influence on the building form chosen, these topics will be examined in three subcategories: sidelighted buildings, toplighted buildings, and court, atria, and lightwell buildings. When choosing the overall building form, it is important to try to anticipate possible changes in the immediate environment.

Strategies

In designing the placement, spacing, and massing of buildings and associated landscaping to take advantage of sunlighting opportunities afforded by a master plan, consider the general characteristics of the possible building types.

Orient and shape buildings to sunlight as well as to the street (figs. 5-11, 5-12, and 5-13). This generally implies that they be elongated along an east/west axis. Buildings requiring illumination early in the day or late

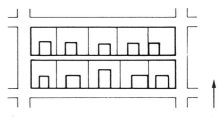

5-12. In the colonial towns of ancient Greece, planners made orderly arrangements that took maximum advantage of the sun. Blocks that ran long in the east-west direction generally contained ten houses, five on each side. The houses varied in their sizes and configurations, but they were consistently built around a south-facing court. Consequently, while the house was always entered from the street, and in that sense had a street front, the house was also oriented to the sun, and had a sun front.

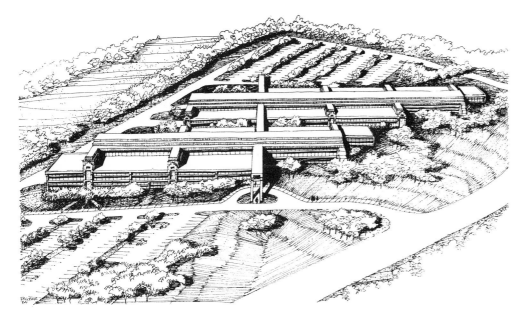

5-13. Texas Employment Commission, Austin, Texas (Graeber, Simmons, Cowan, Architect). Buildings oriented to sun despite a site not oriented along the cardinal points. (Courtesy of Graeber, Simmons, Cowan)

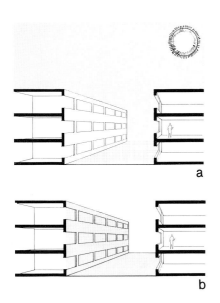

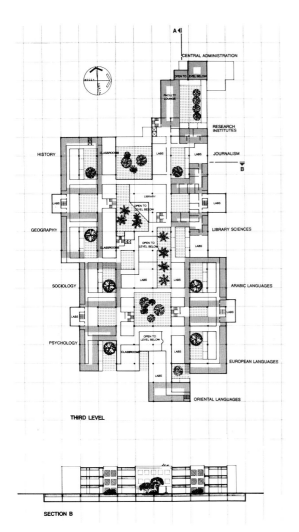

5–14. (a) On a sunny day an adjacent building can be brighter than the sky; (b) on an overcast day an adjacent building is always darker than the sky.

in the afternoon (such as indoor tennis courts) may benefit from elongation on the north/south axis. This orientation is usually desirable only for toplit buildings, where glare control is not a problem.

Place parks and plazas on the sunny side of buildings. In most climates, open areas get more use on the sunny side, and the open space allows for a substantial unshaded foreground for the building. This can increase the quantity of ground-reflected light received, or at least allow the sun to reach the full facade.

Whereas any adjacent building, wall, or trellis is an obstruction in the vocabulary of daylighting design (which assumes overcast conditions), these ''obstructions'' can be used to advantage when designing around sunlight. If sunlit surfaces are light in color, they will generally provide more illumination than the sky (fig. 5–14), as was discussed in chapter 4.

The location of the sunlighting aperture and the associated building form can be categorized as either sidelight, toplight, or atrium. The choice of form will often be dictated by the building's programmatic needs. For example, sidelighting provides light with views; toplighting helps to create uniform light levels; and atria create dramatic spaces in addition to providing illumination deep within building complexes (fig. 5–15).

5–15. Design for a university in the Middle East (case study A1). Proper orientation and elongated forms allow for solar access for all buildings. Sun courts and lightwells provide sunlight deep within the building complex. (Courtesy of Campus Consortium)

These sunlighting methods are not mutually exclusive; each method has its own impact on a building. The selection of any of the sunlighting methods should be guided by an understanding of the implications of that choice from a planning point of view. Therefore, a discussion of the general characteristics of these three methods follows.

PLANNING IMPLICATIONS OF SIDELIGHTED BUILDINGS

The decision to use sidelighting (in the form of windows and translucent walls) has historically been encouraged by the need for exterior views as well as light (fig. 5–16). Ventilation and protection from the elements are easily achieved with wall apertures.

Sidelighting is easiest when buildings are narrow (fig. 5–17). As buildings get wider, those areas away from the perimeter receive insufficient sunlight. This can be alleviated to a degree by increasing the ceiling height or using light-redirecting devices, but the ratio of sunlight opening to floor area remains limited by the geometry of sidelighting.

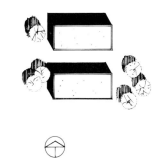

5–16. Sidelighting provides both light and view.

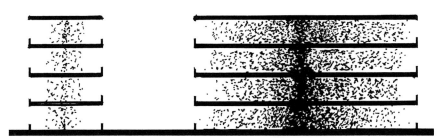

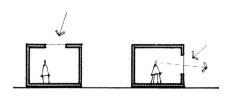

5–17. Sidelighting is easiest when buildings are narrow.

Elongation of the building along an east/west axis facilitates glare control and increases the building perimeter over a square plan (fig. 5–18). Increasing the building perimeter affords more opportunities for sidelighting. Apertures can be located to create unilateral illumination, bilateral illumination, or illumination from multiple directions (fig. 5–19). Sidelighting also allows every floor of multilevel buildings to have both light and view.

The combination of light and view makes orientation very important when planning for sidelighting. Proper sidelighting design must include careful arrangement and orientation of building masses to maximize direct and reflected sunlight on principal facades when heat and light are most desirable and minimize it when undesirable. For heat control, and to make shading and redirection of sunlight most effective, orient sidelighting apertures north and south whenever possible.

Elongated east/west blocks allow for the most simple glare and seasonal energy control. Deed restriction forcing such orientation can give a unifying character to an area, much as hillside sites promote the uniform orientation of buildings.

Sidelighting is easiest when the predominant sun angle is high (south- and north-facing exposure near the equator) and most difficult when the predominant sun angle is low (high latitudes, or east and west exposures

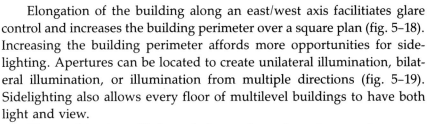

5–18. Orient sidelit buildings with long facades facing north and south for easiest shading.

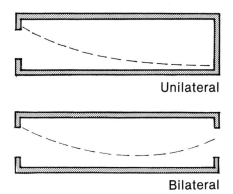

Unilateral

Bilateral

5–19. Sidelighting can be unilateral or bilateral.

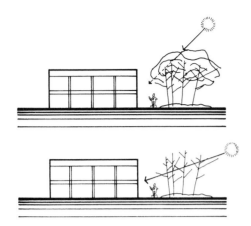

5–20. Deciduous trees can be used to shade hard-to-control, low-angle east and west sun in the summer (top) and winter (bottom).

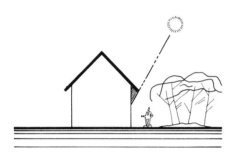

5–21. Allow sun to reach south facade at all times; expect facade to do its own shading as necessary.

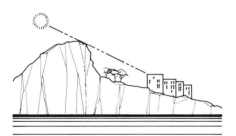

5–22. When possible, take advantage of topography to shade low-angle sun. Tall elements at a distance will shade many floors almost equally, whereas adjacent trees may shade only the ground floor.

5–23. Toplighted buildings are desirable when the building is too large to be lit by sidelight alone.

early and late in the day). This is mostly due to the glare problems that accompany low-angle sun.

Sidelighting can utilize not only the light from the sun and the sky, but also the light reflected from the ground and adjacent buildings. However, extensive expanses of sunlit ground or building surfaces are not often available. More often, sunlight is received directly on the building facade, making the facade itself the most important element for capturing, shading, and redirecting sunlight.

The shady sides of buildings usually receive more light reflected from nearby walls than from the sky. Wall- or building-reflected light is at a maximum when the sun is low; ground-reflected light is at a maximum when the sun is high (see chapter 4).

In densely built areas, courtyards can be designed to catch and redirect sunlight for sidelighting at facades that are in shade. A building complex can be designed to ensure light colors on those surfaces that are most important for reflecting sunlight.

The apertures of sidelighted buildings are easily obstructed by adjacent buildings and trees. Conversely, this attribute can be exploited by using deciduous trees to allow sunlight on buildings when desirable, and provide shading when sunlight is undesirable thermally and glare is difficult to control (e.g., on west facades in summer, fig. 5–20). Depending on trees and neighboring buildings for protective shading generally works well only for single-story buildings. For higher buildings, such shading will tend to be insufficient on some floors and excessive on others. Do not shade the south facade during the summer if working light is desired; instead, design the facade to self-shade, capture, and redirect the sunlight (fig. 5–21).

Sidelighted buildings will benefit most from protective shading elements at great distance, such as a distant tall building or far away mountains, because they can shade an entire building equally and reduce the need for local shading of low-angle sun (fig. 5–22). The presence of surrounding hills can be a great asset in simplifying the problems on east- and west-facing facades. If used extensively, this will create distinctive solutions in such locales.

Privacy and/or security requirements may determine the suitability or form of sidelighting desirable. A more detailed discussion of sidelighting can be found in chapter 6.

PLANNING IMPLICATIONS OF TOPLIGHTED BUILDINGS

Toplighting (via skylights, clerestories, sunscoops, and lightscoops) may be desirable when the user program calls for floor areas too large to be illuminated adequately by sidelighting alone (fig. 5–23). Toplighting allows for very high densities of development, in part because it is the sunlighting option least obstructed by other buildings.

Exterior views are severely compromised with toplighting; therefore it should be used when views are not important programmatically, or desirable views are unavailable. Sunlit interior walls can provide a satisfactory view substitute by meeting biological information needs for contact with nature and orientation in time and space.

When the predominant sun angle is low and maximum heat and light are wanted without the glare of the low sun angle (high latitudes), toplighting is the ideal solution.

Although toplighting is usually limited to a single story, it can be used to illuminate more than one level by expanding in scale and combining with open courts, atria, and lightwells. When used to illuminate only one floor level, however, toplighting allows for the most efficient utilization of sunlight because uniform illumination is easiest to achieve. This freedom in locating apertures for optimum light distribution allows for the use of sunlight with minimum HVAC impact, because a minimum percent of sunlight opening is required to maintain a given minimum light level throughout a space (fig. 5–24).

A toplighting aperture may be adjusted easily to allow for maximum light and heat at any time of day or season. Apertures can also have the flexibility of being independently oriented from the dominant building orientation (fig. 5–25).

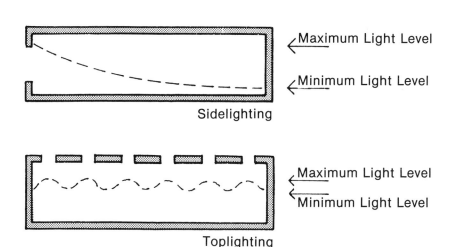

Maximum Light Level
Minimum Light Level

Sidelighting

Maximum Light Level
Minimum Light Level

Toplighting

5–24. Toplighting can provide the most uniform light levels, hence the minimum impact on HVAC.

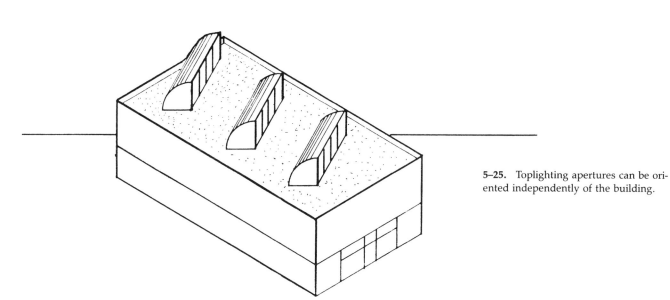

5–25. Toplighting apertures can be oriented independently of the building.

Planning Implications of Toplighted Buildings 69

Placing the aperture in the ceiling frees the walls and floors to meet other programmatic needs. Walls may be important for display (such as in museum or stores) or for security (warehouses). Toplight is useful where the height of equipment, shelving, or necessary partitioning would limit the distribution of sidelight. A more detailed discussion of toplighting is found in chapter 7.

PLANNING IMPLICATIONS OF COURT, ATRIA, AND LIGHTWELL BUILDINGS

Programmatic Options

This sunlighting technique creates architectural spaces that can be realized in various forms. These forms include:

☐ occupied or unoccupied areas;

☐ fully conditioned spaces, thermally tempered spaces, or nonconditioned buffer spaces;

☐ enclosed spaces or spaces that are fully open to the sky.

If these spaces are enclosed and climate-controlled, they may be acoustically, visually, and/or thermally open to adjacent spaces or separated from them. Adjacent spaces may be designed to benefit from the light and/or heat from these shared spaces, or they can be isolated from them.

Characteristics

Shared central spaces should be used to achieve maximum development density while retaining contact with nature and sunlight. This method allows light to reach multiple levels in deep buildings, making them more pleasant than they would otherwise be (fig. 5–26). Proper atrium design can reduce the energy costs for providing visual and thermal comfort in deep buildings.

A primary benefit of this technique is the creation of dramatic use areas as focal spaces for surrounding development. The surrounding area of a successful court or atrium space is often assigned high economic value and may provide economic justification for its construction and operations costs.

If this degree of attention is not called for, this sunlighting method can be integrated into the building program in the form of major spaces (lunchrooms, conference areas) or minor shared areas, such as a stairwell or circulation spine.

When not serving adjacent spaces, sunlight may be used to serve the created open space alone. Illumination will generally be required within the space for trees and for user activities such as circulation.

Shared central spaces can provide sunlit views for the surrounding spaces. If desired, their usefulness can be increased by designing them to redirect sunlight efficiently and provide ambient and task lighting for

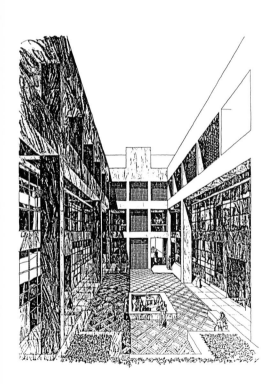

5–26. Courtyards allow light to reach multiple levels deep in building complexes. (Courtesy of Campus Consortium)

surrounding occupied spaces. In such cases, careful control of quantity and direction of sunlight admitted is required. A more detailed discussion of shared central spaces can be found in chapter 8.

BASIC STRATEGIES OF SUNLIGHTING: COMFORT AND ITS ACHIEVEMENT

Having planned strategies for getting sunlight to various types of buildings, how is this sunlight then used? The objectives of optimum use of sunlight in buildings are visual and thermal comfort. These objectives require the control of the immediate, instantaneous effects of direct sunlight to eliminate glare and radiant overheating, redistribute the visible light and infrared heat to illuminate the spaces optimally, and achieve comfortable air temperatures throughout the year. Comfort and delight also require optimizing interior and exterior views.

These concerns exist in all spaces occupied by people. The exact nature of the optimal solutions will vary according to the programmed activities that define the given environment. The following basic strategies and techniques will help achieve the "comfort objectives" to different degrees. Designers must weigh the trade-offs of cost, appearance, and function associated with the strategies chosen for a specific application.

Shading

Shade sunlight to prevent glare and excess heat gain (fig. 5–27). Use optimum orientation to make fixed shading and redirection more efficient and/or easier. On north- and south-facing facades, fixed shading can be effective all of the time for control of glare and HVAC loads. On east and west exposures, fixed shading cannot usually control glare at dawn and dusk. If fixed shading devices are not sufficient, supplement them with movable devices that are used as infrequently as possible. Movable shading devices should be automatically controlled; if manual controls are used, they should be dependable and nonfrustrating to operate, particularly if the movable devices are also needed for privacy, nighttime containment of the space, or control of artificial light.

Why not control the amount of light reaching the space simply by using low-transmission (mirror) glass? In my opinion, this type of thinking has shaped most of the architectural atrocities of the recent past. Mirror glass cannot eliminate the need for shading because 10 percent of the sun's brightness is *still* too much. Mirror glass cannot redirect sunlight, except to neighboring buildings. (Its use is prohibited in Singapore for this reason.) Furthermore, low-transmission glass reduces the light when it is wanted as well as when it is not.

Redirection

Distribute light where needed to minimize the need for supplemental lighting (fig. 5–28). A high average illumination level is not efficient if it is not well distributed (i.e., if the area near the window receives most of the light). Redirect sunlight to optimize the brightness balance of the room

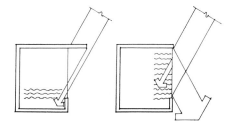

5-27. Shading versus low-transmission glass.

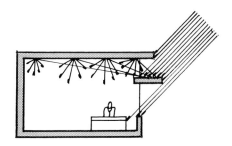

5–28. Distribute light where needed.

by distributing sunlight over the largest possible area. Illuminate three-dimensional objects from all directions; illuminate horizontal surfaces uniformly throughout the room. Minimize contrast with windows.

Control

Control the total amount of light reaching the space to achieve thermal comfort and minimize energy cost for HVAC (fig. 5–29). Overlight in winter when heat is welcomed psychologically and physiologically and when excess heat can be dumped easily. Provide only as much light as necessary for planned activities in summer when excess light creates cooling loads.

Efficacy

Use light efficiently. Once light energy is admitted and "paid for," preserve it with high reflectances. High reflectances are less important if there are only heating concerns (minimal lighting needs and little need for cooling).

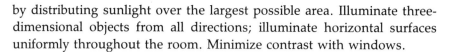

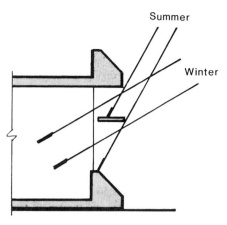

5–29. Control the total amount of light reaching the space seasonally.

5–30. Optimize exterior views by using very large- or very small-scale shading elements.

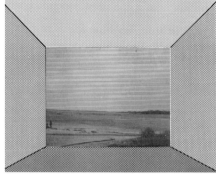 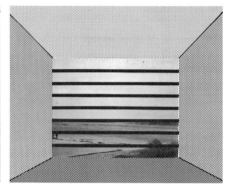

Framing of Views

Optimize exterior views. Frame the best views and block bad views. Use sun-control elements that require no user action, or either the view or the light will suffer. Minimize pattern conflicts between shading elements and views (fig. 5–30). This is best accomplished with shading elements that are large enough to frame the view. Otherwise, the smallest scale elements that present a texture rather than a pattern may be best. Avoid translucent glazing unless it is an interesting, satisfying, artificial "view" in itself (stained-glass windows, for example).

Optimize interior views. Design and illuminate room surfaces so that they become sources of light that are enjoyable to look at. Shape the entire room as a lighting sculpture, as Aalto and Utzon have done (fig. 5–31). A beautiful interior space is also a comfortable one; *to be beautiful is to be functional.*

5–31. Optimize interior views by creating beautiful scenes to look at.

6 Sidelighting: Strategies, Techniques, Devices, and Forms

6–1. Indigenous sidelighting in overcast climates often included stained-glass windows placed as high as possible.

6–2. Sunny climates encourage small, shaded windows located relatively low in the space. (Photograph courtesy of Norman Carver)

Sidelighting is the most commonly used form of sunlighting because it can provide light, view, and ventilation simultaneously.

The previous chapter discussed the ways in which urban design can make sunlighting available at the site and the architectural programmatic considerations that can ensure maximum solar access for sidelighted buildings. But how do we manipulate the light at and within the building? In this chapter, we will discuss in greater detail those strategies applicable specifically to sidelighting and the resulting techniques, design forms, and devices.

HISTORICAL PRECEDENTS

As discussed in chapter 5, sidelighting has historically been the predominant form of using natural light because it fulfills the need for light, views, and ventilation simultaneously. Sidelighting was also the most practical lighting method, given the difficulty of keeping out rain and snow before the development of glass and weathertight glazing systems.

Until the advent of electric artificial lighting, the forms of indigenous architecture reflected the distance that natural light could penetrate the building through windows. Narrow building blocks ensured that sufficient light was available even in the middle of the building. In the predominantly cloudy climate of northern Europe, windows were placed high to distribute diffused sky light. The Gothic cathedrals evolved to achieve the highest and largest windows possible.

It is logical and likely that stained-glass windows were used to give color and interest to the otherwise gloomy overcast sky, as well as to illustrate religious themes. Stained glass also reduces the glare of unshaded windows when the sun shines by reducing the luminance and because, unlike plain translucent material, the information-rich windows are "signal" rather than "noise" or "glare" (fig. 6–1).

In sunny locales throughout the world, the windows in all types of buildings have generally been shaded by overhanging roofs or deep window reveals (fig. 6–2). These shaded windows were generally placed relatively low in walls to best reflect sunlight, rather than extended to the ceilings, even though ceiling heights were increased in larger, deeper rooms. In religious buildings, the light-receiving surfaces were often the ceilings, which thus became the most common and logical location of decorations. The relatively small apertures were either glazed with clear glass or left unglazed. Stained glass was rarely used (fig. 6–3).

These common design solutions evolved because they were the most logical, practical ways to use sunlight to satisfy the lighting needs of those buildings. These simple principles can be varied to achieve the more stringent objectives in today's larger buildings.

6–3. Monastery of Hosios Loukas, Stiris, Greece (ca. 1040 A.D.). Religious buildings in sunny climates decorate the light-receiving surfaces (ceilings) rather than the glazing. (Photograph courtesy of John Lam)

SIDELIGHTING GEOMETRY—OPTIMIZING INDIRECT LIGHTING

In earlier times, building forms reflected the limits of natural lighting and the expectation that critical tasks would be performed near the window. Shading provided relief from glare, and ground-reflected light provided adequate indirect lighting.

Sidelighting in today's large buildings requires maximizing the sun's indirect lighting potential as well as providing shading and glare control. While direct sunlight can be controlled and converted into diffuse direct lighting by using diffusing materials, this approach is to be avoided when possible, if freedom from visual noise and the other conditions of a good visual environment are to be achieved (see chapter 2).

The strategy for achieving the comfortable and delightful interior environments described is to redirect sunlight to primary room surfaces (ceiling and walls), which in turn will illuminate secondary horizontal work surfaces. This will also improve the brightness balance of the space relative to the window view.

To optimize the design of indirect lighting, the designer must identify where the light is wanted, where the best primary and secondary reflecting surfaces are located or can be created, and where the light can originate.

Direct light from the window and illuminated surfaces near the window will best illuminate those surfaces deep in a space that ''see'' or face the windows (fig. 6–4). A surface facing away from the window can only receive light indirectly (as reflected by other surfaces). Only a totally black room would have no interreflected light. An object facing the window of such a room would be completely dark on those sides that did not see the window (fig. 6–5). Without interreflected light, a person in front of a window (light source) will appear only in silhouette.

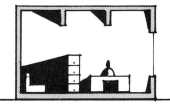

6–4. Without interreflected light, only those surfaces that ''see'' the window are not in shadow.

 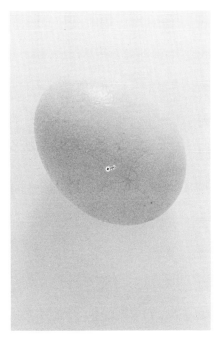

6–5. Egg in black box is lit only by aperture. Egg in white box receives interreflected light from several sides, improving perception of the object.

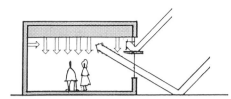

6–6. By redirecting light received from the ground or a lightshelf, the ceiling becomes an indirect source of light.

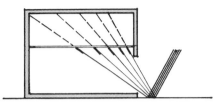

6–7. Increasing the ceiling height allows more light in the rear of the space.

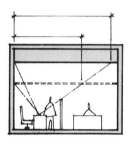

6–8. High ceilings are more easily ''seen.''

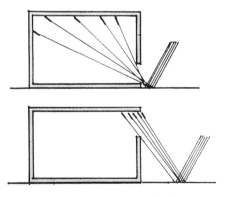

6–9. Locate the light source as far from the ceiling as possible. For upward-reflected light, a low aperture (top) will provide better light distribution than one located higher up (bottom).

Major surfaces within a space must both ''see'' the window and be of high reflectivity to provide this desirable interreflected light. For this reason, furnishings are not dependable as reflectors; they may be of low reflectivity, and their arrangements may trap rather than redirect sunlight. In typical office buildings, even the location of walls may not be predictable. Office landscape systems may have no substantial wall surfaces to reflect light. Floors and low horizontal surfaces tend to be of low reflectivity as well as being potential sources of glare.

Using the Ceiling as the Principal Source of Reflected Light

In the majority of buildings the ceilings and upper walls are likely to be the only areas that can be depended upon as good light-reflecting surfaces. In addition, the ceiling is likely to be the best location for redirecting glare-free light downward onto horizontal surfaces and onto vertical surfaces facing away from the window (fig. 6–6). When using the ceiling as the principal source of reflected light, bear in mind the following:

□ *Locate the light source as far from the ceiling as possible.* To illuminate the ceiling cavity area most uniformly, the light source(s) should be as far below the ceiling as possible. This can be done by raising the ceiling, lowering the light source, or both.

High ceilings can be more evenly illuminated than low ceilings because they can be a greater distance from the reflected light sources (fig. 6–7). High ceilings can also be ''seen'' by desk-top work surfaces more easily (fig. 6–8). However, high ceilings are not very helpful under overcast conditions, except to make higher window locations possible.

If necessary, create integrated building systems to get high ceilings economically. Most contemporary buildings waste potential ceiling height, with excess space above the ceiling (see chapter 9).

Windows and shading/redirecting devices should also be placed as low as possible after consideration of the other comfort objectives, such as glare, view, and privacy (fig. 6–9).

□ *Locate and shape the reflecting devices to best redirect light to the ceiling (rather than to eye level), thus avoiding glare.* This will affect the device's allowable reflectance. For example, if the device is below eye level, glare considerations will dictate that it either be of low reflectance, or shaped to direct light away from potential glare angles.

□ *Use high-reflectance ceiling cavities.* While high reflectances on all room surfaces are beneficial for preserving the sunlight admitted, the configuration of a room determines the relative importance of a given surface's reflectance. For tall narrow rooms, the side walls may constitute the greatest surface area and therefore be the most important area in which to maintain high reflectances. For low-ceilinged deep rooms, the reflectance of the ceiling cavity is most important for light distribution. A simple diagram makes obvious the importance of highly reflective upper room surfaces for achieving efficient light utilization (fig. 6–10). In general, light-colored materials should be used for upper room surfaces.

Under overcast conditions, the sky itself (rather than the indirectly illuminated ceiling cavity) will always be the principal source of illumination. At such times a highly reflective ceiling cavity will not affect illumination levels and distribution as much as it will make a gloomy condition seem less gloomy by improving the brightness balance of the room.

☐ *Maximize the ceiling's effective reflectance.* This can be done by using building systems that minimize the amount of surface area making up the ceiling cavity (fig. 6–11). A given amount of light will be spread more thinly over a configured ceiling than over a flat ceiling of equal projected area. The ceiling will thus become less bright. The reduction in reflected light will be equivalent to painting the flat ceiling with a lower-reflectance paint (equal to its ''effective'' reflectance).

☐ *Shape the ceiling cavity for best light distribution.* Having minimized the amount of surface area by eliminating light-catching pockets, refine the ceiling shape for the desired distribution of light rather than for maximum average illumination. For instance, a low ceiling or a ceiling that slopes downward from the window will produce the highest average illumination levels but the lowest illumination levels deep in the space where they are most needed (fig. 6–12). Other shapes produce even better distribution (fig. 6–13). The best shapes are those with the least surface area, which receive the ground/-facade/-reflected light deepest in the space and are angled to best ''see'' both the floor below and the light source. Refer to generic data at the end of this chapter for more information.

☐ *Maximize other reflectances.* Maximize the reflectance of the ground and of the shading devices to allow the greatest amount of light to be reflected to the ceiling cavity, after consideration of comfort and other practical factors (fig. 6–14).

The relative influences of window placement, ceiling height, room reflectances, and room shapes are difficult to compute but can be measured easily in scale models. Examination of the generic model data presented at the end of this chapter reveals the significance of these factors.

Location of the Light Source: Windows

For the purpose of analyzing the effects of different sidelighting aperture locations, we divided a potential (model) window wall into three areas; low, high, and middle. Orientation, reflectances, scale, and ceiling configuration were assumed to be equivalent in all instances.

Low Windows

Low windows provide the most uniform illumination by distributing re-

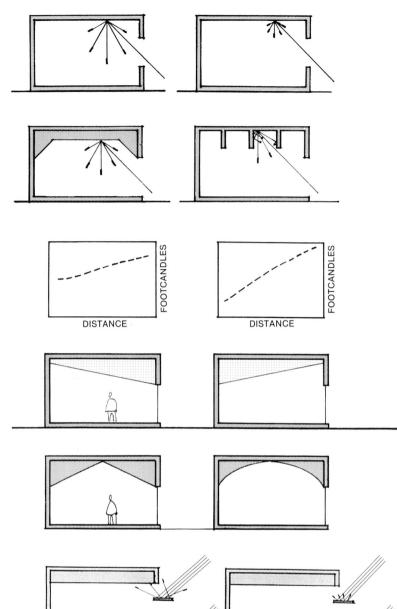

6–10. A highly reflectant ceiling cavity is necessary for efficient utilization of light.

6–11. Highly articulated ceilings have a lot of surface area and trap light (right). Simpler ceilings, with less surface area, distribute light more efficiently (left).

6–12. Ceilings that slope up from the aperture improve illumination uniformity when the back wall is white. Sloping ceilings downward from the aperture increases the average illumination level but keeps the light closer to the window and makes the illumination less uniform.

6–13. Some ceiling shapes are better than a single slope.

6–14. Maximize primary reflectances (left) to distribute more light to ceiling cavity.

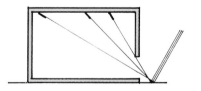

6–15. Low windows provide the most uniform illumination by distributing reflected sunlight deep into rooms.

flected sunlight deep into rooms (fig. 6–15). However, they have several drawbacks as well:

Low windows effectively place the principal *reflected light source* near or below eye level and thus maximize the potential glare for nearby work performed at desk-top level. This is not a problem in spaces where there is no specific task location or where the "task" is enjoying the sunlit scene. The area of the room affected by potential glare and local overheating from *direct sunlight* is minimized with a low window. Direct sunlight penetration is kept close to the window and generally below eye level, to a limited area along the perimeter wall.

When using low windows, the contrast with the unlit upper wall and the adjacent ceiling may seem gloomy. To counteract this, minimize the

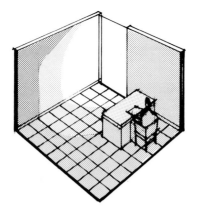

6–16. For any window height, locating the window adjacent to a wall will minimize shadows and aperture contrast.

unlit surface area by sloping the ceiling down to the window head and locating the low windows adjacent to perpendicular walls (fig. 6–16).

The value of the view out a low window depends on its scale. The view from the bottom third of 24-foot wall can be very good, but the view from the bottom third of a 9-or 12-foot wall with the window head only 3–4 feet above the floor is likely to be unsatisfactory (fig. 6–17).

When used as a primary source of illumination, low windows are likely to have some view interference in the form of glare. Light-colored reflecting materials placed low in the space will always be more conspicuous than those placed above eye level. Therefore, allowable reflectance values tend to be lower. In addition, low partitions, and other furnishings may block much of the light from being reflected deep into the room.

Finally, privacy may be an issue with low windows. In low-rise buildings, combining privacy with some view and light can be difficult with a low window.

High Windows

High windows give the deepest penetration of sidelight from direct, diffuse light sources (i.e. overcast skies or translucent glazing) to a horizontal workplane and less light near the window (fig. 6–18). This advantage in the overcast condition has promoted the myth that they are best for distributing sunlight as well.

The advantages of high windows include providing light with privacy and improved security. The extra wall space can be used for display, chalkboards, bookshelves, storage, and so on. Furnishings and low partitions do not block any reflected light from reaching the ceiling, and the higher location of the zone of maximum brightness reduces the potential glare interference for VDTs. High windows permit the highest efficiency of *comfortable* reflected sunlight because the brightest reflecting surfaces are above eye level. Mirrored reflectors at various angles can be used to offset the disadvantages of the less favorable position relative to the ceiling.

The primary disadvantage of high windows is that they provide less favorable light distribution to the ceiling from ground-reflected light. High windows maximize the potential for glare from sky and sun, exposing more of the space to the brightest part of the sky. Light from that part of the sky must be baffled and redirected to the ceiling to minimize contrast (fig. 6–19). In addition, the view out of a high window is likely to be less than satisfactory.

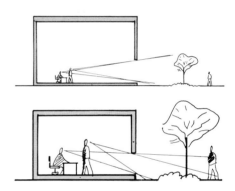

6–17. Low windows may have a view.

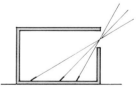

6–18. High windows provide the best distribution of the direct, diffuse light of overcast skies.

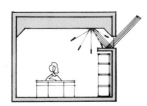

6–19. High windows maximize the potential for glare from sky and sun and must be baffled.

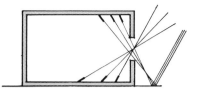

6-20. The middle window location is not optimal for distributing ground-reflected sunlight or overcast sky light.

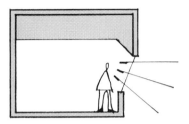

6-21. "Overbite" aperture is similar in performance to overhangs and favors ground-reflected light.

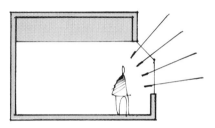

6-22. "Greenhouse-type" window aperture favors light from the sky. Best for shady sides and overcast skies.

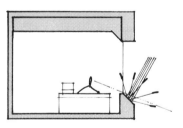

6-23. Sloping the sill away from the building minimizes glare from the sunlit sill and increases the collection of ground-reflected light.

Middle Windows

The middle third of a wall is not as good as the lower third for the deep distribution of ground-reflected sunlight, nor as good as the upper third for the deep distribution of diffused light from the overcast sky (fig. 6–20). However, if it provides sufficient light for the purposes of the room, it is frequently the preferred choice because it generally provides the best view. This means less discomfort glare, because even the brightest exterior scene is still considered "signal" rather than "noise."

Glare from the sunlit sills of middle windows with maximum reflectivity can be minimized by sloping the sills to be below eye level from the most important work positions, yet allowing them to be "seen" by the ceiling. If the sill is as reflective as the ground it will be equal in brightness and more reliable as a light source.

Another disadvantage of middle windows is that the brightness of the view in typical office buildings maximizes the potential for reflections on VDT screens when they cannot be oriented so as not to reflect the windows. If the light input from other windows alone is sufficient, it may be desirable to reduce the luminance or, better yet, the extent of the middle window, particularly if exterior wall surface is wanted for other purposes. Used in this way, they become "view" windows. Middle windows are easily accessible for interior cleaning and operation.

Shaped Apertures and Sloped Glazings

For a given sidelighting condition, it may be desirable to slope the glazing by moving the sill location into the building (to maximize the ground view) or moving it out (to maximize the sky view). Pulling the glazing sill in ("overbite" aperture) will tend to shade the window and provide a better angle of incidence for accepting ground-reflected light (fig. 6–21). Larger benefits may be an improvement in the view due to reduced veiling reflections and less heat gain because of the more oblique solar incidence angle. Sloping the sill out ("greenhouse-type" aperture) increases the effective sky aperture, resulting in a window that is difficult to shade and maximizes incoming daylight (fig. 6–22). This is only recommended on the north sides of buildings (as at TVA, case study B7) and in very overcast climates. In all conditions, the glazing position is much less important than the shape of the aperture. Shaping the aperture is *always* recommended to maximize lighting benefits and minimize problems:

☐ If the sill is light-colored and sunlight redirection is already provided for, slope the window sills out to minimize glare. Slope sills out on the shady side to maximize ground-reflected light (fig. 6–23).

☐ If there is no other sunlight-redirecting device on the sunny side, use wide-level sills to redirect sunlight, hopefully located above seated eye level.

☐ Slope the ceiling to the window head to minimize brightness contrast between windows and walls and improve light distribution.

Sources of Reflected Sunlight

Wherever a window is located, the source of reflected light can be the ground, adjacent building surfaces, or portions of the facade itself.

Ground-reflected light on the sunny side, and light reflected from the facing facade on the shady side, are the easiest to use. If these dependable sources are available, little is needed architecturally to take advantage of the light. An overhang is sufficient to shade the sunny side, and an unshaded window is good on the shady side.

Ground-reflected Light

It is difficult, especially in dense urban areas, to achieve the expanses of sunlit foreground necessary for the ground to be the principal source of light in buildings. "Solar envelope" zoning as proposed by Knowles (discussed in chapter 5) would increase the opportunities to use ground-reflected light (fig. 6–24).

For sufficient ground area to be illuminated, buildings must be widely spaced. Even at the equator, where the high arc of the sun allows penetration to north and south facades without much spacing, the unshaded ground area should extend at least as far away from the window plane as the window is above the ground (fig. 6–25).

It is much easier for low, single-story buildings to have enough sunlit foreground than it is for urban multistory buildings, unless the high-rise buildings tower so far above their neighbors that rooftops effectively become "ground" (fig. 6–26).

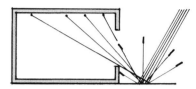

6–24. Ground-reflected light.

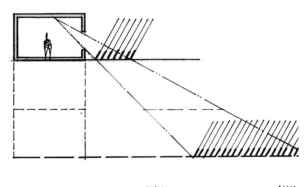

6–25. As buildings get taller, they must "see" more sunlit ground to get reflected light.

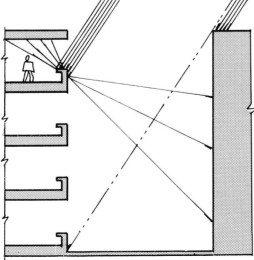

6–26. Ground-reflected light is not always available.

When the building spacing is sufficient, the foreground must also be relatively free of trees and other potential shading elements such as fences, walls, and bushes. This is not always possible or desirable, however. The exposed sunlit ground must be light in color to be as quantitatively effective as integral facade elements can be. Snow and concrete make excellent foregrounds. Gravel is fair. Sunlit ground cover, green grass, brick, and asphalt reflect less than 10 percent, but even this quantity of light (when the sun is high, approximately 8,000 Fc × 10% = 800 Fc) is as much as is received from the north sky and considerably more than is received from the shady side of buildings, trees, hedges, and walls.

Because of these requirements, ground-reflected sunlight for facades facing the equator (i.e., south in the northern hemisphere, north in the southern hemisphere) is a realistic choice only for low structures, for those fronting a beach, lawn, lake, or plaza, or for high-rise buildings protected by restricted zoning heights (fig. 6–27).

6–27. Ground-reflected light from the balcony of Frank Lloyd Wright's Robie house.

Facade-reflected Light

A building's facade is the most likely potential source of reflected sunlight for the space it encloses. This method avoids the stricter site constraints imposed by ground-reflected light. Of course, it is valuable only as long as it is sunlit. Deciduous trees can be planted to shade the sidewalks as long as they do not shade the light-reflecting elements of the facade.

A small sunlit area of horizontal reflecting surface on the facade has the same projected area as a very large expanse of sunlit ground as seen from the ceiling of upper floors (fig. 6–28). In addition, the placement and characteristics of that reflecting surface can be controlled, as will be discussed later in this chapter.

To be of maximum value, that portion of sunlight not directed into the building can be reflected to the adjacent building blocks (fig. 6–29).

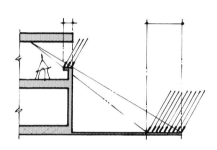

6–28. A building's facade needs only a small amount of reflecting area to get the equivalent benefit of a large area of sunlit foreground.

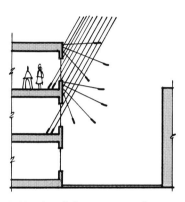

6–29. Any light not accepted into the building may be reflected to the adjacent building(s).

Building-reflected Light

On the shady side of a building, both ground-reflected and building-reflected light are logical supplements to diffuse sky light (fig. 6–30). Ground-reflected light is often available when the sun is high. However, when the sun is low, the ground is in shade. Building-reflected light is sunlight reflected off the surfaces of close adjacent buildings; the greatest light is reflected when the sun is low. These surfaces can be a source of uncomfortable glare because of their brightness at eye level. To take advantage of building-reflected light directly, high windows should be used. When the sunlit surfaces have intrinsic interest, low and mid-level windows are more acceptable because the view is perceived as a pleasurable experience rather than as glare. However, designers rarely have this degree of control over neighboring buildings. More often, neighboring mirror-glass buildings have a negative impact that must be mitigated (fig. 6–31).

Using building-reflected light was a very common strategy before electric lighting. For example, the narrow streets and whitewashed buildings of Greek villages allow a great deal of light in the facing windows without the heat of the sun. Larger buildings with courtyards have historically used their internal facades as sources of building-reflected light. McKim, Mead and White's Boston Public Library building is a good example of this.

These strategies are discussed in greater depth in chapter 7.

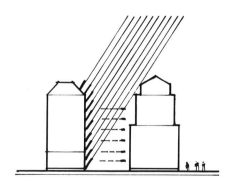

6–30. Building-reflected light.

6–31. The shady side of the masonry building is now in sunlight (reflected from the adjacent mirror-glass building). (Photograph courtesy of Victor Olgyay)

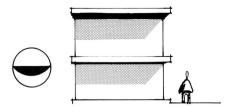

6–32. Horizontal shading devices respond to solar altitude. They shade most at noon, when the sun is highest.

SIDELIGHTING FORMS AND DEVICES

Having discussed the theoretical aspects of window location and determined the building facade to be the most consistently viable source of reflected light for sunlighting, we can now evaluate the devices that best achieve the desired light distribution along with the other sunlighting objectives. These devices can be categorized as horizontal or vertical. The most simple, effective devices for achieving all of the sunlighting goals are horizontal shading/redirecting devices of various types (fig. 6–32).

Shading

Horizontal shading devices can be simpler than vertical shading devices because of the apparent orbit of the sun. Examination of the sun

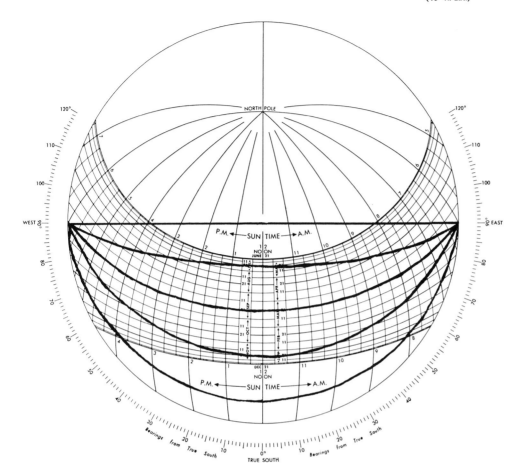

6-33. Sun path diagram. Profile angles (the sun's height above the horizon from a direction normal to the facade) on north and south exposures change relatively little over the course of a day, and only 45 degrees seasonally.

path diagram in figure 6-33 reveals that for window orientations parallel to the equator, the change in the solar altitude relative to the facade (*profile angle*) varies little during the day and by only 45 degrees from summer to winter. Thus, at any latitude, total shading can be achieved on north/south facades by quite narrow, seasonally adjusted horizontal shading devices, and even fixed devices can be of reasonable proportions in tropical and temperate latitudes. At the low sun angles of polar latitudes, the dimensions of fixed horizontal shading devices can only be reasonable when angled downward.

For east- and west-facing windows, fixed horizontal shading can be effective for most of the working day, but generally must be supplemented early and late in the day with other devices.

Vertical shading devices control low-angle sun by blocking the "troublesome" area of the aperture and the accompanying view (figs. 6-34, 6-35). They are simplest and most effective when acting as supplements to horizontal devices. An "eggcrate" facade can allow more view than vertical louvers alone (figs. 6-36, 6-37). If vertical louvers are used alone, the rapidly changing direction in the sun's bearing angle (15 degrees per hour) will require constant adjustment if they are to remain effective. At that rate, 45 degrees of fixed vertical louvering changes from 100 percent to 0 percent effective in three hours.

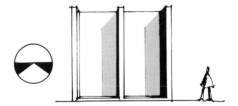

6-34. Vertical shading devices respond to the sun's bearing angle—its movement around the horizon. On a south wall, they shade at the beginning and end of a day.

Sidelighting Forms and Devices 85

6–35. Vertical shading devices control low-angle sun by blocking the ''troublesome'' area on the aperture and the accompanying view.

6–37. A medium-scale eggcrate shading device may disguise the scale of a building.

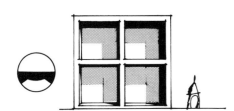

6–36. ''Eggcrate'' shading devices combine the elements of both horizontal and vertical devices. Their shading masks are therefore the combination of their horizontal and vertical constituents.

Redirecting Devices

Horizontal louvers can redirect light to the ceiling. Dynamic specular louvers can beam sunlight to the walls or ceiling as desired. Vertical louvering can only redirect sunlight to walls or low horizontal elements.

Glare Control

Horizontal louvers of any finish are glare-free as long as the reflecting surface is not visible (above eye level). Specular-finish horizontal louvers can direct glare-free light above eye level even when they are visible. Less control of light redirection is possible with vertical louvers. Matte-finish vertical louvers will direct as much light to eye level as to the ceiling. Glossy-finish vertical louvers will direct intense sunlight down toward eye level and can thus be a source of glare in portions of the room. Design these carefully!

Scale of Louvers versus View

Views are least interrupted by the largest size louvers (i.e., building-scale rather than hardware-scale). This allows one to be within the louver, which frames rather than disrupts the view. At the other extreme, the smallest scale of louver can be inconspicuous, appearing as a texture or screen rather than as a competing pattern, as would a medium scale-device (see chapter 11).

Other Advantages of Building-Scale Shading/Redirecting Devices

Large-scale elements are an integral part of the building fabric and can be combined with other elements. Thus, they can be built to be more durable and easier to maintain than hardware solutions. Small-scale elements tend to be more fragile and are best located within the protection of the building envelope. This also implies that any sunlight blocked will become heat in the interior of the building rather than on the exterior. Because of these characteristics, use of large, architectural-scale building elements is preferred for primary sun control. Unlike hardware solutions, which can merely be added on at any stage, they must be part of the initial building design concept. Whether located on the interior or the exterior, large-scale elements are likely to be major architectural formgivers.

HORIZONTAL SHADING/REDIRECTING DEVICES: CONTROL RELATED TO SOLAR ALTITUDE

The Overhang—Single Shading Element

While not as universally useful as some other devices, the simple overhang needed for seasonal shading and glare control can be the best design solution for some conditions. Since the overhang provides shading without redirection of the sunlight, sufficient foreground area must be available to utilize ground-reflected light as the primary source of illumination (fig. 6–38).

That assurance can be created when the foreground has a programmatic use in addition to its sunlighting function. Foregrounds might be used as circulation paths, living terraces, or balconies (fig. 6–39); on mul-

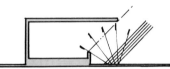

6–38. Because the overhang provides shading without redirection of the sunlight, sufficient foreground must be available to utilize ground-reflected light.

6–39. Frank Lloyd Wright's Robie House. Horizontal overhangs provide total shading of south-facing french doors at midsummer. Very deep overhangs are effective on east and west ends. Balconies and living terraces (of medium reflectance) are effective reflectors.

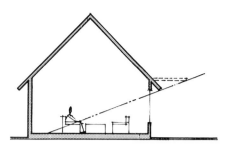

6–40. Sloped roofs minimize the length of overhang necessary to achieve cut-off angle but lessen the sky view as compared to horizontal overhangs.

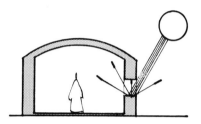

6–41. Small windows may be shaded by the depth of a thick wall; the similarly deep sill redirects light up into the space.

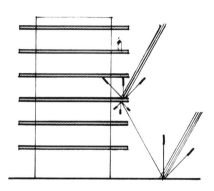

6–42. Extensions of the floors of multistory buildings can provide the necessary overhang as well as some dependable reflective foreground. It is important that this foreground be attractive.

tilevel buildings the overhang of the window below may be large enough to be the foreground for the floor above. Skyscrapers that stand alone "see" large amounts of foreground from the upper floors, minimizing the detrimental effect of the foreground's low average reflectance.

Historically, the most commonly used overhang has been an extension of the roof. With pitched roofs, the natural slope of the roof minimizes the horizontal extension required for shading without reducing the amount of ground-reflected light received (though reducing diffused light from the sky more than a level overhang providing the same shade—fig. 6–40). The indigenous architecture in equatorial climates throughout the world is that of sloping roofs with wide overhangs (necessary for the east and west sides to protect extensive openings that provide ventilation and ground-reflected light).

Indigenous equatorial architecture in hot, dry climates has traditionally been constructed with thick load-bearing walls. These massive walls help temper thermal loads. The windows are generally small because of the dependability of sunlight, minimum lighting requirements, and the desire to minimize solar heat gain. Under these conditions, the window depth itself can provide the necessary overhang. This design also benefits substantially from the inherently deep light-reflecting sill, particularly when white (fig. 6–41).

The floors of multistory buildings have also been extended to create overhangs. This is a natural solution if the extended floor also has value for living space, circulation, and window maintenance (fig. 6–42).

With proper orientation to take advantage of the overhead solar path at the equator, even planters are wide enough to provide total shading for full-height windows and provide delightful foreground views for hotel rooms (fig. 6–43).

Precast concrete and lightweight metal-skinned spandrels can be made three dimensional to shade windows, as they were at the Honolulu County Office Building and the Federal Reserve Building in Boston. Of course, the required dimensions for effective overhangs are determined by latitude and orientation.

Sufficient fixed shading is the most important requirement for successful sunlighting. Otherwise, largely redundant supplementary shading is likely to be needed and misused, negating the benefits of sunlight, especially with today's option of artificial lighting. The form of supplemental shading must be selected to minimize such misuse rather than for its decorative qualities alone.

6–43. Pavilion Intercontinental Hotel, Singapore (John Portman, Architect). Planters are attractive and effective shading devices for north and south facades at the equator. (Photograph courtesy of Kwee Liong Tek)

When deeply recessed windows must be supplemented by curtains and blinds, an irregular array of blinds will not create a disorderly facade. Disorderly blinds in shaded windows are in deep shadow and baffled from full view, unlike disorderly blinds behind unshaded windows. Compare the windows of Boston City Hall with those of the adjacent JFK building (fig. 6–44).

6–44. Disorderly blinds behind shaded windows are in deep shadow and are less conspicuous than disorderly blinds behind unshaded windows. Compare Boston City Hall (left) and the adjacent JFK building (below).

Louvered Overhangs

Overhangs need not be solid to be effective as shading devices; they may be louvered or perforated to achieve different effects. The general characteristic of a nonsolid overhang will be an increase in the sky view over a solid overhang of the same size, thereby benefiting performance slightly under overcast skies. However, the shading pattern of a louvered overhang may allow more direct sunlight to reach the window area.

Horizontal louvers parallel to a south-facing wall will produce an effect similar to several small overhangs, with the advantage that louvers can be angled to allow penetration of sunlight at high angles and block it at low angles, or vice versa (fig. 6–45). Small-scale operable louvers are also possible, though they may be hard to justify because of high maintenance cost and limited usefulness.

Close-Up: Shaded Skyscrapers

Both the Honolulu County building and the Boston Federal Reserve building require supplementary shading because they are not oriented to best advantage.

Although located on one of the major east/west streets, the Honolulu County building faces southwest and northeast (fig. 6–46). Thus, the deeply recessed windows require the use of blinds on winter afternoons. In summer, occupants with northeast exposure must close their blinds at night to avoid arriving at an overheated space in the morning. Alignment with the street would have eliminated such problems.

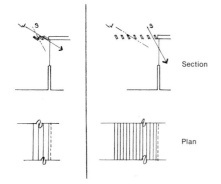

6–45. Horizontal louvers parallel to a south-facing wall can be designed to block either high-angle sun (left) or low-angle sun (right). (From Olgyay and Olgyay, *Solar Control and Shading Devices*; reprinted by permission of Princeton University Press)

6–46. Honolulu County building (Narimore, Bain, Brady and Johnson, Architect): exterior (left); interior (below).

Similarly, sun control in the deeply shaded Boston Federal Reserve building would have been easier if the windows did not face east and west (fig. 6–47). However, I have heard that an unusually conscientious building management is taking maximum advantage of the overhang design. The cleaning staff closes the vertical blinds on the east side and opens the blinds on the west side every evening. The office staff opens the vertical blinds on the east side in midmorning when they are no longer needed and (after some recent retrofitting) the rows of recessed fluorescent fixtures are switched off automatically when sufficient daylight is available. On the west side, the office staff closes the blinds when it is necessary in the midafternoon. Thus, with the green tinted, high-light-transmission glass kept uncovered most of the business day, this shaded building does quite well in using the reflected light from the roofs and landscape far below. However, a north/south orientation would have performed better and required less effort, although providing somewhat different views.

A nighttime view of the Boston skyline suggests the daylight utilization of the Federal Reserve building (fig. 6–48). When the lights are on, its windows appear brilliant in contrast to its neighbors, whose low-transmission glass rejects rather than admits daylight.

6–47. Boston Federal Reserve building (Hugh Stubbins, Architect): exterior (left); interior (below).

6–48. The Federal Reserve building (far right) outshines its neighbors at night.

Horizontal louvered overhangs perpendicular to a south-facing facade can also be adjusted to favor high or low sun angles, but they will vary primarily with the daily change in the sun's bearing angle rather than the seasonal change in the sun's altitude. They produce radial breaks in segmental shading masks (fig. 6–49).

Combining parallel and perpendicular overhang elements produces a grid or pattern shading device. These devices can produce quite complex shading patterns, the danger being that they are often much too open and sculptural, and thus ineffective as shading devices (fig. 6–50).

Increasing the quantity of indirect sunlight is accomplished by totally shading direct sunlight and "catching" and redirecting the sunlight with reflective surfaces (fig. 6–51). The requisite geometries are primarily determined by the orientation and site conditions; on facades parallel to the equator, horizontal devices are generally appropriate. For the difficult low sun angles on the east and west, a louver parallel to the window plane is advisable. Some compromise of view to control glare is inevitable in all east/west conditions. However, this geometry does provide substantial illumination.

Transparent Overhangs

Mirror-glass awnings appear to give the protection of overhangs. In fact, they reduce the solar heat load but give minimal protection against glare from the sun. The Union Carbide building in Danbury, Connecticut (fig. 6–52) was retrofitted with additional blinds immediately after occupancy and thus sacrificed much of the benefit of ground-reflected light. Overhangs must be opaque or light diffusing to be effective. A 90 percent reduction in direct sunlight is not enough—glare will persist.

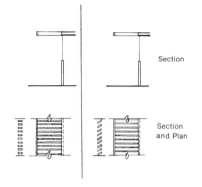

6–49. Louvered overhangs perpendicular to south-facing facades vary primarily with the daily change in the sun's bearing angle. (From Olgyay and Olgyay, *Solar Control and Shading Devices*; reprinted by permission of Princeton University Press)

6–50. Louvered overhangs may be too open to be effective as shading devices.

6–52. The Union Carbide building (Roche, Dinkeloo and Associates, Architect) unsuccessfully attempts to shade windows with mirror-glass overhangs. (Photograph courtesy of Roche Dinkeloo Associates)

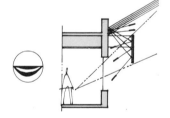

6–51. "Suncatcher" baffles block direct sunlight but allow maximum indirect reflected sunlight.

6–53. Photocell-controlled retractable fabric awnings are a wise solution at the Low Energy Demonstration building in England. (Photograph courtesy of Building Research Establishment)

Temporary Overhangs—Awnings

The functions of the overhang can be achieved using awnings. While less durable and maintenance free than more substantial building elements, awnings also have their advantages. Their first cost can be less and they weigh less, thus storing less heat and cooling off more rapidly after sundown. As translucent or louvered elements they can admit more light and view than solid overhangs.

Retractable awnings can be lowered to give buildings the benefit of shading when the sun is out and raised to provide maximum input of sky light under overcast conditions. This can be a cost-effective approach in predominantly cloudy climates such as that of England. At the Low Energy Demonstration building at the Building Research Station outside London, translucent fabric awnings are lowered automatically to the necessary position (fig. 6–53). In the cooling season, photocells lower the blinds to prevent direct sunlight from entering; in the heating season, they lower the blinds to prevent sunlight from entering above eye level.

Maximum utilization of reflected sunlight was not necessary with the very shallow offices of the double-loaded corridor scheme. For maximum benefit in sunny conditions, awnings should be large enough and opaque enough to negate the need for any additional shading. The inside of opaque awnings should also be light in color to help reflect ground-reflected light into the building and minimize contrast with the outdoor scene.

Twin Overhangs

When the required horizontal dimension for adequate shading is unavailable or becomes impractical for some reason (e.g., very large overhang dimensions are needed in high latitudes and east/west orientations), two or more overhang elements can be combined to obtain the required shading more easily (fig. 6–54). This also allows for better control of the quantity and direction of reflected sunlight reaching the glazing plane without compromising the advantages of a single overhang (minimum interference with views, air movement, or traffic when kept above door height). The double overhang for large spaces has been used throughout the world for centuries, particularly when sheltered circulation was also useful (fig. 6–55).

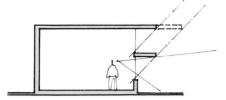

6–54. Double overhangs require a smaller dimension to achieve the required cut-off angle.

6–55. The double overhang is an important theme at the Imperial Palace in Beijing. (Reprinted, by permission, from Yu Zhuoyun, *Palaces of the Forbidden City*)

6–56. Horizontal breaks as a scaling device in a Richardsonian window.

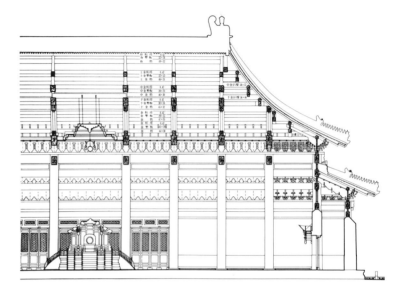

Even when not used for shading, major horizontal division of large windows is often used to effectively create two windows. This strategy allows the upper and lower windows to be treated differently, creating a scaling device or an organizing element in the overall design (fig. 6–56 and case study B3).

The old concept of the twin overhang can be modified to maximize its light distribution function when lighting requirements are stringent. While the reflectance of roof tiles, unpainted concrete, or the exterior cladding of the building may be satisfactory for social spaces, the best distribution of reflected sunlight in the large, deep office buildings of today is achieved through high reflectances, total control of direct sunlight penetration, and careful placement of the second overhang.

While the form of the double overhang has been used in modern buildings throughout the world, I have found few that performed as well as they could have. This is generally because the designers probably did not include optimum use of light as an objective and did not consider the control of solar impacts on the thermal environment. More stringent requirements can be met by refining historical precedents to include considerations for using the sun positively, rather than only providing protection from it.

The Lightshelf

Lightshelves, like double overhangs, provide shading with uncluttered views; they also provide excellent distribution of sunlight with minimum glare (fig. 6–57). Lightshelves reduce the illumination near the window and redistribute the light to increase illumination deeper in the space. Compared to other sun-control devices, lightshelves should be economical on a long-term basis. Their first cost may not be as low as some other devices (such as blinds), but they are likely to be more durable and simpler to maintain.

Compared to unshaded buildings with mirror glass or those with dynamic shading devices, lightshelves should pay for themselves by savings in "purchased energy" for lighting and heating and reduced load for air conditioning. They can add human scale and character to the interior of a building and visual interest to the facade.

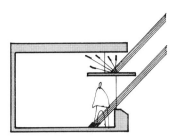

6–57. The lightshelf provides shading with redirection of sunlight.

Design Parameters for Lightshelves

Lightshelves differ from twin overhangs by optimizing the use of reflected light. To design lightshelves effectively, consideration must be given to their height, depth, shading requirements, the location of the glazing, the finishes and reflectances used, and the slope of the shelf, as well as to the actual method of construction. (Of course, such detailed analysis is appropriate when considering *any* sunlighting device.)

Height. Lightshelves should be located as low as practical in the facade to reflect sunlight to the ceiling most advantageously. While lighting performance alone would dictate a height just above eye level (about 5'6'' to 6'), the best height, when other factors are considered, is generally 6'8'' to 7'. This height allows for clearance for doors along that wall, and, if none are anticipated, for alignment with door headers, indirect lighting units, beam bottoms, etc., thus integrating the lightshelf naturally into the room(s). An exception to this is when the lightshelf forms the bottom of a clerestory window above a solid wall. In this case, the lowest height is best. (This was my recommendation for classrooms in Saudi Arabia, case study C3.)

Depth. The required depth of a lightshelf is a function of window height and shading angle requirements (which in turn are determined by latitude and orientation). Lightshelves may also be made deeper than required for shading in order to reduce the illumination near the window and thus flatten the illumination gradient. An extreme example of this can be found in the lightshelves in the Lockheed building in Sunnyvale, California (fig. 6–58), which are thirteen feet deep—as deep as the perimeter offices—to ensure that the occupants of the interior zone will never be cut off from natural light by the partitioning, shades, or blinds used at the perimeter offices (under the lightshelves). This depth requires very high ceilings and reflectances to be effective.

Shading Objectives of Lightshelves

As described above, shading is necessary to prevent glare and local overheating. The upper clerestory portion of a lightshelf facade should block the penetration of direct sunlight onto interior work surfaces at any time of the year, thereby controlling glare and eliminating any need for sup-

6-58. Lockheed building, Sunnyvale, California (Leo Daley, Architect). The very deep lightshelves (13') ensure that the interior zone will receive reflected sunlight from the inward-sloping reflector even if the perimeter offices are walled off and have their blinds closed. (Courtesy of Leo Daly)

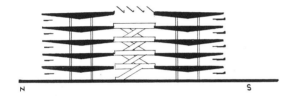

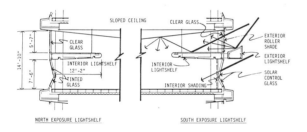

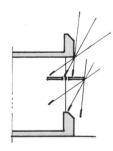

6-59. The clerestory portion of a lightshelf should not allow direct penetration of sunlight at any time. The lower window may allow some sunlight penetration as long as it falls below eye level.

plementary shading (fig. 6–59). With favorable orientation, this objective can be easily accomplished by combining the overhang and intermittent vertical fins.

Total shading is less important for the lower window. If the window is sufficiently shaded to minimize cooling loads for most of the year, some penetration of direct sunlight in winter may be welcomed in temperate climates, as long as it falls below eye level. Except for those persons whose work is absolutely stationary, or involves critical visual tasks, sunlight on the floor is almost always enjoyed.

Since the clerestory window is generally smaller than the lower window, equivalent shading of both windows implies either a lightshelf that projects beyond the rest of the facade or a lower window that is further recessed.

Projection of the lightshelf beyond the clerestory shade is helpful for capturing more sunlight when the sun is high and interior illumination levels tend to be lowest (fig. 6–60). If both projections are equal, most of the lightshelf will be in the shade during the summer on equator-facing facades when the sun is highest (fig. 6–61). This conditon becomes particularly critical at low latitudes when the sun is almost directly overhead.

Extra shading can also be achieved by sloping the lightshelf downward (figs. 6–62, 6–63). However, a downward-sloped lightshelf reflects light away from rather than into the clerestory. Sloping the lightshelf inward helps bounce sunlight deeper inside, with a corresponding decrease in shading effectiveness (fig. 6–64). Care must be taken to avoid eye-level glare in inward-sloping lightshelves. For these reasons, the most effective sunlighting is often achieved with the compromise of a level lightshelf. Additional shading for difficult conditions can be achieved by adding a vertical baffle for a level lightshelf (fig. 6–65).

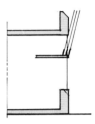

6–60. Project lightshelf from facade to capture high-angle sunlight and provide additional shading for low windows.

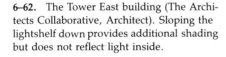

6–61. With flat facades, most of the lightshelf is in shade at high sun angles.

6–62. The Tower East building (The Architects Collaborative, Architect). Sloping the lightshelf down provides additional shading but does not reflect light inside.

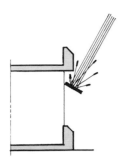

6–63. Sloping the lightshelf down provides effective shading but rejects light.

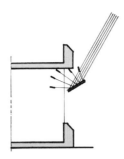

6–64. Sloping the lightshelf in directs light inside building but does not shade as effectively.

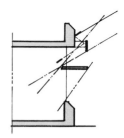

6–65. The lightshelf can be combined with a vertical baffle for additional shading in difficult conditions, such as east/west orientations.

Climate and Glazing Location

While the shading angles are set by latitude and orientation, the position of the glazing should be determined by climate and the amount of solar heat desired. The lightshelf facade configuration, by its division into two windows, allows the glazing of each window to be located independently to optimize the quantity of solar gain for a given condition.

In hot climates, therefore, all glazing should be shaded throughout the year, and only reflected sunlight should be allowed to enter the building (fig. 6–66). This was the objective at the GSIS Building in Manila (case study B3).

In temperate climates there are several options for positioning the glazing. Generally, both windows are shaded throughout the cooling season, and some direct solar heat gain is allowed during the heating season (fig. 6–67). Additional winter glare control can be provided by an internal lightshelf. Another option is to allow the glazing above the lightshelf to be flush with the exterior and unshaded (allowing more solar heat gain at all times) while leaving the lower window recessed to collect solar energy on a seasonal basis (fig. 6–68). This minimizes collection of snow and debris on the lightshelf and allows for easy maintenance of the most critical light-reflecting surface.

In frigid climates with minimal summer cooling requirements, both windows should be flush to the exterior for maximum solar gain (fig. 6–69). The lightshelf thus becomes completely internal, yet retains its functions of controlling glare and distributing light. This configuration is

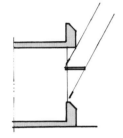

6–66. Hot climates: glazing shaded year round.

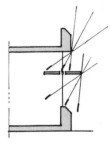

6–67. Temperate climates: glazing shaded during cooling season.

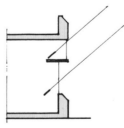

6–68. Temperate climate alternative: keep lightshelf on interior to optimize maintenance; control seasonal gain through lower window.

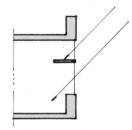

6–69. Cold climates: glazing flush, all sun admitted.

similar to that on the shady sides of buildings in temperate climates, where the lightshelf is used for light distribution rather than for shading.

Even if the glazing is not flush with the building's exterior, it should not be shaded at all during the heating season in cold climates. Any glazing not contributing solar gain is a thermal liability. Sloping the top of the window aperture down to align with the lowest solar angle can optimize the shading/solar gain balance. By channeling the light into the window, little reflected sunlight will be lost to the exterior.

The light distribution from a narrow band of clerestories can be optimized by raising the adjacent ceiling height. A chamfered section enclosing perimeter HVAC ducts is one way to achieve increased ceiling height over the majority of the space and to make a good transition from window to ceiling. The sloped ceiling surface will aid in light distribution and reduce aperture brightness contrast (fig. 6–70).

Reflectance—Exterior Lightshelf

The *dimensions* of the lightshelf are primarily determined by shading requirements. The *reflectances* of the lightshelf should be determined by the lighting requirements at various times (of day and of year).

The reflectance of the exterior lightshelf has a major effect on the amount of reflected sunlight admitted. Normally, maximum reflectances are desirable. Being above eye level, the potential glare of high-reflectance surfaces is never a problem. When cooling loads are important throughout the year, it may be desirable to minimize seasonal illumination variations by making the surface reflectances nonuniform. Designating the outer band of a lightshelf to be light-colored and the inner area to be darker will equalize the quantity of light reflected from the smaller area (illuminated by high-angle summer sun) with the amount reflected by the larger, darker area (illuminated by lower-angle winter sun) (fig. 6–71).

The bottom surface of the lightshelf can be designed to help balance the illumination gradient throughout the room. Darker finishes reduce the levels of ground-reflected light near the window, with minimum impact further into the room (since the back of the room receives most of its reflected light from the high ceiling). Sloping the bottom edge downward will yield somewhat similar results by reducing the quantity of light received directly from the sky more near the window than deep in the room. Turning the front edge also increases shading.

High reflectances can best be maintained on high-gloss finishes that are easily cleaned (hopefully self-cleaning by rain). With specular reflecting surfaces, a distinct inward slope can be very beneficial in distributing light deep into a building and in keeping the lightshelf clean.

Mirrored Sloped Lightshelves

When using sloped specular reflectors (high-gloss paint, glazed ceramic tiles, polished aluminum, or stainless steel) lightshelf angles must be planned so that sunlight is directed slightly above horizontal to the ceiling when the sun is lowest. It is critical that the sunlight is not directed downward, as it will create glare at working levels.

A relatively small area of high summer sun captured by the front edge of a lightshelf can be very effective if beamed deep into a room by

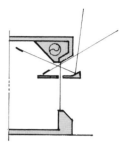

6–70. On the outside, the aperture is sloped at the top to maximize winter gain. On the inside, a chamfered ceiling encloses HVAC, maximizes ceiling height, and minimizes aperture contrast. In summer, when the sun is high, lighting levels can be increased by extending the lightshelf beyond the facade and by the addition of an inward-sloping mirror.

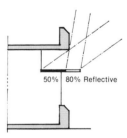

6–71. Balancing seasonal light levels with nonuniform reflectances will reduce the seasonal variation by reducing winter light levels.

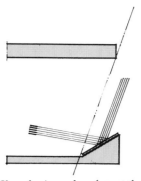

6-72. Sloped mirrored surface at the front edge of lightshelf reflects high-angle summer sun deep into space and makes the most efficient use of the smaller band of sunlight reaching the lightshelf in summer. This will help reduce seasonal illuminance variation by increasing summer light levels.

6-73. Effect of inward-sloping mirror reflector on interior lightshelf in Lam residence. Dotted line shows where light would reflect if mirror was level instead of inward-sloped.

a small band of steeply sloping mirrors. The sloping section may shade some of the other reflecting surface when the sun is lowest, but such shading would not be harmful because illumination would normally be maximum at that time (fig. 6-72).

A note on mirrors: Perfectly polished mirrors must be very flat and uniformly clean or dirty to avoid distracting, distorted patterns on the ceiling. The familiar glass mirrors are the best optically and are the easiest to clean without scratching, but they are also the most fragile. They may be a good choice indoors.

Unbreakable polished metal sheet mirrors must be laminated to thicker backing to be flat enough. Since perfect mirrors will reflect dirt patterns perfectly, they should probably be avoided outdoors if light is to be reflected to uniform ceiling surfaces rather than to the varied surfaces of atrium balconies or floors (see case studies G1, G2). In that case, semispecular rather than perfect mirrors (as found on aircraft wings) are likely to be the best choice.

Reflectance—Interior Lightshelf

Any interior lightshelf should be of maximum reflectance. Once the light is in the building and "paid for," it should be used as efficiently as possible. If less light is wanted, it is better to keep it out of the building altogether.

Here too, mirroring can help, particularly with the deep shading necessary at high latitudes. Since all of the light reaching the inner lightshelf must then be at a low angle, mirroring even a flat interior lightshelf will distribute light inward at equally low angles. A slight downward slope to the mirror greatly benefits light distribution (fig. 6-73 and case study B7).

Close-Up: Precast Sloping Lightshelves

At the Hawaii Medical Service building (fig. 6-74), a gutter scupper system is integrated into the inward sloping precast concrete lightshelves, resulting in a richly detailed facade. The slight slope increases the reflective area "seen" by and the illumination received by the distant ceiling surfaces. Unfortunately, because the rough concrete surface of the reflective part of the lightshelf was left unpainted, much of the potential is unrealized. A white high-gloss surface would direct much more light to the ceiling, deeper into the space. The rough surface allows more scattered light to reflect at eye level. A smooth surface would have been better.

View Windows in Lightshelf Facades

As discussed earlier in this chapter and documented in the generic data, the lower "view" window in lightshelf facades can contribute valuable ground-reflected light to supplement the direct sunlight reaching the lightshelves.

Because it is lower in the visual field, however, the view window may create reflection problems on VDT screens. Reducing the transmission of the glass sufficiently to reduce potential reflections will sacrifice illumination and may create a sensation of gloom when the high-transmission upper window is seen simultaneously. To avoid reflective

6–74. Precast concrete lightshelves for the Hawaii Medical Services building, Honolulu (CJS Group, Architect). The unusual detail created to solve the drainage problem of the inward slope gives the precast concrete lightshelves richness and elegance both on the facade and from the interior. Note the gutter/scupper system.

glare, it is best to control the placement of windows in relationship to work stations, VDTs, and partitioning carefully. Shading in the form of a strategically placed banner or plant may solve a local problem without affecting the rest of the room. Otherwise, the best solution may be to provide shades locally when and where needed. Low-transmission glazing should only be used when high-aperture-contrast situations are unavoidable, such as windows at the end of hallways.

The upper windows in lightshelf facades should always be clear, high-transmission glass. When properly baffled, they should rarely create a glare or reflection problem.

Internal Lightshelves and Human Scale

Internal lightshelves can add a beneficial scaling element to rooms in which high ceilings and large windows are needed for effective sunlighting of deep work spaces. Internal lightshelves allow those near the window to see less sky (and sky glare), but the view deep in the space remains unaffected. An additional benefit is a decrease in aperture contrast, as more light is redirected to the ceiling (fig. 6–75).

Even when not needed for shading of direct sun, internal lightshelves can improve the uniformity of illumination in a room by greatly reducing the illumination of areas near the window and slightly increasing the illumination deeper in the space.

Because lightshelves are generally at door height, they frame rather than divide views from the interior and help building exteriors relate to

6–75. GSIS building (case study B3): mock-up with and without internal lightshelves. Internal lightshelves, though not needed for shading, even out the illumination gradient and are valuable as a scaling element.

6–76. In warm climates, exterior lightshelves may be an integral part of the building structure, as at the Westinghouse building, Orlando, Florida (case study B5).

people rather than hardware, as do some other shading devices (see chapter 11).

Internal Lightshelves and Supplementary Shading

The presence of internal lightshelves tends to force drapes and blinds to be limited to the lower window, even if a gap is left to allow free air movement at the window plane. This is beneficial because the clerestory is thus kept unshaded when the lower window needs to be closed off for privacy or glare control. If the lightshelves provide total sun control, the clerestory window probably needs to be closed off only for special functions requiring blackout conditions.

Construction

There is no best way to construct lightshelves. They may be made of concrete, metal sheets, or composite curtain-wall-type metal panels; interior lightshelves may be framed and covered with drywall or plywood. The finish may be anodized aluminum, paint, or ceramic tiles, depending on how the rest of the building is fabricated. Lightshelves should be economical and durable, and their reflecting surfaces should be easy to maintain.

Construction of exterior lightshelves is simplest in warm climates where the structure can be extended to support them without creating undesirable side effects on thermal performance (fig. 6–76). A gap at the glazing plane can allow valuable ventilation of hot air at the facade, which otherwise might be conducted inside. Such a gap is also useful in reducing collection of debris and for self-washing (as well as manual cleaning) of the glass.

In cold climates, where indoor-outdoor temperature differences are great, heat loss by conduction through the exposed structure can be significant. Therefore, the simpler structural solutions should be avoided in favor of those that will provide thermal breaks to minimize conductive heat transfer (fig. 6–77). (This subject is discussed further in case studies B1, B2, and B6.)

Advantages of Scale

The inherent large scale of lightshelves, compared to smaller-scaled louvers, gives many advantages, both in construction and maintenance.

Lightshelves are large enough so that they must be an integral part of the building fabric and can be built of durable, easy-to-maintain materials. They have few parts to install or clean, and their large scale allows easy access for cleaning the windows. Lightshelves are large enough to be suspended from a few points to span between beams (case study B5) or columns (case study C1) or to be hung as prefabricated boxes.

Lightshelf elements can have multiple functions, serving as spandrel, bracing, or catwalks, in addition to shading and redirecting light. Their hangers can also be vertical louvers (case study B3). Interior lightshelves can also be duct enclosures (case studies B2, B5) or contain light coves and sprinklers (case studies B2 and C1). Lightshelves are large enough to incorporate sculpturally significant details, such as built-in scuppers to counteract an inward slope.

It is very important to make sure that lightshelves are durable, easy to maintain, low in cost, and attractive, because of their significance in the building's construction cost, maintenance, and architectural form. Integrating lightshelves into the overall design allows them to become an element of the design rather than an additional purchased item. Additional construction costs can generally be eliminated with repeat jobs and standardization, which serve to amortize the development and tooling costs. The case studies illustrate many lightshelf constructions that function well for sunlighting and have been economical in construction cost, even in the first generation of their application. (That is, their cost has not upset any budgets, except when treated as an addition to a design already priced without lightshelves.)

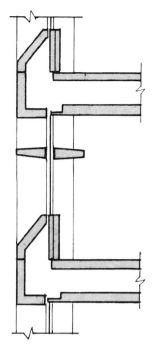

6–77. In cold climates, thermal breaks should be provided to insulate the exterior lightshelves from the structure (see also case study B6).

Some Ineffective Lightshelves

After beginning to propose lightshelves in a number of projects, I began to look around actively, both nearby and during my travels, to see if I could find any precedents. I was interested in seeing how they looked, how they worked, and how they were constructed. I was disappointed to find many examples that had the sculptural forms of lightshelves but did not perform as such and were used with spaces not designed to use reflected sunlight.

In my neighborhood in Cambridge, Massachusetts, I examined the Smithsonian Observatory (fig. 6–78). I found concrete "lightshelves" and

6–78. Smithsonian Observatory, Cambridge, MA (Cambridge Seven, Architect). Note that glass is recessed on top floor and flush on lower floor.

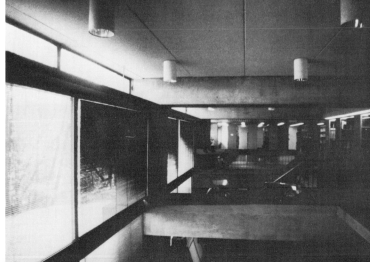

ceilings that were unpainted and windows of low-transmission tinted glass. Since the shading is irregular as well, I assumed that the forms were used more for their sculptural effects than for thermal or light control. Thermal breaks in the concrete construction would have been desirable in the cold Massachusetts climate.

If one looks at the Boston University Law and Education building (fig. 6–79) one will notice the "lightshelves" on the south side—devices that one assumes will control the sun. In fact, they are not effective in controlling glare or thermal loads. The upper window is unshaded. The widely spaced, black-colored louvers do little shading in summer, some (but not enough) in winter, and reflect almost no light to the white ceiling. As a result, the interior blinds tend to be down at all times, as though the louvers were not there.

In Berlin, Germany, the IBM building (fig. 6–80) has lightshelves that have insufficient depth (even in the clerestory portion) to do much controlling of glare at that latitude (52 degrees North). At the nearby chemistry building of the Berlin Technical University (fig. 6–81), the lightshelves are much deeper but are painted black on all surfaces to match the exterior wall finish. They therefore absorb rather than reflect the light. However, the metal panel construction probably minimizes winter heat loss from thermal bridging.

The State Trade School in Zurich, Switzerland (fig. 6–82) was built with a very well integrated precast concrete system throughout. While the public spaces are quite attractive, and the perimeter corridors utilize daylight effectively, the principal spaces—the classrooms—do not capitalize very effectively on the "lightshelves" that give the exterior walls their form. These "lightshelves" are not deep enough to reduce the need for other shading significantly at that latitude (47 degrees North) and as unpainted concrete are inefficient light reflectors. The open louvered ceiling, which is efficient in delivering artificial light from the plenum above, is also equally "efficient" in allowing reflected sunlight to leak into the ceiling plenum.

More recently, I was pleased to see "lightshelves" being installed on a new building being completed in Cambridge—the Harvard Biochemical building (fig. 6–83). This is a handsome building that approaches good sunlighting design. The overall forms are right, but the details fall short. A louvered lightshelf should not have been used, as there is already too much light below the louver. (A louver that is 50 percent open will reflect only 50 percent as much light as a solid louver. However, unlike those at Sert's Boston University building, these metal louvers were painted white.) More important, it does little good to reflect light upward in such spaces unless it is redirected downward. The light-colored ceiling near the window is a good start, but the rest of the ceiling is even more important for balancing the light in the room so as to minimize the need for supplementary artificial lighting. Dark brown paint is ineffective for this purpose.

Some Lightshelves That Work

In my search I met Alfred Roth, a Swiss architect who had always designed around climate. He showed me photographs of lightshelf buildings he had designed for lighting as well as shading. Among them was

6–79. Boston University Law and Education building.

6–80. I.B.M. building, Berlin.

6–81. Chemistry building, Berlin Technical University. Black exterior *and* light-shelves.

6–82. Zurich Trade School: lightshelves are narrow on exterior; louvered ceiling inside does not reflect light.

6–83. Harvard Biochemistry building, Cambridge, MA. Exterior balcony and louvered lightshelf; interior view of lab.

Sabbaga Center, an office building in Beirut, Lebanon (fig. 6-84). The lightshelves covering the south facade were white and deep enough for the latitude (33 degrees North).

In Singapore, a powerful sculptural form dominating the skyline is I.M. Pei's Overseas Chinese Bank building (fig. 6-85). The strong horizontals of the properly oriented lightshelves (deep enough for total shading at 2 degrees latitude) are skillfully employed as an articulated counterpoint to the otherwise unbroken oval shaft—a beautiful and powerful image in a city of shaded buildings. The interior is not as successful (fig. 6-86). Equally strong horizontals in the form of wider horizontal mullions or interior lightshelves might have limited any draperies used to the lower windows and given the interior the strength of character achieved on the exterior.

6-84. Sabbaga Center, Beirut (Alfred Roth, Architect). Lightshelves are appropriate to the climate. (Photograph courtesy of Alfred Roth)

6-86. Interior shading could be integrated better.

6-85. Overseas Chinese Bank building, Singapore (I.M.Pei, Architect). Lightshelves that work, in a distinctive form.

6-87. St. Elizabeth's College Primary School, Hong Kong.

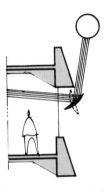

6-88. Dynamic specular lightshelves can lift low-angle sunlight above eye level. When necessary, they can convert to a blocking mode to prevent glare from low-angle direct sunlight, while allowing ground-reflected sunlight.

With a more positive expression of the lightshelf in the interior, industrial windows are much less noticeable in the Hong Kong school shown in figure 6–87.

Dynamic Lightshelves and Suncatchers

When lighting needs or conditions are extreme, lightshelves can be made dynamic for optimum performance. For example, a specular lightshelf can "lift" low-angle sunlight deep within a space above eye level and up to the ceiling. Similarly, high-angle sunlight can be "beamed" wherever it is desired (fig. 6–88). Furthermore, these lightshelves can convert to a "blocking" mode whereby glaring low-angle direct sunlight is intercepted but some indirect light is allowed to enter. This modified "suncatcher" mode is particularly useful on difficult western exposures. The dynamic nature of these devices implies that they be somewhat smaller and lighter than their static counterparts.

A promising automated system for use within the glazing plane that utilizes tracking mirrors of stretched film has been developed for production by Thomas C. Howard of Synergetics, Inc. of Raleigh, North Carolina.

Multiple Horizontal Louvers

Instead of a single lightshelf, a number of architectural-scale horizontal louvers can be used instead when window sizes or shading requirements make a single lightshelf impractical (i.e., too large). For example, at the GSIS building (case study B3), the normal lightshelf configuration was supplemented with fairly large louvers on portions of east and west facades to provide additional shading and redirection at low angles.

The louvers should be large enough to be individually placed for maximum redirection of sunlight to the ceiling with minimum glare (fig. 6–89). The top of the lowest reflective louver should be located so that it is just above the viewer's eye level when seated. If located below eye level, they should be dark-colored to avoid glare. Louvers of this scale should be few enough and sufficiently spaced to create minimum interference with window washing and views (fig. 6–90).

6-89. Multiple horizontal louvers can achieve the desired cut-off angle and be placed for minimum glare and optimum light distribution.

Medium-scale Horizontal Louvers

Mass-produced louvers durable enough to be used for exterior shading are likely to be of hardware scale (i.e., 4–12″-wide blades). There are advantages and disadvantages to working at this scale. As hardware rather than architectural elements, louvers can be added on with less architectural or structural integration. They are likely to be "off-the-shelf" manufactured items that can be electrically or manually operated as well as fixed. A minimum of design effort is required to specify premanufactured louvers; they can be selected from a catalog. However, integration with window details is desirable. When well integrated, louvers fit within the window recesses. In Zurich, for example, the wall details of most commercial buildings integrate recessed pockets for blinds.

Louvers may require less horizontal space than lightshelves. This can have a significant economic impact in tight real estate markets such as in Hong Kong and New York, if the projection outside the glass is counted as part of the floor area allowed. Intelligent zoning regulations could minimize this factor in the future (see chapter 5).

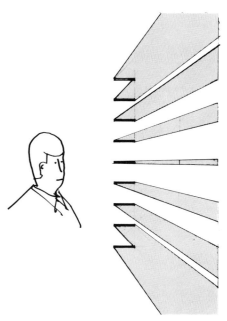

6–90. Too many louvers restrict views.

6–91. Ministry of Education, Rio de Janiero (Oscar Niemeyer, Architect): building facade (right); outward view (left). Painted dark blue, these louvers reflect little sunlight and appear very dark against the sky under overcast conditions.

Medium-scale louvers are likely to be operable; thus, the same louvers can be used on all orientations, with different operating programs for the different shading requirements. They can be totally closed at night and on holidays for maximum insulation value and total shading. In addition, they can provide physical protection and visual privacy upon demand. This is probably a principal factor in their popularity for low-rise housing in many high-density locations, such as Puerto Rico.

The disadvantages of medium-scale louvers are primarily those inherent to their scale. They are not large enough to frame views, not small enough to be perceived as a texture or pattern, and thus tend to obstruct views (fig. 6–91).

Their inherent (vertical) location is not optimal for either light distribution or glare reduction. At the upper window area, the reduced average distance to the ceiling (compared with lightshelves) reflects less uniformly to the ceiling, and at the lower window, bright louvers at eye level are good for light distribution, but bad for glare. Dark-colored louvers lessen glare problems but are useless for light distribution (fig. 6–92).

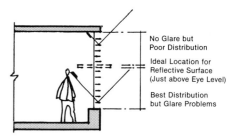

No Glare but
Poor Distribution

Ideal Location for
Reflective Surface
(Just above Eye Level)

Best Distribution
but Glare Problems

6–92. Multiple horizontal louvers suffer from their location. When above eye level, their light distribution is worse than a lightshelf; below eye level, glare can be a problem.

Smaller louvers require more maintenance, as they have more surfaces to clean. They create access problems for cleaning windows and reduce the self-washing of glass by rain. For example, years of trapped debris, bird droppings, and the like are highly visible behind the tightly-spaced louvers of classrooms at the Boston University Law and Education building.

Louvers as Architecture

If louvers are suspended away from the windows, space advantage and design simplicity are eliminated. Smaller-scale louvers are likely to need more frequent support than larger louvers. They cannot span between beams or columns and tend to be made from less durable materials.

The Swiss consider regular maintenance a fact of life and construct systems requiring high maintenance more readily than others. They have created a high-tech louver/wall style in which the free-standing louver/wall structure is the dominant feature of the architecture. The visible facade is the light metal frame that provides support and tracks for the raising and lowering of overscaled venetian blinds. Representative of this approach is the Standard Charter Bank in Zurich (fig. 6–93).

A number of Brazilian buildings also use louvers as "the architecture." Among the largest and most conspicuous of these is the PetroBrazil Headquarters in Rio de Janeiro, with walls of vertical and horizontal metal louvers (see fig. 11–6).

An earlier example is Oscar Niemeyer's São Paulo Exhibition Palace (1962), designed with vertical and horizontal louvers covering the entire facade. These louvers had been removed by the time I saw this building (fig. 6–94). The deteriorated state of the louvers on similar adjacent buildings indicated the probable reason.

6–93. Standard Charter Bank, Zurich. (a) exterior blinds integrated into the spandrel; (b) blinds in freestanding louver wall as the dominant element of the facade.

a

b

6–94. São Paulo Exhibition Palace (Oscar Niemeyer, Architect). (a) rendering of original design; (b) photo from 1982, with louvers removed.

a

b

Both from within and without, hardware-scale louvers are unrelated to human scale. In many cases, it is hard to know how many floors a building has, when viewed from the exterior. Buildings dominated by medium-scale louvers tend to look more like machines than architecture.

Medium-scale Louvers in Double-Envelope Buildings

Double-envelope building construction, such as that used in the Hooker Chemical building in Buffalo, takes advantage of standardized operable louvers; it avoids many of the usual practical and aesthetic drawbacks and contributes to efficient use of energy (fig. 6–95).

6–95. Hooker Chemical building (Cannon Associates, Architect). (Photograph courtesy of Cannon Design)

The usual problems of maintenance and durability were minimized by enclosing the louvers behind glass and within a service walkway. Operation of the louvers is automatic and each facade is separately controlled. The louvers achieve total shading at all times and close up like a flower at night to minimize heat loss. With a well-engineered buffer space to retain or exhaust solar heat, this is a technically sound approach for buildings that must be oriented in all directions (fig. 6–96).

But while an excellent solution for east and west exposures that are impossible to control without some form of dynamic shading, such complexity was not necessary on the north or south sides. A much simpler fixed lightshelf (within the double envelope if desired) would have allowed unrestricted views with less glare and created a more delightful human environment. On those exposures, it was not necessary to look through a confining, bright, distracting screen of louvers, even though the louvers themselves were well made, and their uniform adjustment (photocell-controlled) appears very orderly compared to the usual irregular array of conventional venetian blinds. However, the expanse of floor-to-ceiling windows, made energy-efficient by the double skin construction, helped compensate for some of the visual disadvantages of the blinds (fig. 6–97).

Whatever shading/redirecting device was used, higher ceilings and glazed transoms would have helped. With the interior spaces cut off by full-height partitions at the perimeter offices, the daylight admitted seems wasted when confined to the narrow band of perimeter offices alone.

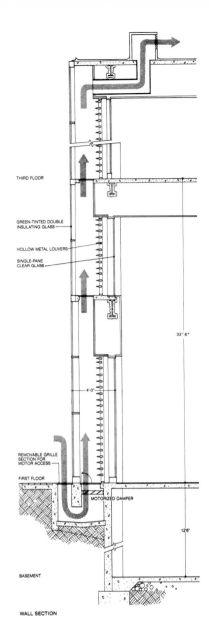

THIRD FLOOR

GREEN-TINTED DOUBLE INSULATING GLASS

HOLLOW METAL LOUVERS

SINGLE-PANE CLEAR GLASS

32'6"

4'-0"

REMOVABLE GRILLE SECTION FOR MOTOR ACCESS

FIRST FLOOR

MOTORIZED DAMPER

12'6"

BASEMENT

WALL SECTION

6–96. Hooker Chemical building: wall section.

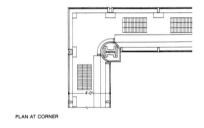

PLAN AT CORNER

4'-0"

6–97. Hooker Chemical building: interior of a typical office.

From the exterior, this double-envelope, louvered building does not appear as a "sun-control machine," as do buildings with exterior, metal, operable louvers. The Hooker Chemical building also appears much more humane than the typical mirror-glass building because the floor levels are clearly defined due to the clear glass used, and one can see signs of activity within, both during the day and at night.

Small-scale Horizontal Louvers

Small-scale louvers (venetian blinds) are most frequently located within the building envelope. They are generally an afterthought to unshaded designs, when neither optimum view nor thermal or lighting performance were given a high design priority.

Blinds share many of the same advantages and disadvantages of medium-scale louvers. The design process for using blinds is virtually nonexistent. They can be installed at any time with no effect on facade details. They tend to screen views and produce glare if light-colored and convert light into heat if dark-colored (in exhange for better views and less glare). From a distance, blinds interfere with views less than do medium-scale louvers, especially if they are black, in which case the small scale is perceived as texture rather than pattern (fig. 6–98).

The ease with which blinds can be adjusted to control the quantity and direction of light and privacy is an advantage to be balanced against their high maintenance requirements and low mechanical reliability. Visual noise inevitably results if all the blinds in a room are not uniformly arranged. Furthermore, difficulties in raising and lowering blinds often result in their being permanently lowered, rather than being lowered only when needed. As interior louvers, venetian blinds reject less summer heat than exterior louvers that provide equal light.

One would expect blinds to have no effect on exterior architectural image when installed within the building. Because light-colored louvers are usually arranged in a disorderly fashion, however, they tend to be conspicuous on the exterior. Dark blinds are often selected or windows are glazed with dark or mirror glass to conceal this disorder as much as for the reduction in cooling loads; in either case, lighting suffers.

6–98. Hooker Chemical building: interior view of venetian blinds.

6–99. Premanufactured metal screens are available with various cut-off angles.

6–100. Shade Screen®.

Sheet-metal screens of various patterns and degrees of aperture became architecturally fashionable in the late 1950s and are still available (though less popular) today (fig. 6–99). By combining horizontal and vertical elements in a modified eggcrate style, these screens may block much of the sunlight with no thought given to the redirection of the light. They are usually not very durable, cannot be repaired easily, and once damaged are even less attractive than they were initially.

Metal screens such as Kaiser Aluminum's Shade Screen® represent the smallest end of the horizontal louver scale. They are dark-colored screens woven of tiny (1/16″ × 7/8″) horizontal louvers (fig. 6–100). While actually quite effective in shading glazing to reduce glare, they are difficult to maintain outside, collect solar heat when located inside the building, and do not assist with light distribution. Once damaged, they cannot be repaired. Their advantages are that they are inconspicuous, easy to add to existing buildings, and also function as insect screens.

Venetian Blinds within Glazing

Researchers at the Massachusetts Institute of Technology tried to develop a venetian blind that would allow for optimal control of direct sunlight for best thermal performance. The device that resulted is an adjustable, upside-down, reflectorized blind sandwiched between two layers of glass. These blinds cannot be pulled up and out of the way like common blinds, but they can be adjusted on their horizontal axis to best redirect sunlight to dark-colored, salt-filled, heat-storage ceiling tiles (fig. 6–101). (The eutectic salts used store heat by melting and then giving up heat as they "refreeze.") They can also aid in reducing local overheating and glare (though this is harder to avoid when the convex side faces up).

Since the objective of these blinds is to store solar heat, biweekly or monthly adjustments of the specular reflectors on the south orientation is sufficient to keep the reflections onto the ceiling above eye level, preventing glare from even the lowest blind (as long as the occupant is not adjacent to the window). Adjacency to the windows at MIT Solar 5 building is controlled by placement of a wide shelf in front. The blinds are not as effective for directing sunlight onto the ceiling deep in the room, because it is impossible to avoid glare from the lower louvers at lower beam angles; this results in substantial "bleed-by" of light, which is not redirected.

Isolation of the blind between two layers of glazing lessens internal heat gains and drastically reduces maintenance problems. Similar window-blind construction may have applications for supplementary shading to large-scale devices on difficult-to-control facades. It is interesting to note that Alvar Aalto used such a construction almost thirty years ago at the National Pensions Institute in Helsinki.

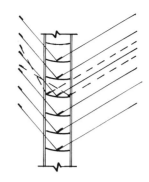

6–101. Top: inverted specular blinds beam sunlight to ceiling, producing less glare than standard blinds; Bottom: interior view.

VERTICAL SHADING DEVICES: CONTROL RELATED TO SOLAR BEARING ANGLE

The shading and light-control characteristics of vertical shading elements were discussed earlier. The specific characteristics of the devices are largely a function of scale, much the same as for horizontal devices.

Large-scale Fixed Vertical Shading Elements—Fins, Columns, Walls, Beams

Many of the advantages of larger scale that apply to horizontal shading devices also apply to vertical devices. In general, vertical devices are not good sources of reflected light, so larger scale is no advantage in this regard. Architectural-scale elements are likely to be more durable and easier to maintain than smaller elements. In addition, they frame rather than break up views (fig. 6–102). For panoramic views, of course, vertical shading should not be used if it can be avoided.

Larger scale, vertical architectural elements are most useful for sun control in combination with horizontal elements such as lightshelves. Vertical elements such as fins, walls, columns (fig. 6–103), or deep beams should be integrated with horizontal elements to form "boxes" (see figure 6–77). Angling east- and west-facing vertical fins toward the north or south will increase their usefulness somewhat, with a corresponding decrease in direct east/west views.

Because vertical elements are used for blocking sunlight rather than for its positive redirection, their color has less effect on illumination levels than is the case with horizontal elements. Maximum-reflectance louvers redirect the maximum amount of illumination but may also create glare. However, such glare is likely to be short-lived, because the brightness on vertical surfaces is constantly changing with the rapid movement of the sun. When combined with horizontal shading elements, only small areas are likely to be exposed at any time (except when intentionally captured by suncatcher baffles).

6–102. Intercontinental Pavilion Hotel, Singapore (John Portman, Architect). Vertical baffling works best at the largest scales. The north and south blocks of guest rooms shade east- and west-terraced and trellised rooms.

6–103. Reed College Library, Portland, Oregon (Harry Weese, Architect). Columns function as vertical baffles on east and west facades. The effectiveness of the columns as shading devices (in combination with trees and light-shelves) is demonstrated by the continued lack of need for additional shades after fifteen years of use.

6–104. Vertical baffles always direct sunlight downward.

Unlike lightshelves, vertical surfaces cannot reflect selectively to the ceiling. Specular vertical surfaces will always reflect sunlight downward at potential glare angles (fig. 6–104). For avoidance of glare, matte surfaces are best.

Medium-scale Vertical Louvers— Fixed and Dynamic

Medium-scale vertical louvers are similar to other vertical louvers in their inability to distribute light selectively to the ceiling and the need for constant adjustment to follow the changing direction of the sun throughout the day to control sunlight. They are most useful in east and west facades (figs. 6–105, 6–106).

In other respects, medium-scale vertical louvers share most of the advantages and disadvantages of medium-scale horizontal louvers. They are most effective in blocking low-angle sun that cannot be controlled easily with horizontal louvers (at very high latitudes), particularly in combination with a lightshelf that redirects sunlight to the ceiling. Dynamic medium-scale louvers can also be very effective in blocking low-angle sun and redirecting it to walls when needed (though at the expense of views). They become less visually confining when fully opened at other times. Because of their cost and somewhat limited usefulness, however, they should be integrated with some other programmed need (e.g., privacy, total blackout requirements, maximum thermal performance as shading and insulation) to be justified.

Smaller-scale, Dynamic Vertical Louvers

Fixed vertical louvers alone cannot block direct sunlight at all times throughout the day unless they are so closely spaced that the rooms enclosed feel prisonlike. To obtain a more reasonable input of light when vertical louvers are used alone, adjustable louvers should be used. The effectiveness of vertical louvers depends on their position relative to the sun's position on its path around the horizon (its bearing angle). For this reason they need to be adjusted hourly throughout the day; horizontal louvers respond to the seasonal changes in the sun's altitude above the horizon and can be adjusted seasonally. In office buildings, control of vertical louvers should be automatic. In residential applications, manual control is acceptable because patterns of use are less predictable and the occupants are more likely to adjust the louvers when necessary.

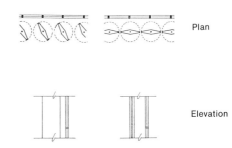

Plan

Elevation

6–105. Louvers on left shade at beginning and end of the day; louvers on right are closed to produce total shading. (From Olgyay and Olgyay, *Solar Control and Shading Devices*; reprinted by permission of Princeton University Press)

6–106. Medium-scale adjustable vertical louvers used on the west exposures at Peabody Terrace apartments, Cambridge (Josep Luís Sert, Architect). (Photograph courtesy of John Lam)

6–107. Louver drapes.

Interior Louvers

Vertical louvers used indoors have some important advantages over those used outdoors, especially if they are in the form of louver drapes. Although not as efficient in heat rejection as exterior louvers, louver drapes have an important advantage in that they can be pulled aside when not needed (i.e., most of the time when supplementing large-scale shading elements).

Vertical louver drapes seem to be more reliable in operation than venetian blinds. Larger-scale vertical louver drapes tend to have more pattern than texture against the view, although when dark-colored and perforated they can be seen through more easily than one would expect. When made of fabric, they offer some visual softness and acoustic absorption. Like draperies (and unlike venetian blinds), vertical louver drapes do not look particularly disorderly when irregularly arranged (fig. 6–107).

GLAZINGS

For effective sunlighting or passive solar design we should minimize reliance on the glazing itself for sun control. Glazed areas have significant heat loss. The purpose of glazing in sunlit buildings is to let light in. Clear glazing is the best way to admit the amount of light desired (fig. 6–108). (As discussed in chapter 3, green-tinted and Low-E glazings are more expensive but are also appropriate.) Shading, rather than reflective glass, is the best way to reduce heat gain.

As discussed in chapter 2, low-transmission glass produces an effect of gloom and ambiguity, regardless of the weather and time of day. It reduces the effectiveness of daylight but cannot reduce intensities enough to provide comfort in direct sun. Thus, supplementary shading will be required with low-transmission glass despite reduced light levels and a gloomy atmosphere. Heat-absorbing glass may have undesirable reradiation effects. Mirror glass produces a particularly uncomfortable ("fishbowl") effect at night, whereby one sees one's own reflection in the window, rather than the view outside.

The so-called "shading coefficient" (defined as the ratio of solar gain in BTUs to that admitted by clear glazing) is used by industry to evaluate the effectiveness of low-transmission glazing. This mesurement does not account for the amount of visible light relative to heat gain, or for any of the spectral characteristics of a glazing. This standard would rate an insulated opaque wall as having an ideal shading coefficient and is therefore useless as a measurement of glazing-lighting performance.

Low-transmission glass is useful when the amount of light is not as important as the view. It still must be shaded to reduce heat gain and glare, however. It is particularly valuable when a large view is desired without the brightness of the exterior—for example, a view window in a museum gallery.

Many glazing materials are available that have diffusing or directional qualities. Direct sunlight striking translucent fiberglass becomes diffuse direct light, potentially very bright and glaring. It is only when a surface of this type has enough visual interest to be attractive that it ceases

Clear
89% Transparent
1 Sq. Ft.

50% Transparent
1.8 Sq. Ft.

10% Transparent
8.9 Sq. Ft.

6–108. Use clear glass for the most light with the least amount of heat loss.

to be an unpleasant distraction (fig. 6–109). Translucent glazings are best when temporary or when privacy rather than view is desired.

6–109. Stained glass adds visual interest to translucent glazing.

Glass block was formerly produced with horizontal ridges that directed incoming sunlight up to the ceiling and away from the line of sight (fig. 6–110). Although clever and inexpensive, this directional glass block did not allow for any view, and the redistribution of light was less than ideal (usually a source of visual noise). Redirecting devices in glazings are never as good as larger-scale reflecting devices, and diffusing devices inevitably produce a shallow penetration of sunlight. For some purposes, clear glass block can be an attractive source of light, combining a degree of privacy with some view and light. When set in mortar, the width of the bed is purported to offer a degree of shading, but in practice this amount is rarely sufficient.

Clear glass maximizes views and a sense of contact with the outdoors, and allows seasonal admission of heat gain (when desirable) through correct shading geometry. More often than not, clear, insulated glass is the most inexpensive and appropriate glazing.

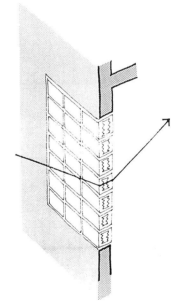

6–110. Directional glass block.

FILTERING AND BLOCKING DEVICES— SUPPLEMENTARY DYNAMIC SHADING

Devices that block and diffuse but do not redirect light tend to have a myriad of influences take priority over their sunlighting characteristics. Filtering and blocking devices are used to attain privacy, to "black out" rooms, and for security and aesthetic reasons. When these devices are used to control light, they are normally expected only to prevent a negative situation (glare or overheating) rather than to optimize the natural illumination. As such, the most important factors to consider when selecting a filtering/blocking device are its reliability and ease of use. If a device is not reliable and easy to use, it is likely to remain in place when it is not needed and prevent the utilization of natural light. For the same reason, I prefer totally opaque blocking devices to translucent ones, because they are more likely to be opened by the occupants when not needed.

Shutters

Traditional slatted window shutters offer some protection from stormy weather and vandals, but minimal view or light. In the Caribbean, the indigenous louvered awning/shutters were designed as shading devices, allowing ground-reflected light and some view when the awnings are raised (the louvers are parallel with the ground at that time), and privacy and protection with ventilation when they are closed (fig. 6–111). When dark-colored, these awning/shutters interfere with the view less than when light-colored, but must depend more on ground- and roof-reflected light.

The shutters traditionally used in early American buildings allowed infinite control of privacy and light. They were constructed with numerous individually foldable sections, the louvers within each section being adjustable. These shutters were frequently integrated with the window recesses so that they were barely noticeable when fully open (fig. 6–112). They may still be the best choice today for some residential applications but are unlikely to be properly used in a work environment where there is generally no one managing the window systems.

Window Shades

If additional movable shading is used to supplement windows already shaded by lightshelves or overhangs, it should move from the bottom up, rather than from the top down, as do traditional shades (fig. 6–113). In this way direct light is blocked and ambient indirect light is

6–111. Slatted shutters in Bermuda.

6–112. Shutters at Longfellow House, Cambridge are integrated with window recess.

6–113. Shutters at the Royal Crescent (Bath, England) are integrated to disappear as part of the window reveal when opened.

least affected. Unfortunately, attractive hardware of this type is more complicated than the standard variety (without the doubled cord showing), but has been achieved elegantly on a custom basis (see Johnson Controls, case study B4). Hopefully, this type of hardware will become more readily available in the future.

Window shades can be designed to have a significant insulative value. In large offices, such shades should probably be automated if they are to be effective. Unfortunately, they tend to be either bulky (quilted types) or rather unattractive on the outside surface (reflective types).

Draperies

Draperies are the most traditional window treatment, being interesting to look at and allowing for wide variation in personal taste. Draperies are an obvious choice for view windows and are the blocking device most likely to be opened by the occupant when not needed. They can be made translucent (allowing privacy with filtered light), opaque (for total privacy, room blackout, and local shading), or insulating. When used primarily for shading (rather than for privacy or insulation), draperies should be free-sliding in small sections to allow local shading without blocking ambient light. In otherwise hard-surfaced rooms, drapes provide useful sound absorption. They do not look disorderly when not adjusted uniformly in a room or on a facade. On the negative side, when drapes are open they may block much of the light and view from individual windows unless they are stacked entirely to the side.

Opaque and Translucent Sliding Panels

Rigid sliding panels have an extensive history in Japan, where *shoji* have long been the window treatment of preference (fig. 6–114). Very light in weight, wooden *shoji* slide freely in waxed wooden tracks. Although the rice paper ''glazing'' in *shoji* is translucent and diffusing, the richly detailed and proportioned wooden frames make *shoji* a pleasure to observe—a finely crafted picture rather than an overly bright distraction.

6–114. *Shoji* are not gloomy like most plain white translucent walls because they can be opened. Design details and rich materials add visual interest. (Photograph courtesy of John Lam)

6–115. *Moucharabies* model light softly.

Shoji screens often have small areas of transparent ''view'' glazing at seated eye level. Because of their ability to move, they offer privacy and protection as desired and can disappear when no longer needed.

In the Middle East, the traditional *moucharaby* developed as an architectural device to screen the brightly sunlit exterior views to pleasurable levels (fig. 6–115). Consisting of numerous wooden cylinders joined with spherical joints, *moucharabies* are unglazed and are placed in unglazed openings, allowing ventilation and filtered light with a minimum of heat. The rounded forms grade the light very softly, unlike screens cut out of flat surfaces. These devices can be meaningfully adapted to today's needs and context. (I endorsed their use in combination with lightshelves for classrooms in Saudi Arabia—case study C3.)

In residential applications, where one wants privacy and ventilation and where controlled redistribution of light is unimportant, the softly filtered light from rounded forms characteristic of *moucharabies* would be appropriate anywhere. Such forms could easily be mass produced in molded plastics. The principle of rounded forms could also be applied in larger-scale elements, such as concrete block units for screen walls.

Sliding panels can be highly insulative and can offer security as well. Like *shoji*, if translucent panels are used, they should be interesting as abstract designs and should be three dimensional with a louverlike quality rather than flat. (Otherwise, they may be considered visual noise.) Translucent panels have the disadvantage of not disappearing when not in use, as do window shades.

Opaque sliding panels are particularly appropriate when total blackout is often desired and good insulation is useful. They are used in a number of hotels in southeast Asia (e.g., the Jakarta Hilton).

I found the window treatment of the Fujita Hotel in Kyoto, Japan, very good for the guests and probably for the owners as well. It consisted of a combination of both traditional *shoji* for light with privacy and some insulating value and sliding wood panels for blackout and better insulation. Very logically, the window opening was only the central 50 percent of the wall width, since no more than that could be exposed at any time. Too often, full-width windows are used under similar circumstances.

Interior Furnishing, Layout, and Partitioning

Sunlight distribution should influence interior layouts and detailing. Partitioning, equipment, and furnishings should not block any more light than necessary and should be light in color when practical. (These concepts should be self-evident for the reader, but they are so often neglected that they merit reiteration.)

While premium is generally given to perimeter offices (especially corner offices with windows on two walls), it is desirable that natural light be able to penetrate into the interior zones of today's very deep buildings. The best way to achieve this is to place spaces that need complete enclosure, such as conference rooms, away from the building perimeter. Assuming a plan does call for dividing walls parallel to the window wall, these walls should be fully glazed or at least (if visual as well as acoustical privacy is needed), glazed from the transom to the ceiling (fig. 6–116). Open office planning allows for maximum use of transom-height and lower (4.5–6') walls with minimum blocking of light. Transom-height walls are also ideal for the integration of indirect artificial lighting.

Full-height partitioning obstructs less light from windows if perpendicular to the window. Such partitions are usually acoustically important, separating offices or classrooms rather than open-doored areas, corridors, or support spaces.

Light distribution should influence other aspects of interior planning as well. For example, most libraries designate a large amount of space for book storage in stacks. If these stacks are arranged parallel to the window plane, the second aisle will require supplementary artificial lighting. For deep penetration of sunlight, library stacks should run perpendicular to the window walls. This has the added benefit of providing window views to those in the stacks (see case study H1).

Light-colored furnishings can be important for light distribution and can also make a space feel well illuminated. For example, black law books on black library shelving make the stacks appear dark even if well illuminated. White shelves make the space feel well lit, even if the books remain dark. White shelves may also reflect useful light to the index numbers low on the spines. White tops of stacks provide a lot of reflective "lightshelf" area.

Luminance distribution in a room should be considered when laying out work stations and placing VDT screens. Avoid placing them so that they face windows unless there is an intervening partition.

Plants, banners, and the like can provide local shading in special cases.

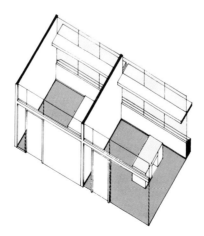

6–116. Partitions parallel to windows should be glazed to allow sunlight to reach interior spaces. If they must be opaque, transom-to-ceiling area should be glazed.

GENERIC MODEL DATA

Several years ago, in order to teach my students at Harvard and MIT about the geometry of sunlighting, I built a number of generic models to help them test, examine, and communicate the relative quantitative effects of various sunlighting concepts, both sidelighting and toplighting. For this reason, the design of the models was not that of any realistic building but rather a format that facilitated the comparison of alternatives. For instance, the facade was divided into three equal sections (high, middle, and low), each equal to 10 percent of the floor area (fig. 6–117). All reflectors were white, even though the ground adjacent to a low window is, in reality, unlikely to be white.

Illumination levels and gradients of various room shapes and window locations should be observed *relative* to each other. Estimates of realistic illumination levels under the sunlight conditions tested—for example, noon at the equinox and 45 degrees north latitude (when the 45-degree cut-off white reflector is completely sunlit)—can be made by extrapolation from the test data. For instance, if both lower and middle windows are to be used, their data should be combined.

For estimating the effects of seasonal change, one can assume that midsummer levels of illumination would be 50 percent of the test values, since the sun would be 22.5 degrees higher at that time and only one-half of the reflector surfaces would be illuminated. Similarly, 30 percent should be added to the test values for the winter, assuming that the louver width would be increased accordingly to provide complete shading and redirection.

In examining the data presented, remember that light has no scale factor. For the same reasons that measurements of an accurate scale model can be completely accurate in forecasting the performance of a real building, the values shown for a 40' × 40' × 16' room are essentially the same as those for a 20' × 20' × 8' room or an 80' × 80' × 32' room. The only difference is the position of the plane of measurement, because of difference in scale; the light meter should be placed at desk height for the scale intended. (Measurements at *floor* level need no adjustment for scale.)

6–117. The generic model.

To minimize this factor, the plane of measurement was level with the top of the lower window (figs. 6–118, 6–119). This assumption made little difference, except for those measurements that were taken near the window. The light meter should have been lower for these measurements (i.e., at a scale such that the top of the window was higher than thirty inches). At this height, the meter would have "seen" more window and hence more light.

6–118. The model interior from above showing location of Li-Cor photo sensors.

6–119. The model interior as seen from a viewing port.

Much can be learned by actually doing such generic model studies divorced from a real design in which one limits the alternatives. For example, if one were testing an actual design and comparing design alternatives, one would not divide a window into three areas—a procedure used for theoretical analysis only. My students have been able to get useful results using fairly crude instrumentation—hand-held light meters. The measurements presented here, however, were obtained with automated, computerized instrumentation that is not only infinitely faster but eliminates the potential errors from the wide daylight fluctuations common to all but the clearest or most heavily overcast days.

The generic data for sidelighting under sunny conditions demonstrate the effects of various elements on the room's illumination. The curves plot illumination at the center line of the room. Tabulated results indicate efficiency (average illumination in footcandles) and uniformity (average/minimum).

Group 1: Ground, Facade, and Room as Reflectors

These data illustrate the potential value of the facade (horizontal reflectors) as the most dependable source of reflected sunlight, unless the foreground would be equally free from shadows and could be of equal reflectance (e.g. white sand beach or consistently snow-covered ground):

☐ If the foreground is white, it is as effective as white reflectors at the building facade.

☐ If the foreground is black (or in shade), sunlit white reflectors can increase illumination by 500 percent.

☐ When the reflected sunlight introduced into a room from white foreground or white louvers is effectively utilized, most of the illumination at the workplane away from the windows comes from indirectly illuminated room surfaces (white walls and ceiling) rather than directly from the window.

☐ In deep, wide rooms (as modeled) the ceiling is the most important room surface for redirecting light to the workplane. Light-colored walls increase illumination near the walls and thus improve uniformity and total illumination. The percentage effect on average illumination is understated because measurements were taken only at the center line of the room and not near the side walls.

☐ When reflected sunlight is well utilized, the lowest window can be the most efficient for total illumination provided as well as the most effective in providing uniform illumination.

1 GROUND, FACADE, AND ROOM AS REFLECTORS

A BLACK FOREGROUND

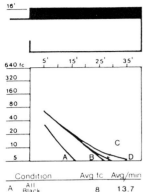

	Condition	Avg fc	Avg/min
A	All Black	8	13.7
B	White Ceiling	20	9.1
C	White Ceiling & Back Wall	20	5.1
D	White Ceiling, Back, & Side Walls	22	4.0

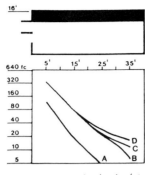

	Condition	Avg fc	Avg/min
A	All Black	30	20.1
B	White Ceiling	88	13.0
C	White Ceiling & Back Wall	89	7.5
D	White Ceiling, Back, & Side Walls	92	5.5

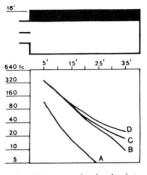

	Condition	Avg fc	Avg/min
A	All Black	28	18.9
B	White Ceiling	105	11.1
C	White Ceiling & Back Wall	109	6.2
D	White Ceiling, Back, & Side Walls	120	4.7

B WHITE FOREGROUND

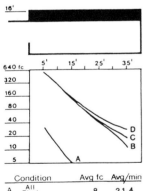

	Condition	Avg fc	Avg/min
A	All Black	8	21.4
B	White Ceiling	144	12.8
C	White Ceiling & Back Wall	147	7.9
D	White Ceiling, Back, & Side Walls	157	5.8

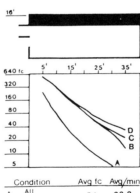

	Condition	Avg fc	Avg/min
A	All Black	54	23.8
B	White Ceiling	159	11.6
C	White Ceiling & Back Wall	158	7.1
D	White Ceiling, Back, & Side Walls	173	5.1

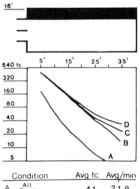

	Condition	Avg fc	Avg/min
A	All Black	41	21.9
B	White Ceiling	139	11.4
C	White Ceiling & Back Wall	145	6.2
D	White Ceiling, Back, & Side Walls	155	4.7

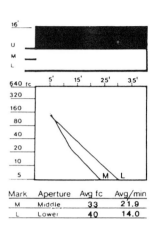

Mark	Aperture	Avg fc	Avg/min
M	Middle	33	21.9
L	Lower	40	14.0

Group 2: Changing Ceiling Heights

These data confirm the value of increasing ceiling height to increase illumination away from the window, reduce illumination near the window, and thus make illumination throughout the room more uniform wherever the windows are located (i.e. high, middle, or low).

☐ The higher the ceiling, the more uniform the illumination:

☐ The most uniform reflected sunlight is always from the lowest window. Changing from an 8-foot ceiling to a 16-foot ceiling improves the uniformity by a factor of 4. Increasing from 8 to 12 feet improves uniformity of illumination by a factor of 3.

☐ In high spaces, the least uniform illumination is from the upper windows.

☐ The greatest degree of uniformity is achieved from the lowest window with the highest ceiling and room reflectances (avg/min. of 1.5).

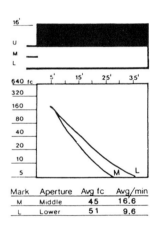

Mark	Aperture	Avg fc	Avg/min
M	Middle	45	16.6
L	Lower	51	9.6

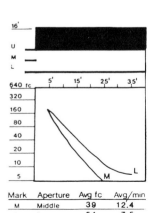

Mark	Aperture	Avg fc	Avg/min
M	Middle	39	12.4
L	Lower	54	7.5

2 CHANGING CEILING HEIGHTS (Sunny Condition)

A REFLECTANCES : ceiling 80% walls 20% floor 20%

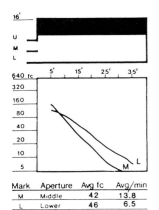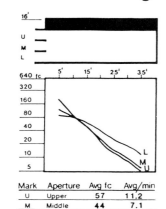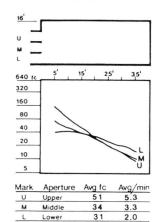

Mark	Aperture	Avg fc	Avg/min
M	Middle	42	13.8
L	Lower	46	6.5

Mark	Aperture	Avg fc	Avg/min
U	Upper	57	11.2
M	Middle	44	7.1
L	Lower	46	3.9

Mark	Aperture	Avg fc	Avg/min
U	Upper	57	8.0
M	Middle	43	4.9
L	Lower	42	2.8

Mark	Aperture	Avg fc	Avg/min
U	Upper	51	5.3
M	Middle	34	3.3
L	Lower	31	2.0

B REFLECTANCES : ceiling 80% walls 50% floor 20%

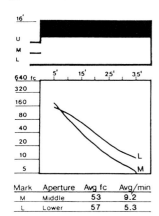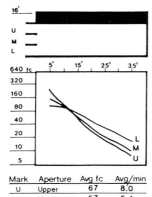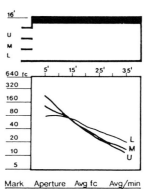

Mark	Aperture	Avg fc	Avg/min
M	Middle	53	9.2
L	Lower	57	5.3

Mark	Aperture	Avg fc	Avg/min
U	Upper	67	8.0
M	Middle	57	5.4
L	Lower	57	3.2

Mark	Aperture	Avg fc	Avg/min
U	Upper	70	6.0
M	Middle	54	3.9
L	Lower	53	2.4

Mark	Aperture	Avg fc	Avg/min
U	Upper	49	4.3
M	Middle	43	2.7
L	Lower	41	1.8

C REFLECTANCES : ceiling 80% walls 80% floor 20%

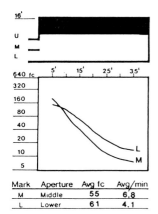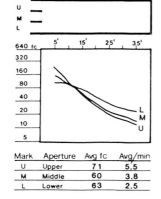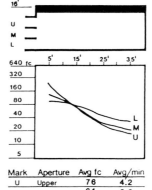

Mark	Aperture	Avg fc	Avg/min
M	Middle	55	6.8
L	Lower	61	4.1

Mark	Aperture	Avg fc	Avg/min
U	Upper	71	5.5
M	Middle	60	3.8
L	Lower	63	2.5

Mark	Aperture	Avg fc	Avg/min
U	Upper	76	4.2
M	Middle	61	2.8
L	Lower	63	1.9

Mark	Aperture	Avg fc	Avg/min
U	Upper	62	3.2
M	Middle	32	2.0
L	Lower	31	1.5

Group 3: Changing Ceiling Shapes

These data show that changing from a flat ceiling to a shaped ceiling with the same average height can improve uniformity very noticeably:

☐ The best uniformity is attained when most of the ceiling slopes upward from the window and some portion of the ceiling best "sees" both the window and the work plane at the rear of the room. The most effective shape is arranged on the left, the least effective on the right.

☐ The most effective shape improves uniformity by a factor of 3, compared to a flat ceiling.

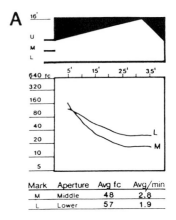

Mark	Aperture	Avg fc	Avg/min
M	Middle	48	2.8
L	Lower	57	1.9

Group 4: Beamed Ceilings

These data show that:

☐ Widely spaced beams perpendicular to the windows can improve average illumination and uniformity compared to a flat ceiling with equal height clearance. The averages are reduced because of reduced levels near the window.

☐ Beams perpendicular to the windows are more efficient and produce more uniform illumination than those parallel to the windows.

☐ Increased spacing improves efficiency and uniformity.

☐ A two-way grid provides somewhat more efficiency and better uniformity than similarly spaced beams parallel to the windows, but is not as good as beams perpendicular to the windows.

☐ A two-way grid is less efficient than a flat ceiling.

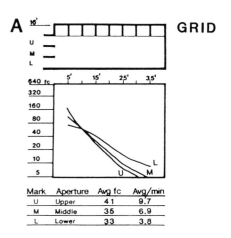

GRID

Mark	Aperture	Avg fc	Avg/min
U	Upper	41	9.7
M	Middle	35	6.9
L	Lower	33	3.8

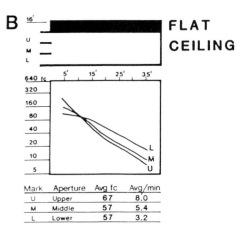

FLAT CEILING

Mark	Aperture	Avg fc	Avg/min
U	Upper	67	8.0
M	Middle	57	5.4
L	Lower	57	3.2

3 CHANGING CEILING SHAPES (Sunny Condition)

REFLECTANCES : ceiling 80% walls 50% floor 20%

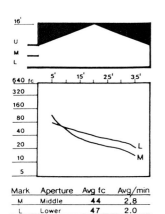 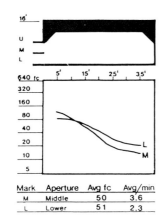 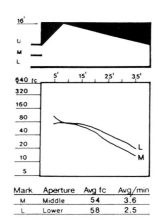 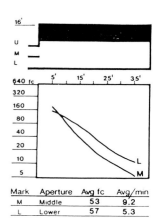

Mark	Aperture	Avg fc	Avg/min
M	Middle	44	2.8
L	Lower	47	2.0

Mark	Aperture	Avg fc	Avg/min
M	Middle	50	3.6
L	Lower	51	2.3

Mark	Aperture	Avg fc	Avg/min
M	Middle	54	3.6
L	Lower	58	2.5

Mark	Aperture	Avg fc	Avg/min
M	Middle	53	9.2
L	Lower	57	5.3

4 BEAMED CEILINGS   (Sunny Condition)

REFLECTANCES : ceiling 80% walls 50% floor 20%

PARALLEL

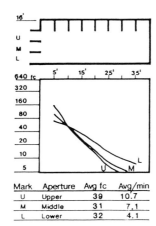 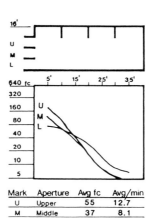

Mark	Aperture	Avg fc	Avg/min
U	Upper	39	10.7
M	Middle	31	7.1
L	Lower	32	4.1

Mark	Aperture	Avg fc	Avg/min
U	Upper	55	12.7
M	Middle	37	8.1
L	Lower	35	4.8

Mark	Aperture	Avg fc	Avg/min
U	Upper	66	7.8
M	Middle	48	5.6
L	Lower	44	2.9

PERPENDICULAR

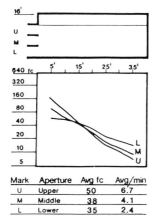 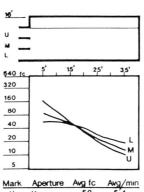 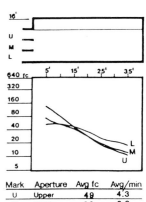

Mark	Aperture	Avg fc	Avg/min
U	Upper	50	6.7
M	Middle	38	4.1
L	Lower	35	2.4

Mark	Aperture	Avg fc	Avg/min
U	Upper	59	5.1
M	Middle	46	3.2
L	Lower	42	2.0

Mark	Aperture	Avg fc	Avg/min
U	Upper	49	4.3
M	Middle	36	2.8
L	Lower	38	2.0

Group 5: Combined Effect of Room Shape and Color

These data compare the effect of ceilings sloping upward or downward from the window in rooms with light ceilings and dark walls and those with dark ceilings and light walls:

☐ Sloping the ceiling downward will always make illumination less uniform because it always increases the light near the windows.

☐ Sloping the ceiling upward always makes the illumination more uniform.

☐ The best uniformity from upper windows is achieved with the lightest colored upward-sloping ceiling.

☐ The best uniformity from the windows is achieved with a dark-colored ceiling sloping upward to white walls. The dark ceiling reduces illumination near the window. The upward slope allows the light to reach the large area of white wall deep in the space to get the best uniformity along with the lowest average illumination levels. This combination is characteristic of many buildings in sunny tropical climates.

5 COMBINED EFFECT OF ROOM SHAPE AND COLOR (Sunny Condition)

A REFLECTANCES : ceiling 80% walls 20% floor 20%

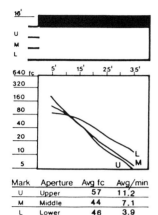

Mark	Aperture	Avg fc	Avg/min
U	Upper	57	11.2
M	Middle	44	7.1
L	Lower	46	3.9

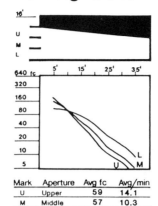

Mark	Aperture	Avg fc	Avg/min
U	Upper	59	14.1
M	Middle	57	10.3
L	Lower	56	5.8

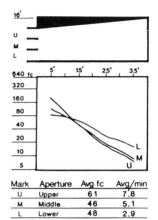

Mark	Aperture	Avg fc	Avg/min
U	Upper	61	7.8
M	Middle	46	5.1
L	Lower	48	2.9

B REFLECTANCES : ceiling 80% walls 50% floor 20%

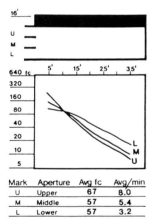

Mark	Aperture	Avg fc	Avg/min
U	Upper	67	8.0
M	Middle	57	5.4
L	Lower	57	3.2

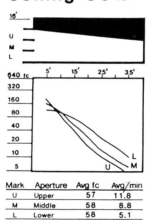

Mark	Aperture	Avg fc	Avg/min
U	Upper	57	11.8
M	Middle	58	8.8
L	Lower	58	5.1

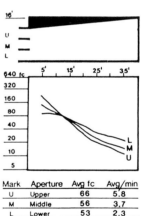

Mark	Aperture	Avg fc	Avg/min
U	Upper	66	5.8
M	Middle	56	3.7
L	Lower	53	2.3

C REFLECTANCES : ceiling 20% walls 80% floor 20%

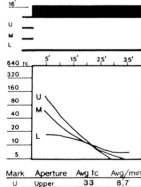

Mark	Aperture	Avg fc	Avg/min
U	Upper	33	8.7
M	Middle	19	3.7
L	Lower	12	1.6

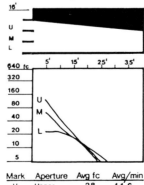

Mark	Aperture	Avg fc	Avg/min
U	Upper	28	11.6
M	Middle	18	8.9
L	Lower	12	3.5

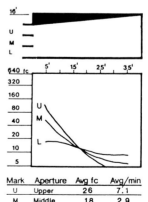

Mark	Aperture	Avg fc	Avg/min
U	Upper	26	7.1
M	Middle	18	2.9
L	Lower	13	1.4

Group 6: Overcast Conditions

Under overcast conditions, illumination levels are reduced, and the effects of window height and room reflectance are quite different than under sunny conditions. The effects are those of direct lighting from the sky rather than indirect lighting from the ceiling and walls. For these reasons, the data show:

☐ The upper window provides most of the illumination.

☐ The lower window provides little illumination (unlike under sunny conditions, when it can be the most effective).

☐ Lightshelves can improve uniformity by reducing illumination substantially near the window and boosting it slightly deeper in the room.

☐ For upper windows, lightshelves improve the uniformity but they also reduce the average substantially.

☐ For lower windows, lightshelves can improve both the uniformity and the average illumination.

☐ Under overcast as well as sunny conditions, increased ceiling height improves uniformity from any window when room reflectances are high.

6 OVERCAST CONDITION

REFLECTANCES : ceiling 80% walls 80% floor 20%

A Flat Facade

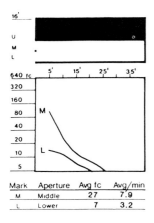

Mark	Aperture	Avg fc	Avg/min
M	Middle	27	7.9
L	Lower	7	3.2

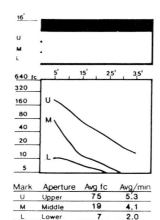

Mark	Aperture	Avg fc	Avg/min
U	Upper	75	5.3
M	Middle	19	4.1
L	Lower	7	2.0

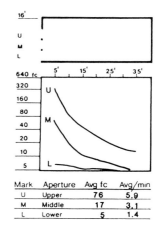

Mark	Aperture	Avg fc	Avg/min
U	Upper	76	5.9
M	Middle	17	3.1
L	Lower	5	1.4

B Light Shelf

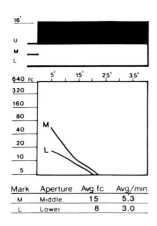

Mark	Aperture	Avg fc	Avg/min
M	Middle	15	5.3
L	Lower	8	3.0

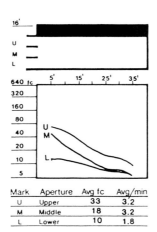

Mark	Aperture	Avg fc	Avg/min
U	Upper	33	3.2
M	Middle	18	3.2
L	Lower	10	1.8

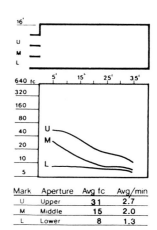

Mark	Aperture	Avg fc	Avg/min
U	Upper	31	2.7
M	Middle	15	2.0
L	Lower	8	1.3

Overview of Generic Sidelighting Data

☐ For best illumination under both sunny and overcast conditions, use a combination of low windows (best for sunny conditions) and high windows (best for overcast conditions).

☐ Use reflectors at the facade to reflect light into the room as well as to provide shading and glare control; use high reflectances and high ceilings to distribute light to the workplane most efficiently and uniformly.

☐ Use shaped ceilings or widely spaced beams perpendicular to the windows to improve light distribution.

SUMMARY

Concepts and devices for sidelighting have been discussed at length in this and the preceding chapter. While those most applicable to various buildings will vary, there are some concepts and devices I find universally useful:

1. *Orient most windows to face north or south* to make effective use of sunlight easiest. Such orientation allows the simplest fixed shading/redirecting elements to provide complete control. In contrast, east and west exposures require at least some use of dynamic shading devices to control glare and overheating.

2. *High room reflectances*, particularly those of upper walls and ceilings, are essential for efficient use of reflected sunlight. Avoid highly configured ceilings with many light-catching cavities that reduce the *effective* reflectance of the ceiling. Keep exposed beams widely spaced and perpendicular to the window walls.

3. *High ceilings* are necessary to distribute light more uniformly to the deep spaces characteristic of many modern buildings. They are beneficial but less necessary for shallow rooms. High ceilings can be achieved economically if given high priority in the integration of building systems (chapter 9).

4. *Large-scale architectural shading elements* such as the classic overhang are the most effective, dependable, durable, and economical over time. They frame rather than compete with views. They add interest and richness to a building's exterior form, but as major elements, they need to be well designed and integrated into the building fabric. This is most likely to happen if they are included from the beginning of the design process.

5. *Lightshelves, combined with high ceilings, are the best devices for shading and redirecting sunlight* in a manner that integrates with other elements of the architecture, fulfills user needs, and creates comfortable, spacious, delightful sunlit spaces. To be effective for distributing light, high reflectance on the top surfaces is essential. On north and south exposures, lightshelves can be designed to

require no additional movable shading for control of glare or heat. On other exposures they can be effective most of the time but need to be supplemented for short periods. As large-scale architectural elements, they are an important formgiver for sidelit buildings. The many case-study examples in which they are used indicate how widely applicable they are and demonstrate the range of design expression possible.

6. *Reliability is very important for dynamic shading devices.* If unreliable, they remain in place (and adjusted for the worst condition) permanently. Although best on the exterior for heat control, an interior location is preferable if reliability and maintenance are better. Hence, my preference for using large-scale fixed elements when possible, with smaller-scale movable devices only as a supplement or as an unavoidable alternative.

7 Toplighting: Strategies, Techniques, Devices, and Forms

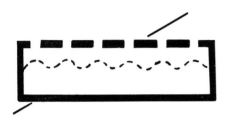

7-1. Toplighting can provide uniform luminous distribution with minimum glazing area.

For low-rise buildings, toplighting can be the most efficient form of sunlighting, as measured by illumination levels in relationship to HVAC loads (heating and cooling). This is due to the fact that the distribution of illumination can be made very uniform while the glazing area can remain minimal (fig. 7-1).

CHARACTERISTICS AND CHALLENGES OF TOPLIGHTING

Toplighting is of minimal use in tall multilevel buildings because it can illuminate only one or two floors. Its multilevel implementation is discussed in detail in chapter 8.

The most obvious advantage of toplighting over sidelighting is the freedom to place natural light sources wherever illumination is desired, either uniformly distributed or in whatever pattern is dictated by the programmed activities of the space. This flexibility makes it simple to achieve uniform illumination. Unlike sidelighting, there is usually no need, when toplighting, to overlight one area in order to get sufficient light for the adjacent areas. Despite these advantages, other challenges remain for toplighting design, both quantitative and qualitative.

The quantitative challenge is that common to all sunlighting—to optimize the relationship between lighting and HVAC under the wide daily and seasonal variations in sunlight availability. The best toplighting solution is likely to be different for each particular building configuration and each set of programmed activities and related lighting and thermal comfort requirements, latitude, climate, and microclimate.

The qualitative challenge is to create beautiful, pleasant, appropriate visual environments that satisfy the occupants' needs for orientation in time and space. Sunlighting should be used to create delightful environments rather than simply to save energy. Direct sunlight on interior walls can be used to give the occupants of windowless spaces a "view" that provides some information as to exterior weather conditions and time of day.

As explained in chapter 1, office and factory buildings should maximize long-term worker satisfaction and thus productivity—a primarily qualitative challenge. Therefore, the highest priority should be to provide enjoyment from sunlighting, particularly in spaces that tend to be dreary and can only be rectified by toplighting.

These challenges were either not present or were less important in earlier periods of history, before air conditioning and artificial lighting had made large floor areas feasible, and when the criteria for human comfort and/or the visual demands of the programmed work were less stringent. The design solutions that evolved worked well for the conditions and the available technology of those times. We must now meet today's increased expectations by combining historical precedents for sunlighting forms with the potential of current technology.

HISTORICAL PRECEDENTS

Skylights

The precedents for skylights include unglazed apertures open to the sky overhead for light and ventilation, as in the extensive bazaars of ancient Persia and the Pantheon of Rome (figs. 7-2, 7-3). These openings were small (2–5 percent of floor area) but adequate, particularly on the sunny days that prevail in these climates.

In visiting the bazaar at Isfahan, Persia (now Iran) I found the illumination on a sunny day functionally adequate for public circulation but somewhat gloomy to my taste and contemporary Western expectations. This condition could be easily rectified by more highlighted displays in the bordering shops. Lighter colors on walls and ceilings would also help distribute interreflected light.

The dullness of the dark ceiling and wall surfaces was largely offset by the biologically important information that was provided. The unglazed openings overhead gave an absolutely clear view of the blue sky, and the small, changing patches of sunlight on room surfaces were infinitely more satisfying than the same average quantity of illumination would have been from translucent skydomes or fluorescent light fixtures. The occasional windows and doorway openings to courts were more important for their information value than for the additional illumination they provided.

The use of small horizontal openings to provide light and ventilation in thermally massive, vaulted roof structures is uniquely appropriate to the predominantly sunny, dry, desert climate, with its hot days and cool nights. Small horizontal openings in high, vaulted ceilings are still logical today under similar conditions. This combination ensures that the ceiling vault and upper walls will be the primary reflecting surfaces, minimizing glare and providing visual interest.

In contrast, extensive areas of skylights were used in late nineteenth-century European and American museums. The sunlight reaching the galleries was controlled by an attic full of operable louvers above a glazed ceiling. The negative effect of such large areas of skylights on thermal comfort in summer was reduced by the thermal isolation of the gallery space from the independently ventilated attic. (See museum case studies for comparison with some contemporary museum designs.) In present-day America, skylights are most commonly used in industrial buildings with minimal heating, cooling, or lighting requirements.

7-2. Very small unglazed skylight at Isfahan.

7-3. The Pantheon, Rome.

Clerestories

Early in history, the interior zones of large spaces were also supplemented by toplighting from clerestories in the form of open (Isfahan) or glazed (Hagia Sofia) apertures. Sunny climate and function dictated that the openings be small (fig. 7–4).

In eighteenth-century England, while skylights were the common solution for circulation spaces, shopping malls, and railroad stations, industrial buildings were more likely to use north-facing clerestories in sawtooth roofs. The form of toplighting selected might have been dependent on considerations of glare control rather than control of solar gain. Even under dirty, smoggy conditions, the glare of sunlight was not welcomed in work spaces. However, direct and indirect solar heat gain from skylights or south-facing clerestories would probably have been welcomed.

7–4. The dome of the mosque at Isfahan, Iran. (Photograph courtesy of Tom Lam)

GEOMETRY OF TOPLIGHTING: FORMS OF TOPLIGHTING FOR TODAY'S CONDITIONS

Both skylights and clerestories are applicable today, but their selection, size, detailing, and relationship to other room surfaces need to be reconsidered for each application, recognizing the differences in objectives and means. Optimizing the performance of toplighting today implies using light indirectly. As with sidelighting, incoming sunlight must be baffled and redirected in order to avoid glare and local overheating and to provide the light distribution and delightful interior environments desired.

In toplighting, the walls are often the most important illuminated surfaces. By intercepting direct sunlight, walls can redistribute the light to the desired surfaces and areas. Because of the crisp and changing patterns of sunlight on these illuminated walls, they can be a satisfying substitute for a window view. Walls can be seen throughout large spaces, satisfying biological information needs for orientation. By contrast, a patch of sunlight on the floor coming from a shared central skylight may be visible only in a local area.

Ceiling height is also important with toplighting. Unlike sidelighting apertures, toplighting apertures can be distributed as needed. Fewer apertures are necessary, and the light distribution will be more uniform with increased ceiling height, especially when the sunlight is diffused by reflecting surfaces or diffusers (fig. 7–5). Sloping the ceiling up to meet the aperture will minimize contrast between the aperture and the space receiving the illumination. These geometrical considerations can be met with a variety of shapes and devices.

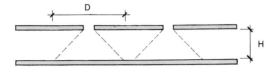

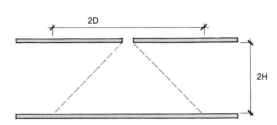

7–5. Diffused light distribution from toplighting apertures increases in uniformity with increased ceiling height (fewer apertures are necessary).

Horizontal or Near-Horizontal Glazing for Toplighting: Skylights

Horizontal skylights favor overhead light, and their performance is independent of orientation. Their performance under sunny conditions is dependent on solar altitude (fig. 7–6).

Advantages

The advantages of horizontal skylights include the following:

- ☐ They can be placed almost anywhere on any roof with minimal impact on structure or framing. Like window blinds, they can be added at any stage of the design process, even after the building is completed and occupied. Little design effort is required beyond size selection of cataloged or standard details. Larger-scale greenhouse-style glazing is also simple to specify as a premanufactured item.

- ☐ For a given glazing area, skylights are likely to have a very low first cost because they need little architectural provision beyond omitting an area of roof and installing a mass-produced product.

- ☐ They can provide the most efficient lighting for dark, overcast conditions when the sky vault is uniformly bright. Under these conditions, a skylight oriented directly overhead "sees" the most sky and receives and distributes the light most directly to the space below (fig. 7–7).

- ☐ Clear skylights give maximum views of the sky. Translucent glazing will help distribute light on clear days but must be in a well to baffle the glare of the overly bright, sunlit diffusers.

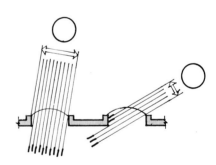

7–6. The performance of skylights under sunny conditions is dependent on solar altitude.

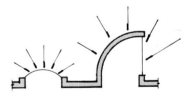

7–7. Horizontal skylights "see" the most sky and are therefore the best method for collecting and distributing diffuse, overcast sky light.

☐ Skylights may be the best option in equatorial locations where their horizontal orientation will maximize collection of the incident sunlight from a high solar altitude. Under such conditions, a very small area of glazing in a deep well can illuminate a large area effectively. The skylight should be no larger than necessary to provide the desired illumination under *sunny* conditions (i.e., the aperture should be $+/-1$ percent of the floor area). If sized for overcast conditions, the overheating that would occur under sunny conditions would create additional cooling requirements and offset any savings from lighting.

Disadvantages

The disadvantages of horizontal skylights include the following:

☐ They perform poorly in temperate and frigid climates (high latitudes). This is not a problem at the equator where there is little seasonal difference and one can design for the overhead condition. Horizontal glazing admits maximum sunlight and heat in summer when the sun is high and minimum sunlight and heat in winter when the sun is low. Clearly, this is the reverse of the generally desired condition for both thermal and lighting considerations. Many of the best-known architects have created dramatic toplighted sculptural statements that must have assumed sunless skies and then attempted to ameliorate the self-imposed problems with technical solutions, sometimes with little success. One example is the fully glazed greenhouse ceiling/roof at the Cambridge University History Faculty building (James Stirling, 1967). This building is an environmental disaster, cold and drafty in winter and hot as an oven in summer. A fraction of the glazed area, if well employed, could have created a more comfortable thermal and visual environment at a fraction of the construction and operating cost (figs. 7–8, 7–9).

7–8. Cambridge University History Faculty building (James Stirling, Architect). (Courtesy of Paul Scoville)

7-9. Cambridge University History Faculty building. Broken-down blinds are a constant reminder of the need for shading in this overglazed space.

☐ They have the potential to create glare problems. If clear glazing is used, beams of direct sunlight from overhead are welcomed in circulation areas but unacceptable in most work areas. The high angles of sunlight received by horizontal skylights are difficult to redirect by naturally occuring architectural elements, such as beams and walls (fig. 7–10). Sunlit translucent glazing can also be a source of glare and, like informationless translucent fluorescent fixtures, much more annoying than similar areas of *reflected* light from interesting "real" surfaces. As sources of direct lighting, translucent surfaces are bright relative to other room surfaces. Translucent glazing that diffuses the light to the space and reduces direct glare also eliminates the beneficial information of sunlight (time, weather conditions).

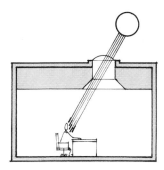

7-10. Skylights should avoid sending direct sunlight onto work surfaces or their occupants. If placement is inappropriate, the sunlight must be baffled or diffused.

☐ Unit skylights, either clear or translucent, placed to illuminate the workplane directly with maximum efficiency (i.e., centered in a space) tend to leave the wall and ceiling surfaces unlit and gloomy. Shaping the ceiling cavity to improve light distribution offsets the initial economy of off-the-shelf skylight units (fig. 7–11). The use of unit skylights does not encourage architectural integration between beams, ducts, and the like.

☐ Horizontal glazing is more vulnerable to leakage problems than vertical windows; building codes may require expensive wired or laminated safety glass.

7-11. A coffered ceiling improves the light distribution and relative aperture brightness contrast of a unit skylight as compared to a flat ceiling with a deep well.

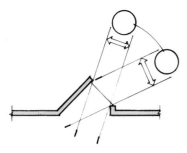

7–12. Sloping a skylight toward the equator improves the winter/summer performance ratio. Sloping it away from the equator achieves the steadiest light, in winter and summer, under sunny and overcast conditions.

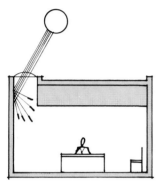

7–13. Locate skylight to illuminate walls.

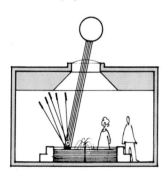

7–14. Reflecting pools, sculptures, or polished floors can be used to redirect sunlight to the ceiling.

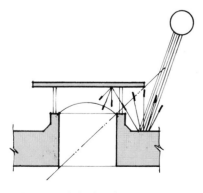

7–15. Horizontal shades (fixed or seasonal) effectively create clerestories from skylights.

Using Skylights to Best Advantage

The following guidelines will help optimize skylight performance:

☐ In temperate climates, tilt and orient skylights as much as possible to reduce the seasonal disadvantages. For example, a south-facing skylight at a 45-degree slope in Boston would improve the summer/winter ratio (of light to heat admitted) from 5:1 to 2:1 (fig. 7–12). With a 60-degree slope, illumination at noon in summer and winter would be equal.

☐ Coffer the ceiling up to the skylight to improve light distribution and reduce aperture contrast. A small skylight can have remarkable impact if integrated with a large coffer. Lift the entire ceiling around the skylight, or whatever area is possible. It is better to use fewer skylights with good distribution than a large number with poor distribution.

☐ Except in public spaces where views of the sky or adjacent buildings are a principal objective, use small areas of clear glazing rather than large areas of low-transmission glass. Smaller areas of glazing are less expensive, need smaller areas of shading devices, are easier to control, and permit less heat transfer in and out of the building. Achieve visual connection with the external world through visible penetration of sunlight rather than maximum area of visible sky.

☐ Locate skylights to bring sunlight against walls or other light-redirecting surfaces (fig. 7–13). These will then illuminate the work surfaces indirectly, minimizing contrast with the skylights, and helping to create bright, cheerful spaces. Sunlight and sky light falling on a wall will benefit a much larger space than will the same-size opening in the middle of a room. Reflecting pools, sculptures, or even polished nontask floor areas can be effective in redistributing the light from clear skylights (fig. 7–14).

☐ Design baffling to control glare and redirect light to large areas of room surfaces. Baffling can be located outside the skylight, at the glazing plane, or in the zone of transition between the aperture and the end-use surface (figs. 7–15 through 7–20). Local interior shading devices such as trellises, trees, banners, and umbrellas offer selective protection.

☐ Control the amount of light entering the space with dynamic shading that redirects unwanted light back to the exterior, rather than converting it to heat within the space (fig. 7–21).

☐ For best performance, use adjustable louver/reflectors that redirect the light precisely where desired.

☐ Unless functional glazing system elements are interesting or beautiful, baffle them from view with large-scale architectural or decorative elements. Avoid the visual noise that results from complex structural forms juxtaposed with uncoordinated glazing details.

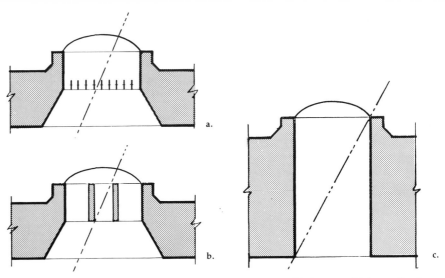

7–16. Skylights may be shielded by exterior louvers such as these at the Mellon Gallery at the Yale Museum (Louis I. Kahn, Architect). However, louvers are visually busy, require constant maintenance, and greatly reduce the efficiency of the skylights in exchange for steadier illumination. This seems to be a very inefficient and convoluted way to get the effect of a simple north-facing clerestory. (Photograph courtesy of John Lam)

7–17. Interior control at the glazing plane: (a) fixed or operable louvers; (b) larger fixed or operable louvers or beams; (c) deep well openings alone.

7–18. The reflector used in the skylight system of the Kimbell Art Museum (Louis I. Kahn, Architect) is a sound concept inefficiently executed. The relatively dark-colored surfaces of the unpainted concrete skylight well and ceiling vault give a pleasant glow that is insufficient for lighting the exhibits even at noon on a sunny day in midsummer. There would be more light if the skylight well was painted white.

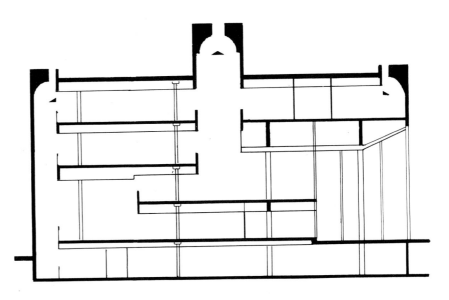

7–19. The library of this Middle Eastern University (case study A2) employs the same reflector wedge concept as the Kimbell Museum. However, because all surfaces will be white and the space between the skylight and reflector much greater, it should deliver much more light. (Courtesy of Campus Consortium)

Geometry of Toplighting   145

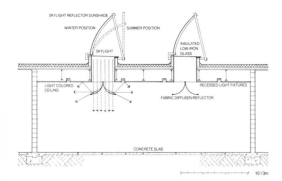

7-20. Dynamic reflector/shades can maximize the daily and/or seasonal performance of skylights.

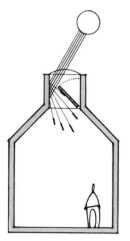

7-21. A simple dynamic shading device is a single insulated panel that modulates light levels seasonally (or as needed). (See also Case Study D1)

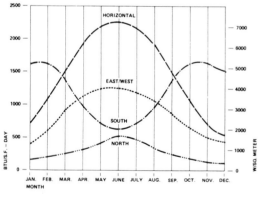

7-22. The effects of orientation: seasonal thermal gain from different clerestory orientations versus a horizontal skylight. (Courtesy of Syska & Hennessy)

Vertical Glazing for Toplighting: Clerestories, Sunscoops, and Lightscoops

Clerestories

Clerestories favor low-angle light, either facing the equator at high latitudes (winter in temperate climates), or at dawn and dusk on east and west exposures. Orientation is the critical determinant of their thermal performance (fig. 7-22).

Clerestory monitors for toplighting have advantages over skylights for energy conservation and ease in controlling glare. Since they are more difficult to add on than are skylights, and have a greater effect on architectural forms, they must be integrated with the overall design at an earlier stage.

Sunscoops

Sunscoops are clerestory monitors oriented toward the sun (fig. 7-23).

In temperate climates and high latitudes, clerestory monitors oriented toward the equator will automatically achieve the usual temperate climate objective of more light in winter than summer to reduce heating and cooling loads. A sunscoop can get twice as much light in winter as in summer; a horizontal skylight might get only one-fifth as much (see fig. 7-9). Such orientation also makes glare control simple. Glare control can be best provided by a nearby parallel wall that blocks and redirects any sunlight penetrating at any angle from large unshaded clerestories (see case studies F1 and H1). Such a construction allows occupants to enjoy seeing sunlight on wall surfaces without receiving direct glare.

Because of their ability to provide glare-free lighting much more easily than windows, sunscoops are ideal in very high latitudes where the sun is very low in the winter and maximum light and heat from the sun is always desired (e.g., in Alaska, where the sun is at 10 degrees elevation on a December noon) (fig. 7-24).

Sunscoops can control the quantity of sunlight with the same shading devices used in sidelighting—overhangs, louvers, and the like (fig. 7-25)—and baffle the light by using deep monitor shapes in combination with beams, coffered ceilings, high placement of the clerestory within the monitor, and deep, interior lightshelflike sills (figs. 7-26 through 7-30).

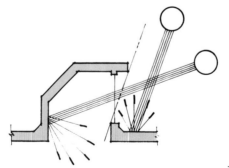

7-23. Sunscoops receive direct sunlight and sky light as well as roof-reflected light.

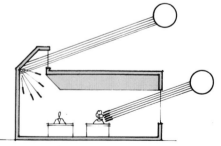

7-24. Sunscoops are better than windows for controlling the potential glare of low-angle sunlight.

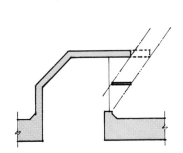

7–25. Sidelighting-type exterior louvers, overhangs, and fins can provide baffling for sunscoops as well.

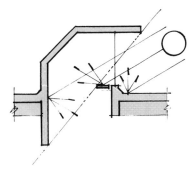

7–26. Various combinations of overhang, wide sill (lightshelf), and beam (a dropped bulkhead) can be balanced to provide necessary cut-off angle for sunscoops.

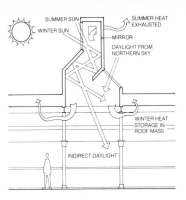

7–27. As with skylights, deep splayed wells can baffle sunlight from sunscoops. In the One University Plaza monitor, a skylight was integrated as well. (Reprinted by permission of *Progressive Architecture*)

For maximum efficiency, use a minimum area of clear glazing in continuous bands for easiest summer shading and minimum heat loss in winter. When the roof is the immediate foreground, white marble chips or polished reflectors can be located to increase light selectively in summer or winter. The light input through sunscoops can also be increased by maximizing reflections from adjacent walls. The actual shape of the monitor has little effect on performance; orientation and effective reflectances are much more critical.

Lightscoops

Lightscoops are clerestory monitors oriented away from the sun (north in the northern hemisphere) (fig. 7–31). Of questionable value in frigid climates, lightscoops utilize sky light and roof-reflected sunlight and require little if any shading to eliminate all direct sunlight (fig. 7–32). Both sunscoops and lightscoops are useful and can be easily shaded in equatorial latitudes.

The advantages of lightscoops are as follows:

☐ They give the steadiest level of illumination with a minimum of glare. If adjacent roofs are dark-colored, lightscoops will receive more light on overcast days than on clear days. Light-colored adjacent roofs (or suncatchers) can alter that balance.

☐ They contribute virtually no solar heat gain.

☐ They require minimum shading and baffling to control light.

The disadvantages of lightscoops are as follows:

☐ They admit the lowest amount of light per unit of glazing.

☐ The light admitted is diffuse sky light, which is nondirectional and does not penetrate as deeply into a building as sunlight. The color of sky light is ''cooler'' than that of sunlight, and although steady, may be uninteresting.

☐ Little or no solar heat gain is achieved in heating season. Heat lost through lightscoops can be significant. Highly insulative glazing should be considered.

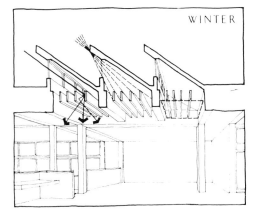

7–28. At the Mt. Airy Library in North Carolina (J. N. Pease, Project Architect; Mazria/Schiff, Associate Architect), the design of the sunscoop baffles allows for glareless maximum winter solar gain but also creates a low and visually busy ceiling. (Reprinted by permission of *Progressive Architecture*)

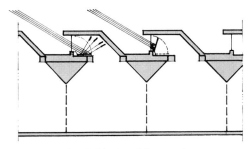

7–29. At the Tarble Arts Museum (case study D2), we baffled south sunlight with lightshelf panels that will fold up as dynamic insulated panels.

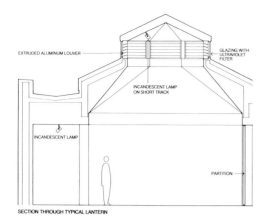

EXTRUDED ALUMINUM LOUVER

INCANDESCENT LAMP
ON SHORT TRACK

GLAZING WITH
ULTRAVIOLET
FILTER

INCANDESCENT LAMP

PARTITION

SECTION THROUGH TYPICAL LANTERN

7–30. Portland Museum of Art (I. M. Pei and Partners, Architect). Exposure to sunlight from all directions can make illumination levels steadier from dawn to dusk. However, symmetrical treatment of fixed louvers is extremely inefficient. Louvers designed for the lowest sun angles from the east and west provide excessive shading on the south side and are redundant on the north side, where no louvering is necessary. (Reprinted by permission of *Progressive Architecture*)

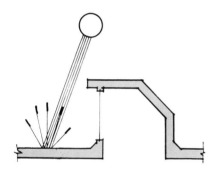

7–31. Lightscoops are clerestory monitors oriented away from the sun, receiving sky light and roof-reflected light. They provide the lowest and steadiest light levels with minimum annual heat gain.

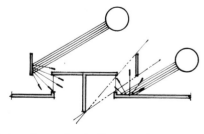

7–33. Suncatcher baffles provide both shading and redirection on east and west exposures.

7–32. North-facing lightscoops with tinted glass at Boston University Library (Josep Luís Sert, Architect) are an unfortunate choice in Boston, where the heat and light of winter sunlight are always desirable

Lightscoops can be used to advantage under the following conditions:

☐ In museums, where steady light levels may be more important than winter thermal gain.

☐ In warm climates, where heat is never needed. (See, for example, case study D3.)

☐ In buildings such as museums, where high light levels are never desired.

The decision to orient a clerestory monitor away from the sun is often determined by architectural necessity rather than by lighting needs. If more light is desired, reflect light into the windows from a high-reflectance roof when the sun is high and from suncatcher baffles when the sun is low.

Suncatcher Baffles

A shading/redirecting device of exceptional usefulness in toplighting is the suncatcher baffle (fig. 7–33). This is an exterior device that converts direct sunlight to indirect sunlight. Positioned to redirect sunlight into a window, suncatchers can significantly increase the illumination in north-facing windows (fig. 7–34). On east- and west-facing windows, suncatchers both shade and redirect sunlight, significantly reducing daily illumination fluctuations (fig. 7–35). Although they also reduce illumination on overcast days, on sunny days suncatchers always increase the illumination on the shady side.

A suncatcher in combination with a lightscoop can reduce the inequality between sunny (south) and shady (north) exposures and also increase the average illumination of the space.

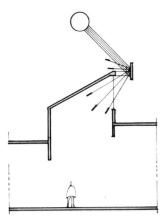

7-34. Suncatcher baffle in north orientation.

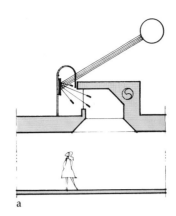

a

b

7-35. Suncatcher baffles at the Hawaiian Life building (Ossipoff and Snyder, Architect). (a) section; (b) exterior view. In this renovation of an existing building, a lightweight, white plastic suncatcher panel with a pipe frame was designed for the new east-facing monitor.

Lightscoop/Sunscoop with Suncatchers

When monitors face east and west, they act as both sunscoops and lightscoops during a sunny day (fig. 7-36). In this case, suncatcher baffles can make the light fairly uniform during the course of a day by blocking some of the light from the sunny side and capturing it on the shady side. At noon, suncatcher baffles increase the illumination by redirecting much of the roof-reflected light that otherwise would have gone into the sky into the space.

The design of suncatcher baffle proportions is similar to lightshelf design in that it is a compromise between the optimum conditions for receiving and reflecting sunlight. To minimize reductions in illumination under overcast conditions, suncatchers should be kept some distance away from the window. A good rule of thumb is that the suncatcher-to-window distance should be more or less equal to the size of the suncatcher (fig. 7-37). Projecting the suncatcher above the roof maximizes the amount of low-angle light captured; projecting it below the roof maximizes the amount of baffle ''seen'' by the interior. Therefore, a single blade is more efficient than multiple fins with an equal cut-off angle because more area is sunlit, and all of the sunlit baffle area is seen by the window (fig. 7-38 and case study B5.)

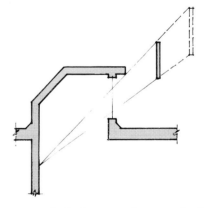

7-37. The further away the suncatcher baffle is placed, the larger it must be for any point of the wall to ''see'' the same amount of sunlit surface.

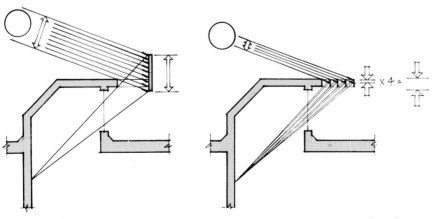

7-38. For a given surface area, one large louver is more efficient than several small ones both in capturing and redirecting sunlight.

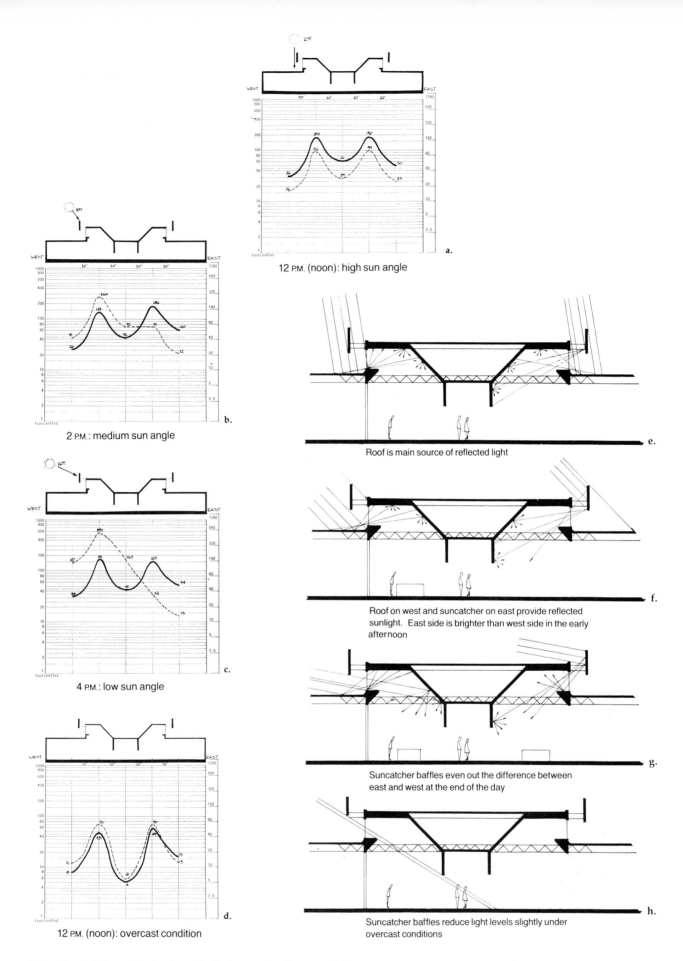

12 P.M. (noon): high sun angle

a.

2 P.M.: medium sun angle

b.

4 P.M.: low sun angle

c.

12 P.M. (noon): overcast condition

d.

Roof is main source of reflected light

e.

Roof on west and suncatcher on east provide reflected sunlight. East side is brighter than west side in the early afternoon

f.

Suncatcher baffles even out the difference between east and west at the end of the day

g.

Suncatcher baffles reduce light levels slightly under overcast conditions

h.

7-36. Suncatcher baffles in east/west orientation. The effectiveness of this device was illustrated by model studies for renovating at Cummins Engine Factory in Madison, Indiana (Eisenman and Robertson, Architect). With east-and west-facing clerestories above the two adjacent production lines, the illumination and heat gain at 4 P.M. (c) would be sixteen times greater on the sunny side (j) than on the shady side (k). With the addition of suncachers (solid line), both sides would be about equal (l,m). The suncatchers increase illumination by 100 percent at noon (a), but reduce illumination by 50 percent on an overcast day (d).

i.

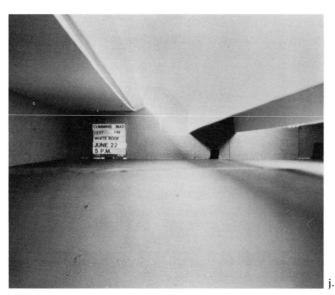

j.

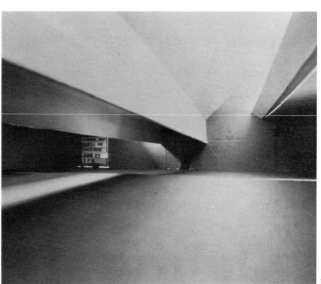

k.

l.

m.

TOPLIGHTING GENERIC STUDIES

The toplighting studies on the following pages compare equal areas of glazing (10 percent of floor area) with a range of configurations at the center of a space and at two edges. Designs tested were based on the supposition of no direct sunlight penetration to the workplane. Therefore, glazing was clear only if the sunlight would be controlled by the lightwell or walls; otherwise, the glazing was translucent. Assumed location was 42 degrees north latitude (Boston).

Group 1: Central Fenestration Oriented N-S

☐ Horizontal skylights (A) admit the most light when the sun is high (summer noon) and the least when it is low (in winter). Usually this is not desirable for lighting or HVAC.

☐ Vertical clerestories oriented south admit the most light when the sun is low (in winter) and a fraction of that in summer. This is good thermally, but there may not be enough light in summer.

☐ Sloping skylights to the south (B and C) maximizes light at the equinox and gives the steadiest level of light throughout the year. This may be the best choice when equal light is desired in summer and winter to minimize lighting-energy cost without HVAC penalty.

TOPLIGHTING STUDIES (Sunny Condition)

REFLECTANCES : ceiling 80% walls 80% floors 20%

1 CENTRAL FENESTRATION ORIENTED N–S

A DIFFUSE HORIZONTAL SKYLIGHT

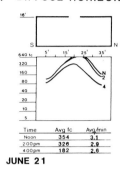

Time	Avg fc	Avg/min
Noon	354	3.1
2:00pm	326	2.9
4:00pm	182	2.6

JUNE 21

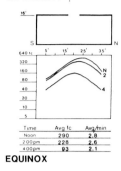

Time	Avg fc	Avg/min
Noon	290	2.8
2:00pm	228	2.6
4:00pm	93	2.1

EQUINOX

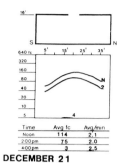

Time	Avg fc	Avg/min
Noon	114	2.1
2:00pm	75	2.0
4:00pm	3	2.5

DECEMBER 21

B DIFFUSE 45° SKYLIGHT

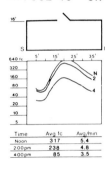

Time	Avg fc	Avg/min
Noon	317	5.4
2:00pm	238	4.8
4:00pm	85	3.5

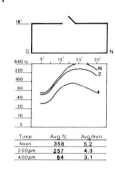

Time	Avg fc	Avg/min
Noon	358	5.2
2:00pm	257	4.3
4:00pm	84	3.1

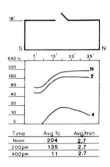

Time	Avg fc	Avg/min
Noon	204	2.7
2:00pm	135	2.7
4:00pm	11	2.7

C DIFFUSE 60° SKYLIGHT

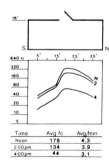

Time	Avg fc	Avg/min
Noon	178	4.3
2:00pm	134	3.9
4:00pm	44	3.1

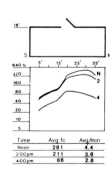

Time	Avg fc	Avg/min
Noon	281	4.4
2:00pm	211	3.6
4:00pm	66	2.8

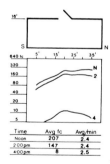

Time	Avg fc	Avg/min
Noon	207	2.4
2:00pm	147	2.4
4:00pm	8	2.5

D DIFFUSE VERTICAL CLERESTORY

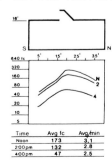

Time	Avg fc	Avg/min
Noon	173	3.1
2:00pm	132	2.8
4:00pm	47	2.5

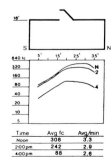

Time	Avg fc	Avg/min
Noon	308	3.3
2:00pm	242	2.9
4:00pm	88	2.6

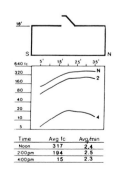

Time	Avg fc	Avg/min
Noon	317	2.4
2:00pm	194	2.5
4:00pm	15	2.3

E   CLEAR VERTICAL CLERESTORY

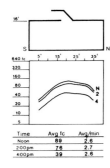

Time	Avg fc	Avg/min
Noon	89	2.6
2:00 pm	76	2.7
4:00 pm	39	2.6

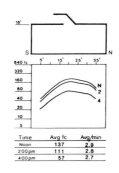

Time	Avg fc	Avg/min
Noon	137	2.9
2:00 pm	111	2.8
4:00 pm	57	2.7

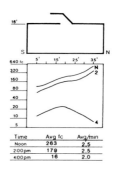

Time	Avg fc	Avg/min
Noon	263	2.5
2:00 pm	179	2.5
4:00 pm	16	2.0

F   CLEAR VERTICAL CLERESTORY

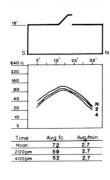

Time	Avg fc	Avg/min
Noon	72	2.7
2:00 pm	59	2.7
4:00 pm	52	2.7

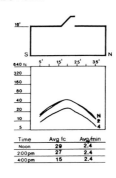

Time	Avg fc	Avg/min
Noon	29	2.4
2:00 pm	27	2.4
4:00 pm	15	2.4

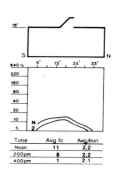

Time	Avg fc	Avg/min
Noon	11	2.2
2:00 pm	8	2.2
4:00 pm	1	2.1

G   CLEAR VERTICAL CLERESTORY WITH SUN CATCHER

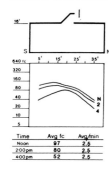

Time	Avg fc	Avg/min
Noon	97	2.5
2:00 pm	80	2.5
4:00 pm	52	2.5

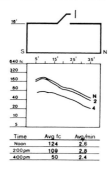

Time	Avg fc	Avg/min
Noon	124	2.6
2:00 pm	109	2.8
4:00 pm	50	2.4

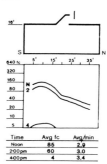

Time	Avg fc	Avg/min
Noon	85	2.9
2:00 pm	60	3.0
4:00 pm	4	3.4

Group 2: Central Fenestration Oriented E-W

☐ As would be expected, horizontal skylights (A) admit many times more light in summer than in winter, with large variations throughout each day.

☐ Clear vertical clerestories with suncatchers (C) provide much steadier illumination throughout the year and throughout each day, although at much lower levels than the horizontal skylights.

☐ Clear double clerestories (B) with total glazing area equal to (C) also provide steady illumination but less efficiently.

2   CENTRAL FENESTRATION ORIENTED E-W

A   DIFFUSE HORIZONTAL SKYLIGHT

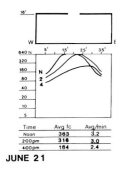

Time	Avg fc	Avg/min
Noon	363	3.2
2:00pm	316	3.0
4:00pm	164	2.4

JUNE 21

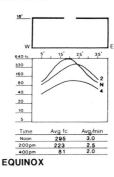

Time	Avg fc	Avg/min
Noon	295	3.0
2:00pm	223	2.5
4:00pm	81	2.0

EQUINOX

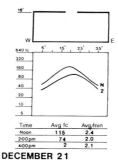

Time	Avg fc	Avg/min
Noon	115	2.4
2:00pm	74	2.0
4:00pm	2	2.1

DECEMBER 21

B   CLEAR VERTICAL DOUBLE CLERESTORY

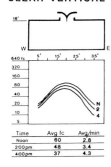

Time	Avg fc	Avg/min
Noon	60	2.8
2:00pm	48	3.4
4:00pm	37	4.3

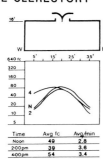

Time	Avg fc	Avg/min
Noon	49	2.8
2:00pm	39	3.6
4:00pm	54	3.4

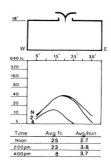

Time	Avg fc	Avg/min
Noon	25	2.7
2:00pm	23	3.8
4:00pm	8	3.7

C   CLEAR VERTICAL CLERESTORY WITH SUN CATCHER

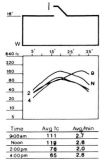

Time	Avg fc	Avg/min
9:00am	111	2.7
Noon	119	2.6
2:00pm	76	2.0
4:00pm	65	2.6

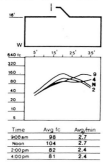

Time	Avg fc	Avg/min
9:00am	98	2.7
Noon	104	2.7
2:00pm	82	2.4
4:00pm	81	2.4

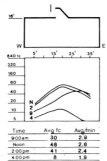

Time	Avg fc	Avg/min
9:00am	30	2.9
Noon	48	2.6
2:00pm	41	2.4
4:00pm	8	1.9

Group 3: Edge Fenestration Oriented E-W

In this group the diffuse skylights were sloped to illuminate the adjacent walls, with the diffuser surface largely out of sight. This was compared with vertical clear glazing with direct sunlight controlled only by the walls.

☐ The diffuse skylights (A) provide the most light at noon but provide less at the beginning and end of each day than do clear vertical clerestories (B).

☐ The addition of suncatchers to clerestories (C) achieves the steadiest illumination throughout each day and the most uniformity throughout the room. The suncatchers increase the illumination at noon and make both walls equally bright whatever the direction of the sun, with some sacrifice in total efficiency.

3 EDGE FENESTRATION ORIENTED E-W

A DIFFUSE 45° EDGE SKYLIGHTS

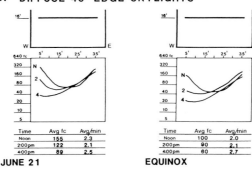
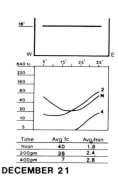

Time	Avg fc	Avg/min
Noon	155	2.3
2:00pm	122	2.1
4:00pm	89	2.5

JUNE 21

Time	Avg fc	Avg/min
Noon	100	2.0
2:00pm	90	2.1
4:00pm	60	2.7

EQUINOX

Time	Avg fc	Avg/min
Noon	40	1.8
2:00pm	36	2.4
4:00pm	7	2.8

DECEMBER 21

B CLEAR VERTICAL EDGE CLERESTORIES

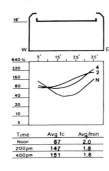
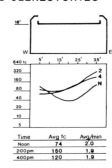
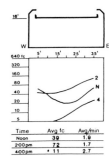

Time	Avg fc	Avg/min
Noon	87	2.0
2:00pm	147	1.8
4:00pm	151	1.8

Time	Avg fc	Avg/min
Noon	74	2.0
2:00pm	150	1.9
4:00pm	120	1.9

Time	Avg fc	Avg/min
Noon	39	1.9
2:00pm	72	1.7
4:00pm	11	2.7

C CLEAR VERTICAL EDGE CLERESTORIES WITH SUN CATCHERS

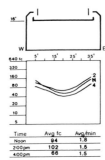
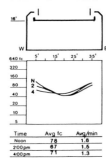
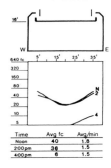

Time	Avg fc	Avg/min
Noon	94	1.8
2:00pm	102	1.5
4:00pm	66	1.5

Time	Avg fc	Avg/min
Noon	78	1.8
2:00pm	67	1.5
4:00pm	71	1.3

Time	Avg fc	Avg/min
Noon	40	1.8
2:00pm	36	1.5
4:00pm	6	1.5

Toplit Shared Central Spaces: Courts and Atria, Lightcourts, Litria, and Lightwells

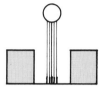

8–1. Court.

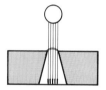

8–2. Atrium.

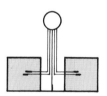

8–3. Lightcourt.

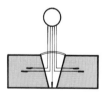

8–4. Litrium.

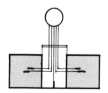

8–5. Lightwell.

While the previous chapters were concerned with the particulars of fenestration for sidelit and toplit buildings, this chapter is concerned with the potential for massing a large building or complex of buildings around a central space. Courtyards and atria are central spaces created primarily for human pleasure, though they do have some sunlighting implications; they will be discussed briefly. Lightcourts, litria, and lightwells have evolved from the courtyard and atrium forms. They express the utility of sunlighting; the light-reflecting and controlling qualities of their central spaces are maximized in order to provide sunlighting for the surrounding spaces. These spaces will be examined in detail.

DEFINITIONS OF SHARED CENTRAL SPACES

Court: an outdoor area open to the sky and largely or entirely surrounded by buildings or walls (fig. 8–1).

Atrium: the central room of a building open to the sky at the center; today, the atrium is usually multistoried and glazed (fig. 8–2).

Lightcourt: a courtyard that is designed to optimize the sunlighting in the enclosed building(s) (fig. 8–3).

Litrium: an atrium that is designed to optimize the sunlighting in the adjacent spaces (fig. 8–4).

Lightwell: a vertical opening through one or more floors in a building, created for the primary purpose of distributing natural light to adjacent spaces (fig. 8–5).

HISTORICAL PRECEDENTS

Designing to accommodate the sun through the use of toplit central spaces has been a feature of architecture for many centuries. Greek houses faced into courtyards. The Roman ''atrium'' was a skylit space within the house that served as the center of the home and contained the family shrine.

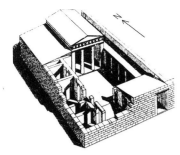

8–6. In ancient Greece, rooms were organized around the peristyle.

8–7. The central atrium in the Maison de la Chasse, Bulla Regia, Tunisia. (Photograph courtesy of Richard Kennedy)

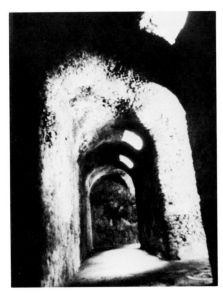

8–8. The lightwell in a corridor of the Maison de la Peche, Bulla Regia, Tunisia. (Photograph courtesy of Richard Kennedy)

The Romans also often extended their houses out, enclosing the back garden with a colonnade to create a peristyle (fig. 8–6).

An interesting example of the atrium building form is found in the ancient Roman underground houses of Bulla Regia in Tunisia (fig. 8–7). The open atria in these structures (more like our modern courtyards) usually contained a tiled mosaic reflecting pool, which, in addition to providing a degree of evaporative cooling, served to reflect sunlight into the adjacent underground rooms. The Bulla Regia structures are also noted for their careful use of lightwells (fig. 8–8). These asymmetrical wells gathered the maximum amount of sunlight possible, but because the solar gain would have been unwelcome in this hot, arid climate, the light was used indirectly with less heat gain. Many of the wells were constructed so that one could not see a line of sight up to the sky; direct sunlight had to bounce several times within the well before entering the space.

Later in history, and a continent away, cast iron and steel structures supported large areas of overhead glazing to keep out rain, snow, and cold in the shopping malls and railroad stations of London, Milan, and other northern cities (fig. 8–9), where cloudy climates prevailed and large expanses of glass were affordable. For such spaces, any direct sunlight that could penetrate the smog, fog, and dirty glass was probably more than welcome at any time. Natural ventilation provided sufficient summer comfort.

In qualitative terms, much can be learned by observing the design of these malls. Looking directly overhead at the glazing in these structures is not a pleasant experience. One sees a clutter of small, dirty panes of glass with cracks patched with tar and a disorderly array of partly open windows. But these details are not normally noticed because of the extent of large-scale architectural elements (girders and beams) that baffle the views of these unattractive details. One perceives illuminated building surfaces with interesting details, not glazing hardware.

8–9. (a) Galleria Vittorio Emmanuele, Milana. (b) Burlington Arcade, London, glazing baffled by structure. Light-washed architectural surfaces appear less dull and gloomy than the overcast sky outside. (Photograph *a* courtesy of Victor Olgyay)

In those structures where extensive areas of glazing and hardware were totally exposed, the skylights tended to be handsomely executed, interesting, positive design features, rather than purely functional ones. Some prominent examples of such structures include the Royal Pavilion in Brighton, the Crystal Palace, and the Galleria Milan. These public spaces were generally not specifically designed to temper the adjacent spaces.

Grand buildings were also created around courtyards, often for the pragmatic purpose of increasing the amount of building perimeter with natural light and ventilation. The Boston Public Library, designed by McKim, Mead and White (1887–93), is typical of this building form. Appearing from the street as a large bulk, it is actually perforated by a central courtyard that creates a thin cross section (figs. 8–10, 8–11).

8–10. The Boston Public Library, (McKim, Mead and White, Architect). (Photograph courtesy of Shepley, Bullfinch, Richardson and Abbott)

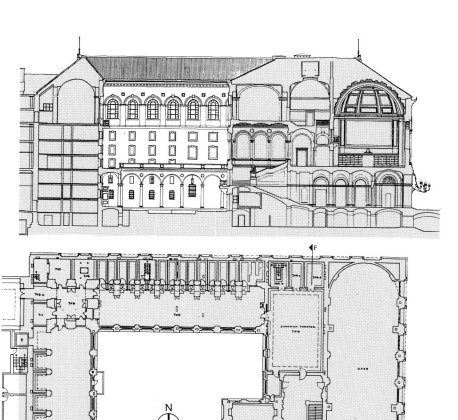

8–11. Boston Public Library: plan.

8–12. Axonometric of the Wainwright building when built.

In densely built areas, these perforations often occurred on a less grand scale; uninhabited lightwells were commonly used to make deep buildings habitable. To maximize their usefulness, the spaces needing ventilation and light were clustered around these wells. Lightwells were also occasionally used as circulation areas.

An example similar to the Boston Public Library is Adler and Sullivan's Wainwright building in St. Louis (1890–91); in this case the building is U-shaped rather than O-shaped in plan (figs. 8–12, 8–13, and 8–14). Subsequent renovations of the Wainwright building have created a more efficient building envelope design by glazing the open courtyard and creating an enclosed atrium. Frank Lloyd Wright's Larkin Soap building in Buffalo (1904–5) effectively anticipated the renovations of the Wainwright building with its modern toplit atrium (figs. 8–15, 8–16). Because this space was conditioned, the floor of the atrium could be used as additional functional work space. Ironically, the Larkin building, with its sensitive environmental design (sealed and mechanically ventilated), also assisted in the evolution of sealed buildings and the accompanying electrical and HVAC systems that eventually would allow twentieth-century designers to virtually ignore external environmental forces.

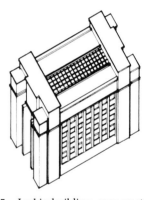

8–15. Larkin building: axonometric.

8–13. Wainwright building after glazing of courtyard.

8–14. Wainwright building, interior of atrium; note white-painted interior walls.

8–16. Larkin building: interior. (Photograph courtesy of the Taliesin Foundation)

COURTS

Courtyards are used for circulation and informal "al fresco" relaxation. Their use is dependent on season and weather. Landscaping can create a courtyard out of "leftover" space between buildings (fig. 8–17). Courtyards can be large for relatively little cost because landscaping is the only cost. They should be enjoyable spaces for people (fig. 8–18).

8–17. Courtyards are often created by space left over between "built" buildings.

8–18. Courtyards provide an attractive view.

Sunlighting and Courts

Courtyards are useful to sunlighting because their open spaces preserve the solar access of the adjoining buildings; they allow sunlight to reach the facades so that sidelighting strategies can be used. Depending on the distance across the courtyard, the buildings may use each other's facades as sources of building-reflected light. If the ground materials are light-colored, courtyards are good foreground sources of ground-reflected light. Remember that courtyards are primarily for human enjoyment; the facade or ground materials are to be chosen for reasons of human comfort and delight in the courtyard itself, rather than to provide reflectances ideal for sunlighting surrounding buildings.

ATRIA

The design and construction of atria and courtyards are very different, although similar activities may take place within them. An atrium results when the interior space of a building is "opened up" to the outside. Atria in warm climates may be unglazed, as the original Roman atria were. Atria are usually isolated from the outdoors by glazing. Activities may take place year round in an atrium, depending upon the extent to which the space is heated or air-conditioned. The need for mechanical ventilation or total air conditioning makes it important to control the amount of sunlight admitted according to seasonal heating or cooling needs.

When atria are sealed and fully air-conditioned, glazing areas should be minimized to reduce the thermal penalty; it is important to use whatever light is admitted efficiently. To minimize the benefits relative to the costs, atria are often tall and thin. There is a great difference between the economies of a given amount of sunlight for a given floor area of a two-story hotel lobby and for a fifty-story atrium with the same floor area at lobby level. Tall hotel atria often slope in at the top to a minimal aperture. Despite the cost, a dramatic and delightful atrium is cost effective because of the premium-value space it creates.

Sunlighting and Atria

The qualitative lighting objective in atria is to create sparkle—the visual interest of a sunlit outdoor scene. To help accomplish this, some direct sunlight should be allowed to hit the architectural surfaces to create sharp shadow lines (fig. 8–19). Clear glazing will allow a glimpse of sky to be seen. In cold climates, more sunlight in winter than summer is desirable, both for cost savings and the positive emotional response it evokes.

The most stringent quantitative objectives are to optimize growing conditions for trees and plants and to maintain thermal comfort for minimal energy cost. The minimum light levels should be determined by what is necessary to sustain trees and plants. Direct sunlight on trees will eliminate the greatest need for supplementary artifical illumination.

8–19. Direct sunlight on architectural surfaces will create sharp shadow lines and read clearly as ''sunlight.''

The form of an atrium sunlighting aperture reflects its application. Low, wide atria are easy to illuminate and can benefit from selective strategies such as clerestories (figs 8–20, 8–21). As with any sunlighting application, reduce light and solar gain by reducing the glazed area or by orientation, rather than by using mirror glass. Narrow atria require careful attention to receive sufficient light. ''Beaming'' the sunlight with mirrors can be invaluable (fig. 8–22). When sizing the glazing in narrow atria, remember that the benefits and costs are shared by the whole space. A skylight that is 30 percent of the lobby floor area may be less than .5 percent if the fifty floors of balcony corridors are figured in. On this basis, clear glass can more often be justified if it makes the space more pleasant.

Frequently, the challenge is to get sufficient light down to lobby level where the plants and people are (fig. 8–23). To maximize the reflectances of surfaces such as balcony railings, make them light-colored and solid.

Light-reflecting sculptures can also be used to provide focus, interest, and scale to an atrium and can assist in the distribution of sunlight (fig. 8–24). Because sculpture is usually interesting, it can be very bright without being glaring (fig. 8–25).

While plants provide much of the excitement of an atrium, it is important that they not obstruct the glazing or important light-reflecting surfaces. Otherwise, the plants on lower floors will need to be replaced constantly.

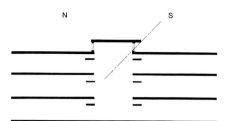

8–20. North/south vertical glazing offers a high degree of seasonal control.

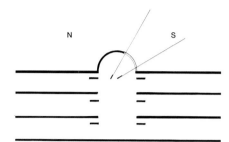

8–21. A slanted aperture can be best when equal light is desired in the cooling and heating seasons.

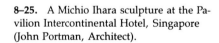

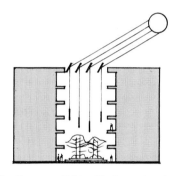

8–22. Beam sunlight with dynamic mirrors in atria with difficult orientations or proportions.

8–25. A Michio Ihara sculpture at the Pavilion Intercontinental Hotel, Singapore (John Portman, Architect).

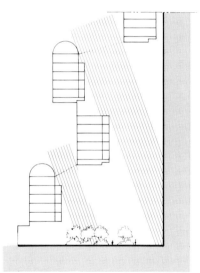

Sun Penetration on June 21 at Noon

8–23. The proportions and orientation of the atrium at the Marriot Marquis Times Square Hotel in New York City allow very little direct sunlight from the main skylight to reach the floor; a smaller lower skylight makes a significant contribution by directing sunlight to the garden.

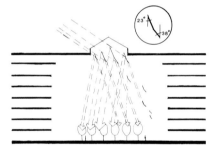

8–24. In the atrium at Park West, Dallas (Haldeman, Miller, Bregman, Hamam, Architect), the addition of reflective sculpture could balance the sunlight and aid tree growth on the shady side.

LIGHTCOURTS

Lightcourts are courtyards that maximize the potential of using sunlight to light adjacent buildings. They are open exterior courts intentionally designed to capture and deliver controlled light to the surrounding buildings. The shapes and reflectances of lightcourts will respond to sunlighting requirements rather than to the desire to create lush landscaping. Of course, lightcourts can be designed to provide for circulation and seasonal lounging as well.

Unlike courtyards, lightcourts may be designed exclusively to provide light and not as attractive outdoor living spaces at grade or for the creation of pleasant views for the surrounding buildings. Therefore, lightcourts may be built in a purely utilitarian manner. For example, the old Waldorf Hotel in London was built around a lightcourt that supplied light and ventilation to the surrounding guest rooms as well as to a greenhouse attic and the decorated translucent ceiling of the garden court at lobby level. While the publicly visible exterior walls of the building were richly detailed (fig. 8–26), the exterior walls around the lightcourt obviously were not intended to be seen except hazily through fixed translucent curtains of guest rooms and stained glass windows of public spaces. Without these filters, one looking across the lightcourt would see unattractive walls covered with exposed plumbing and would look down onto ventilation equipment and the crudely detailed greenhouse roof (fig. 8–27).

I was interested to note the use of front lightcourts in the townhouses of London and Bath. These courts are sunken to basement level and generally contain no trees (there were trees in the park across the street, however). Open iron rails and light wall finishes maximize the light available to the lower-level kitchens and work spaces.

8–26. Exterior detail of Waldorf Hotel, London.

8–27. Lightcourt detail, Waldorf Hotel, London.

Sunlighting and Lightcourts

Lightcourts should be designed to allow the maximum amount of direct and reflected sunlight to reach adjacent facades. In addition, lightcourts should shade low-angle sunlight that is difficult to control at the facade and redirect that light into the buildings (case study B3).

Forms and Devices to Achieve Sunlighting Objectives

Optimizing sunlighting in lightcourts requires that all elements be considered for their possible contribution to redirecting light into the enclosing buildings.

Orientation and Massing

In planning for lightcourts, the massing of the adjacent buildings should be adjusted to allow the lightcourt to capture sunlight when and where it is desired. Orienting the lightcourt axis east/west will result in the equator-facing facades receiving the maximum number of hours of sunlight. The north/south facades receive sunlight at high angles that are easy to shade and redirect into the building.

Reflectances

Any light not accepted into the sunny-side facade should be redirected to the shady side by the use of light-colored surfaces. This is of increased importance in narrow spaces, where the upper building surfaces that first ''see'' the light *must* be light-colored. Ground materials should be selected and placed to reflect light into the adjacent buildings; pavement, water features, sitting areas, and sculptures should all be sensitive to the concern of reflected light. Trees may be used to provide shade in the courtyard as well as pleasant views, but they should be placed carefully so that they do not shade critical light-reflecting surfaces such as the building facade.

Suncatcher Trellises

Light-colored trellises may be better than trees if shade is necessary, as trellises can simultaneously redirect the sun onto the surrounding building surfaces above themselves.

Suncatcher trellises are best used to shade windows from low-angle sun that is difficult to control with fixed shading at the facade itself (fig. 8–28). Lightshelves and suncatcher trellises make a splendid solar-control combination. North/south trellises allow high-angle sunlight to penetrate but convert low-angle sunlight from the east and west to diffused reflected sunlight. It is important to shade only as much as necessary. At the GSIS building, for example (case study B3), the cut-off angle is 45 degrees one way (fig. 8–29). Light above 45 degrees is controlled with lightshelves at the facade. There should be no shading of the high-angle sunlight reaching the north and south light-redirecting facade elements at midday. Solid spandrels of high reflectance may be shaped and oriented to act as suncatchers, to redirect light to adjacent and facing facades if not into the room they enclose. When more precise control is desired, tracking mirrored louvers can be used in lightcourts. With outdoor exposure, however, maintenance is more difficult and wide movements of reflected light by wind action are unavoidable.

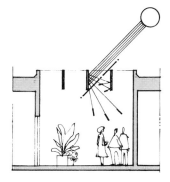

8–28. Suncatcher trellises control low-angle sun that is difficult to control at the facade itself.

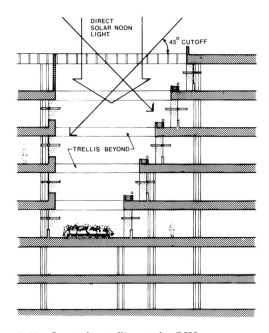

8–29. Suncatcher trellises at the GSIS building (case study B3) are combined with lightshelves for a complete sunlighting system.

LITRIA

A litrium is a form of atrium that provides the benefits of sunlighting to its adjacent spaces. While an atrium provides the delight of a glimpse of sunlight to people in the atrium, a litrium admits sufficient sunlight to illuminate the spaces adjacent to the litrium.

Architectural Context

Litria are useful when lighting in adjacent spaces is qualitatively and economically important (in offices, classrooms, etc.), and the space of the litrium itself is a desired architectural feature. Depending on the HVAC and programmatic considerations, the adjacent spaces may be physically open to the litrium or thermally and acoustically separated. The litrium floor may be used either as a work space or a public space.

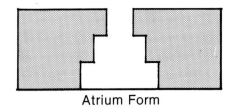

Atrium Form

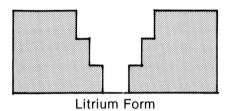

Litrium Form

8–30. Litria should be equal in width at top and bottom or wider at the top than at the bottom.

In order to minimize shadows and open the space to sunlight, litria should have a geometrical form that is equal in width at top and bottom or wider at the top than at the bottom (fig. 8–30). They should never be narrower at the top. The orientation of the litrium space and aperture is critical to maximize control of light; the guidelines for massing and orienting lightcourts are appropriate to litria as well.

Lighting

Litria are fundamentally different from atria in that much more light is desirable. This is due to the much greater area (the surrounding floors) that is using the light and the working illumination requirements of this area. The direction, quality, and quantity of light must be carefully controlled for maximum effectiveness. It is generally better to distribute light in litria to the interior facades, into work spaces, and onto the shady side, rather than to the floor (fig. 8–31). As in lightcourts, glare control in litria is important for the adjacent offices, but is also important at floor level if there is a work space there.

8–31. Light admitted into litria should be directed into work spaces rather than to the floor.

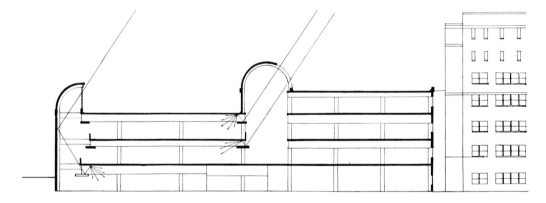

HVAC

Efficient use of light and high reflectances are more important in litria than in lightcourts because they are enclosed spaces. As with atria, the enclosed spaces in litria may be conditioned, tempered, or buffered as necessary to suit the programmatic needs. As a by-product of the additional light they receive, litria will usually have a larger solar/HVAC load than atria. It is therefore very important to take advantage of seasonal light variations to get as much sun as possible during the heating season. This will help save money in electric lighting and heating as well as increase the pleasure of "basking" in the sun during the winter (fig. 8–32). Conversely, severe operating cost penalties can result if litria are incorrectly designed, and more sunlight is admitted than is useful.

8–32. The litrium at Soddy Daisy High School (case study C1) has a large south-facing clerestory that provides maximum light and heat in winter, less light and heat in summer.

If light is being well utilized during the summer, the cooling load necessitated by the additional sunlight can be justified economically (see case study H1). There is an unfortunate tendency to reduce the amount of light too much in summer to minimize the cooling load, necessitating the constant use of purchased electric light (which produces more heat than a similar amount of sunlight). If litria use sunlight efficiently, they can have a more positive effect on cooling loads than atria, because they require electric illumination both for themselves and for the surrounding spaces.

In litria, even more than in atria, it is important to use whatever sunlight is admitted as light *before* it becomes absorbed by darker surfaces as heat. *Use it twice.*

Forms and Devices to Achieve Sunlighting Objectives

The specialized lighting requirements of litria begin with careful design of the sunlight aperture to suit the intended use and climate. Skylights, clerestories, sunscoops, and lightscoops should all be considered; more often than not, however, the most appropriate aperture will be a combination of sunscoops and lightscoops. A well-designed sunscoop-shaped aperture will flood a litrium with sunlight in the winter and allow an appropriately limited amount of summer sun to enter. The effectiveness of lightscoops can be augmented with the addition of suncatcher baffles. Other exterior architectural elements such as overhangs, fins, baffles, and roof reflectances should be exploited as well (figs. 8–33, 8–34).

The glazing considerations and recommendations for litria are identical to those described for atria, with an increased emphasis on the actual quantity and distribution of the sunlight.

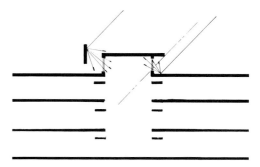

8–33. Suncatchers, baffles, and overhangs make litria apertures more effective.

8–34. Suncatcher baffle on the Westinghouse World Headquarters building: (a) exterior; (b) interior. (See also case study B5.)

a

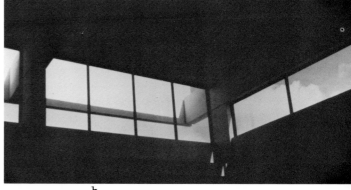

b

The exacting degree of light control required in a litrium may merit the use of tracking mirrored louvers to beam sunlight (fig. 8–35). Litria provide an ideal environment for locating louvers so that they are sheltered from wind and pollution. An interior location will sacrifice some thermal benefit compared with an exterior location, but this will be more than offset by the vastly simplified maintenance. The louvers should have a polished specular surface on one side (to beam sunlight) and a light matte finish on the other (for the heat-rejecting mode). Dynamic louvers may have insulative value for reducing nighttime heat loss. When beam-

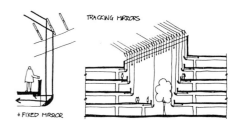

8–35. Mirrored louvers can be used to beam sunlight to adjacent work spaces.

ing sunlight from litria to work areas, use secondary specular reflectors at the work space/litria interface to ensure the sunlight is beamed to an appropriate receiving surface above eye level (see case study B7).

Because litria supply light to adjacent interior work spaces, the interface between work space and litrium deserves special consideration. The interior facades of the litrium can be glazed to isolate it thermally and acoustically from the work space, while still allowing light to enter. If the litrium is to be conditioned, the facades may be left open and unglazed (see case studies B1, B5, and B7). This option is somewhat more energy efficient, as the light loss incurred by the second layer of glass is removed. However, this option may be restricted by fire codes.

With or without glazing, the configuration of the *interior* sunny wall of the litrium should be designed as an *exterior* sunny wall: it should be shaded and may have lightshelves. Litria provide a protective environment in which mirrored lightshelves may be used without excessive maintenance. The interior shady facade will receive light reflected from the sunny wall and will benefit from increased atria view and interior lightshelves that reflect light up to the ceiling.

It is reasonable to assume that not all areas of the litrium and surrounding work areas will have the same lighting needs. After general ambient light is provided for, local conditions should be attended to. As in atria, litria should use local shading as needed. Fabrics can be used on the interior for this purpose, as can trees and furniture.

Litria and atria almost always contain plants, which should be arranged to work *with* the sunlighting system. Keep them clear of important light-reflecting surfaces, and use them for shading as needed. This may create a conflict since most plants can be maintained most easily with direct light.

LIGHTWELLS

A lightwell is generally a utilitarian, uninhabited shaft or slot within a building, whose primary purpose is to provide natural light and ventilation to adjacent spaces. As such, lightwells have fewer architectural considerations than the other types of toplit shared spaces.

Architectural Context

Small lightwells can add excitement and relief to the interior of deep buildings. With a relatively small planar area of 25 to 400 square feet, the "event" of a lightwell may be emphasized or remain discreet. Lightwells may have operable glazing opening into them from the work space, or mirrored lightshelves and other sunlighting elements may form an interface between the lightwell and the work space. When lightwells are glazed and uninhabited, maintaining maximum reflectances (specular surfaces) can be easy. A common programmatic use of lightwells is their integration with vertical circulation. When this is the case, glass block or open steel mesh can be used for stair treads and platforms. This will allow deep penetration of ambient light.

The aesthetic benefits of lightwells are somewhat limited. At best, they offer views of sunlit surfaces that provide some biological information and communication with the outdoors. Lightwells can provide minor communication across their width, via small windows, although they are not noted for this. In many buildings, they are so discreet that they are not visible at all.

Lighting

Lightwells can provide sidelight to adjacent spaces and toplight to bottom spaces (figs. 8–36, 8–37). When used only for toplighting, the interiors can be mirrored for maximum reflectance (fig. 8–38). Because of the small size of lightwells, the sunlighting aperture is almost always a full skylight. Tracking mirrors can be used to maximize collection and control of sunlight in narrow apertures and spaces; however, this is rarely cost-effective at this scale. Because of their tall, narrow proportions, glare is unlikely to be a problem.

HVAC

Lightwell apertures may be glazed or open to the sky. When open, lightwells can offer ventilation and vertical circulation of building systems. They may also be glazed or open to the work space. When the area between lightwell and work space is glazed, lightwells serve as thermal buffers with no thermal penalty for overlighting.

8–38. Mirrored lightwells have been proposed for the Canadian National Gallery (Moshe Safdie, Architect) to light the lower galleries.

8–36. New York State Education building, Albany (Palmer & Hornbostel, Architect): lightwell with side-lighting apertures.

8–37. New York State Education building: the grand first-floor rotunda ceiling, toplit from lightwell.

⑨ Sunlighting Building Systems

In chapters 6 and 7, the importance of high ceilings for optimizing the distribution of sunlight was explained, and the forms and devices that can be used in conjunction with higher ceilings were presented. However, relatively low ceilings (8'–8'6" or, on occasion, 9') are what one generally associates with those buildings that could most benefit from optimum sunlighting—office buildings.

Why are these ceiling heights typical? Low ceilings have become the norm because they are easy to design. No coordination of building systems is required when four to six feet of building height are used between the ceiling and the floor above. A flat low ceiling does make partitioning simple and economical, and high ceilings are not so important if daylight is not being used and illumination is from closely spaced recessed fluorescent fixtures.

However desirable they are for sunlighting, can owners afford higher ceilings? I believe they can not only afford them on a cost-in-use basis, but that they can be had with no increase in first cost or in total building height. Essentially, there are two ways to achieve higher ceilings:

1. add to floor-to-floor height;

2. make more efficient use of building volume (ceiling space).

The first way (adding to the floor-to-floor height) is costly and therefore is rarely used for general building types. Floor-to-floor heights are usually minimized to reduce construction costs or to increase the rentable space within the allowable building volume.

The second way of achieving high ceilings requires that all building systems be designed to meet the goals of efficient space utilization. *If building system designs are integrated, most of each floor can have 11' to 12' ceilings with no increase in floor-to-floor height over a conventional building.* In some cases it is possible to actually *reduce* floor-to-floor height simply through more efficient integration of systems.

Most contemporary air-conditioned buildings are very wasteful of building volume. Look at a typical building just before the acoustic ceiling tile is installed; you will find that the low ceiling height was established by the *combined* depth of the deepest duct, beam depth, and recessed lighting, even though the major ducts actually occupy very little area (less than 5 percent) of the ceiling area (fig. 9–1). In such homogenized designs (fig. 9–2), each system—structural, mechanical, lighting, and ceiling—is given its own layer so that designers need not bother to coordinate their placement. The result is a waste of valuable ceiling height. A building with a floor-to-floor height of 14′ typically devotes 5′ to the above systems.

9–1. In most contemporary buildings, ceiling height is established by the combined depth of the deepest duct, beam, and light fixture. In this case these elements have been intentionally left exposed (Pompidou, Museum, Paris—Piano and Rogers, Architect).

Two undeniable benefits of this wasted volume are flexibility in placing partitions against the flat ceiling and almost unlimited freedom to move services within the ceiling due to the great redundancy of volume. By physically integrating the concerns of the primary structural and HVAC systems (and, to a lesser degree, partitioning, secondary structure, acoustics, plumbing, and so on), spatial efficiency can frequently be increased even with flat ceilings and no sacrifice in flexibility. Integrated systems with exposed structures can achieve the ultimate spatial efficiency. I believe that their beauty and operating economy outweigh any associated loss in flexibility.

This chapter will discuss how to achieve articulation and harmonious ordering of the various building systems and how these principles can help achieve the goals of sunlighting.

While the following principles and techniques are economically indispensable in sunlit buildings, most other buildings can benefit as well.

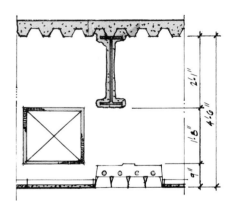

9–2. Section of the systems within the ceiling of a typical steel-framed building.

OBJECTIVES AND BENEFITS OF INTEGRATING BUILDING SYSTEMS FOR SUNLIGHTING

Maximum Ceiling Height

As previously explained, high ceilings improve the distribution of reflected sunlight and indirect supplementary electric light, as well as allowing for high windows.

High-reflectance Ceiling Cavity

High reflectance means maximum lighting efficiency. It is easier to ensure high-reflectance finishes throughout ceiling cavities when they are distinctly articulated from other surfaces. Natural architectural breaklines (e.g., from deep exposed structures) can help ensure achievement of the desired finishes in the coffer regardless of the finishes (fig. 9–3).

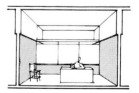
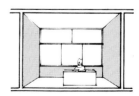

9–3. Natural architectural breaklines (such as those that are created from deep exposed structures), can help ensure and extend high-reflectance ceiling cavities.

Integrating Building Systems 171

Integration of Sunlighting Elements

This is the primary opportunity to integrate sunlighting elements into the architectural form. In addition to allowing high ceilings, integrated structural and HVAC systems can provide physical support for large sunlighting elements such as lightshelves, vertical fins, and suncatcher baffles and help achieve visual cohesiveness, so that these devices appear to be a natural part of the architecture instead of tacked-on devices.

Structure as Shading

Exposed structures can become an integral part of a building's total shading pattern. Columns can provide vertical baffling; girders can be used for lightshelves (fig. 9–4).

Integration of Electric Lighting

Supplementary electric lighting elements can be integrated, aligned, and supported by making them a part of the architecture, illuminating the same surfaces as the sunlight.

In addition to the above, there are numerous distinct architectural and perceptual benefits to articulated/integrated designs. High ceilings give visual spaciousness and less constriction and claustrophobia in large spaces. Perception of structure is reassuring, and delegation of services to certain areas can improve service access for maintenance. Architectural diversity and interest is encouraged, and options are created by the addition of elements and lines.

To achieve these objectives, we have to work with the following systems (usually covered up with ceiling tile):

Primary structure—girders, beams;

Secondary structure—slabs, joists;

HVAC—main ducts, feeder ducts, VAV boxes, flex ducts, pneumatic lines, hot and cold water piping;

Electrical—lighting fixtures, conduits;

Plumbing—sprinkler piping, roof leaders, sanitary piping, etc.

The degree to which these systems can be integrated is often dependent on the amount of design (actual or conceived) that has occurred prior to the establishment of effective sunlighting or high ceilings as a design goal.

FIRST STRATEGY (if general design of building is set)

This strategy involves no change to the structural system but requires more efficient organization of elements below the structural plane. The controlling element, HVAC ducts (the largest, most challenging system to integrate), should be concentrated in areas less critical to sunlighting performance.

9–4. Girders are positioned to provide shading at the Wellesley Science Center. They would be even more effective for distributing light if the top surfaces and the emergency exit grating above were light in color (Perry Dean and Stewart, Architect).

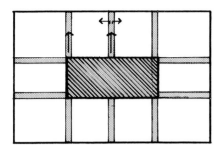

9–5. Radial distribution of major ducts.

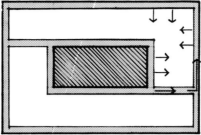

9–6. Major ducts arranged in loops.

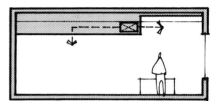

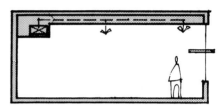

HVAC Treatments (with no change to structure)

The discussion of HVAC systems is limited to those that have centralized air handlers and a network of ducts. Other systems, such as a four-pipe system with fan coil units, take up much less space, although placement of the equipment should be coordinated with the needs of sunlighting.

HVAC elements can be organized in two general ways: the most common is a radial pattern in which the perimeter is served by ducts emanating from the core (fig. 9–5). The second pattern consists of two or more "loops" connected by several radial "spokes" (fig. 9–6). With either method, ducts running out to the perimeter (perpendicular to windows) are best placed parallel to the primary structure. Ducts that must run perpendicular to the structure should be smaller and carefully placed to minimize the combined depth. The largest ducts should be routed between beams; duct size should be reduced before rather than after crossing the deepest structural members. Ducts and recessed lights should be planned so that they do not overlap. In many buildings, these steps alone can serve to increase the height of flat ceilings.

Ceiling heights can be articulated in the following ways to provide high ceilings where desired and lowered ceilings for services, where needed:

□ Raise ceiling at perimeter (fig. 9–7). Relocate ducts if necessary to increase the width of the raised perimeter zone. Keep large ducts in the interior;

□ Use separate ducts for interior and perimeter zones (fig. 9–8);

□ Create false beams to enclose ducts in order to maximize the high ceiling area (i.e., to feed the perimeter zone).

Ducts can be moved out of the ceiling plenum to decrease the thickness of the ceiling sandwich:

□ Float ducts in space and expose them with minimum blocking of light (see case study B4);

□ Combine ducts with lightshelves to help glare control and light distribution (fig. 9–9 and case studies B2 and B5).

9–7. Ceiling heights can be articulated without moving ducts; moving major ducts inward increases area of high ceiling; minor runs can be enclosed in "beams."

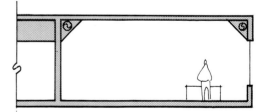

9–8. Separate ducts for interior and perimeter zones.

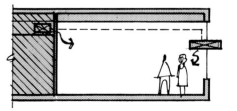

9–9. Combine ducts with lightshelves for perimeter HVAC loop.

First Strategy 173

Lighting Treatments

Interior building surfaces can be streamlined for maximum effective reflectances:

☐ Enclose highly articulated ceiling structures (waffle slabs, exposed joists) to minimize trapped light;

☐ Avoid recessed fixtures where they would cause ceilings to be lower; use indirect lighting mounted lower in the space. Also consider surface-mounted or pendent fixtures and local task lighting.

Other Systems

Other systems should be located in such a way as to minimize interference with sunlighting:

☐ As with HVAC, concentrate placement of plumbing, sound systems, and the like in areas less critical for sunlighting performance; avoid excessive system depths.

SECOND STRATEGY (if design can be integrated from the beginning)

A structural system should be selected and developed that is totally integrated and articulated. This is the most effective strategy, allowing the underside of the floor slab above to be the ceiling.

When selecting a structural system, the building program is a primary consideration; for example, the large spans in a gymnasium will necessitate a different system from that required for fully partitioned offices or classrooms. The physical requirements of proposed types of mechanical and electrical systems must be allowed for, and the *net perceived ceiling height* should be considered (i.e., a 12' ceiling may feel like an 8' ceiling if a network of pipes and ducts exists at the 8' level).

Some structural systems that favor integration and articulation are listed here and described in detail below.

For unilateral and bilateral sidelighting:

Flat slabs

Deep exposed concrete beams

Paired beams

Boxed steel framing, trusses

Two-level structures

For multilateral sidelighting:

Flat slabs

Modified slabs

Haunched beams

Steel framing with haunched beams

For toplighting:

Concrete ''tree systems''

Large-scale channeled concrete structures

Boxed steel structures

STRUCTURAL SYSTEMS FOR UNILATERAL OR BILATERAL SIDELIGHTING

When a space is sidelit from two opposing sides, the most important requirement is that the primary structural system run perpendicular to the primary window wall(s). This will ensure the greatest daylight penetration. One-way structures are perfectly suited for the requirements of bilateral sidelighting.

Concrete Slab Systems

Flat Slabs

For short spans, flat slabs are the thinnest system. When the primary structure is a flat slab, there is freedom to locate services, but a suspended ceiling is still necessary unless all services can be exposed or services can be organized and boxed into lowered soffits or false beams. Use the thinnest flat slab possible to leave the most space available for services. Flat slabs can be combined very successfully with paired beams to channel services.

Waffle Slabs

Waffle slabs should be avoided. They require depth but do not allow horizontal services to penetrate. Waffles are very good at trapping light because of their extensive surface area (fig. 9–10).

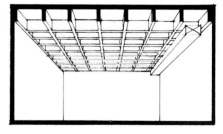

9–10. Avoid waffle slabs that trap light, require depth, and do not allow horizontal services to penetrate.

One-way Joists, Ribbed Slabs, Pan Joists

The structural benefit of one-way joists, ribbed slabs, and pan joists is a somewhat reduced weight for increased spans. Some services can be contained within them, they are thicker than flat slabs, and their additional surface areas trap light (although somewhat less than do waffle slabs). Pan joists are somewhat better for lighting than waffle slabs and may be adequate for enclosing local services (fig. 9–11). Minimize shadows by running ribs perpendicular to fenestration.

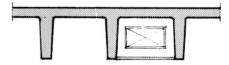

9–11. Pan joists can enclose local services.

Deep Exposed Concrete Beams

Beams must run perpendicular to the primary windows for reasonable light penetration.

Consideration should be given to the perception of space created

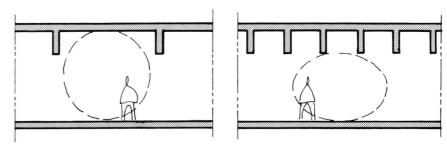

9–12. Wide beam spacing versus close beam spacing.

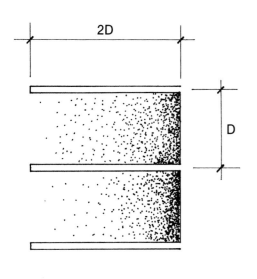

9–13. Plan view of beams and light distribution. Wider beam spacing distributes light deeper into space.

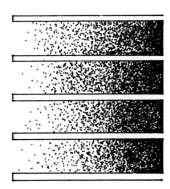

9–14. Extended beam depth at the Blue Cross/Blue Shield building (case study B1) allows plenty of distance from the ceiling for indirect lighting.

when placing beams. Wide beam spacing gives a more open feel than close beam spacing (fig. 9–12). Widely spaced beams (even if much deeper than smaller, closely spaced beams) do not reduce the effective ceiling height and relate better to human scale, but are worse for hiding services.

The spacing of beams is critical to their effect on sunlighting. Widely spaced beams trap less light and are better for light distribution than closely spaced beams, which are inefficient in reflecting light. To distribute light effectively from a lightshelf, beam spacing should be no less than ½ to ⅓ of the maximum seating distance from the window (fig. 9–13). Closely spaced beams will trap more light.

There are also advantages to increasing the *depth* of widely spaced beams. Deep exposed beams at maximum spacing oriented perpendicular to windows channel light into a space (case studies B1, B7). In the interior of a building (distant from windows), widely spaced beams are likely to receive more light than the adjacent ceiling because light from continuous windows will strike the beams at a less oblique angle. As important potential reflecting surfaces, such beams should be light in color. Light-colored deep beams will modulate light and improve brightness and illumination gradients. Deep beams can frame large clerestories and provide vertical louvering for them, minimizing sky glare. They can also be cantilevered to support lightshelves at the correct height (case studies B5, B7). Deep beams provide an opportunity for inconspicuously and economically integrating supplementary indirect electric lighting elements at the maximum distance from the ceiling, allowing for good light distribution. Beams may be made (or appear to be made) deeper than structurally necessary to achieve the above advantages. This may be particularly important in conjunction with the relatively shallow cross sections of steel constructions (fig. 9–14).

Paired Beams

A structural system of paired beams is proving to be one of the best systems for sunlighting. The unequal spacing provides regular channels to enclose ducts and other services and leaves the wider space "clean" for distributing and controlling light. Paired beams can therefore have higher effective ceilings than smaller, more closely spaced beams (fig. 9–15). The combination of paired beams and lightshelf-as-duct can allow the ceiling height to be virtually floor-to-floor (case study B5). The beam spacing module must be developed to accommodate the programmed space requirements. For example, a school's structure must be easily partitioned for stardard-sized classrooms. To increase the depth of the ser-

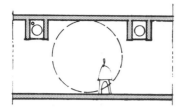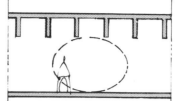

9–15. Paired beams (left) increase perceived ceiling height by creating room-sized coffers.

vice channel and create a larger natural clerestory, paired beams may also be oversized. Although making beams deeper than necessary will add to the structural cost, the total building cost may be lower because of reduced partitioning cost and simplification of other details such as support of lightshelves, better alignment or window framing, and so forth.

Boxed Steel Framing

Beams

Speed of erection, the need for thermal breaks, cost, or other reasons may make a frame of steel beams advantageous. In this case, the spatial and light distribution of deep exposed concrete beams and the service enclosure features of paired structures can be combined by boxing in the beams with fireproofing much larger than otherwise necessary to create false ''deep beams'' with sufficient clear space for the mechanical and electrical services (case studies B1, H1).

Trusses

If trusses are dictated by longer spans or economics, they too can be enclosed to contain services neatly and make deep one-way channels good for unilateral and bilateral sidelighting or for effective and efficient toplighting (case study D2). If the desired finished form is triangular, delta trusses may be the best choice because their lateral stability eliminates the need for cross bracing and provides the most unobstructed service channels.

Two-level Structures

For very large unimpeded blocks of bilateral sidelighted space, two-level structural systems may be the most logical. In such cases, the major structure of widely spaced deep beams can run perpendicular to the window walls, and a secondary structure can be placed on top to create a plane of continuous service channels connecting vertical service cores at the ends of the building. This secondary structure could be of steel beams and decking or concrete double ''T''s (case studies B1, B7).

STRUCTURAL SYSTEMS FOR MULTILATERAL SIDELIGHTING

For multilateral sidelighting, where windows on at least two sides are perpendicular to each other, flat ceilings are the only practical solution. If exposed beams run parallel to the windows, sunlight will be limited to the perimeter. Articulated systems are only acceptable for small buildings where most of the floor area is effectively perimeter. For larger buildings, the best solution is to use a flat ceiling and attempt to limit the thickness of the ceiling sandwich as much as possible. The best structural systems are modified two-way systems or columnar type systems. Two-level structural systems are not useful for achieving flat ceilings with minimal building volume.

Flat Slab

The ideal multilateral sidelighting system is a thin flat slab, with the largest ducts and services located in areas less critical for sunlighting. However, unless spans are very small, slabs cannot remain very thin, as they will not be strong enough to span large distances. (fig. 9–16).

9–16. Flat slabs are the ideal multilateral sidelighting system as long as services can be contained in areas less critical for sunlighting.

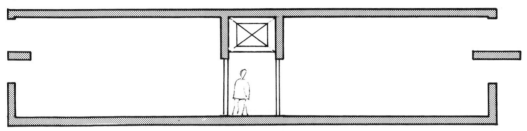

Modified Slabs

Larger spans can be achieved by using slabs of varying thickness. Dropping the column caps and thickening the slab at those points will allow the slab to be thinner in the middle. The thinner slab areas are used to run the ducts and other major services to minimize the thickness of the ceiling sandwich. A suspended ceiling can then be used to reduce surface area and improve acoustics (fig. 9–17).

9–17. Modified slabs can house ducts at their thinnest points.

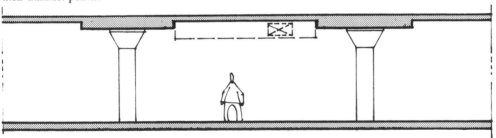

Haunched Beams

For larger spans or greater earthquake resistance, use haunched concrete beams instead of dropped column caps to allow for duct space with minimum average ceiling depth (see fig. 9–18 and case study B3).

Steel Framing with Haunched Beams

Even though a structure of steel beams can be shallower than one of concrete beams, the most efficient use of building volume would be to use the haunched beam principle suggested above for concrete. According to structural engineer William LeMessurier, such structures are most

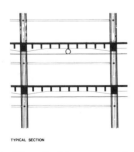

TYPICAL SECTION

9–18. Haunched beams can also contain services under their shallow zone.

efficient in the use of steel because the material is placed where most needed. However, the extra fabrication cost over standard beam systems probably cannot be justified unless the cost of wasted volume would be very high (as in buildings with many floors).

STRUCTURAL SYSTEMS FOR TOPLIGHTING

Concrete Tree Systems

"Tree" systems are integrated building systems with great potential for toplighting vast areas with great flexibility in planning. As independent cantilevered structures related to Frank Lloyd Wright's "mushrooms" in the Johnson Wax building and Felix Candella's "umbrellas," modules can be omitted to form courtyards or irregular edges, or individual units may be at different heights.

However, unlike the "mushrooms," tree structures contain coffers for integral indirect lighting or for skylights and are created to edge services placed between them neatly, in totally unimpeded open channels that can run in both directions. These functions are achieved by having "branches" radiating from the "trunk" to support perimeter edge beams. With such a structure, the panels filling the tops of the coffers can be omitted or pierced at any time for toplighting, and continuous clerestories or skylights can be placed between trees whenever the entire gap is not needed for mechanical ducts. In either case, the beams provide beneficial baffling. Great unity can be given to a project by the structural consistency of being able to use the same coffer form for indirect artificial lighting, daylighting, or a combination of the two, and by having unimpeded and neatly enclosed service channels in between or around every tree (figs. 9–19, 9–20).

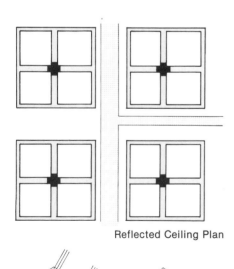

Reflected Ceiling Plan

Section

9–19. Systems can be routed between structural "trees."

9–20. The slabs of "tree" structures may be pierced at any point for toplighting apertures. (Governor State University, Park Forest, Illinois—Caudill, Rowlett and Scott, Design Architect).

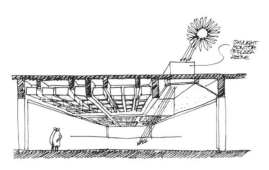

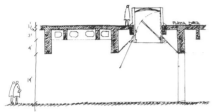

9-21. Large-scale concrete structures can also route services and be used advantageously for toplighting (see case study D1). (Courtesy of ARCOP)

Large-scale Channeled Concrete Structures

Other large-scale channeled concrete two-way structures can be flexible in routing services, but they are generally not as good as tree systems because the continuous clear spaces are likely to be limited. They are, however, more rigid. Similar to ''trees,'' large-scale channeled concrete structures are better for toplighting than for sidelighting (fig. 9–21).

Boxed Steel Structures

Steel systems should follow the same rules of direction and spacing as outlined for concrete structures. Because of the greater strength of steel, there is more flexibility in the sizes and shapes of the structural members used. Steel structures should be enclosed to maximize the desired light distribution characteristics (case study D2). Beams that must be fireproofed may be boxed in to increase their depth and hide services as well (case studies B1, H1). Long-span delta (triangular) trusses may be a good way to frame sunscoops when the lighting design suggests a triangular shape (figure 9–22). Boxed steel structures are easily insulated (a significant advantage over concrete), and provisions can easily be made for thermal breaks.

9-22. Steel delta trusses are ideal for extruded toplighting structures. Enclose steel structures for best light-distribution characteristics.

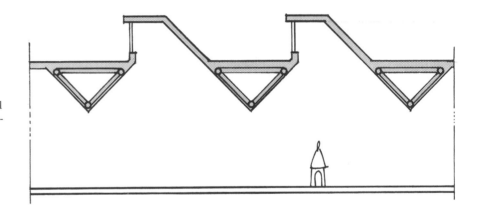

Secondary Structure

Secondary structures spanning major beams and girders are likely to be closely spaced. They may be steel beams or bar joists supporting steel decking or concrete slab, or they may combine beams and slabs in the form of single or double ''Ts'' (fig. 9–23). Whether or not the secondary structures are used to enclose HVAC ducts or other services, they should be covered by ceilings to achieve efficient sunlighting or indirect artificial lighting. Minimizing the surface area maximizes the effective reflectance (see fig. 3–16).

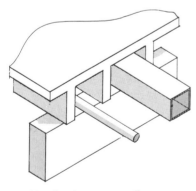

9-23. Two-level structures allow passage of services perpendicular to the primary structure.

Hollow-cored Slabs

Cored slabs (poured in place or precast planks) can span significant distances inexpensively. It is possible to run some limited services (such as wiring) through the cores one way; however, this is generally impractical as access is difficult (fig. 9–24). The bottom of precast plank may be an attractive high-reflectance finished ceiling. Because of their limited

9-24. Hollow-cored slabs are minimally useful for carrying services.

value for enclosing services, hollow slabs are logical only in building types with a limited need for these secondary service channels (i.e., houses, schools with through-the-wall air conditioning—see case study C1) or in more demanding buildings in which the plumbing, ducts, and other larger and more accessible requirements are accommodated within the primary structure via double beams, boxed steel beams, or within floating elements such as hollow lightshelves (case study B2).

In summary, building systems should:

☐ Control light distribution and glare;

☐ Enclose ducts and other HVAC equipment with a minimum of wasted volume;

☐ Integrate lightshelves, other sunlighting devices, and supplementary lighting elegantly.

Such integrated building systems cannot be achieved by the usual sequential design processes but require a team process in which *all* disciplines are involved with the project simultaneously and from the beginning.

SUPPLEMENTARY ELECTRIC LIGHTING SYSTEMS

Artificial lighting should be designed to supplement daylight selectively—to maintain a moderate level and distribution of ambient light that will dispel gloom and provide for the range of ordinary activities. Ceilings and other large areas of room surfaces can be illuminated so as to flatten out the normally uneven daylight gradients on these surfaces (figs. 9–25, 9–26). This will also improve indoor/outdoor contrasts. Indirect lighting minimizes the contrast and color difference between daylight and electric light. Downlighting does not help in this respect (figs. 9–27, 9–28).

Lighting hardware and the brightness patterns it generates should be designed to harmonize with the architectural forms and sunlight patterns of a given condition (fig. 9–29). Supplementary illumination should

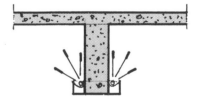

9–25. Indirect lighting fixtures on beams do not interrupt spaces; they provide brightness gradients that blend well with reflected sunlight because they illuminate both beam and ceiling.

9–26. Beam-mounted indirect lighting at the Carrier building (case study B2).

9–27. Direct lighting along beam illuminates only the beam, not the ceiling.

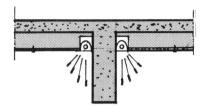

9–28. Direct lighting along beam does not blend with daylighting as well as indirect lighting (see fig. 9–25). Inappropriate fixture design produces distracting "scallops."

9–29. Library, Kimbell Museum, Fort Worth, Texas (Louis I. Kahn, Architect). Pendent supplementary fluorescent lighting perpendicular to vault axis conflicts with vault form, skylight form, and daylight distribution; it would have been better integrated with the skylight baffles. Note reflected sunlight from low strip windows.

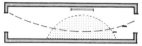

Natural Light Level
Supplementary
Electric Illumination

9–30. Supplementary illumination should be designed to fill in the gradients where natural light is lowest.

continuously fill in illumination gradients, following the "fit" of the sunlighting curves. For example, a bilaterally illuminated space produces a characteristic "saddle-shaped" sunlight distribution curve; supplementary illumination should therefore be greatest in the middle of the space and more moderate toward the perimeter (fig. 9–30). Similarly, sunscoops, skylights, and other apertures will all have distinct sunlight distribution curves for a given configuration and should be supplemented accordingly.

Locally controlled "task lighting" can be provided for special tasks for which the ambient light is insufficient or inappropriate. Such task lighting can be in the form of ceiling-mounted spots, pendant lamps, table lamps, and under-the-shelf fixtures.

Integrating lightcoves with the structure almost guarantees a high-reflectance ceiling cavity by making the beams an integral part of the lighting coffer. Fixtures should be contained in the beams or lightshelves if possible (or attached to or aligned with them). Electrically illuminating the same surfaces as the sunlight illuminates is the simplest solution visually speaking. When using the ceiling as a source of indirect illumination, it is important to use high-quality ceiling materials and careful detailing. For example, matte-finish T-bar joints are discreet when illuminated, but gloss-finish T-bar joints are glaring and distracting. Integration of electric lighting fixtures with beams and lightshelves should follow the alignment of the header/transom lines.

SUPPLEMENTARY LIGHTING CONTROL SYSTEMS

Interface between User and System

Electric lighting control systems provide the economic and energy savings in sunlighting designs. The amount of savings increases as more ambient light is provided by natural means and a similar quantity of electric light is displaced. Depending on the given condition, energy controls can be either manual or automatic.

In small buildings, or buildings where a maintenance staff (or persons with a vested interest) can be depended on to operate them, manual controls can be adequate. Controls should be provided that encourage use by providing switching for lighting in small areas, with switches located to discourage thoughtless use. User adjustment of sun-control devices (opening drapes, shades) can be "forced" by providing photoelectric controls that do not allow supplemental ambient lighting when adequate daylight is available.

Automatic controls can adjust sun-control devices as well as supplementary electric lighting. Sun-blocking devices (shades, movable insulation) and dynamic sun-redirecting devices can be controlled by simple time clocks or by photosensitive relays. So-called smart buildings can provide total energy management systems, which, controlled by a central computer, can start HVAC systems just prior to the advent of the working day, control electric lights based on occupancy and exterior conditions, and monitor security as well.

In most daylit office buildings, our primary concern is to coordinate the quantity of interior supplemental illumination with the amount of illumination provided by sunlight. This can be accomplished easily with a combination of photosensors to measure the quantity of sunlight, a microprocessor-based "logic" unit (which can be programmed to know how much natural light should be present in each area in relation to the exterior sensors), and a switching/dimming system to control the electric lights accordingly. Such systems should provide for some user control by providing a manual override for switching small areas.

Location of Light Fixtures

As previously explained, supplemental electric lights should be an integral architectural element, their location conforming to the forms and needs of the building. Generally, fixtures nearest the sunlighting apertures will be required the least; in sidelighting, for example, this implies that the perimeter lighting will be switched off first, and the center lighting last. This can be accomplished with fixtures running either parallel or perpendicular to the windows, as long as the switching arrangement is consistent with the predominant lighting gradients (fig. 9–31).

Location of Sensors

If the building is of an extruded nature, the spaces are open, or the partitioning is regular and the occupancy uniform, sensors can be located

9–31. Lighting switched off at the perimeter of the Blue Cross/Blue Shield building during the day (case study B1).

a SWITCHING

b "IDEAL" DIMMING

c FLUORESCENT DIMMING, STANDARD BALLAST

d FLUORESCENT DIMMING W/ ON-OFF, STANDARD BALLAST

e FLUORESCENT DIMMING, DIMMING BALLAST

9–32. The switching and dimming system chosen will affect the relative light level contributed from daylight (parabolic curve) or artificial lighting. The total actual level in each case is the sum of artificial and daylight illumination. (Reprinted by permission of *Solar Age*)

on the interior to measure illumination and switch or dim lights in large areas when the illumination exceeds a certain level. Illumination should be measured from a surface of interest (such as a desk top) and be consistent with the needs for that area as delineated in chapter 2. If partitioning or occupancy is very irregular, switching and dimming should be in small areas.

Sensors can also be located in a scale model of the space, mounted on the exterior of the model building. This is a very reasonable approach to take if there are many different facade conditions or if the space is particularly complex. (See case study B3.)

Dimming and Switching Systems

Switching is the least expensive lighting control system and can provide a large savings in energy use if properly used. Switching also produces the most noticeable changes in illumination ("lighting discontinuity"), which can be distracting for the occupants. If the switch occurs only once or twice a day, however, switching may be the best option (fig. 9–32).

With the natural fluctuations of sunlight, the quality and distribution of daylight in the room allows the light levels to drop below the established level for short periods of time without being noticed.

Dimming achieves the most graceful blending of artifical and natural light and can be virtually unnoticeable in use. Savings are generally more than with switching because they occur over a wide range, providing a more even overall lighting of the space. Dimmers consume some energy even when the lights are effectively "dimmed off." In addition, some lamp manufacturers will not guarantee their lamp if on a dimmer circuit. Unfortunately, most dimmers do not operate over the full range of light levels but switch on at the 50 percent light level. Improvements in dimming equipment and the eventual reduction in prices will probably make dimming systems more universal.

Dimming can be combined with switching for maximum energy savings and graceful transitions from artificial to natural illumination. This system is more expensive initally than either switching or dimming alone; however, it is a tiny part of an overall building budget and should provide a quick payback.

Don Aitken determined that dimming systems were cost-effective to a 50 percent dimming level and provided a three-year payback in retrofits for lighting energy saved. This payback period decreased to one year when cooling load savings were included. In a study for the Denver Tech Center (case study B6), the simple payback for the proposed dimming system (integrated with sunlighting and reduced installed cooling equipment) was determined to be thirteen months for the lighting cost alone, had the proposal been realized.

UTILITY LOAD MANAGEMENT

The final opportunity for integrating building lighting systems occurs beyond the walls of the building—with the surrounding buildings, community, and utilities. In large buildings where the peak load is for summer cooling, utility peak-load-demand switching can provide substantial savings for both the building and the utility. When the utility experiences peak load demand for the entire system (usually on summer afternoons), the building receives a ripple signal from the utility, which switches off the perimeter lighting. This reduction in peak demand means that the utility does not have to invest in expensive new reserve power plants, and the building will avoid paying for the most expensive peak energy price (see chapter 1).

In sunlit buildings, however they are controlled at other times, perimeter lights should be turned off during peak utility load times—on sunny summer afternoons.

$\textbf{10}$ Sunlighting Design Processes and Tools

Previous chapters have introduced the basic principles and forms of sunlighting. The case study section of the book will describe some actual buildings and their sunlighting features. This chapter examines the processes and tools that my firm and its clients have used to develop and test these forms.

THE TEAM DESIGN PROCESS AND SUNLIGHTING

The idea of design by team is not new. As William Caudill discusses in his book *Architecture By Team*, his firm (Caudill Rowlett Scott) began to talk about and refine the team design process in the early 50s (fig. 10–1). Their concept of the ''squatters'' brings the important people—client, architect, and other specialists—together in one place to design the building as a team in a few days. The benefit of the ''squatters'' process for any building is that it helps the architect and the client clarify at an early stage the values the project should exemplify. Because key representatives of the client are involved in the design process, the design that results becomes ''our'' design (as opposed to ''the architect's'' design). This often turns the clients into advocates for the design.

In chapter 9 integrated building systems were discussed. It should be clear that their level of complexity demands a team design process from the beginning. When designing sophisticated buildings with the kind of multiple, simultaneous goals discussed in chapter 1, the value of a team process becomes self-evident.

Using sunlighting adds another layer of complexity to the building's design. Not only must a building fulfill the client's needs; it must also respond to the variability of the sun's changing direction and intensity. People's reactions to the sun are also variable, according to the context. The decision to use sunlighting as a design strategy has an impact on, and must be followed through on, many levels. The sun affects the orientation and massing of the building on the site. Using sidelighting demands the high ceilings that integrated systems can provide. It is difficult to integrate structural and mechanical systems to achieve the high ceilings needed for indirect lighting economically; incorporating sunlighting makes it even more difficult. The direction of structure relative to the fenestra-

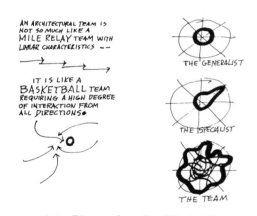

10–1. Diagram from Caudill's *Architecture by Team*. (Reprinted by permission)

tion thus becomes a major factor. The type of interior partitioning can aid or compromise sunlighting.

Follow-up on the final details of a project is essential—I have seen many designs fall short of their potential because the reflecting surfaces of lightshelves were never painted white or white gravel was not used on the roof surrounding a sunscoop. Sunlighting cannot be just the domain of another specialist—its values must be shared by all members of the team: they must want to create "our" sunlit building. It is ideal when members of the team can evaluate existing buildings together. It is well worth the expense, because it will develop common objectives and make it less likely that they will be unwittingly compromised later in the process.

SUNLIGHTING TOOLS

Sunlighting designs are site specific. They must respond to the context, both of the exterior site and of the interior program.

While the context and the principles outlined in this book may suggest sunlighting solutions, it is necessary to develop and evaluate solutions specific to the building being designed. The information provided here and your own further modeling of generic concepts will provide the basis for developing specific designs. Quick thumbnail diagrams based on sun angles derived from consulting *Graphic Standards* or using the L.O.F. sun angle calculator (available from Libby, Owens, Ford Company) will help you to understand the geometries involved. Examples of diagramming light have been given in chapter 3 and throughout this book. Using scale models is the best way to evaluate the designs that are developed.

Remember that the tool you choose should be appropriate to the task at hand. For the conceptual design phase, design tools need to be quick and interactive in order to allow the evaluation of alternatives without a great investment of time or effort. They can be quite crude; you need only information that is accurate enough to allow rational choices between alternatives. If we know that option *A* will produce better daylighting than option *B*, we need not, at the conceptual design stage, have very accurate values for either. In some cases, the important information is not really quantifiable at all, but is qualitative or perceptual. During the concept refinement phase, more accurate information may be needed, and more investment of time and effort is justified in evaluating the chosen concept. For the presentation phase, the client needs to be convinced of the effectiveness and success of the design. Since this success is often measured both quantitatively (in illumination gradients, KWH, or dollars) and qualitatively, a combination of tools may be required both to develop accurate quantitative projections and to express the qualities of the environment designed.

Programming

Once the actual process of design begins, the programming stage is obviously critical. Specific details about the use of each space or class of spaces will help determine their shape and detailing. As discussed in chapter 2, a descriptive performance criterion for lighting is much more useful than numerical footcandle specifications. Such a process can be extremely tedious and time-consuming. However, the exercise of having gone through such a systematic, detailed conceptualization process once is invaluable. An experienced designer goes through such a process almost unconsciously in the design of every space and is able to sum up occupants' activities, their biological needs, and the respective environmental implications in simple summary statements of objectives and design concepts.

Site Analysis

After the project's program has been well defined, the actual design can begin with the evaluation of the site and the exploration of architectural options. As many of the largest decisions in terms of overall form are set by the combination of program, site, and climate, this is the context within which the integration of building and comfort objectives must be considered. Site evaluation should include an analysis of microclimate and solar access. In the case of a building that is intended to rely on the sun and the sky for some of its light or heat, it is important to determine the shading on the site from surrounding buildings, vegetation, and terrain. A 360-degree map of the site horizon as seen from points of interest in the proposed building is needed. This can later be used in section studies, model testing, or overlays on sun path charts. While this information can be obtained with a compass and transit or Abney level, a device such as the one illustrated greatly simplifies mapping the local horizon and shading (fig. 10-2).

10-2. Evaluating solar access with the *Solar Pathfinder*® by Solar Pathways, Inc.

Concept Diagrams

After the relevant site characteristics have been noted, the conceptual design phase can begin with the integration of building and comfort objectives in the context of program, site, and climate. At this phase the directional nature of sunlight makes architectural section drawings an appropriate method of studying sunlighting designs. Buildings of a simple extruded nature can often be adequately explored by a single typical section (fig. 10-3). More complex geometries require multiple sections, plans, models, and so forth.

Plotting sun angles in section studies can evaluate the needs and suitability of sun control and redirection strategies. By diagramming light (chapter 3) it is possible to draw the intended effects of a given architecture and then adjust the architecture to produce the desired lighting condition. Since any window view is a potential source of glare, it is necessary to plot the actual sun angles for a given condition to find out if a problem exists. The sun angles relevant to a given situation can be ascertained quickly using a L.O.F. sun angle calculator or similar device.

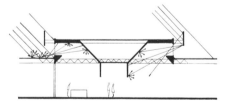

10-3. Diagramming light on a building section.

Scale Models

It may seem surprising to advocate the use of physical models for testing in an age when we have come to rely with confidence on mathematical models in many fields. In the case of daylighting, however, much or most of the lighting calculation data base was in fact derived from model studies, and these were of a limited number of conditions, some not realistic. Obviously, the most relevant model study is of the proposed design itself rather than an extrapolation from other studies.

Due to the extremely short wavelength and high speed of visible light, there is virtually no scale factor for lighting in scale models. This means that in a scale model constructed with reasonable accuracy and with representative glass transmission and surface reflectances, measured light levels from daylight will be identical to those in the real building modeled, given identical exterior illumination. In addition, by tilting the model, sun angles representative of a variety of latitudes and times of day may be simulated.

Both qualitative observations and quantitative measurements may be made from models. Since controlling the sun is the key to design studies, they should be conducted outdoors in natural light conditions. Artificial skies give a false sense of security in that they are steady and easily controlled, but they do not simulate the sun and sky accurately, if at all. Constantly varying light conditions make outdoor testing more difficult, but the benefits are worthwhile. The evaluation is much more realistic because of the similar variations in real buildings. Lighting differences that are hard to observe in a model will be equally difficult to observe in a building. The educational experience of doing real sky testing only once should create an indelible recognition of this phenomenon.

Making the Model

Crude "generic" models are useful to increase the base of understanding and experience for both experienced designers and students. They are also an effective quick way of evaluating alternatives during the conceptual design phase. They should be constructed out of sturdy and forgiving materials (such as homosote) to allow and encourage easy testing of alternatives (fig. 10–4). The geometries and surface reflectances should be approximately correct. I cannot overemphasize how important the reflectances are.

The typical white foamboard model makes any lighting arrangement seem reasonably even—a false impression unless the room will actually be all white. As with all sunlighting models, generic models should be light tight. Particularly with window areas that are small in relation to the floor area, small pinholes or cracks, or even the translucency of "solid" materials, can affect the results of testing. Light leaks will tend to even out illumination levels and obscure places where the variation in light levels within a space might prove objectionable.

Design models are the mainstay of the design evaluation, refinement, and illumination estimation processes (fig. 10–5). Accuracy is now of primary importance in modeling window size and mullions, in representing exterior reflecting surfaces and interior reflectances, in details, and in the massing of interior furnishings. Certain aspects of the model may be made interchangeable to test the effects of different facade designs, clerestory shapes, or the qualities of a sloped lightshelf. To reiterate: *if a design model is accurately constructed and tested, the normalized model illuminance measurements will correspond accurately to those in the final building.*

10–4. Generic model with various facades for testing sidelighting. (Photograph courtesy of John Lam)

10–5. Design model for a museum. (Photograph courtesy of John Lam)

The following is a helpful checklist for model construction:

☐ *Reflectances* of surface finishes should be modeled accurately to ensure representative appearance and data. Color need not be accurate except for presentation purposes. Specularity of a surface (i.e., the degree to which it is specular or diffuse) is also important.

☐ *Materials* used to make solid portions of the model must not be translucent to any degree nor have any light leaks. Some common materials such as foam board and thin cardboard transmit light and must be covered or painted to be opaque.

☐ *Openings* must represent the actual glazing area and position to be used. Ideally, a plastic glazing with equivalent light transmitting and reflecting characteristics should be used in a model. As a practical compromise, openings in the model may be left unglazed and a glazing transmission factor may be applied to the data afterwards.

☐ *Scale* of the model should be as large as convenient for handling, such as ½'' = 1'-0'' for large spaces or 1'' = 1'-0'' for small spaces. This will permit control devices such as louvers to be modeled accurately and facilitate the use of meters and cameras in the model.

☐ Provide *access* and *viewing ports* for meters and cameras. A lightproof hood or dark cloth is necessary during viewing for measurements or photography.

☐ Scale *furnishings* should be included in the more finished models to gauge their effect on illumination and glare control. They also enhance the model's appearance, giving scale and realism to the space. Realistic furnishings should make photographs of the model almost indistinguishable from the real space.

☐ Build the model strong enough to withstand moving, tilting, wind, and moisture.

Test Conditions—Orienting the Model

As explained in chapter 4, the sun's location and intensity vary throughout the day and the seasons. Because the variations are predictable, they can be simulated by tilting the model relative to the sun. Fixing a sundial to the model is the easiest way to determine the degree of tilt necessary (fig. 10–6). It is best to tilt the model no more than necessary; it is better to time the tests to take advantage of natural changes in the sun's altitude throughout the day. When a model is very large (as it was for TVA—case study B7 and GSIS—case study B3) it may also be impractical to tilt the model very much.

Comparisons of alternate designs will be most accurate if the geometric adjustments are minimal. For instance, if a model needs to be tilted only a few degrees to attain the desired sun angle, changes in the horizon characteristics will be less. Fortunately, when testing designs that utilize sunlight effectively, the contribution from direct sunlight is so dominant

10–6. Tilting the model with the aid of a sundial. (Photograph courtesy of John Lam)

that errors from inaccurate simulation of the rest of the ground and sky are minimal. Thus, if the time available is short, we can tilt the model as much as necessary instead of waiting for the ideal conditions under which little tilting is needed.

Variations in the sun's expected intensity relative to its intensity during testing conditions must be adjusted or "normalized" mathematically. (For example, if you are testing in July with 8,000 footcandles and the condition you are simulating is a December morning with 3,000 footcandles, the measurements must be multiplied by 3/8). If the actual glazing was omitted from the model, a *glazing factor* must be applied. A *maintenance factor* is applied to reflect loss in transmission due to dirty windows or atmosphere.

Ideally, tests and observations of the model should be conducted under totally clear and totally overcast skies, as these are the extreme conditions. At those times the illumination is likely to be very stable and the adjustments easier. Observing the model under partly cloudy skies is also useful to get a more complete understanding of real-world conditions, with the widely varying illumination that one normally does not even notice.

Observing and Testing the Model

When the model is properly constructed and oriented, both qualitative observations and judgments and quantitative measurement can occur.

10–7. Viewing the model through a viewing port. (Photograph courtesy of John Lam)

Qualitative Observations. Qualitative judgments are important. It is necessary to "put oneself inside the model" as much as possible. View and photograph through viewing ports, using blackout cloth to prevent extraneous light from entering the model (fig. 10–7). Careful observations may suggest alternative schemes or adjustments to the model that should be made *before* the laborious process of quantitative testing is begun. Consider if the light distribution is as desired. Are there distracting shadows or dim areas? Evaluate the contrast between the brightness of room surfaces and the window's brightness. How will artificial lighting be integrated?

Photographing the different schemes and the different seasonal and time-of-day scenarios will facilitate direct comparison. A wide-angle lens (e.g., 20 mm) is essential for photographing the model. It is very useful to place a legend describing the sky condition, time of year, and time of day within view on the model; otherwise, trying to reconstruct which slide represents which condition can be quite an experience. The inclusion of scale figurines and furnishings will help make your model indistinguishable from the actual building (see figs. B4–9, B4–10, D2–7, D2–8). Although the model itself is not constructed specifically for presentation, photographs of a sunlit design model can be a powerful presentation tool. Slides of the model may bring the concept alive in a way that drawings and sketches do not, particularly for laymen unaccustomed to visualizing in three dimensions. Visualizing the impact of light gradients is difficult even for most designers.

Model photographs are more useful for presenting design alternatives than viewing of the model itself. While viewing the model can create interest and excitement, problems of logistics and timing make *comparative* viewing and discussion of alternative designs under varying conditions almost impossible. With a photograph, everyone can be looking at and discussing *exactly* the same scene.

Quantitative Testing. Quantitative testing of the model is useful for several reasons. While we do not believe that single-number footcandle requirements are the criterion to describe what we like in a space, numerical measurements facilitate comparison of different schemes and evaluation of their respective economic impact. For one thing, mathematics is the only practical way to compensate for differences in the sun's intensity during model testing conditions relative to site conditions. Numerical measurements allow comparison of different conditions and of the distribution of light within the space. Careful modeling can be used to predict how much supplementary (electric) lighting will be required and when—sunlighting's economic impact.

Occasionally, when specific footcandle levels are relevant—as in museums with conservation requirements—model testing is an excellent way to determine if sufficient but not excessive illumination levels can be achieved. Modeling makes it possible to try various forms of dynamic shading and evaluate their impact on light levels (see case study D7).

Instrumentation

While the instrumentation required for quantitative testing and the concepts of adjusting the data are very simple, the practical realities are quite different. The number of steps involved in measuring, recording, adjusting, and presenting the data in a useful format make the process time-consuming and labor intensive. An additional complication is the fact that in most locales, perfectly clear days are quite rare. Even on days that appear perfectly clear to the naked eye, unnoticeable clouds make the sunlight intensity fluctuate rapidly and constantly and thus can multiply the number of measurements necessary to get consistent results.

Nevertheless, although time-consuming and expensive, real sky testing can be accomplished with nothing more than a simple hand-held or remote-reading illumination meter, worksheets, and a programmable calculator. Because I was forced to come up with data quickly on my initial sunlighting design projects, most of the data produced (and presented in the case studies) was gathered in this manner. Fortunately, we had sufficient budgets.

The problem with real sky testing is the fluctuation in sky conditions; for each test the different sensor locations need to be read under identical conditions. In addition to interior readings, you need an exterior reading in order to normalize the data. The exterior readings from before and after each test should be within 10 percent; otherwise, the variation has been too great and the test must be done over. If you have only one sensor, you will need a good system for repositioning it quickly and accurately. We used a stick with markings that slides back and forth in a track in the model (fig. 10–8). If you have a multichannel meter and several sensors, you will not have to move the sensors (fig. 10–9). Even this manual reading of the meter and hand recording of the data is a process infinitely slower than a microprocessor-based system that can read and record the sensors almost simultaneously (fig. 10–10). It is important that the sensors be located at an appropriate site such as horizontal at desk height for offices or vertically at picture location for museums. It is also important that the sensors are color- and cosine-corrected.

10–8. Repositioning stick and manual meter. (Photograph courtesy of John Lam)

10–9. Multiposition meter with sensors and data form.

10–10. Microprocessor-based system; one push of the button does it! (Photograph courtesy of John Lam)

Recently, William Lam Associates has made accurate model testing more affordable by creating a portable computerized instrumentation package that will work under the constantly changing light of the real world and rapidly check and normalize the figures, even under partly cloudy conditions. This eliminates many of the inherent advantages of an artificial sky with simulated sunlight, of which there are very few in the world.

Our system is based on a portable microcomputer that automates much of the data-gathering process. The computer takes repeated high-speed scans of the sensors inside and outside the model, averages the interior readings, normalizes the data for the simultaneous exterior conditons, and prints out both the numerical values and a graph of the data, saving all important information for that test on diskette (fig. 10–11). With this system, a single test takes only a few seconds, so that accuracy can be maintained without interference from the variations inherent in real sunlight and other exterior conditions. The immediate availability of results also makes the model an interactive, "what if" design tool. With

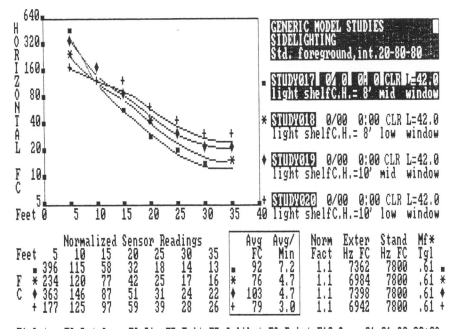

10–11. Computer printout.

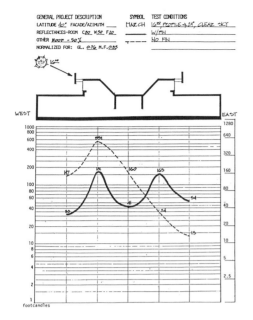

GENERAL PROJECT DESCRIPTION   SYMBOL   TEST CONDITIONS
LATITUDE 40° FACADE/AZIMUTH ____   MARCH   16° PROFILE ±24°, CLEAR SKY
REFLECTANCES–ROOM C.80 W.50 F.10   _____   W/FIN
OTHER ROOF – 50%   - - - -   NO FIN
NORMALIZED FOR: GL. 0.76 M.F.0.85

10–12. Section and testing results.

10–13. Plan and isolux graph; contour lines and shading show different levels of illumination.

this system, the most time-consuming task for the tester is to change design options in the model or to tilt it to obtain the proper bearing and altitude relative to the sun.

Presenting and Interpreting the Data

Some information can be read directly from the raw data, but it is easier to evaluate the significance of the data if it is organized in a format that facilitates easier comparison, such as a graph.

The graph should show levels of illumination at different places in the space. If illumination is graphed versus distance, the design's illumination curve will show the changes in the distribution of light in one dimension. It is helpful to place a scaled section drawing of the model above the data. This immediately indicates the relation of illumination values to the space (fig. 10–12). As explained in chapter 2, the *perceived* variation in illumination intensities will be more accurately conveyed if footcandle values are plotted on a log scale. The flatness of the curve represents the evenness of distribution of light. This is the most important qualitative characteristic of a lighting design.

With an irregularly shaped plan or a scheme that uses multilateral illumination, it is important to represent the changes in intensity in more than one dimension/axis. In this case, an isolux graph should be drawn over a plan view. This is similar to a survey map; it shows changes in levels through the use of contour lines (fig. 10–13).

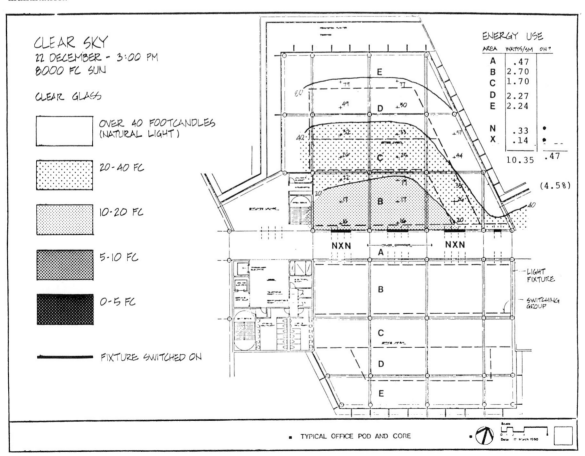

CLEAR SKY
22 DECEMBER – 3:00 PM
8000 FC SUN

CLEAR GLASS

OVER 40 FOOTCANDLES (NATURAL LIGHT)

20–40 FC

10–20 FC

5–10 FC

0–5 FC

FIXTURE SWITCHED ON

ENERGY USE

AREA	WATTS/SM	ON?
A	.47	
B	2.70	
C	1.70	
D	2.27	
E	2.24	
N	.33	•
X	.14	•
	10.35	.47

(4.5%)

LIGHT FIXTURE

SWITCHING GROUP

NXN   NXN

TYPICAL OFFICE POD AND CORE

In addition to the consistency of distribution, the amount (magnitude) of illumination is also important. Remember that we are most interested in data within the working range of human perception. Therefore, the difference between 1 footcandle and 10 footcandles is very significant, but the difference between 10 and 40 footcandles is barely noticeable. A change from 50 to 200 footcandles is even more insignificant in interior spaces, and measurements above 200 footcandles are generally not relevant for most spaces. The average illumination in a space *is* a useful number, especially if excessively large numbers are discounted. (Excessively high levels may represent small pool of direct sunlight falling on the sensor or measurements too close to the window, for example.) In qualitative terms, one number that *is* useful is the average to minimum ratio, because it indicates the perceived differences in brightness within a space.

Data from the model that indicate the average levels achieved by sunlighting is quantitatively important, because it is often necessary to maintain a minimum level of general, "ambient" illumination. If sunlighting is not sufficient, the artificial lighting will be turned on. If we can predict when artificial lighting will be turned on or off, we can quantify one aspect of how sunlighting will save energy. In practice, the nature of control systems and user actions have an equally important (and unpredictable) influence on whether the lights are turned on or off.

For this reason, modeling only provides the basis for a very crude "guesstimate" of lighting energy use. The lighting designer's guess— "Gee, we think that a fourth of the artificial lights will be switched on half of the time on overcast days"—is then combined with other data (such as weather data and HVAC analysis) in megacomputer programs such as the D.O.E.'s #2, or BLAST to create predictions as to building energy use and operating cost (fig. 10–14).

In some cases it is necessary to calculate the dollar benefits of sunlighting strategies in order to sell their increased initial cost. This was the case with several of the buildings discussed in the case studies. In any case, I believe that it is easier to sell the qualitative benefits of sunlighting, because calculating the economic benefits rests on many complex and "soft" assumptions. This may change over time as more buildings are monitored to see how *actual* performance compares with the *predicted* performance.

Mock-ups

The ultimate in modeling is a life-size mock-up. If the complexity of the project justifies it and the design concept has been established with confidence, building a full-scale mock-up of a representative portion of a building can be invaluable for studying the design details as well as for client communication. Although often perceived as an extravagance, the cost of a mock-up can sometimes be absorbed in the competitive bidding process. The mock-up used for the GSIS building in the Philippines (case study B3) was felt to be worth every penny, both by the owner and by the contractor who built it, because it provided the opportunity to test and finalize construction details (see fig. B3–20).

The mock-up also conclusively showed the client the desirability of the interior lightshelves and the importance of matte-finish T bars—con-

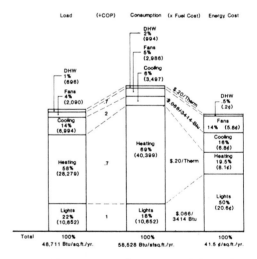

10–14. Energy use prediction. From left to right, graph shows installed BTU capacity; operating BTU use; and dollar cost.

cepts that are difficult to communicate without being in the space. In addition, there are always unexpected benefits in building a mock-up.

The greatest danger when creating a mock-up is that not enough care will be taken to finish the space accurately. If the mock-up is left unfurnished or unpainted, it is likely that the client will have a very negative impression, for reasons quite unrelated to what is being tested, and the original intent will be jeopardized. Care and forethought in communicating the mock-up's limitations can help to prevent this. Access to an incomplete mock-up should be carefully controlled to ensure that the necessary briefing has taken place.

Final Comments

Models are an easy and commonsense way to evaluate complex designs. Too often, models are only built to present finished ideas or to evaluate the building facade. The bias against exploiting the potential of models is strong. I have actually sat on a jury for a museum competition and listened to other members of the jury argue at length about the natural lighting potentials of the various schemes when a trip outdoors with the already available models would have instantly resolved their questions. For this reason, I believe that slides of the models under real conditions would facilitate discussion and comparison and should be required along with the models.

A useful exercise that will improve your understanding of daylight modeling is to model and test an existing space. This allows you to compare your perceptions and test results from a model with its full-scale version (figs. 10–15, 10–16).

10–15. Model photo.

10–16. Photo of actual building.

POST-OCCUPANCY EVALUATION

In any building, a post-occupancy evaluation is useful to see how well the design intent has been carried out and to examine how the building and its occupants interact. It is particularly helpful in assessing the value of techniques created for a new combination of objectives, such as sunlit buildings. Some quantitative criteria you might use are:

☐ Is the building meeting its lighting and energy goals as expected?

☐ Are there conspicuous areas of excess light or underlighting?

☐ Are the supplementary shading devices and electric lighting control systems functioning effectively?

☐ Is the lighting functionally adequate?

☐ How might the building be made more efficient?

Some qualitative criteria are the following:

☐ Is the lighting comfortable and enjoyed by the occupants?

☐ Is it attractive?

☐ Are there areas that are gloomy or dim?

☐ Are there areas that are glaring? Has it been necessary for additional shading (such as blinds) to be installed?

☐ How might the building be made more pleasant?

A thorough scientific post-occupancy survey is an ideal but infrequent occurence. A casual hour or two walk-through by an observant member of the design team can produce much essential information. It can remind the building's management to follow up on incomplete details; it can provide issues to consider for future designs. In the case of sunlit buildings, it is particularly important to notice whether people move shades and turn off lights in response to changing conditions. It is often necessary to encourage the occupants to regain control over their environment. Participation in the control of shading and lighting by the occupants can improve their feeling of comfort. Sensitive building management can make a significant impact on building energy use. Visits to finished buildings will influence my assumptions for future buildings. For example, for designs in the U.S. I would now prefer automatic control of dynamic shading and lighting with local override possible.

11 Sunlighting and Architecture

The aesthetically successful use of sunlighting in buildings requires that the associated forms and devices be conceived as an integral part of the architectural design, as much as floors, walls, and beams. Materials and finishes that have a role in shading or redirecting light must be in harmony with the total palette selected for the building. The scale, proportion, and rhythm of sunlighting devices should contribute to the whole, in deference to the larger order of the design (fig. 11–1).

My field observations and evaluations of a number of completed sunlit projects, both successful and otherwise, suggest that there are some general guidelines that can be applied to the design of sunlit buildings.

11–1. The Ventura Coastal Corporation headquarters office building in Ventura, California (Rasmussen & Ellinwood, Architect) gets its character from the horizontal lightshelves and the interesting transition to the unshaded north side. Each orientation's interior and exterior forms are directly expressive of sunlighting design. The window-facade treatment of the offices is appropriately interrupted for a buffer-space lobby area. (Photograph by Michael Urbanek; courtesy of Scott Ellingwood Associates)

USE A SINGLE, EFFECTIVE SUNLIGHTING/ENERGY CONCEPT

Designers working with sunlighting for the first time may become over-enthusiastic and attempt to use as many methods and devices as they can include in the design. The result can look like a catalog of all the possible sunlighting forms and devices, sometimes combined with passive and active solar devices as well (fig. 11–2). As with any design, the use of a strong central theme with variations is more unified and satisfying.

a

b

11–2. While the individual spaces are pleasant enough, the Mt. Airy Library (Mazria and Charlotte, Architect) suffers from too many sunlighting techniques (sometimes overlapping) for such a small building. For example, clerestory forms that are simple in one interior zone (a) are filled with additional louvers in the next; the visually "busy" toplighting system is extended to the perimeter (b) where the handsomely detailed window/wall alone would have been sufficient (as demonstrated in the adjacent perimeter spaces).

Making the best use of the selected technique will reduce the number of supplemental techniques necessary. A single technique well executed will often be the most cost-effective solution as well. Additional techniques, beneficial by themselves, may be only marginally beneficial (or redundant) as supplementary elements.

SELECT AND OPTIMIZE THE SUNLIGHTING METHOD FOR A GIVEN DESIGN PROGRAM

It is very important to select a sunlighting technique that is in harmony with the intended character and program of the building. For example, forms such as litria have an enormous impact on the entire design; they create a major central space which in turn orders the entire space-planning process. The first and most critical requirement of a successful sunlighting technique is the enthusiastic support and commitment of the client. A client who is opposed to the open office landscaping or glazed partitions necessary for light distribution from a litrium cannot derive maximum benefit from a litrium building.

The successful technical design of a sunlighting system will not ensure an elegant and satisfying work of architecture. Good sunlighting performance can be optimized by the proper building orientation, by having shading redirecting devices of the right proportions for that orientation, climate, and programmed needs; and by having an appropriate amount of aperture. But producing good architecture requires that sunlighting performance be balanced against other design considerations such as site conditions, views, placement, and design features of neighboring buildings. Order, scale, proportion, and clarity are additional design considerations. The technical design considerations of successful sunlighting only add to the already overwhelming complexity of architectural design and challenge the talents of the best designers.

The scale and volume of atria welcome the addition of major sculpture, as part of the building forms themselves as well as independently created sculptures (fig. 11–3). Interior landscaping of an atrium enhances the sense of contact with the exterior and takes advantage of the high light levels within such spaces. If the atrium is intended to have the character of an outdoor space, selection of materials and finishes should be appropriate to an exterior environment (fig. 11–4).

11–3. 84 Wyman St., Waltham, MA (Anderson, Beckwith, and Haible, Architect). Atria are a natural location for displaying sculpture. Here, sculpture (by Michio Ihara) is integrated with the sunlit wall.

11–4. Galleria Post Oak Shopping Center, Houston (Neuhaus & Taylor, Architect). The use of indoor materials—carpeting and plaster—makes this space seem like an indoor space despite the amount of direct sunlight admitted onto the skating rink in this hot climate.

11–5. Medium-scale devices interfere with views.

If a litrium is created to provide lighting for adjacent office spaces, it cannot, as a by-product, help but be the major space and focus of a building, demanding a high level of design quality in terms of materials, finishes, and detailing.

If the work spaces illuminated by the litrium are open to it without glazing, the intimate relationship between the offices and the litrium makes the design quality of all elements of the litrium, including its landscaping, even more important than that of a courtyard within sealed buildings. In the latter case, one *might* look out of the window or walk in the courtyard. The litrium *demands* that one does.

But both the landscaping and the materials and finishes of the litrium should not handicap excessively the use of natural light in the adjacent spaces—the major purpose for which the litrium was created.

SELECT SUNLIGHTING ELEMENTS WHOSE SCALE IS APPROPRIATE TO THE OVERALL BUILDING CONTEXT

As discussed in chapter 6, sunlighting devices of various scales may be employed; the scale chosen must be considered in relation to the occupants of a building, to the structural system and module, and to the overall building context. A small number of larger-scale elements are best for sunlighting performance. A facade that utilizes overhangs and light-shelves or larger-scale louvers to shade and redirect the sunlight is more effective than one that relies on medium-scale louvers. More important to building users, large-scale devices tend to frame views, while medium-scale devices break up and compete with views (fig. 11–5). At the other extreme, very small-scale louvers (miniblinds) are relatively inconspicuous, appearing as a texture or screen rather than as a competing pattern.

Architecture versus Hardware

A seeming fascination with hardware is evident in many buildings where shading or redirecting of light is accomplished by add-on devices such as louvers. These devices seldom have any inherent visual interest yet tend to attract attention by their incongruity with the forms and materials of the building. They thus assume undue importance within the context of their use. While the light weight and the temporary appearance of brightly colored canvas awnings are appropriate and attractive for sidewalk cafés or even low-rise office buildings, they would be hopelessly out of place on the sides of a granite high-rise office building. Similarly, the use of relatively fragile metal awnings or louvers on an otherwise "permanent" facade will seem contradictory at best; the entire sense of building quality will be affected. While these devices are designed to be operable, it is important to recognize that they are subject to failure and misalignment (fig. 11–6). Off-the-shelf items often have a character of anonymous ubiquity that lessens the individuality of a design.

A more satisfying solution is to design the *building* to perform functions of shading and redirecting light, within the context of the structural system and exterior materials of the building. Extended beams and floor slabs can provide shading and baffling. Lightshelves of concrete or metal can provide both shading and redirection of light, and at the same time be an integral and permanent part of the building facade.

Textural Scale

When it is necessary to provide small-scale operable shading devices to supplement permanent devices (such as on a west facade where the complete shading of late afternoon sun is difficult to achieve), they should be located on the inside of the building for protection, exterior appearance, and ease of operation and maintenance. Such interior shading devices generally sacrifice very little in terms of energy performance (compared with exterior devices) when they are supplemental rather than primary shading devices.

It is important to remember that when retracted, small-scale devices such as roll-up shades and venetian blinds are not things of beauty or visual interest; emphasizing them only detracts from the architecture. Visual baffling in the form of a valance or ceiling pocket will make such devices less conspicuous by placing them outside of the normal field of vision (fig. 11–7).

On the exterior, the deeply shaded windows of sunlit buildings help bring order to a facade because they shadow any interior disarray. For example, recall the contrast between Boston City Hall and the adjacent JFK building, where disorderly blinds behind unshaded windows form a dominant pattern on the facade (see fig. 6–44).

11–6. Mechanical sunlighting elements are subject to failure and misalignment. They also tend to make buildings look like sun-control machines or hardware displays.

BE SENSITIVE TO THE ARCHITECTURAL IMPLICATIONS OF SUNLIGHTING FORMS

The most pervasive implication of sunlighting design is the three-dimensional articulation of building elements. The spatial qualities of light require that its use and control be three-dimensional. The most efficient and economical way to obtain the forms necessary to control sunlight is to make them an integral aspect of the architecture, articulating beams, floors, and columns, to achieve sunlighting goals. The resulting forms are in direct opposition to the planar, smooth-skinned, scaleless boxes designed in defiance of the sun. Because these forms are highly articulated, they may be conspicuously ugly if ungraciously designed, or very handsome in the hands of skillful designers.

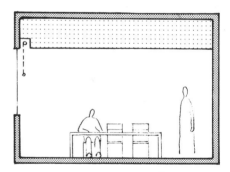

11–7. Visually baffle small-scale elements on the interior in recessed slots.

Environmental Influences

Sunlighting design implies careful control of solar gain and interior climatic conditions. As such, each building should reflect the environmental conditions of the site. Granted, there will always be solutions that can defy any environmental influence on their form by a technological tour de force (like the double envelope of the Hooker Chemical building, see fig. 6–95), but the more economical and reliable approach is to adapt the building's form to the site. This implies that the different elevations of a building will have different configurations or proportions. Regional differences will evolve as designers respond to local sunlight availability and climate.

Human Scale

Sunlighting performance benefits from the high ceilings created by the integration and articulation of structural and mechanical elements. The resulting interior spaces are more generous and interesting, and there is a genuine relationship between structure, space, and human scale. The value of a lightshelf as a human-scale reference device should be self-evident—the proportions that determine the size and location of the light-shelf are those of human beings. In turn, interior lightshelves can serve to establish an organizing line for door heads, window mullions, glazed transoms, partial-height partitions, and indirect or valance lighting (fig. 11–8). Regardless of the absolute dimensions, the addition of elements proportioned for the use and needs of humans will result in a more comfortable and intimate space.

This is true on exteriors as well as interiors: the human-scale influence ''demystifies'' buildings by enabling people to count the number of floors a building has and thus establish a sense of their relationship to the building. At night, the depth of the sunlighting aperture creates lantern forms, illuminated by the interior lights spilling out through the high-transmission glass (fig. 11–9).

11–8. The human scale determines the location of organizing lines.

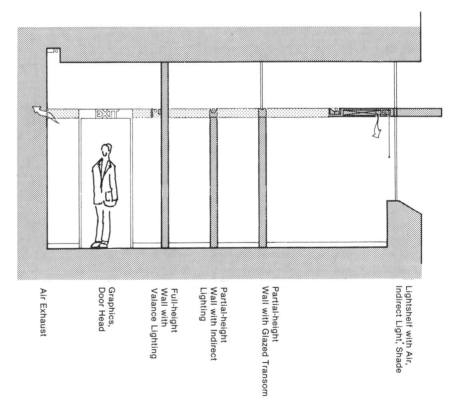

Air Exhaust

Graphics, Door Head

Full-height Wall with Valance Lighting

Partial-height Wall with Indirect Lighting

Partial-height Wall with Glazed Transom

Lightshelf with Air, Indirect Light, Shade

INTEGRATE AND COMBINE DEVICES
FOR VISUAL SIMPLICITY

If you were to ask an architect about his or her design for a particular room, it might be described in terms of its spatial or emotional character, its programmatic "fit," or even the contextual, historical basis for the color scheme. The architect would probably not address the issues of light fixtures, speakers, air diffusers, or venetian blinds. In many buildings, however, these items inadvertently command more visual attention than any other design element. In part, this is due to architects' abandonment of their role as designers in the areas of lighting and HVAC. These areas are ceded to engineers and salesmen, whose priorities are quite different, and who are not likely to be sympathetic to the design.

It is my belief (and probably that of any architect who cares about the quality of the interior environment) that these supplemental hardware items are similar to small-scale shading devices in that their visual presence should defer to the architectural elements and furnishings. (A chandelier or other light source that is intended as a focal point is an obvious exception.) The only way this can be assured is for these elements to be recognized and planned for as part of the building. Integrating these elements into the design will allow them to be visually baffled.

For example, in buildings designed for sunlighting, a major portion of the supplemental artificial lighting should ideally illuminate the ceiling and blend imperceptibly with the reflected sunlight. While suspended linear indirect fluorescent fixtures could provide such light efficiently, such fixtures tend to break up the space and create a lower, implied ceiling plane. A better strategy is to make use of the available architectural elements to support, blend with, house, and conceal lighting hardware. Inexpensive fluorescent strip fixtures can be combined with lightshelves and beams by providing an architectural pocket for the purpose. All the elements we do not want to see (light fixtures, speakers, air grilles) should be hidden in the shadows of pockets or reveals. Conversely, the surfaces and objects we enjoy seeing should be highlighted.

11-9. The "lanterns" of the Tarble Arts Center (case study D2) at night.

USE HIGH-QUALITY MATERIALS

More often than not, sunlighting design designates the ceiling as the primary source of indirect lighting from sunlit sources or fluorescent fixtures. As the most apparent source of illumination, the ceiling materials used are critical to the character of a space. When there is a choice, use the highest quality materials and craftsmanship in those areas where they will be noticed. When acoustical tile ceilings are used, concealed spline grids are preferable. If exposed "Ts" are used, they should have a nonglare, matte finish. Tiles with regressed edges tend to make "Ts" less dominant.

Acoustical tile is often chosen as the ceiling material not for its acoustical properties but to allow easy access to the ceiling plenum. With a carefully integrated building system, the areas requiring access are confined to a small area, freeing up the majority of the ceiling for installation of plaster or gypsum board (fig. 11–10). In concrete framed structures, the ceiling finish can be as minimal as paint on the underside of the floor slab above (except for office landscape areas requiring maximum acoustic absorption).

Integrated systems create ceilings with variety and visual interest. In addition, integrated systems, by their nature, require less ceiling material than monolithic suspended ceiling systems, and thereby make more expensive, higher quality materials more affordable.

11–10. A well-integrated building system at Complex G, Quebec Government Center (Fiset & Deschamps, Gautier, Guite, Jean-Marie Ray, Architect).

DIAGRAMMATIC DESIGN VERSUS POETRY

A good technical solution is not necessarily aesthetic, of course, but it need not be an impediment to beauty either. Looking at the schematic diagrams of sunlighting techniques in this book, you might think that the proposed architectural devices and forms could become very monotonous if widely applied. I must confess that the case studies presented suggest that trend at first glance. This is not surprising, since they represent the first generation of such applications in the work of a single consultant. However, the rigorous application of sunlighting concepts should increase rather than decrease the opportunities for design talent and taste

11–11. Poetry in motion. Sweeping curves combine beauty and function in Aalto's Mt. Angel Library, Oregon.

to be demonstrated. There is no reason for all sunlit buildings to look alike; indeed, they need not "look" obviously sunlit at all.

Understanding the concepts involved allows designers to achieve diagrammed sunlighting goals with the poetry of inspired means. The work of Aalto and Utzon is exemplary; their beautiful sweeping curves function without compromising their diagrams, which may well have shown straight lines (fig. 11–11). The dominant horizontal exterior lines of Wright's Robie house were enhanced by the need for deeper shading on east and west facades. The elegant floating lightshelf forms and their interruption by a central greenhouse-buffer entrance lobby at the Ventura, California, office building designed by Scott Ellinwood create a delightful contrast to the typical boxlike buildings of the area. When integrated solutions are sought to solve multiple problems in the most economical attractive fashion, enrichment of details naturally occurs. Witness the elegance of the lightshelves at the Hawaiian Medical Services building, which are sculptured to channel rainwater (fig. 11–12).

Solving interior problems adds richness as well. Steps in the ceilings to accommodate pockets for flexible museum lighting, as at the Tarble Arts Center in Charleston, Illinois, make much richer, more interesting forms than the monotonous pure geometric coffer forms of I.M. Pei's West Wing addition to the Boston Museum of Fine Arts (figs. 11–13, 11–14).

Perhaps new, unexpected forms will evolve as sunlighting concerns are blended with other programmatic requirements. Problem solving can create interesting designs based on simple diagrammatic concepts. Affection for preconceived forms should be avoided. Buildings should not

11–12. Hawaii Medical Services building, Honolulu. A creative solution to a pragmatic problem (the need to channel rainwater) adds the richness of detail.

11–13. Tarble Arts Center (case study D2). Positive integration of supplementary lighting, air diffusers, and lightshelves into the design of the coffers gives them richness and elegance.

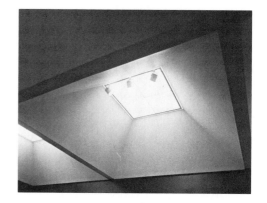

11–14. The "pure" geometry of the coffers at the Boston Museum of Fine Arts is interrupted inelegantly by unintegrated fixtures seen against the uniform and uninteresting glow of the white translucent diffusers.

seek their identity and beauty from faddish styles and arbitrary abstract forms; many creative solutions can result from responding to multiple goals such as the energy and human comfort aspects of sunlighting, local context, and site restrictions.

Designers should be able to use sunlighting strategies without creating a conspicuous "sunlighting building" look. Perhaps the best design is one that appears to be an adaptation of local indigenous building forms (figs. 11–15, 11–16).

11–15. HOK's airport design in Riyadh is an excellent example of sunlighting as an integral part of an elegant work of architecture. The toplighting aperture, in particular, is integral to the structure. Clerestory windows and light-reflecting ceilings are richly composed and detailed. The forms created seem appropriate to the character of Middle Eastern architecture rather than a mere imitation of historical details.

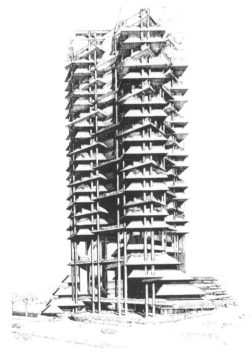

11–16. In his Dharmala Office Building, Paul Rudolph created a high-rise variation on the indigenous roof forms, which utilize overhangs for shading and ground-reflected light for illumination. In this building, the facade will provide shading and building-reflected light; the soffits will be finished with white tiles to maximize reflected light. Indirect fluorescent light will blend with reflected daylight on the high ceilings of the perimeter rooms. (Courtesy of Paul Rudolph)

SUNLIGHTING AND ARCHITECTURE—AN EXAMPLE OF POSITIVE INTEGRATION

In his design for the new National Gallery of Canada in Ottawa, architect Moshe Safdie has illustrated that following the rules of good sunlighting design with balanced judgment need not restrict a designer to mechanistically repetitive forms.

Although the greatly reduced glazing areas and the consistency of their orientation make this museum quite different from those following the classical mold of the last century (such as the Louvre and the Boston Museum of Fine Arts), it will be appreciated no less as a "classic" piece of architecture from without and has far superior galleries within (figs. 11–17, 11–18).

11–17. Safdie's National Gallery of Canada, model view. The design is a "classic" museum form with visible skylights. (Photograph courtesy of Moshe Safdie)

While the galleries within the impressively scaled multistory block are consistently oriented to face only north and south (for easiest sunlight control), Safdie has created an interesting variety of interlocking gallery cross sections. Tested in models and full-scale mock-ups, these gallery types will all use the modest amount of sunlight and skylight admitted efficiently and simply (figs. 11–19 to 11–22).

11–18. A ''grande'' circulation arcade. (Courtesy of Moshe Safdie)

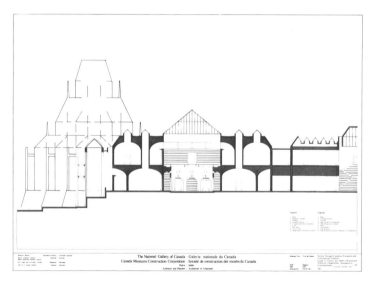

11–19. Section shows a variety of toplit galleries lit by both skylights and clerestories. Extensive glazing is limited to the circulation areas, atrium, and arcade. (Courtesy of Moshe Safdie)

11–20. Daylit model shows building cross-section. (Photograph courtesy of Moshe Safdie)

Unlike Kevin Roche's overglazed Lehman Wing at the Metropolitan Museum of Art in New York, extensively glazed roofs at the National Gallery of Canada are limited to public circulation spaces where the sunlight from such extensive glazing can be used and appreciated without handicapping displays or damaging art objects. Judging from the variety of spaces and structural forms combined in a building with a classical demeanor, it appears that thoughtful consideration of sunlighting principles need not handicap the invention and aesthetic judgment of the most talented architects.

I believe that some of the following case studies similarly demonstrate this potential. Others accomplish at least some elements of note.

11–21. Model view of typical toplit gallery. (Photograph courtesy of Moshe Safdie)

11–22. A typical side/toplit gallery: (a) model; (b) mockup. (Photographs courtesy of Moshe Safdie)

a.

b.

PART: II CASE STUDIES

GROUP A Urban Design and Site Planning

The orientation of streets, building alignment, and solar envelope zoning, as advocated in chapter 5, are not easy to control given the usual constraints of the real world. Control of design on the scale of city planning is most easily accomplished under strict administration. It is more frequently *possible*, under somewhat equivalent situations, when a single design team is responsible for the design of an entire community.

Examination of two such contemporary projects indicates that consistent orientation favorable to sunlighting can and is being done. Probably not coincidentally, both projects are in Saudi Arabia, where the visible evidence of past attention to the sun is difficult to ignore.

In the first example, referred to as "A military academy in the Middle East," the buildings themselves gain from their orientation for shading, but not from conscious efforts to optimize the benefits of sunlighting. Although involved with the project from the beginning, I must admit that at that period of time (1974) my attention as a building systems consultant was focused predominantly on creating integrated building systems with artifical lighting. I did not try to maximize the potential of sunlighting.

In the second case (still in the design phase), here referred to as "A university in the Middle East," the architects and planners have maintained excellent orientation and spacing of the buildings and also indicated conscious attention to using sunlight for building illumination through lightwells and light-reflecting courtyards. In this case, I hope to take full advantage of the sunlighting potential created. The proposed application of sunlighting in a typical academic building in this master plan is presented in case study C3.

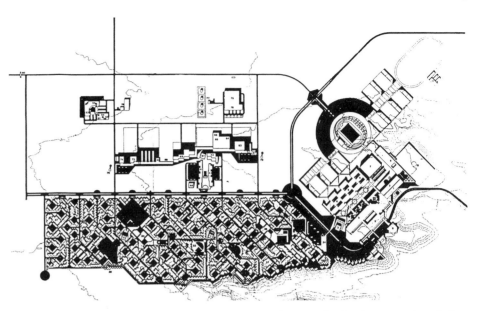

A1–1. The site plan. All buildings are aligned with the cardinal points, even though the major circulation is aligned otherwise. (Courtesy of CRS)

A1–2. Family housing illuminated by reflected sunlight through shaded openings, with the largest openings facing north and south and smaller bands facing east and west. (Courtesy of CRS)

A1 A Military Academy in the Middle East Riyadh, Saudi Arabia

CONTEXT

Latitude 24.2°N

Architect: Caudill Rowlett Scott/
McGaughy, Marshall &
McMillan—joint venture
architects (Charles Lawrence,
Louis Finlay, and Truitt Garrison)

Consultants: William Lam
Associates—lighting and
building systems

Construction completed: 1984

This was a project with few design constraints. The design team began by selecting the community site within an assigned property of 200 square miles. The site selected was a plateau overlooking a very small village to the south. With no particular views, landmarks, trees, or any constraints except the desire to be visible from the roads below, the layout of the entire community was up to the discretion of the design team.

The design team had responsibilities that included programming and the design of academic facilities and housing for 3,000 students plus faculty and staff, and all of the supporting facilities of an isolated community one hour's drive from the nearest city. The project needed to get its own water and dispose of its own waste. Thus, the constraints were self-imposed by the program and architectural objectives.

A primary influence was the client's request to recognize the Saudi lifestyle in the design. CRS senior VP Charles Lawrence (and several of his associates) had extensive experience working in Saudi Arabia, having previously designed the College of Petroleum and Mining and a great deal of Saudi housing for Aramco. Thus, the planning throughout both the academic and housing complexes reflected the influences of densely packed buildings and shaded streets. Since scarce water made dependence on large trees for shading unrealistic (water is recycled), the project was designed with the assumption of relatively little vegetation and hence a greater dependence on orientation, overhangs, trellises, and other forms of man-made shading.

DESIGN

Housing

The site plan (fig. A1–1) shows multilevel family housing units designed around courtyards. The predominant orientation of glazing is to the north and south, even though the major circulation paths are 45 degrees from the cardinal points. The reflected sunlight into buildings of the limited dimensions of residential-scale rooms should be adequate without special provisions (fig. A1–2).

Central Campus—Academic Buildings and Cadet Housing

The elongated blocks of academic buildings and cadet housing arranged around a series of trellised courtyards are even more clearly aligned in an east/west direction (fig. A1–3). The north/south-oriented trellises created by extensions of the structural system across all courtyards (figs. A1–4, A1–5) only partially baffle the noontime sun (which can be easily controlled at the facades), but provide more complete baffling of the low sun from east and west.

These buildings are well shaded by overhangs and baffle walls. Even with limited fenestration, the perimeter rooms of the cadet housing are reasonably daylit, but the academic buildings are too deep to be illuminated adequately by reflected sunlight without deliberate design effort to do so. Instead, they were designed with well integrated indirect fluorescent lighting that at least blends well with whatever natural light is admitted (fig. A1–6).

SUNLIGHTING POTENTIAL

It is easy to see that the overall planning scheme optimizes the possibilities for sunlighting in any buildings in which natural lighting is given the high priority it deserves. Although the direction of major avenues of circulation changes with topographic and other influences, the actual buildings are not compromised and remain consistently oriented north/south. While it might appear that sunlighting would be easy in complexes of low buildings such as these, the opportunities afforded by access to sunlight are not created without deliberate effort at the planning stage, as is evident here.

Since my interest in sunlighting began long after this project had been designed, the buildings are well shaded but do not take maximum advantage of sunlighting potential. With the favorable orientation and solar access created by the master plan, however, any renovations or future buildings can easily do so.

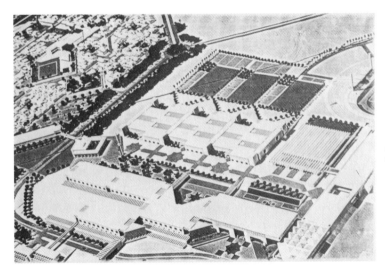

A1–3. Academic buildings and cadet housing. (Courtesy of CRS)

A1–4. Courtyard shaded with extended structure. (Courtesy of CRS)

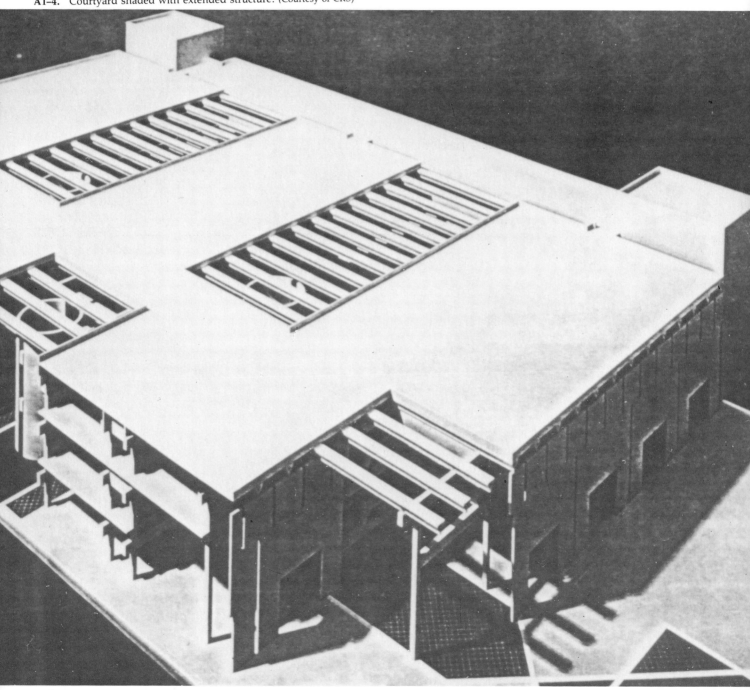

A1–5. Courtyard from the inside.
(Courtesy of CRS)

A1–6. Interior of academic building.
(Courtesy of CRS)

A2 A New University in the Middle East

Latitude: 23°N

Architect: Campus Consortium
Consultants Ltd./The Webb
Zerafa Menkes Housden
Partnership/Arthur Erickson
Associates—joint venture
architects

Consultants: William Lam
Associates—lighting

CONTEXT

In designing a new university for 12,000 students, the architects inherited a previous master plan but had few design restrictions from the earlier work, since little had been constructed.

I had been part of the original team that had designed a mega-structure-type integrated precast concrete building system (related in plan to that of Berlin Free University) for the men's campus. In this scheme, academic buildings and housing were totally separated.

Years later, with a change in administration and requests for a more "low-tech," indigenous approach, a new team lead by Arthur Erickson created a design much more strongly based on the architectural traditions of the region.

In joining Campus Consortium Consultants Limited during the design development phase, I was pleased to find that the architects had established a master plan and schematic building designs for the men's campus that seemed to recognize fully the sunny, hot, but humid coastal climate (fig. A2–1). Their project report, an excerpt of which follows, related the planning and architectural concepts used to those of traditional Arab settlements:

> It was noted that courtyards with at least two sides as narrow as two-thirds their height provided adequate shade within the yard at most times of the day.
>
> In courtyards having two sides considerably longer than the others, it was observed that the long walls (which consisted of the largest percentage of the total court wall area) remained in shade the most when the long axis of the courtyard was east/west. This orientation was thus well suited for those courts that were intended to have many openings in their walls. The courts within each department of a faculty are a good example of this type of use.
>
> The long, narrow courts with their long sides along the north/south direction provided maximum shading on the floor of the yard, while exposing the wall to considerable amounts of sunlight. This type of orientation works well for those courts or streets that have a heavy pedestrian use and whose walls are shy of openings and essentially inward looking. All the central streets and courts in each of the faculties are good examples of space of this nature.
>
> Consequently, two different orientations for courtyards were established. Those which serve as visual relief and a source of light and view but are not heavily used themselves should be oriented east/west along

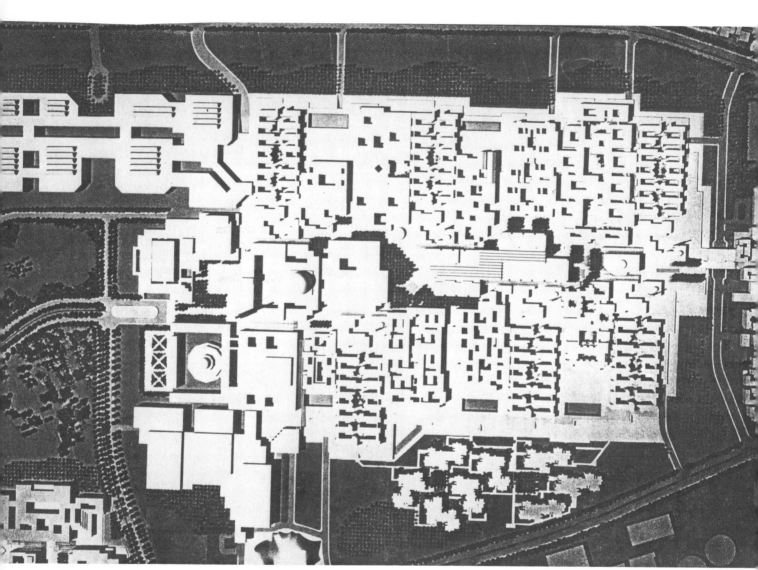

A2–1. Master plan. (Courtesy of Campus Consortium)

their long side so as to give maximum sun protection to their transparent walls while offering a bright, garden-like view to the rooms around it. The others, which offer a shaded ground area for heavy pedestrian use while their walls become an opaque insulation to the sun (thus lighting the shaded areas indirectly by reflecting the sun), must be oriented along the north/south axis wherever possible.

Islamic design principles were to be the core of the project's design philosophy, including the Madrasa (Institute of Higher Learning) tradition of combining learning, worshipping, and living as a continuous fabric in each faculty, the organization of Arab settlements, and traditional architectural forms for dealing with the climate.

While detailed design of sunlighting had not yet been done, the building forms created at the planning level had been influenced by shading and ventilation studies as well as by traditional forms. Although optimizing the illumination of interior spaces had not been thoroughly studied, the resulting design based on shading considerations and traditional courtyard ventilation did turn out to be good potential sunlighting as well, and assured that effective detailed design would be possible.

Men's Campus

The basic concepts behind the design of the men's campus were the following:

☐ Auto circulation and parking below the podium, blending with grade at its edges;

☐ On the podium, a settlement of closely spaced, low (3–4 story) masonry buildings in the wall architecture style of the Arab world;

☐ Main pedestrian circulation on an east/west axis. Widest paths and main plazas on this axis give maximum sunlight exposure to walls that are easiest to control (north- and south-facing);

☐ Secondary circulation paths between faculties on a north/south axis to keep them shaded and cool. Closely spaced walls to shade and redirect sunlight to the facing windows (act like suncatchers) (fig. A2–2);

☐ Within faculties, most rooms to face north and south to inner courtyards. North/south suncatcher trellises could be used to shade east- and west-facing windows and redirect light to all rooms; and

☐ Building blocks to be narrow enough to have daylight penetration to most spaces or to be provided with lightwells, mostly elongated east/west (fig. A2–3).

The men's campus was planned as a dense settlement of academic facilities and student housing. It includes twelve faculties or institutes (faculty of economics and administration, faculty of engineering, faculty of earth sciences, etc.), each including classrooms, offices, mosque, and dormitories.

With such a mixture of uses within each institute and a range of in-

A2–2. Courtyards sized and oriented to act as both shading devices and sun catchers. (Courtesy of Campus Consortium)

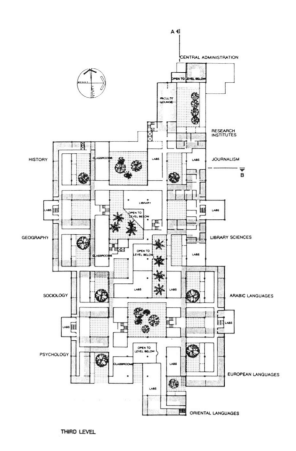

CENTRAL ADMINISTRATION

OPEN TO LEVEL BELOW

FACULTY LOUNGE

RESEARCH INSTITUTES

HISTORY

CLASSROOMS

LABS

LABS

JOURNALISM

LIBRARY

OPEN TO LEVEL BELOW

LABS

LABS

GEOGRAPHY

CLASSROOMS

LIBRARY SCIENCES

OPEN TO LEVEL BELOW

LABS

SOCIOLOGY

LABS

LABS

ARABIC LANGUAGES

LABS

PSYCHOLOGY

OPEN TO LEVEL BELOW

EUROPEAN LANGUAGES

CLASSROOMS

LABS

ORIENTAL LANGUAGES

THIRD LEVEL

A2–3. Building blocks elongated on an east/west axis. (Courtesy of Campus Consortium)

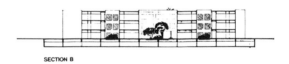

SECTION B

stitutes of very different sizes and functional requirements, the various faculties are all quite different in layout, although similar in style.

Sunlighting Design

Fenestration and building systems indicated in the schematic design documents indicated general approaches but not studied solutions. In both cases, the final designs will probably be much different. However, since the sun's movement was recognized in the orientation and massing of buildings and layout of streets and plazas for solar access and shading, the original fenestration and building systems need merely be refined to take advantage of the opportunities created.

Our master plan report for the lighting of campus and buildings included sidelighting concepts for sunlighting and artifical lighting, involving both fenestration and interior building systems, that should be applicable throughout the range of buildings planned. The design process has been halted awaiting administrative reorganization. When design development is resumed, the toplighting concepts will also undergo refinement.

The concepts I developed for sidelighting in a typical academic building in this development are presented in school case study C3.

GROUP B Offices

Office buildings are probably the most important opportunity for using sunlighting to benefit society in this period of history. A great deal of energy can be saved. More important, work can also be a more delightful and productive experience in airy, high-ceilinged spaces than in the gloomy, low ceilinged, light-fixture-dominated spaces most common today.

In the United States, office lighting currently represents a substantial portion of the electric energy used in buildings, due to the amount of office space that exists, hours of use, high illumination levels, and almost total neglect of natural light.

In typical office buildings, lighting represents over 50 percent of the energy used. Because electric energy (for lighting) is much more expensive per unit of energy (Btu) than coal, oil, or gas (used for heating and cooling), lighting represents an even higher portion of energy dollar costs. In addition, lighting costs include replacement of lamps and maintenance of lighting fixtures.

While artificial lighting must, of course, be provided and used at night, on dark days, and in portions of a building, its use can be minimized, and in many cases almost eliminated, by exploiting the sun. Our national electrical energy load is at its peak demand on hot, sunny, summer days. By reducing cooling costs through shading, and offsetting heat gains from equivalent electric lighting, the savings from using well designed sunlighting in both the existing and new stock of offices can be important both to the economics of individual owners and that of the country. In addition, fewer generating plants are needed if peak loads are reduced.

Other countries of the world, which cannot afford to follow wasteful U.S. practices in office building design, should continue to design around natural light (rather than join the "high-tech style parade" to be "modern"), but could refine their techniques by more careful study to optimize performance, especially to accommodate open planning, should they develop the need for large, deep floor areas. Typical office buildings in most countries (and in U.S. before the advent of office landscaping in the '70s) are quite narrow, with rooms only about fifteen feet deep, and buildings with double-loaded corridors less than forty feet wide. Many buildings in the U.S. are more than twice as deep and therefore much more difficult to light from distant perimeter windows.

Good sunlighting is important to office workers everywhere, since most spend long work days at visual tasks, with limited freedom to move their work positions or the tasks themselves to accommodate glare conditions (unlike library visitors or children at school). For routine office work, but perhaps even more for creative thinking and conferring, the biological information needs for pleasant, comfortable, stimulating visual environments (the qualitative aspects of lighting) are at least as important as adequate, glare-free illumination.

On the other hand, the increasing use of VDTs throughout the work space, and the need to minimize reflections on the screens, will make design problems more difficult.

This group of case studies represents our first attempt to design office buildings around sunlighting principles. They are all deep buildings. They represent a range of scales from a small, typical suburban office/warehouse (Johnson Controls) to very large office complexes of well over a million square feet (TVA and GSIS). The buildings are located in a range of climate zones, from hot climates near the equator (Manila), to the variety of temperate climates of the U.S., including Florida, Tennessee, New England, and Colorado.

While all the case studies began with the same overall lighting objectives and concepts, different contexts and priorities of planning, timing, economics, and location created different results.

An ideal office building maximizes the use of sunlight, uses a moderate level of artificial lighting to supplement the natural light for ambient lighting, and depends on locally controlled task lighting for special areas and occasions.

The ideal sunlit office building would require no user adjustments to control glare, ambient light distribution, or distribution of solar heat. Control of the sun by fixed architectural elements would maximize the benefit from sunlight and window views.

In principle, the simplest strategy for maximizing heat and light in winter and minimizing heat in summer is the use of clear glass with south-facing clerestories and easily shaded north- and south-facing windows with lightshelves and high ceilings. In elongated buildings with such orientation, relatively small overhangs and lightshelves are sufficient to shade and redirect the sun, particularly near the equator.

The following case studies all *began* with these concepts.

B1 Blue Cross/Blue Shield of Connecticut—Corporate Headquarters North Haven, Connecticut

CONTEXT

Latitude: 41.5° N; climate: 6,139 degree days

160,000 square feet @ $80/sq. ft.

Architect: The Architects Collaborative Inc. (Leonard Notkin, Principal; Michael Slezak, Project Architect)

Consultants: Souza & True, Inc.—structural; Van Zelm Heywood, Shadford Engineers—mechanical and electrical; William Lam Associates—lighting

Construction completed: March 1984

This is a very straightforward application of sunlighting in a litrium building. The techniques used could be simple because the design started with the most logical plan form—elongated south- and north-facing blocks with services located at the far ends (fig. B1–1).

Since some of the team had worked together previously on the design of the TVA project (case study B7), there are naturally some similarities between the two, but there are also many differences because of the different contexts. This was not to be a state-of-the-art, energy-conserving demonstration building as was TVA, but simply a good working environment for a corporate client with a moderate budget. The building's energy goals were self-imposed by the design team.

Before I began my participation on this project, the TAC group had already developed the elongated atrium plan with favorable shape and orientation and had indicated a high-celinged transverse section using lightshelves. Steel framing had been selected for reasons of construction speed and because, in this cold climate, concrete frames cannot be exposed without the thermal penalty of winter heat loss through conduction.

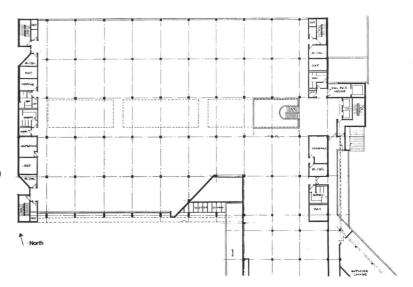

B1–1. Plan. (Courtesy of TAC)

↑ North

DESIGN CONCEPT

I saw my task as one of helping to refine a fairly good scheme. In order to avoid the complexity of the tracking louver system that had been proposed for TVA, TAC planned narrower office blocks (60–70') illuminated from a litrium totally covered by unshaded north-sloping skylights (scheme A, fig. B1–2). I objected, because such a scheme would receive proportionately more sun in summer than in winter. Instead, I proposed a south-facing sunscoop (scheme B) to reverse such results (fig. B1–3). The mechanical consultant was delighted to see the reduction in summer air-conditioning load but felt that *maximum* winter solar heating performance was not necessary because of the high internal loads he predicted. Therefore, subsequent testing of the alternatives included a design (scheme C) in which the same amount of clerestory glass faced north and south under a flat roof (fig. B1–4)—a scheme that the architects preferred for design and construction reasons.

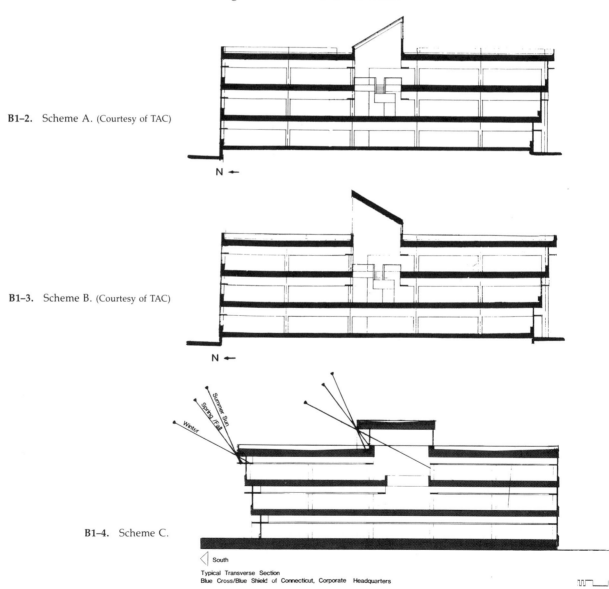

B1–2. Scheme A. (Courtesy of TAC)

N ←

B1–3. Scheme B. (Courtesy of TAC)

N ←

B1–4. Scheme C.

◁ South

Typical Transverse Section
Blue Cross/Blue Shield of Connecticut, Corporate Headquarters

MODEL TESTING

A two-bay slice of buildings and litrium was modeled at 1/2'' scale and tested (fig. B1–5). The illumination measurements rated both options (schemes B and C) fairly equal. Neither would need supplemental ambient light on sunny days, summer or winter. On bright overcast days, both would need a bit of supplemental light in the middle zone. The bilateral scheme was selected because it was expected to be slightly better for illumination under overcast conditions and summer air-conditioning loads. The overriding reason for the decision, however, was architectural preference.

Had I already tested the suncatcher concept at this time, I would have recommended the addition of suncatchers on the north side to equalize the quantity and the sunlit character of the light received by north- and south-facing offices on the edge of the litrium space (with a little additional air conditioning). Visually balancing the extension of the roof plane, if not the function and details, might also have made for a more interesting exterior image (somewhat similar to the Westinghouse Headquarters, case study B5).

The south litrium wall of the north block was designed like an outside wall, with the glass omitted. Model testing indicated that with this particular building geometry, a flat white surface for the tops of the lightshelves was better for light distribution than a mirrored surface.

Model testing included evaluation of the use of lightshelves on the north (litrium and exterior) exposures where they were not needed to shade and redirect sunlight. While they did not add significantly to illuminating the central zone, we recommended them for a number of

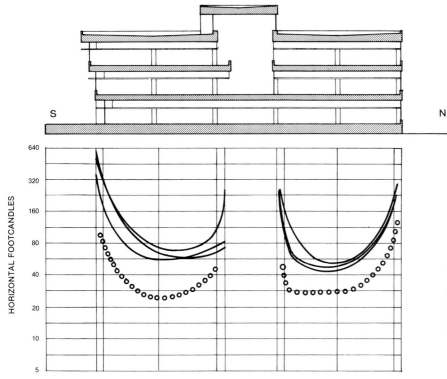

B1–5. Model testing results showed adequate ambient light throughout the building on both sunny days (solid lines) and bright overcast days (dashed lines).

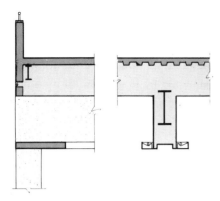

B1-6. Details of the interior lightshelf at the balcony and the deep false beam/light fixture.

qualitative reasons: flattening the illumination gradients, brightening the ceilings, reducing glare from the sky, and giving a more human scale.

Another qualitative objective I achieved was to increase the depth of the drywall false beams encasing the steel girders in order to visually integrate them with the indirect fluorescent cove lighting that edged them and the interior lightshelves that spanned between them (figs. B1-6, B1-7, B1-8). Light distribution from both cove lighting and lightshelves is optimized by maximizing their distance from the ceiling; thus, the need for deep beams. Minimizing the depth above the ceiling to use the building volume most efficiently was accomplished by placing the joists on top of the girders so that ducts could be placed between them.

B1-7. Typical north perimeter office. (Courtesy of TAC/Richard Mandelkon, photographer)

B1-8. The work station at the atrium edge enjoys sunlight visible on the beam at this time.

a.

THE BUILDING

Despite its innovative features, this is a very quiet looking, "background" building. The monolithic, highly finished, high-quality concrete and careful detailing typical of TAC, and an impressive entrance, are what one perceives at first glance. On closer inspection, one notices that the facades of precast concrete spandrels and exterior lightshelves present an interesting, invitingly humane appearance on the exterior as well as on the interior—a richness derived from function rather than applied decoration (fig. B1–9). Unlike the effects of surface decoration on flat facades, the qualities of sunlighting forms and surfaces are appealing at night as illuminated lantern forms. The unshaded north facade is appropriately different (fig. B1–10).

The illumination turned out differently than predicted, both quantitatively and qualitatively. Illumination levels were reduced by 50–75 percent by omission of the recommended white paint on the tops of lightshelves and white gravel on the roof. Consequently, the results were good but not optimal. The management has not yet programmed the use

b.

B1–10. Unshaded north facade.

of the energy-conserving zoned switching system that was provided, but I expect that it will do so in time.

The users are happy to be in such a lively, comfortable, spacious environment from which they can enjoy the view of the countryside with no need for shades or blinds to control glare during most of the year, and enjoy pleasant circulation within (fig. B1–11).

Design studies had predicted that the minimal amount of direct sunlight not intercepted and redirected in winter (when the sun is lowest) would be welcomed, since it can penetrate only below eye level (fig. B1–12). Unfortunately, omission of the interior lightshelves has resulted in the need for full-height dynamic shading in winter. Without the dominant horizontal of the interior lightshelf (fig. B1–13), the south wall is also less attractive than the north side or atrium edges, which do have interior lightshelves. This is a lesson I had learned earlier from the GSIS mock-ups (see case study B3).

CONCLUSION

By typical office building standards, the net-to-gross ratio of visible ceiling height to floor-to-floor height is very good here. However, it is not as good as it could have been using paired beams and lightshelves for air distribution as at Carrier (case study B2) and Westinghouse (case study B5).

After visiting the building in midsummer, I have urged the architects to complete more of the building as designed—to add white paint on exterior lightshelves and white gravel on the roof surrounding the clerestories; I am hopeful that this will be done. In retrospect, I would have eliminated the shading overhang on the south-side clerestories of the litrium or introduced some small, clear skylights, in order to allow some direct sunlight to enter the space as often as possible. The extra light this would have provided would have benefitted the trees within and delighted the building's occupants; the cost of the additional heat gain, which we were very concerned about, seems minimal by comparison. In summary, this is a fine building that could be better. If the details of the sunlighting design are carried through, the energy savings projected for the building could be realized.

B1–11. Litrium: (a) at upper level; (b) view toward offices. (Photograph *a* courtesy of John Lam; photograph *b* courtesy of TAC/Richard Mandelkon, photographer)

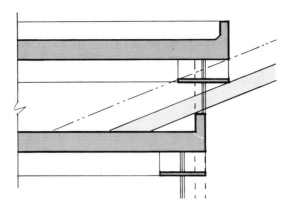

B1–12. South wall section diagram at 2 P.M., December 15, shows how interior lightshelf (as designed) controls glare at eye level.

B1–13. Interior view at south wall. Omission of recommended interior lightshelf results in a less intimate scale and the need for full-height blinds. (Photograph courtesy of John Lam)

B1–14. Integrated beam lightcoves create restful spacious workplaces at night. (Courtesy of TAC/Richard Mandelkon photographer)

B2 Melvin C. Holm Center— Carrier Executive Office Building Weighlock Park, Dewitt, New York

Latitude: 43.1°N; climate: 6,678 degree days

Architect: Quinlivan Pierik & Krause (John D. Quinlivan, Principal; David McNeil and Robert M. Haley, Jr., Project Architects)

Consultants: John P. Stopen & Associates—structural; Robson & Woese, Inc.—mechanical and electrical; William Lam Associates—lighting; Scott Mathews—energy

Construction completed: May 1982

CONTEXT

My consultation on this project began after the architects had developed a schematic design based on daylighting for three blocks surrounding a litrium (fig. B2–1). The northern block was well oriented, but the other two were arranged to define an entrance rather than for easiest control of the sun (too much east and west exposure). The proposed window sections (fig. B2–2) would provide some large-scale fixed shading but not enough to eliminate the need for additional blinds. The planned reflective windows would decrease the light in winter as much as in summer. Desirable high ceilings were planned, but the proposed litrium, with 100 percent horizontal glazing, would maximize the light and heat in summer instead of winter.

I proposed the addition of an energy consultant sympathetic to passive solar techniques. Scott Mathews was hired. As in the Blue Cross/Blue Shield building, the energy goals were not set by the client but by the design team.

REVISED DESIGN CONCEPT

The first team design session resulted in a modified wall section and in a reshaping of the blocks to the simplest effective arrangement for sunlighting—two east/west-elongated blocks separated by and open to a conditioned litrium (fig. B2–3, B2–4). This scheme is quite similar to that of the Blue Cross/Blue Shield building (case study B1), which reduced the building perimeter exposure, maximized heat in winter, minimized it in summer, and made the sunlight easier to control.

The two buildings are *similar* in plan arrangements and orientation and widths of the blocks as well as in their steel and drywall construction and the integration of supplementary ambient lighting coves and interior lightshelves. Both buildings were designed to make maximum use of light from the litrium by placing work stations rather than circulation along the north and south atrium edges. Both use lightshelves on north exposures where they are not needed for sun control but for their qualitative benefits.

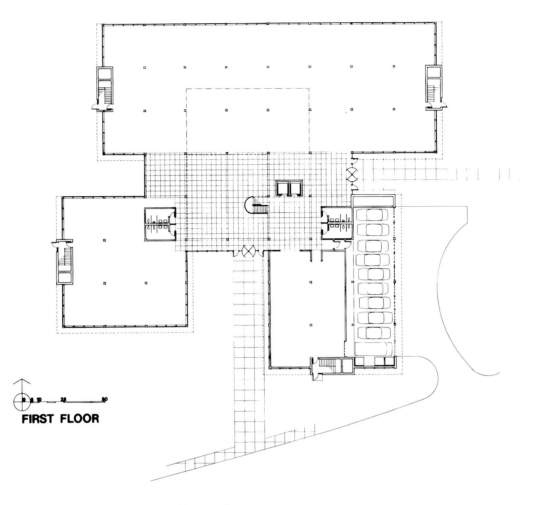

FIRST FLOOR

B2–1. Original plan. Building blocks, connected by a totally glazed greenhouse, are inconsistently oriented. (Courtesy of QPK Architects)

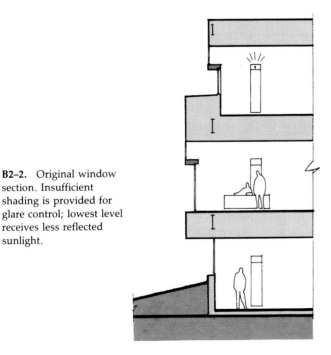

B2–2. Original window section. Insufficient shading is provided for glare control; lowest level receives less reflected sunlight.

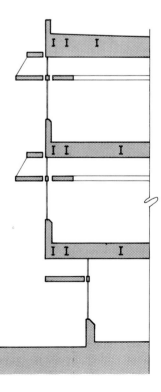

B2–3. Revised south wall section for more shading and reflected sunlight for all floors.

232　**Offices**

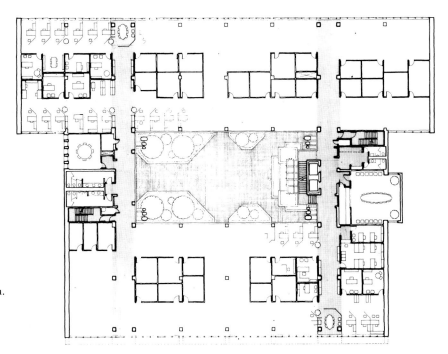

B2–4. Revised plan consistently orients elongated blocks and atrium. (Courtesy of QPK Architects)

SECOND FLOOR PLAN

The buildings *differ* in that the Carrier building has a wider atrium (but of almost equal proportions to that in the BC/BS building) for illuminating three floors instead of two (fig. B2–5). Its litrium glazing favors the south for heating advantages in the more severe Syracuse climate. The south clerestories in the litrium are shaded by large-scale horizontal louvers rather than a single overhang.

Some interesting features of the Carrier building are the means by which it maximizes the utilization of building volume:

☐ Taking advantage of the litrium for exposing the vertical duct runs (fig. B2–8);

☐ Using irregular bay sizes for major lateral distribution. Restricting low ceilings to the narrow bays created for services so that high ceilings are possible elsewhere (see B2–4 and B2–12);

☐ Using lightshelves for local air distribution. This allows the ceiling plenum to be very shallow. In addition, the radiant heat from the warm lightshelf ducts increases comfort (fig. B2–7). The optional interior lightshelves on the north exposures thus pay for themselves qualitatively.

Another difference in the Carrier building was provision of total summer shading for the lower as well as upper windows. The resulting distinctive shape, with lightshelves projecting beyond the upper shading elements, catches more of the high summer sun and increases the illumination at that time.

Melvin C. Holm Center 233

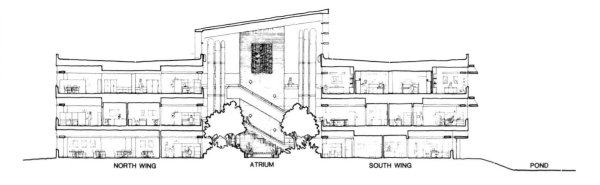

SECTION

B2–5. Revised atrium illuminated predominantly from south-facing clerestories and shaded in summer via multiple concrete louvers.

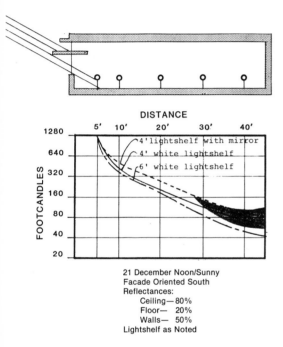

B2–6. Illumination data (from model testing) for December noon, sunny conditions, facade oriented south. Shaded area shows estimated atrium contribution. Reflectances: ceiling—80 percent; floors—20 percent; walls—50 percent

B2–7. Interior lightshelf doubles as duct radiant heater for improving thermal comfort.

MODEL TESTING

The very limited consulting budget allowed us to test only a small section of exterior south and north walls. We extrapolated from BC/BS data to estimate the contribution from the litrium side (fig. B2–6).

In addition to documenting differences in light distribution from various ceiling heights, we tested a range of interior lightshelf widths. While a 4-foot width gave the best gradients, the width selected was 3 feet because the greater width would have created a need for additional sprinklers.

B2–8. Exposed vertical ducts conserve building volume and act as "sculpture."

THE BUILDING

An initial delay in construction occurred because the building, detailed for concrete construction, had to be redesigned in steel when the local precast concrete manufacturer went out of business. As a result, instead of the lightshelves being an integral part of a cast concrete facade system, they are separate elements attached to the facade and the ends of the steel beams within. The connection between the lightshelves and the beams was made thermally discontinuous by using neoprene separators.

CHANGES AND COMPROMISES

Changes in Programmed Use and Partitioning

During the construction period, the programmed use of the building changed from a support building with a need for open spaces to a corporate headquarters programmed primarily for private offices and only narrow bands of office-landscape-type partitioning. The owners elected not to have the recommended design for partitioning the inner offices. They asked for conventional low-ceilinged spaces instead of full-height spaces with glass partitions such as those used at GSIS (case study B3), which would allow daylight penetration. With the resulting narrow pe-

B2–9. South-side perimeter offices.

rimeter spaces, the amount of sunlighting provided at the south perimeter is much more than needed (fig. B2–9).

Placing the solid block of offices in the middle of the floors also eliminated the bilateral illumination effect that the litrium perimeter spaces would have enjoyed.

The top floor perimeter of the north block was also compromised by the use of smaller, conventional-size windows to create the more traditional settings desired by the firm's top executives (fig. B2–10). This change was unfortunate for the building but beneficial for research, allowing the opportunity for direct comparison with the rest of the building: the executive offices seem gloomy in comparison to the adjacent interior secretarial area with its indirect fluorescent lighting from the top of file cabinets—an effect not dissimilar to the indirect daylight and cove lighting of the base building.

Construction Compromises

As a cost-saving measure, standard unpainted concrete was substituted for the white concrete specified, and normal gravel roof ballast was used instead of the white marble chips around which the design had been based. Sunlighting levels were greatly reduced (by a factor of 3 to 4) in summer, when all light entering the space must first be reflected from those surfaces. In summer, the planned illumination was only one third of winter levels. Thus, the compromise is less important in winter when the levels are inherently much higher and some sunlight enters the space directly. Even then, the increased light and heat input would be beneficial.

Fortunately, this situation can be easily corrected any time the owner wishes, whether for qualitative reasons (to create more pleasant spaces) or for direct savings in operating costs.

The recommended indirect fluorescent cove lighting was used and produced the expected natural blending with the indirect daylighting. One noticeable design flaw is the shadows caused by separation of lamps by gaps where photocells and relays were to be placed. The photocells have not yet been installed because of cost reductions. Actually, the cost for automatic switching of the supplementary artificial lighting (in the manner I originally suggested) could be a small fraction of that for the abandoned design, since only one or two photocells could control the entire south side of the building (as at Johnson Controls, case study B4). Since all rooms should receive approximately the same amount of light, a photocell for each fixture would be extravagantly redundant.

Sufficient and readily accessible wall switches have been provided so that energy can be saved whenever anyone cared to do so.

B2–10. Executive office.

CRITIQUE

Despite the changes in use and the construction compromises described above, this is still an excellent example of the potential for office buildings designed around sunlighting. I cannot imagine that many who have visited or worked in this building would choose to work in a "typical" office building with its unshaded dark glass accompanied by a disorderly array of blinds and a ceiling full of fluorescent fixtures operating on the sunniest days (fig. B2–11).

I was shocked to visit the building's litrium on a sunny summer day and to find incandescent floodlights aimed at trees in the litrium to make up for the low light levels during that season, when a little paint on the louvers could have increased the illumination by 300–400 percent. I assume that someday someone will decide to apply the needed paint on a few lightshelf and louver surfaces and thus realize the full potential of the sunlighting design.

The exterior architectural image is enriched by the boxlike shading/lightshelf elements. I would have preferred that the spandrels be of brick (or brick-colored stucco as used by Aalto at the MIT dormitories), so that the south facade would continue the color and appearance of the other facades. If, instead, the south facade were part of a lightcourt, the light-colored spandrels used would be valuable for reflecting light to facing north windows, as do the white balcony surfaces within the litrium (fig. B2–12).

The boxlike projections are a very natural vocabulary for attachment to existing buildings. This approach to detailing is perfectly legitimate, and at times may be more economical (though quite different) from the approach used at BC/BS (case study B1), TVA (case study B7), and DTC (case study B6), where the shading and lightshelf elements are an integral part of, rather than attachments to, the facade.

B2–11. Offices by the litrium edge receive light from the vertical white balcony surfaces opposite as well as from the atrium clerestories and ceiling.

B2–12. South facade.

B3 Government Service Insurance Systems Headquarters Manila, Philippines

Latitude: 15° N; climate: 6,325 cooling degree days

1.35 million square feet

Architects: The Architects Collaborative, Inc. and Jorge Y. Ramos & Associates (Howard Elkus (TAC) and Jorge Ramos (JYRA), Principals; Sherry Caplan (TAC), Project Manager; William Higgins (TAC) and Gener Flancia (JYRA), Project Architects)

Consultants: Gillum-Calaco—structural; Cosentini Associates—mechanical; William Lam Associates—lighting; Van Der Ryn, Calthorpe & Partners—thermal analysis; Firepro, Inc.—life- and fire-safety; L.G. Copley Associates—acoustical; Bolt, Beranek & Newman, Inc.—wind engineering

Construction completed: May 1985

CONTEXT

The average temperature in Manila is 89°F. In this climate, where solar heat gain must be minimized, the first scheme considered for this very large government office building was a series of extruded litrium buildings with easily shaded north- and south-facing fenestration. The concept was naturally related to the TVA building, the design of which several of the team members had been previously involved with.

However, consideration of the architect's desire for maximizing harbor views to the north, combined with the clients' lack of any functional need for atrium space (for communication, etc.), suggested a series of north-facing courtyards with the accompanying challenge of controlling the light and heat entering large expanses of east- and west-facing windows (fig. B3–1, B3–2, B3–3).

DESIGN CONCEPT

The solution employed was a combination of lightshelves and suncatcher/baffle trellises spanning the courtyards (fig. B3–4). Light striking the louvers at angles higher than the 45-degree cut-off angle would pass by and be reflected by the lightshelves. Sunlight at angles lower than 45 degrees would be converted to indirect sunlight by the light-colored trellises, which were designed *not* to be covered with vegetation.

Model testing data verified that the suncatcher trellises would be as effective as expected (fig. B3–5). Natural illumination on sunny days would be quite steady (despite the daily sun path) and almost sufficient to eliminate the need for ambient *or* task lighting throughout most of these very large floors of open offices. More task lighting would be needed in the few areas where office-landscape-type partitioning was to be used.

Lightshelves were used on both north and south elevations because at 15 degrees north latitude, the sun's path is in the south in December and in the north in the summer.

The dimensions of lightshelves and vertical fins were precisely designed to achieve total shading for each facade (fig. B3–6). Additional shading was necessary at the east and west ends of the project and at the

240

B3–1. Model view from the northeast. (Courtesy of TAC; photograph by Sam Sweezy)

B3–2. Plan. (Courtesy of TAC)

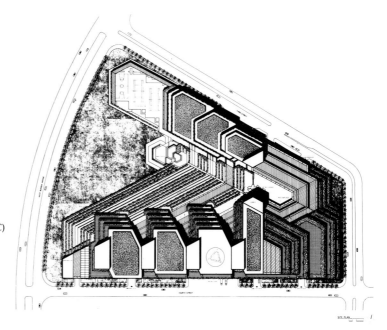

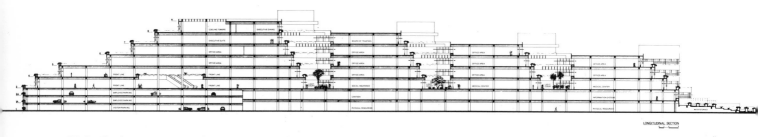

B3–3. Section. (Courtesy of TAC)

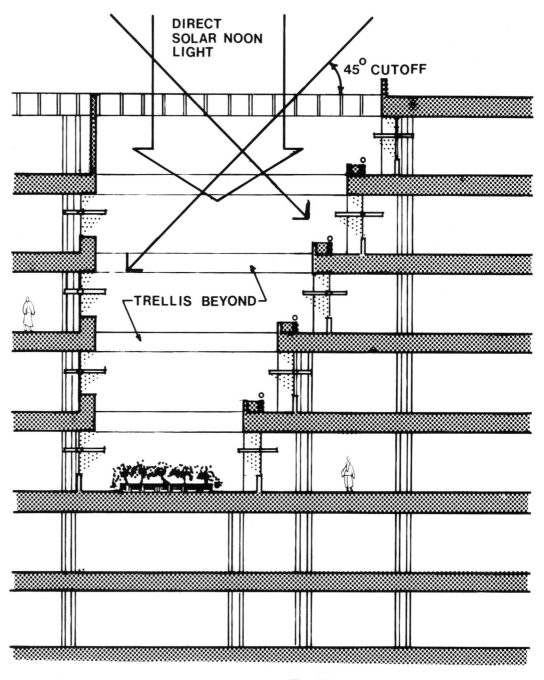

B3–4. Trellised lightcourt section. (Courtesy of TAC)

Trellised Lightcourt Section

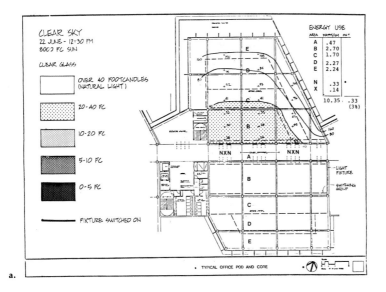

a.

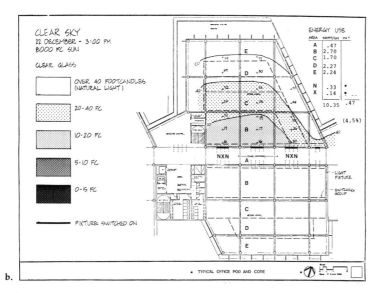

b.

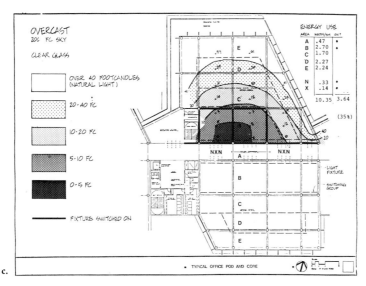

c.

B3–5. Because of the building's nonextruded shape, large sections had to be modeled (rather than the typical module) and the data presented in isolux plan (rather than in section): (a) lighting energy use at noon on a sunny day in June was projected as 3 percent of the maximum ambient lighting designed for the area; (b) at 3 P.M. in December, 4.5 percent should be on; (c) on a bright overcast day (or a cloudy day), lighting energy should be 35 percent.

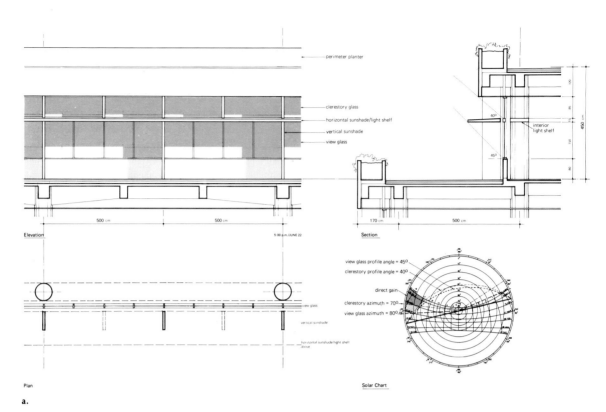

perimeter planter

clerestory glass
horizontal sunshade/light shelf
vertical sunshade
view glass

interior
light shelf

400

450 cm

450

170 cm   500 cm

Elevation   5:00 a.m./JUNE 22   **Section**

view glass
vertical sunshade
horizontal sunshade/light shelf
shelf

Plan

view glass profile angle = 45°
clerestory profile angle = 40°

direct gain

clerestory azimuth = 70°
view glass azimuth = 80°

Solar Chart

a.

NORTH WALL

0 4 8   16

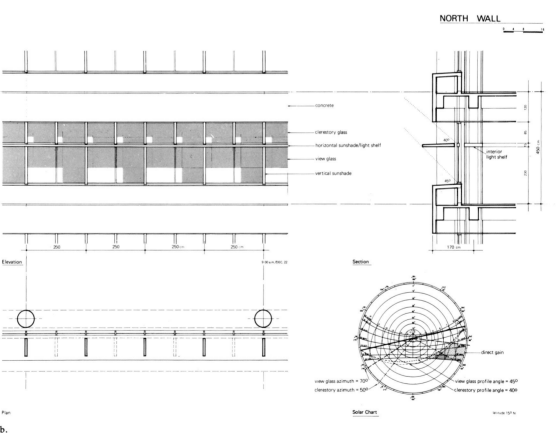

concrete

clerestory glass
horizontal sunshade/light shelf
view glass
vertical sunshade

interior
light shelf

400

450 cm

450

250   250   250   250 cm   170 cm

Elevation   9:00 a.m./DEC. 22   **Section**

Plan

direct gain

view glass azimuth = 70°   view glass profile angle = 45°
clerestory azimuth = 50°   clerestory profile angle = 40°

Solar Chart   latitude 15° N

b.

SOUTH WALL

0 4 8   16

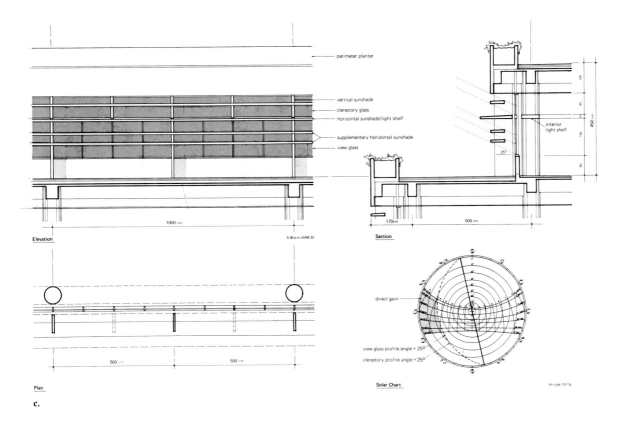

perimeter planter

vertical sunshade
clerestory glass
horizontal sunshade/light shelf
supplementary horizontal sunshade
view glass

interior light shelf

Elevation

5:00 p.m./JUNE 22

Section

1000 cm

170cm   500 cm

Plan

500 cm   500 cm

c.

direct gain

view glass profile angle = 25°
clerestory profile angle = 25°

Solar Chart

latitude 15° N

B3–6. Each facade has a different orientation and shading condition. (Courtesy of TAC)

WEST/EAST WALL (west shown)

corners of the courtyards that were not protected by the trellises. In those areas, additional horizontal louvers were provided to block direct sunlight until it dropped below 22.5°; its reduced intensity and rapid vertical movement in the late afternoon (typical near the equator) would minimize the undesirable solar gain.

While provision of dynamic shading to eliminate the small amount of direct sunlight bleeding past the louvers could not be economically justified on the basis of air-conditioning savings, dynamic shading of the western afternoon sun was considered essential for the thermal comfort of the occupants. Even if the additional shading were needed for only a few minutes a day, the ambient air temperatures and the attitude of people in tropical countries to being in direct sun (particularly when thermostat settings are on the high side of the comfort range) necessitated total solar control. The same amount of sunlight exposure in a frigid winter climate (with lower thermostat settings) would probably be welcomed despite the accompanying glare. Dynamic shading was not deemed necessary on the eastern exposures because any sunlight penetration would occur before office hours.

Assessment of these conditions and the subsequent communication to others of the potential glare and overheating problems were aided by model photographs showing the pattern of "bleed-by." The design team considered the form of dynamic shading a very important issue. Electrically operated window shades were recommended because they could be operated automatically as part of the energy management system, and a uniformly aligned appearance could be maintained for each facade both from within and without. Automatic control would ensure their use only when needed. By avoiding manual operation, we hoped to avoid the perception of window shades as a status symbol that would be demanded throughout the project even where not needed for sun control, creating both unnecessary capital cost and reduced sunlight utilization. Clear glazing was specified for all windows. Solex glass, which admits a greater proportion of light than heat, was considered but would not have been cost-effective in these windows, which are already so well shaded.

Sliding windows were designed to provide emergency ventilation, so that the building would be fairly self-sufficient during the frequently expected brownouts (fig. B3–7). However, these were omitted for cost reasons in the final building.

Building Systems Integration

Soon after the overall plan form of courtyards was conceived, a design integration session was held by the entire design team. It was immediately obvious that the deep, exposed structure approach suitable for the original atrium scheme would only work for spaces with fenestration from two opposite directions and perpendicular to the structure. The spaces proposed for GSIS would have fenestration from several sides and daylight distribution would be severely compromised by the deep, exposed structural system.

Thus, the challenge was to create a structural/mechanical system to maximize the height of the suspended flat ceilings and minimize the ceiling-to-floor thickness in the most cost- and space-efficient manner. In a less earthquake-prone locale, the answer might have been to start with a

B3–7. Natural ventilation diagram. (Courtesy of TAC)

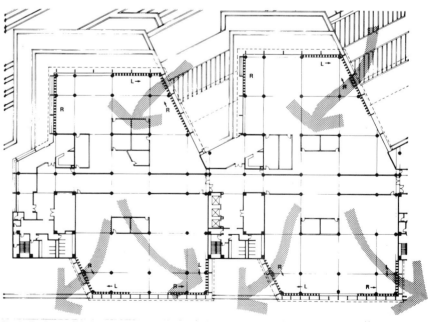

North-Northeast Winds

— operable sliding window

NATURAL VENTILATION DIAGRAM

structure of flat slabs with dropped column caps, leaving side paths for ductwork in between (see fig. 9–17). To provide adequate earthquake resistance, however, the structural engineers proposed a two-way frame of haunched beams (fig. B3–8). This allowed maximum clearance for major ductwork in both directions at the center of each bay and permitted the ceiling plane to be just below the lowest part of the structure. Floor-to-floor height was further minimized by the creation of a HVAC and pedestrian circulation spine (fig. B3–9). Closely spaced columns allowed the creation of a channel for the primary HVAC service ducts. The ceiling height could also be comfortably lowered in that zone since activity needs in the corridor do not require the same quantity or quality of illumination as those in office areas. Thus the ceiling-to-floor thickness is much less than it would be if a more conventional structure of uniform depth had been used, such as waffle or pan joists. By using the team design approach, structural, architectural, HVAC, and programmatic concerns were skillfully integrated, resulting in a cost-effective system with maximum ceiling height and utilization of the building volume.

Artificial Lighting

Supplementary indirect ambient lighting troughs spanning between the columns were designed to become an integral part of partitions when centered on the same columns (figs. B3–10, B3–11). Related details were developed for attachment of similar lighting to the core walls or on any partition for increased ambient lighting in smaller interior spaces.

The grid layouts of indirect fluorescent lighting that grew out of the building's structural system and shape made for a complex switching arrangement (fig. B3–12). Fixtures encircling the perimeter of each bay will be controlled by a low-voltage relay system that will be assignable at any time to various types of control zones, depending on the use of that zone,

TYPICAL SECTION

B3–8. Typical section showing haunched beams. (Courtesy of TAC)

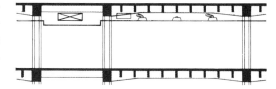

B3–9. Section through circulation spine and typical bay (structure is shaded to show clearance for services). (Courtesy of TAC)

B3–10. Model view of typical "pod." (Courtesy of TAC; photograph by Sam Sweezy)

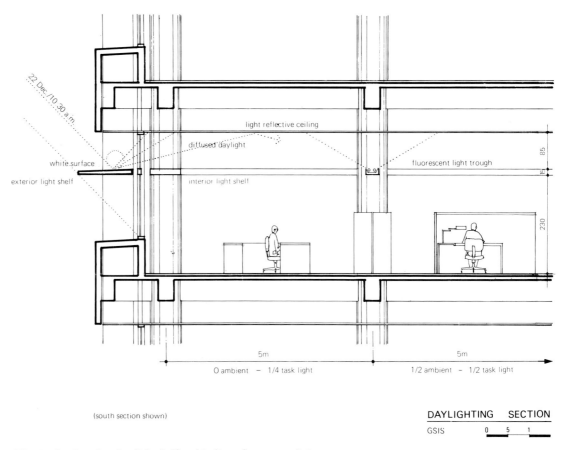

Labels in figure:
22 Dec./10.30 a.m.
white surface
exterior light shelf
light reflective ceiling
diffused daylight
interior light shelf
fluorescent light trough
85
15
230

5m   5m
0 ambient — 1/4 task light   1/2 ambient — 1/2 task light

(south section shown)

DAYLIGHTING SECTION
GSIS   0   5   1

B3–11. Section showing lightshelf and indirect fluorescent lighting trough. (Courtesy of TAC)

the degree of partitioning, and the location relative to fenestration of various kinds. Each bay will be assigned to a time-of-use zone and to a daylight control zone.

In a small building such as the Johnson Controls building (case study B4) with a single orientation, the two or three photocells needed to switch the artificial lighting according to the variation in natural illumination could be most conveniently placed within the space. In this case, there were so many combinations of fenestration, partitioning, and building use that the decision was made to put a few photocells on the roof in a series of model rooms representing the various types of fenestration being controlled—north, south, east, west, east-trellised, and west-trellised. Digital output from these photocells would be related to daylight control zone groups to which each bay could be assigned and reassigned at will. For instance, a north-facing zone at the building would be considered to have a daylight level equal to a north-facing model module. The second bay in from the window would be considered to have some established fraction of the model reading. A northwest corner bay would be assumed to receive the combined light of a north and a west model module.

Local switches will allow overriding of the computer-controlled energy management system, if at any time the system is not "smart" enough to anticipate illumination needs, or if there proves to be any difficulty in maintaining such a sophisticated system.

DESIGN PROCESS

Parametric Study

Before checking the design concept with instrumented model studies, a very rough but conservative estimate of the daylight contribution of a typical floor was made. This enabled us to estimate the annual energy consumption of lighting and HVAC to see if sunlighting could be cost-effective in a hot tropical climate. These were simply educated guesses of likely daylight distribution and use of electrical energy for supplementary ambient and task lighting.

Based on ambient lighting of 30 footcandles and task lighting at 1/2 watt/square foot, the estimate showed that the GSIS building, as designed, would have significant energy savings relative to conventional designs or the D.O.E. design goals for buildings in Florida (fig. B3–13).

Quantitative Model Studies

Model measurement simulating Manila conditions indicated that the assumptions used for the first energy analysis (see fig. B3–5) were as conservative as expected.

Qualitative Model Studies

Additional model studies were made to test the design integration of lightshelves and lighting troughs for indirect artificial lighting and their relationship to the proposed partitioning.

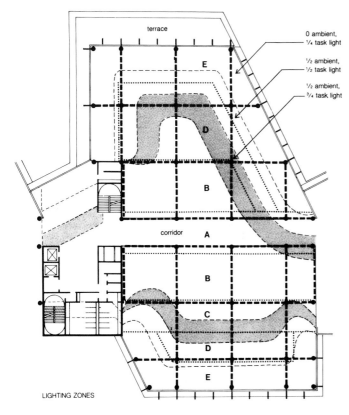

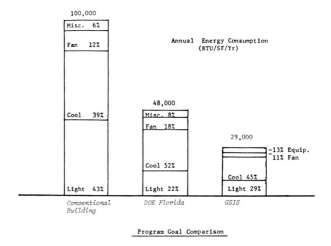

B3–12. Lighting zones. (Courtesy of TAC)

B3–13. Estimate of annual energy consumption (BTUs/sf/year). (Courtesy of TAC)

These two lighting elements created a useful organizing line for the partitioning system.

Potential glare and local overheating were also evaluated. This analysis might have been done by computer, but since the models had already been built for other purposes, a photographic study was more economical and easier (fig. B3–14). Too often, architects build models but never look at them outside of the drafting room to evaluate their performance under real conditions.

A full-scale mock-up was built later and proved without any doubt that additional shading was essential (for the few minutes a day needed) to provide total thermal comfort for the occupants.

B3–14. Qualitative model studies: (a) on the southeast exposure there is no sunlight penetration at eye level after 8 A.M. No additional shading is needed; (b) on the northwest exposure there is sufficient sunlight penetration during office hours to require additional shades.

a.

b.

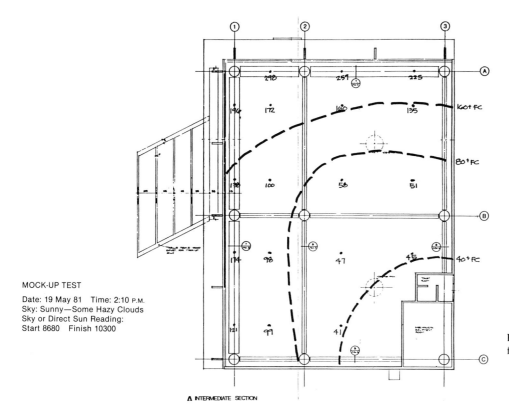

MOCK-UP TEST

Date: 19 May 81   Time: 2:10 P.M.
Sky: Sunny—Some Hazy Clouds
Sky or Direct Sun Reading:
Start 8680   Finish 10300

Λ INTERMEDIATE SECTION

B3–15. Quantitative data from the full-scale mock-up.

Full-Scale Mock-up

Measurements of a full-scale mock-up constructed from the actual building materials verified the sunlighting performance predicted from an equivalent section of the model (fig. B3–15). The comparative readings were very close, considering that the model had been tested in Cambridge, Massachusetts, simulating the conditions in Manila. The mock-up showed convincingly the advantage of sunlighting over traditional shading practices; the light level 40 feet from the window in the mock-up was substantially greater than the light level measured on the shaded windowsill of the architect's office nearby.

In traveling to Manila to view the mock-up, I was able to check on the reason for the drawn curtains and the exclusion of daylight in many Manila office buildings (including the existing neoclassical GSIS offices). Brief questioning of the occupants of several buildings confirmed that the curtains were drawn by those sitting near the windows to keep cool rather than because Filipinos prefer dark spaces and do not enjoy bright outdoor views—speculations voiced by some of the team early in the design process. This observation was reconfirmed by a survey I made a few days later in Hawaii. In the Honolulu County building, the shades have been used much more frequently in controlling solar heat gain since recently enacted government standards require thermostats to be set on the top end of the comfort range.

In addition to verifying the quantitative aspects of sunlighting performance, the full-scale mock-up was important for the further refinement of details (figs. B3–16, B3–17).

B3–16. Mock-up: exterior.

B3–17. Mock-up: interior.

An important qualitative evaluation was made of the interior light-shelves, which are not as necessary in Manila as they are at higher latitudes in temperate climates, where low-angle winter sunlight is admitted for beneficial solar heat gain. In this case, we had proposed the light-shelves to make the lighting more uniform, reducing the lighting near the window substantially and increasing it slightly further in. We also considered them a valuable scaling element, giving offices near the window a more intimate scale and less exposure to the potential glare of excessive expanses of windows. The presence of interior lightshelves also equalizes the amount of sky seen by those near the window, who have a complete view of *only* the lower window, and by those further inward, who see both the lower window *and* the clerestory window unrestricted by the lightshelf.

In order to assess their worth, the interior lightshelves in the mock-up were made to be easily removable (figs. B3–18, B3–19). One comparative look by the designers, owners, and staff convinced all that the light-shelves were essential for the stated reasons, as well as for the way they connected and integrated with the artificial lighting and partition systems.

The importance of matte-finish T bars in the acoustic ceiling and for good detailing of air diffusers was also demonstrated. The full-scale mock-up provided an opportunity for testing the acoustics of the glazed partitioning system, which demonstrated that tight acoustic seals at the ceiling were not necessary for the particular use patterns of this project (fig. B3–21). Building the mock-up from real materials gave us the op-

B3–18. Mock-up: interior with interior lightshelves.

B3–19. Mock-up with interior lightshelves removed.

B3–20. Mock-up: exterior view.

B3–21. Mock-up showing treatment of glazed partitions, quality of supplementary lighting, and integration of lighting hardware.

a.

B3–22. View from the southeast: (a) distant; (b) close-up. (Photographs courtesy of Howard Elkus)

portunity to test the construction details of exterior and interior light-shelves, as well as the artificial lighting details.

The design won an Owens-Corning Energy Conservation Award in 1982. The jury commented:

> The architects have been very innovative with their lighting in an effort to keep cooling loads as low as possible. . . . The cooling load is by far the highest of any we encountered. But the designers' annual energy target is one of the lowest.

B3–23. View from the main court with the north side of office blocks at right. (Photograph courtesy of GSIS)

b.

Summary

This is an effective low-tech design that seems perfectly natural in its setting. While from the exterior its construction does not look dramatically different from other existing new office buildings in the area, the functional concern with sunlighting has produced a building with an exceptionally pleasant work environment, with minimum energy use, and maximum protection against brownout periods. The nearly completed terraced architectural forms of the project, designed to control the Philippine sunlight, evoke indigenous methods of responding to the sun (figs. B3–22 to B3–28).

a.

B3–24. Lightcourts with suncatcher trellises: (a) from the northwest; (b) view out from a lounge (before painting). (Photograph *a* courtesy of GSIS)

b.

B3–25. The trellises make for a dark, gloomy space unless painted white. (Note the difference between painted and unpainted areas.) (Photograph courtesy of GSIS)

B3–26. Close-up view from the northwest. Note the additional horizontal louvers where west exposure is not protected by trellis. (Photograph courtesy of GSIS)

B3–27. Typical interior space. (Photograph courtesy of GSIS)

B3–28. Suncatcher trellises were carried over to the entrance area, creating interesting patterns. They will appear very different when painting is completed. (Photograph courtesy of GSIS)

Latitude: 40.8° N; climate: 5,983
heating degree days

15,000 square feet @ $56.00/sq. ft.

Architect: Johnson Controls, Inc.
Corporate Facilities Group;
Principal Architect: Douglas
Drake; Project Manager, Federal
Energy Programs: John Schade

Consultants: Donald Watson,
FAIA—consulting architect;
William Lam Associates—lighting;
Dubin-Bloome Associates, P.C.—
consulting engineers; Brent
Neilson—Johnson Controls
lighting and HVAC system
designer

Construction completed: 1983

CONTEXT

This prototypical office/warehouse building for a manufacturer of energy controls demonstrates the possibilities of practical, cost-effective sunlighting/passive solar techniques for creating both economic benefit and human delight (fig. B4–1).

The simplicity and small scale of the building made it easy to study the impact of each of the building's components, both quantitatively and qualitatively. The demonstration value of this innovative design was enhanced by the participation of a very well-rounded and articulate energy consultant and an owner with an unusual interest in the project and competence in its instrumentation, which was partially funded by the U.S. Department of Energy Passive Solar Commercial Buildings Demonstration Program. These circumstances created an unusual level of documentation of both the design process and the first year performance of the completed building. In addition, this project has been selected by the DOE for a second year of monitoring to collect statistical data for use as a calibration tool for its new computer energy calculation program, *BLAST*.

PROGRAM

The design team had been challenged to make cost-effective improvements on an already efficient base-case prototype (developed by the Johnson Controls in-house corporate facilities planning department for branches throughout the country). The existing design already incorporated many energy-conserving features such as high-quality insulation, highly insulating windows (triple-glazed) and south-facing windows.

Because of the already very low base-case cost for heating and cooling (which was further reduced by the availability of relatively inexpensive gas), early studies by the energy consultant, Don Watson, revealed lighting as the predominant energy cost and therefore as presenting the greatest opportunity for savings. Although lighting amounted to only 24 percent of the *actual energy consumed*, it represented 63 percent of the total *energy cost* (fig. B4–2).

Watson described the design process in the following words:

B4–1. View from southwest.

The overall energy goal was . . . established to reduce electric lighting by daylighting design and then to consider a practical mix of passive solar heating and natural cooling measures. The second step in the energy design was to compare options to reduce the heating and cooling load. Approximately twenty-five options were compared, such as adding insulation, changing building shape, changing window size, changing the amount of shading, as well as thermostat setbacks. It was found that none of the passive solar techniques, if used alone, would affect the heating energy significantly (fig. B4–3).

The best combination of options submitted for contractor costing indicated that for the one-story configuration (necessary for the warehouse/office operation), a 53 percent reduction in heating and cooling loads was possible from increased roof insulation and earth berming. This set the parameters for the amount of glazing and solar control that become the guidelines for the third step in the energy design process—detailed daylighting analysis.

After first critiquing the project as a member of the consulting team provided by DOE for the demonstration program, I was pleased to have the opportunity to continue with design input. Asked to consult on the overall concept for very minimal fee, my single lighting design concept session with the Watson team resulted in the elimination of several building sections under consideration as being unnecessarily complex in construction and aesthetics (sawtooth designs) or having an unfavorable ratio of summer-to-winter heat gain and light levels (skylight designs) (fig. B4–4).

DESIGN CONCEPT

For the planned 70-foot-deep office block, I suggested a combination of window/lightshelf south wall and a south-facing sunscoop north wall (a masonry wall common to the adjacent warehouse areas that could also be used for effective thermal storage) (figs. B4–5, B4–6). Sloping the ceiling upward toward the north was proposed both to improve the distribution of light reflected from the south window (ground and lightshelf) and to expose more of the sunlit north wall to the space. A ''sun's-eye view'' was drawn to convey the building's exposure to the sun at different times.

MODEL TESTING

Model testing by the architects on the roof of the Yale architecture school (following the guidelines for model testing presented in chapter 11), confirmed that the simple building section developed at the concept session could provide the target ambient lighting during sunny summer days and, as desired, several times more than this in the winter (fig. B4–7). The model testing also demonstrated the quantitative and qualitative benefits of sloping mirrored material (possibly in the form of sculpture on the north wall). Testing also demonstrated the negative lighting effects of a proposal for placing a dark-colored, heat-collecting, return air duct in the

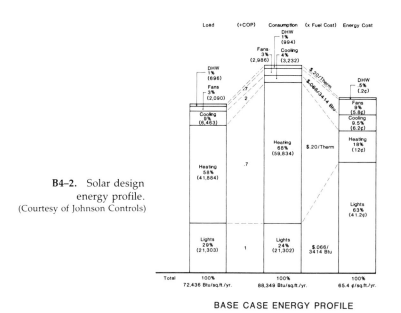

B4–2. Solar design energy profile.
(Courtesy of Johnson Controls)

BASE CASE ENERGY PROFILE

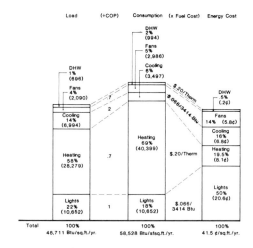

SOLAR DESIGN ENERGY PROFILE

B4–3. Analysis of various energy-conserving options. (Courtesy of Johnson Controls)

A Series	Annual heating MBtu	% Heat improvement	Annual cooling MBtu	% Cool improvement	Annual heat/cool MBtu	% Total improvement
0 Base case square plan Wyoming, MI specifications	623	0	114	0	737	0
1 Same as base, except rectangular plan south wall ⅓ glazing 144 LF	625	−.003	116	−.02	741	−.01
2 Same as base, except plan as shown on Johnson Controls schematic, July 16	652	−.05	121	−.06	773	−.05
3 Base case w/ Trombe Hall ⅔ south wall	585	+.06	114	0	699	+.05
4 Base case w/ 100% glazing south wall	614	+.01	149	−.31	763	−.04
5 Base case w/ 4'-high clerestory and interior mass	594	+.05	136	−.19	730	+.01
6 Base case 1½″ insulation on outside of wall	608	+.02	91	+.20	699	+.05
7 Base case Double base-case R-values wall and roof	471	+.24	68	+.40	539	+.18
8 Base case w/ 5'-high earthberms on W, N, & E walls	595	+.04	100	+.12	695	+.06
9 Base case except warehouse temperature 60° F to 85° F	550	+.12	103	+.10	653	+.11
10 Combination: 0 + 5 + 6 + 7 + 8: skylight, double R-values on outside and earthberms	410	+.34	99	+.13	509	+.31

NOTES: Simulation based upon Salt Lake City NOAA weather tape, 1952. Infiltration rate assumed at 1 Ac/hour. Temperature band setpoints 68%F heating, 80%F cooling. South glazing is unshaded and without night insulation. Interior zones Warehouse, Office, and Sales on same setpoints and occupancy schedule, except as noted.

Design Development Options: Entire Building

B Series	Annual heating MBtu	% Heat improve-ment	Annual cooling MBtu	% Cool improve-ment	Annual heat/ cool MBtu	% Total improve-ment	Solar fraction	Btu/SF/DD SF = 14,884 DD = 6280
00 Base case* 68–75F setpoints	623.4	0	96.2	0	719.6	0	05	7.7
01 Base case 68–80F setpoints	619.3	01	45.4	53	664.7	08	09	
02 Base case 00 w/ 50% south glass	616.5	01	98.9	– 03	715.4	01	09	
03 Case 02 south glass w/ sun-shading	619.5	01	93.6	03	713.1	01	08	
04 Case 03 south glass w/ night-shades	614.7	02	93.6	03	708.3	02	08	
05 Base case 00 w/ clerestory	593.1	05	104.4	– 09	697.5	03	15	
06 Case 05 clerestory w/ sunshading	592.3	05	102.9	– 07	695.2	04	14	
07 Case 06 clerestory w/ night-shades	587.6	06	103.0	– 07	690.6	05	14	
08 Base case 00 w/ earthberms	607.6	03	86.9	10	694.5	04	08	
09 Base case 00 w/ R 15.8 walls	602.6	03	83.4	13	686.0	05	08	
10 Base case 00 w/ R28 roof	477.1	03	58.6	29	535.7	26	11	

*Base case is square plan 14,884 SF divided into warehouse, office, and sales zones; w/ 33% glazing on south wall; R 9.7 walls; R 7.5 roof; 35 occupants on varying schedule; Equipment & Lighting Load 4 W/SF; Infiltration Rate 1 Ac/hr. Weather Data: NOAA T-11 tape for Salt Lake 1952, 6280 DD; solar irradiation reconstructed from NBS Sun Routine.

Proposed Design Options: Entire Building

C Series	Annual heating MBtu	% Heat improv-ment	Annual cooling MBtu	% Cool improve-ment	Annual heat/ cool MBtu	% Total improve-ment	Solar fraction	BTU/SF/DD SF = 14,884 DD = 6280
C1 Proposed design* 68–75°F setpoints	412.5	51	111.4	– 15	526.9	37	.21	5.6
C2 Proposed design w/lighting 1.5w/sf	420.9	48	104.1	– 08	525.0	37	.21	5.6
C3 Proposed design w/ night shades	407	53	111.6	– 15	519.5	39	.21	5.5

Proposed Design Options: Office/Sales Only

C Series OFFICE/SALES	Annual heating MBtu	% Heat improve-ment	Heat Btu/SF SF = 10,164	Annual cooling MBtu	% Cool improve-ment	Cool Btu/SF SF = 10,614	Annual heat/ cool MBtu	% Total improve-ment
C1 Proposed design* 68–75°F setpoints	215.3	46	20,300	93.4	– 25	8,800	308.7	29
C2 Proposed design w/lighting 1.5w/sf	220.8	45	20,800	87.6	17	8,300	308.4	29
C3 Proposed design w/ night shades	210.7	47	19,900	93.6	– 25	8,800	304.4	28

*Proposed design is base case with 50% south glass w/ sunshading, with clerestory w/ sunshading, with R 15.8 walls insulated on outside of mass, R 28 roof on office, with earthberms; lighting @ 3W/SF except as noted.

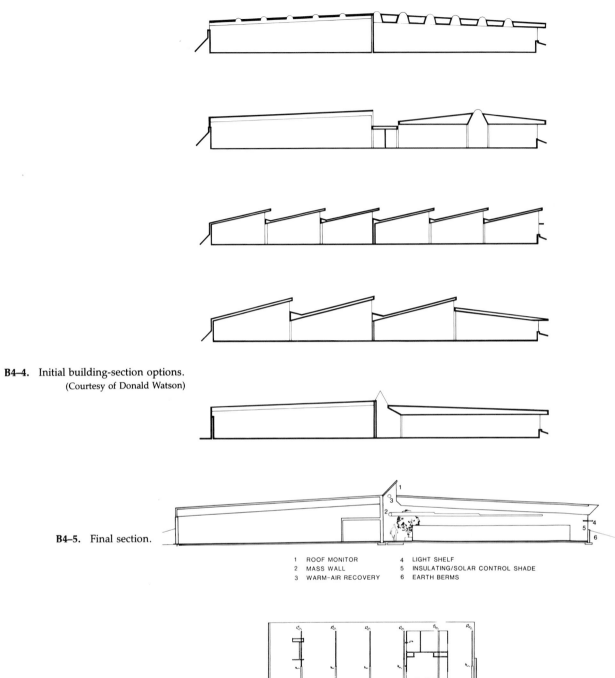

B4–4. Initial building-section options.
(Courtesy of Donald Watson)

B4–5. Final section.

1	ROOF MONITOR	4	LIGHT SHELF
2	MASS WALL	5	INSULATING/SOLAR CONTROL SHADE
3	WARM-AIR RECOVERY	6	EARTH BERMS

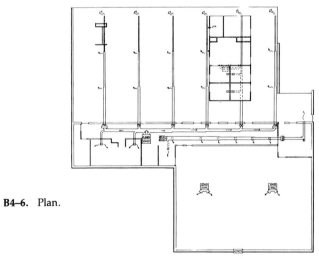

B4–6. Plan.

sunscoop area (50 percent reduction of illumination in that area). Similarly, any temptation to paint the sunscoop wall in a dark color was abandoned.

Lightshelves of various dimensions and finishes were studied. The final configuration shades the south wall completely during June and July but provides only partial sun control during May and August. A larger shading device (which would shade the window wall during the entire summer) would have depressed light penetration below a usable level, especially under overcast sky conditions.

The cut-off provided was not quite as much as I would have provided for maximum visual comfort. Instead, Watson chose to supplement the architectural solution with dynamic shading, utilizing an ''up-from-the-bottom'' night insulation deemed cost-effective for optimum energy performance. (Unlike insulation that is drawn ''down from the top,'' which is ineffective unless fully closed, insulation drawn from the bottom provides a ''dam'' for cold air when partially closed.)

Model testing allowed evaluation of the visual qualities of exposed round ducts placed in the space as a means of cost saving and energy efficiency. This method avoided penetration of the insulation and vapor barrier of the ceiling, as generally happens when the ducts and lighting are located in the ceiling. ''Floating'' the ducts in the space also allowed for a higher ceiling at no cost. Supplementary artificial ambient and task lighting were assumed to be integrated into office landscape partitioning (fig. B4–8).

As mentioned in chapter 10, the realism created by placing a few well-made pieces of furniture in the model can be an important selling tool. In this case, one can hardly see the difference between photos of the model and the completed project (figs. B4–9, B4–10). A subtle difference demonstrated by the photographs is the aesthetic benefit of the chamfered wall above the lightshelf in the model, but omitted in the constructed building.

THE BUILDING

As indicated by the photographs, the reality of the built environment was as I had expected and as was predicted by modeling. When I visited the building in late summer, 1983, the building had been in use for a season and was being enjoyed by the users as a delightful environment.

An excerpt from the final management evaluation report reads:

> Perhaps more important than the amount of energy savings is the fact that the quality of the resulting environment is very high. The overall impression of the office area is that it is extremely pleasant, well lighted, and comfortable. The daylighting, together with the view (to Salt Lake City's surrounding mountains) provide variety and relief not normally available in most working environments.

The management was also pleased that the energy performance for the initial period proved to be better than the design estimates. This improvement is explained by a number of factors including conservative energy assumptions, differences between actual and predicted weather, extremely efficient operation (made more so by lower-than-predicted oc-

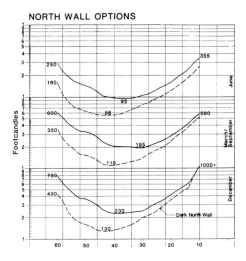

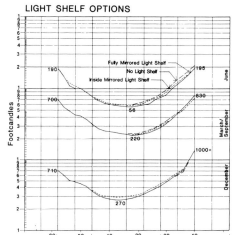

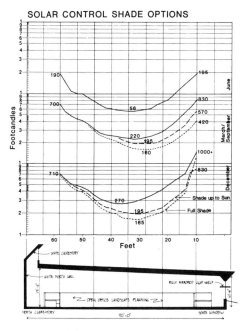

B4–7. Daylighting model measurements. (Courtesy of Donald Watson)

B4–8. Artificial lighting integrated with partitioning.

B4–9. Model. (Courtesy of Donald Watson)

B4–10. Completed project.

cupancy for this initial period, awareness by the users that energy savings are important, and, most important, automated controls developed by the Johnson Controls Salt Lake City office). Lighting energy use was extremely low, far below original projections (fig. B4–11). Paul Lauer, who was in charge of monitoring at Johnson Controls, reported that the total energy bill for the office and warehouse last year was only 50 percent more than for his own house.

The result of the interior lighting of lightshelf plus clerestory is to eliminate the need for electric lighting for the south window perimeter zone and the north clerestory zone during most of the occupied hours year-round. Furthermore, the interior office band (a 20-foot zone in the middle of the office) does not require ambient light during sunny days from fall to spring (fig. B4–12). At the north end of the room, control of glare by the masonry wall allows more direct sunlight to be admitted and therefore produces higher illumination levels at this zone (fig. B4–13).

B4–11. Predicted versus actual energy usage in BTUs per square foot.

	January	February	March	April	May	June	July	August	September	October	November	December
	Actual / Predicted	Actual / Predicted	Actual / Predicted	Actual / Predicted	Actual / Predicted	Actual / Predicted	Actual / Predicted	Actual / Predicted	Actual / Predicted	Actual / Predicted	Actual / Predicted	Actual / Predicted
HEATING	3249 / 6002	3619 / 4846	2406 / 4746	2577 / 1414	865 / 342	213 / 61.4	163 / .94	44 / .93	213 / 107	1129 / 845	2019 / 4441	3004 / 5251
COOLING	0 / 0	0 / 0	0 / .46	0 / 146	46 / 1064	97 / 1064	122 / 1932	188 / 1923	84 / 1028	14 / 382	1.2 / 1.9	-0- / -0-
DOMESTIC HOT WATER	49 / 66	39 / 66	44 / 66	27 / 66	25 / 66	30 / 66	32 / 66	35 / 66	33 / 66	39 / 66	40 / 66	37 / 66
BLOWERS AND HVAC	774 / 267	716 / 267	795 / 267	1013 / 266	1446 / 266	699 / 266	752 / 266	999 / 266	698 / 266	704 / 267	661 / 267	702 / 267
OFFICE MACHINES	124 / 416	112 / 416	124 / 416	120 / 416	123 / 416	119 / 416	123 / 416	125 / 416	120 / 413	124 / 416	115 / 416	87 / 416
LIGHTING	134 / 888	121 / 888	127 / 888	44 / 888	186 / 888	107 / 888	99 / 888	123 / 888	115 / 888	106 / 888	117 / 888	129 / 888
BUILDING TOTAL *	4737 / 7639	5114 / 6482	4027 / 6385	/ 3198	3013 / 2480	1651 / 2703	1944 / 3571	1996 / 3563	1906 / 2774	2549 / 2866	2467 / 6082	3004 / 6888

* Total includes all electrical and gas BTU's used by building including monitored points above.

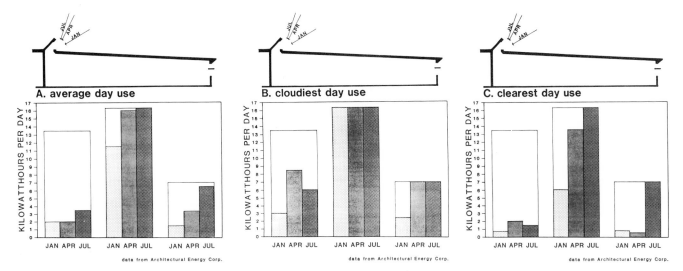

B4–12. Graph of actual electric lighting use for January, April, and July, derived from "An Analysis of the Thermal and Daylighting Performance of the Johnson Controls Inc. Branch Office Building in Salt Lake City, Utah" by Andrew J. Yager, and Donald J. Frey for the U.S. Department of energy: (a) average daily use; (b) worst case, dark overcast day; (c) best case, sunny day.

CRITIQUE

As the first completed and occupied building I had seen employing my recommendations for sunscoops and lightshelves, I was relieved that it met my expectations as an environment in which I would want to work. Though a very modest building in terms of the materials used, the details developed by the architects were generally very good.

One sunlighting element that I was happy to learn about was the sheet metal interior and exterior lightshelf (figs. B4–14, B4–15). It appears as an elegantly simple and economical construction suitable for the small-scale, wood-framed window system and suggests a possible approach for using lightshelves for retrofitting buildings with individual windows (rather than the large expanses of windows spanning column to column as shown in many of the other case studies presented).

Having seen the building in the summer, however, when the sun is highest and the sunlight admitted into the building is at a minimum, I have recommended three small but significant changes for future versions:

1. Increasing the extension of the exterior lightshelves on the south wall to protrude beyond the soffit would have provided more shading for the lower window but *increased* the amount of reflected sunlight (figs. B4–16, B4–17). The existing configuration, with its soffit sloped to maximize the winter light and heat received by the upper window, leaves the lightshelf totally shaded in the summer months. By extending the lightshelf, the winter/summer difference would have been reduced and the need for supplementary ambient lighting eliminated on sunny summer days, as it already is during the rest of the year. Alternately, the

B4–13.

B4–14.

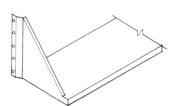

B4–15. Lightshelf bracket.

B4–16. South wall: exterior.

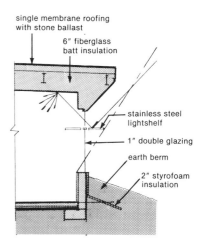

single membrane roofing
with stone ballast

6" fiberglass
batt insulation

stainless steel
lightshelf

1" double glazing

earth berm

2" styrofoam
insulation

B4–17. Section through the south wall.

soffit could be reshaped to produce similar results but without the increased lower window shading.

2. Unlike that at the south wall, the overhang at the sunscoop at the north wall is not needed at all for visual comfort since all direct sunlight is received by the wall (fig. B4–18). As in several other of our first generation sunlighting projects (e.g. Carrier, case study B2), we tended to be too conservative about cooling loads at the expense of lighting effects. In retrospect, I would reduce or eliminate the overhang here to allow a sliver of sunlight to penetrate at midsummer. This would increase the cooling load slightly but also help eliminate any need for electric lighting when demand charges are highest, and, more important, add to the delight of the interior environment. Even at midsummer, a view of sunlight in the building is really appreciated by most people as long as they do not experience glare or overheating. (We have been more generous with summer sun in later sunscoop designs, such as the University of Missouri Medical School library, case study H1.)

3. In hindsight, we should have increased the natural illumination in the center of the building with a row of very small (2'-diameter) horizontal skylights, which are most efficient in summer and on overcast days when the predominant south-facing windows are least effective. However, I agree with Watson that such an addition could not be justified on the economic basis of eliminating the minimal use of supplementary light required, because electric lighting equipment must be provided for nighttime use in any case.

a.

B4–18. North wall: (a) interior; (b) section.

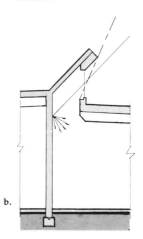

b.

POSTSCRIPT

The office/warehouse is a building type in which the potential for good sunlighting is frequently wasted. Such buildings almost always have good solar access. Using the common wall between warehouse and office for reflecting sunlight and thermal storage is a simple and effective technique that can often be accomplished easily, in retrofitting as well as in new construction (fig. B4–19).

The technique of limiting the extent of south exposure and introducing south clerestories at the north side or center of a building can also be utilized much more in residential design. Architects Kelbaugh and Lee did so in their design of the home of the former (fig. B4–20). Delivering sunlight to the north wall not only makes north-facing rooms more pleasant but is best for distributing heat and light.

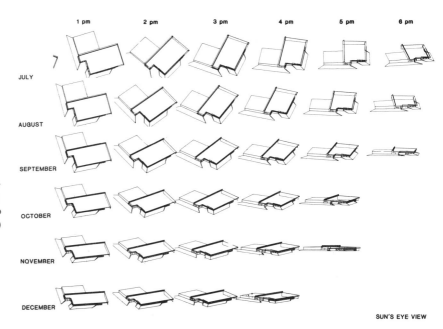

B4–19. This "sun's-eye view" of the building is an elegant way to present information about the building's exposure to the sun. (Courtesy of Donald Watson)

B4–20. A residential application of a sunscoop combined with a north-side masonry wall. (Photograph courtesy of Doug Kelbaugh)

World Headquarters/Westinghouse Steam Turbine-Generator Division Orlando, Florida

CONTEXT

Latitude: 28.5 N; climate: 773 degree days

257,000 square feet @ $57.82/sq. ft.

Architect: William Morgan Architects (William Morgan, Principal; Tom McCrary, Project Architect)

Consultants: Roy Turnkett Engineers—mechanical and electrical; Tilden, Lobnitz & Cooper—structural; Herbert/Halbeck—landscape architects; William Lam Associates—lighting; Jaffe Acoustics—acoustical

Construction completed: September 1983

Because other considerations in the initial planning of this building had established a building orientation that was difficult from the standpoint of sunlighting, I undertook this project with reluctance. The results demonstrate that such disadvantages can be overcome by careful building design. The results can never be achieved as simply as in a building with ideal solar orientation but can still be much more satisfactory than typical solutions that reject rather than utilize the sun.

To take advantage of lake views and the best foundation conditions, the architects had chosen a crescent-shaped atrium-type building oriented predominantly to the east and west (figs. B5–1, B5–2). The most obvious design solution might have been to create a hardware-oriented building with automated louvers (on the exterior or between double skins such as at the Hooker Chemical building (fig. 6–94) or one whose varied fixed architectural elements reflected the varying orientations along the facades (aesthetically interesting but likely to be expensive). However, the design team was able to find a single architectural form that was very effective (supplemented on the interior by inconspicuous dynamic shading elements in some areas, used for short periods of the day).

In addition to its design solutions for east and west orientations, this building is noteworthy for achieving the high ceilings desirable for sunlighting, with the highest possible net-to-gross height ratio, through an integrated structural/mechanical lighting and sunlighting system.

DESIGN CONCEPTS

Sunlighting

My design input began with accepting the overall plan form and section and seeking means to optimize the sunlighting performance. Adjustments were necessary for controlling heat and light distribution to the office blocks both from the exterior perimeter and from the conditioned atrium separating them.

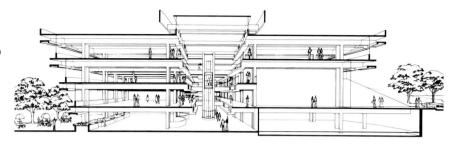

B5–2. Section. (Courtesy of William Morgan)

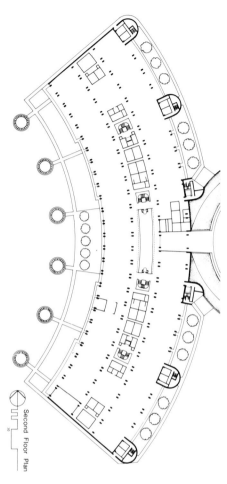

B5–1. Plan. (Courtesy of William Morgan)

Second Floor Plan

The Office Blocks

The job was simplified by some design decisions indicated by the architect's first schematic design:

The stepped section on the exterior provided an advantageous 45 degrees of shading for the lower windows (fig. B5–3). Switching from small-scale louvers to single lightshelves was proposed to improve the distribution of reflected sunlight as well as the outward view (fig. B5–4).

It was decided to keep the levels of office floors of equal width, in order to make the center atrium space more of a litrium (wider at the top than at the bottom). This gave a constant exposure to the combination duct/lightshelves lining the interior edges. The lightshelves were lowered as much as possible to improve their effectiveness in reflecting light to the office ceilings.

The structural/mechanical/lighting system (of paired light coves and beams enclosing mechanical services) previously developed by some of the design team for the Jacksonville State Office building and the Tallahassee District Court of Appeal was used with equal success in this building.

In addition to supporting the lightshelves, the paired radial beams turned out to be very advantageous for sunlight control for this curving building. While the lightshelves alone were sufficient on the southern and northern exposures, the deep beams added useful vertical louvering for the otherwise uncontrollable low-angle sun on the east and west exposures. The curving shape was beneficial in that any solar load pene-

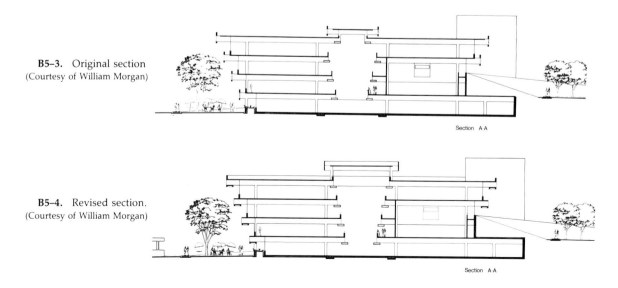

B5–3. Original section (Courtesy of William Morgan)

Section A A

B5–4. Revised section. (Courtesy of William Morgan)

Section A A

trating the building would be distributed over time to different parts of the facade, thus lowering the building's peak cooling load (as in the domed structures typical of the Middle East).

Recognizing the importance of controlling sunlight for occupant comfort, even when not necessary for air-conditioning cost, I conducted model studies to identify when and where sunlight penetration would be bothersome enough to require supplementary blinds. I found that the extensive shading by the proposed lightshelves and beams would be sufficient for most of the eastern exposures because any bothersome penetration would generally take place before office hours. However, I recommended that electrically operated window shades be provided for some of the western and southwestern exposures (figs. B5–5, B5–6). I felt that automatic operation would ensure that the shades would always (and only) be lowered for the relatively short periods of time needed.

The objective for the litrium design was not only to minimize direct sunlight penetration (in this climate with year-round cooling requirements), but also to capture a sufficient and constant amount of reflected sunlight to provide adequate ambient lighting for all areas exposed to the litrium. I recommended increasing the clerestory window height and increasing the sunlight reflected into the clerestory windows on the sunny side by using a white roof. On the shady side, a solid suncatcher baffle was projected above the roof to catch the light (fig. B5–7).

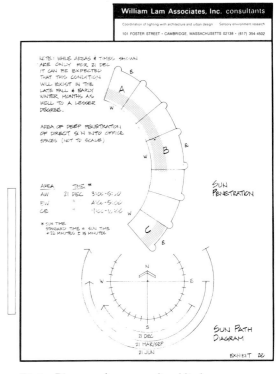

B5–5. Diagram of areas needing blinds.

MODEL TESTING

In model tests we found that we were able to stabilize the illumination received throughout the various sections of the building at various times on sunny days. Note the equality of illumination on sunny and shady sides at any time (fig. B5–8).

The data indicated that with a white roof under sunny conditions, both sunny and shady sides would have adequate ambient reflected sunlight. On overcast days, supplemental lighting would be required for the central zones. Such performance should produce real economies both for lighting and air conditioning for both total energy costs and for peak load penalties.

Prior to testing for dynamic shading needs, we tested 1/2-inch scale models to evaluate the concept quantitatively. A small section of the building was tested under winter conditions in Cambridge; next, a more representative (larger-scale, full cross section) model was tested in Florida. Testing at the actual latitude required less tilting of the model to simulate the seasonal variations and thus had fewer potential sources of error.

Building Systems

As previously discussed, the system of paired beams was useful for shading, light distribution, and support of the lightshelves. It also made possible ceiling heights only a floor slab thickness less than floor-to-floor heights (a net/gross ratio of .91). Electrical distribution was to be an undercarpet system.

Such an achievement was possible in this large, spread-out building

a.

b.

c.

B5–6. Model photographs illustrate the extent of sunlight penetration at southwest exposure *A* at 4 P.M.; at west exposure *B* at 5 P.M.; at southeast exposure *C* at 9 A.M.

B5–7. Suncatcher baffle at the litrium glazing.

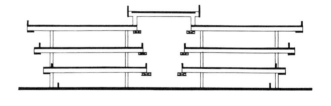

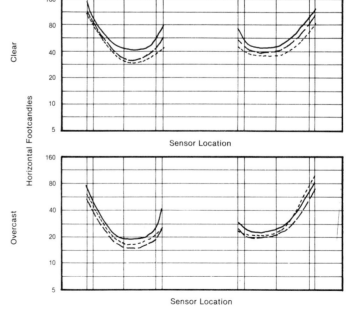

B5–8. Model testing data.

because the paired beams could be used to channel services from the several cores (on one side of the building) to feed the duct/lightshelves at the atrium edges, which in turn could feed other paired beam channels—altogether a very efficient use of space and parts.

Because of the mild climate, the construction of exterior elements could be very simple. The beams were continuously exposed without the necessity for thermal breaks between interior and exterior. Lightshelves were simply attached to those beams. Additional shading and light-reflecting surface area could have been gained by extending the lightshelves to the window plane, but they were omitted to aid window washing. Although an interior lightshelf was not needed for shading, a horizontal mullion at lightshelf level would have been useful for the attachment of drapery or other shading of the lower windows. Because such shading was only needed in a small portion of the building, providing ideal mounting conditions throughout the building would have been an extravagance.

CHANGE IN OBJECTIVES—MODIFICATION OF THE BUILDING CONCEPT

The final building design retained the original exterior forms and most of the building systems components dictated by sunlighting objectives. However, during the construction document phase, some elements were revised so that the interior environment created and the pattern of building energy use would be quite different than originally conceived. These changes, made after my design input had ended, seem to represent a redirection of objectives from maximum utilization of sunlighting to that of almost total commitment to continuous use of electric lighting. They included the following:

- ☐ The proposed clear glazing was changed to heat-absorbing glass, reducing the potential light admitted by 50 percent.

- ☐ The proposed white roof (very important for reflecting sunlight into the litrium clerestories) was executed instead with ordinary gravel. This change probably reduces the illumination received from the sunny side by as much as a factor of three.

- ☐ The proposed switching of the supplementary electric ambient lighting by zones parallel to the daylight sources was changed to zones perpendicular to the windows. Instead of controlling artificial lighting gradients to fill in the low areas of sunlighting gradients, the final switching effectively permits the lighting to be all ''on'' or all ''off'' in any section of the building.

- ☐ The proposed indirect lighting was designed to blend with reflected sunlight on the ceiling. The change to downlighting highlights the beams rather than the ceiling and makes the presence of electric lighting more dominant.

- ☐ With a change in program, two of the three original litria were eliminated and the spaces filled with additional offices.

B5–9. Litrium interior.

b.

SUMMARY

The objectives of sunlighting and the skill of the architect combined to create very powerful yet human-scale architectural forms that are interesting yet undecorated. This building proves that functional can be beautiful (figs. B5–9, B5–10).

The problems of providing effective sunlighting in a curving building with many orientations (including difficult east and west facades) are here solved architecturally with minimum dependence on or visual dominance by hardware systems (figs. B5–11, B5–12).

The simple, economical, exposed structural/mechanical/lighting systems used provide the high ceilings desirable for sunlighting with efficient use of building volume and materials.

The completed project is an excellent building that has created a positive image for Westinghouse in Orlando. Although the visual/luminous environment created differs from the planned sunlighting objectives, the Turbine Headquarters building nevertheless accomplishes much that is noteworthy.

B5–10. (a) Northeast view; (b) southwest view.

a.

B5–11. Perimeter office.

a.

B5–12. Window view: (a) framed by large-scale sunlighting elements; (b) interrupted by blinds (unneeded most of the time).

b.

B6 Denver Technological Center Prototype Building Denver, Colorado

Latitude: 39.7° N; climate: 6,016 degree days

240,000 square feet

Architect: Carl A. Worthington Partnership (Carl A. Worthington, Principal; Douglas Shmitt, Project Architect)

Consultants: BHCD Engineers, Inc.—mechanical; Garland Cox Associates, Inc.—electrical; Richard Weingardt Consultants—structural; William Lam Associates—lighting

Construction not yet begun

CONTEXT

The Denver Technological Center was planned as an 850-acre development with a working population of 30,000 and a project area equal in size to downtown Denver. Working with the Carl A. Worthington Partnership and DTC developer on the lighting and visual communications aspects of site development and urban design, I saw an opportunity to help create an entire community that took advantage of sunlighting where the climate offers the greatest potential.

The cold dry climate of Colorado, with more than 70 percent possible sunshine and a large diurnal temperature range, seemed an ideal opportunity for maximizing use of the sun, particularly with an electric energy rate structure that penalized peak power use by a ratchet clause (see fig. 1–6).

I proposed solar envelope zoning in combination with control of building orientation to maximize the use of sunlighting throughout the development. Because it was very early in the development phase, with the few buildings already constructed restricted to the perimeter of the development area, planning for the eventual core blocks consisted of little more than a diagram of superblocks by occupancy types (financial, medical, and so on). The site model showed buildings seemingly dropped at random on the various blocks, pierced by a diagonal circulation spine that connected the two ends of the core development (fig. B6–1).

Recognizing that the ground-level development had to recognize this diagonal alignment, I suggested that orientation of all major building blocks to the sun (with maximum window exposure to north and south) could have some aesthetic as well as economic advantages (as discussed in chapter 5), by creating an organizing device equivalent to the consistent orientation forced by hillside locations. The idea was thought to be interesting, and to test its potential, I was asked to consult on a building then being designed. This project was very important to me, as it was my first attempt to ''sell'' sunlighting in speculative office buildings.

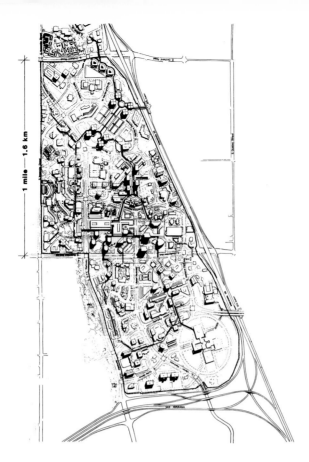

B6–1. Original master plan. (Courtesy of Carl Worthington Partnership)

PROTOTYPE OFFICE BUILDING

Integrated Sunlighting Wall System Design

Two integrated wall system designs for sunlighting in cold climates were developed: three-dimensional precast concrete units in the form of full floor panels (fig. B6–2) and spandrel panels (fig. B6–3) were designed to integrate shading, exterior lightshelves, and thermal insulation in an architecturally satisfying manner. These prototypes seemed suitable and economical enough for widespread application once the original tooling was amortized (fig. B6–4).

Even with tooling amortized on a single building, a very favorable payback of three years was projected because of the operating cost savings due to sunlighting: cost studies showed that the expected increased cost for the integrated sunlighting wall system would be approximately $1,000,000 but also indicated offsetting savings could be achieved from the use of clear instead of mirrored glass, reduced air-conditioning tonnage requirement (due to reduced peak loads resulting from shading), and minimum electric lighting requirements on summer days (fig. B6–5). Unfortunately, the developer for this specific parcel was more interested in first cost and decided to stay with the simpler but less effective conventional flat precast spandrel design previously developed (fig. B6–6), due to the fact that the building was designed for office tenants, not an institutional owner-user tenant.

The total projected construction cost was not unreasonable (even with all of the tooling and other development costs for the complex panels amortized on this single building). Had we *started* with the sunlighting design, rather than having to create an alternate for direct comparison

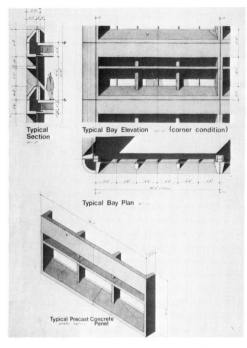

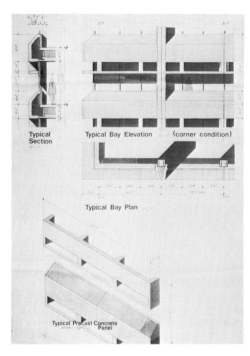

B6–2. Typical precast concrete panel: full-floor unit. (Courtesy of Carl Worthington Partnership)

B6–3. Typical precast concrete panel: spandrel type. (Courtesy of Carl Worthington Partnership)

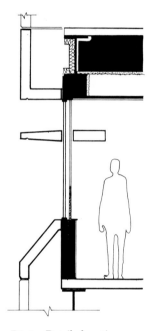

B6–4. Detailed section showing thermal breaks.

FLAT SKIN = 575 TONS AC
LIGHTSHELF = 410 TONS AC

165 TON DROP
OR 29% DROP

= $40,000 SAVINGS

NET COST

LIGHTSHELF
CONSTRUCTION = +70,000
(+ CONC., GLASS, GWB)

HVAC − 40,000

Premium = $30,000

B6–5. Cost breakdown.

with a less expensive first design, it might well have been built, especially if the building was for an owner/user.

At any rate, this project did provide some valuable experience. I learned about two very good ways to integrate lightshelves with other wall requirements in cold climates where thermal bridging should be avoided.

"Bermuda Ceiling" System for Gaining Ceiling Height

In addition to my learning about construction of the facade, this project confirmed my expectations as to one good way to get high ceilings in typical high-rise, tower-shaped buildings. Typically, the ceiling height is dropped to clear the largest air-conditioning duct, despite the fact that it occupies only a very small part of the ceiling area. This was made clear to the design team by a glance at the installed ductwork and the obvious opportunity for gaining ceiling height over most of the space in a high-rise building (by the same engineers) then under construction across the street.

Buildings less than 40 feet deep between core and perimeter window wall are usually serviced from a single loop of main duct located midway between core and perimeter. Placing that duct at the perimeter, or providing two loops at perimeter and core locations, will permit the rest of the ceiling to be higher, thus gaining the reflected light distribution advantages and visual elegance of a "Bermuda ceiling" (fig. B6–7).

Since the girders are usually perpendicular to the perimeter, there is often a lot of empty space between them to feed the main loop of duct and the local diffusers (most numerous near the exterior wall). The added cost of increased lengths of main ducts should be more than offset by the value of the spatial and lighting benefits from ceiling height gained in relation to total building height, if not by shortened local ducts and the reduced lighting and cooling costs of better sunlighting.

Unfortunately but understandably, the design team did not decide to take advantage of this technique. A conventional flat ceiling of reasonable height was attainable at a lower construction cost and excellent cost payback. The decision was probably also affected by fear of the unknown reaction of the ''speculative office building'' market.

POSTSCRIPT

In retrospect, reducing the payback period to even less than the forecasted three years (by taking advantage of the possibility of gaining the economies of reduced building height with equal visual effect) might possibly have prevented the developer from choosing the lowest first-cost design over long-term value.

Concentrating the major ducts at the perimeter and core seems to be a good alternative to the height-saving dual-use lightshelf/duct used at Carrier, which can be utilized with thin or discontinuous lightshelves, or when no lightshelves are being used. This knowledge, and the design development of the two good precast concrete lightshelf wall construction systems, make this project important, though it will never be built. Widespread application of these concepts could well make them less expensive initially, as well as more economical in the long run, and provide a higher quality standard office building.

Unfortunately, due to the 1982 economic downturn in Denver, this building was not constructed.

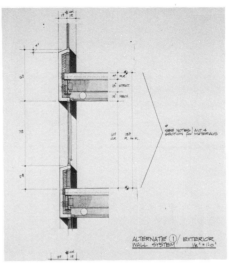

B6–6. Flat wall section as built. (Courtesy of Carl Worthington Partnership)

B6–7. Locate ducts at perimeter for ''Bermuda ceiling.''

B6–8. Elevation for the proposed design for the DTC building using the full-floor precast panel. (Courtesy of Carl Worthington Partnership)

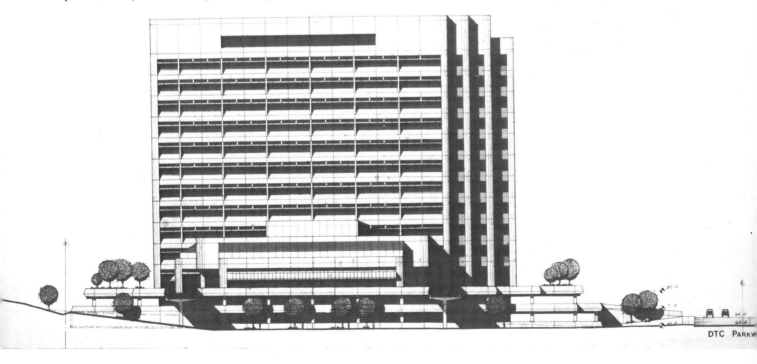

B7 Tennessee Valley Authority Chattanooga Office Complex Chattanooga, Tennessee

Latitude: 35°N; climate: 3,500 heating degree days

1,200,000 square feet

Architect: Caudill Rowlett Scott/The Architects Collaborative, Inc./Van der Ryn Calthorpe & Partners/TVA Architectural Design Branch/Derthick & Henley/Franklin Group

Consultants: Syska & Hennessey, Inc.—mechanical and electrical; Bolt, Beranek & Newman, Inc.—acoustical; LeMessurier/SCI—structural; Stan Lindsey & Associates—engineering; William Lam Associates—lighting; Travis Price—energy; Bill Oliphante & Associates—landscape architecture

Construction completed: 1986

CONTEXT

Although the first project in this group to be designed, this case study is presented last because it is the most conceptually complex and was the most compromised in execution. Aside from the innovative proposal for "beam sunlighting," it uses similar concepts to those in the case studies already presented.

Much has been published about the beam sunlighting concept designed for this building, and much interest has been generated in the verification of its validity. Unfortunately, it is doubtful that anyone will find out how well this concept will perform from this building since it was not built as designed. Almost all of the architectural features were built as conceived, except for the devices around which the architectural forms were developed—the beam sunlighting system of tracking mirrors and clear glass.

Omitting the tracking mirrors and glazing the atria with mirror glass fundamentally compromises the function of the atria. The so-called solar courts are misnamed: as built, these courts attempt to reject and defend against the sun rather than receiving and directing the sun for benefit (fig. B7-1).

As the lighting and building systems consultant, creator of the beam sunlighting concept and proposer of the integrated building systems concept adopted and refined by the design team, I will chronicle the process of the design evolution as I recall the events, comment on the design execution, and suggest lessons to be learned.

THE DESIGN PROCESS

My participation in the project began with a telephone call from Withers Atkins, chief architect at the Architectural Design Branch at TVA, who had heard of my workshops at Energy Inform and the SERI Passive Solar demonstration programs. He told me of his desire to create a very large TVA office complex in Chattanooga that would "advance the state of the art" in the quality of the built environment as well as in energy use. Given a very tight timetable, he wanted suggestions on how to proceed.

I suggested that an interdisciplinary team including a construction manager was necessary for such an assignment and proposed some possible team members.

Several weeks later, I was pleased to be invited to the first (programming) design session and to find a really outstanding design team assembled.

TVA had assembled a very large group, consisting of short-term consultants, who were asked to present their views at the programming session, and long-term consultants, who would continue working throughout the design process. The long-term team included three architectural firms—Caudill Rowlett Scott, The Architects Collaborative, and Van der Ryn/Calthorpe—as well as several technical consultants who were trained as architects (Bill LeMessurier, structural; Bob Newman, acoustical; Travis Price, energy; and myself, lighting and building systems).

Even with my long experience with the team process, it was the largest group I had worked with. Several members who were inexperienced in the team process expressed misgivings about reaching any decisions with such a roster. I assured them that the process would work, and with less friction and more unaniminity than they could imagine. The totally open design process and the personalities of the group members guaranteed that any invalid ideas would be discarded and that logic rather than personal taste would prevail.

The process worked as long as the team remained intact—in this case through design development. The consenses that naturally evolved during the full group meetings were summarized and made final by the executive committee, which consisted of Charles Lawrence (CRS), Sarah Harkness (TAC), and Si Daryanani (S&H).

All of the major programmatic decisions and the design concepts were established during a series of three week-long sessions (programming, urban design, and schematic design) of the full team. Back-up work between those sessions, by individual team members and by subgroups, was limited by the amount of time (less than two weeks) between these major meetings. Design development was done by TAC and CRS, interspersed with smaller subgroup sessions.

B7–1. A section through the presentation model of the TVA Chattanooga office complex. This "solar court" form, designed to accept, control, and direct the sunlight, was fundamentally compromised in its execution. (Photograph courtesy of TAC)

PROGRAMMING

Programming was completed in the first session, which took place in Knoxville. This was due in large part to the excellent brief prepared in advance by the TVA staff. The design team was pleased to find a statement of broad and specific goals that they could endorse enthusiastically:

ENERGY CONCEPTS:

Energy Demonstration

TVA is in the energy business. As a government agency it has a responsibility to demonstrate energy-conscious design in all of its facilities.

Total Energy Impact

TVA wants to reduce the total energy consumption of the region. The building design must address energy consumption on all levels of activity, from the national to the individual, and promote concepts that will reduce the per capita energy consumption when applied on a broad scale.

Reduction of Peak Power Usage

The building systems should use an absolute minimum of expensive, fossil-fuel-intensive peak power. Backup systems that respond to weather conditions should not use electric peak power. Peak power reduction is a high priority of TVA since it will reduce capital outlay costs and consequently electric utility rates.

Solar Rights Ordinance and Building Codes

This project should address and try to solve the problems of using solar energy in cities by helping the city of Chattanooga develop new energy ordinances that will facilitate future efforts. Building codes should also be reviewed for possible conflicts with energy conservation goals and workable changes sought. These changes can have considerable impact on the later project phases.

Use of Natural Energies to Supply Building Needs

The use of natural energies over fuel-intensive energies is a high priority for TVA. Passive and active solar, natural daylighting, methane generation, and human energy for circulation are concepts that must be explored.

Energy Versus Operational Efficiency

Although TVA's building managers are anxious to seek out new energy saving operations methods, excessive functional problems or maintenance problems to save energy are not considered realistic.

Energy Versus Employee Comfort

TVA feels that the human comfort of its employees takes precedence over energy savings.

Reexamine Design Parameters

The design team must reexamine the traditional energy design parameters such as temperature and humidity range, light levels and ventilation rates, etc., and address human comfort ranges based on activities.

ENERGY EDUCATION:

Public Involvement with the Energy Demonstration

The building design must maximize public exposure to and involvement with the energy demonstration. A graphic or literal explanation should be obvious to all building users.

The design eventually produced by the team directly reflected these programmed objectives, particularly the challenging summary statement:

Advance the State of the Art

The consultant team has been selected to provide a balance of new energy thought, representing many areas, and established design experience to produce a successful project that addresses the total scope of energy and human concerns. Our goal is not a building that represents contemporary energy design thinking. TVA wants to advance the state of the art in energy-conscious architectural design and building management and provide a model for future development in the Valley and the nation. The project should have concepts that can be used on a broad scale by this region's building industry and users.

Using the CRS "squatters" procedure (see Caudill: *Architecture by Team*) for efficient team design sessions, any team member with an idea to contribute sketched or wrote it down on a card, which was tacked up on the conference room walls for discussion. Ideas that were rejected were removed, and those ideas adopted were left to be Xeroxed and distributed for the record (fig. B7–2). Review of those "instant notes" suggests that energy efficiency was almost guaranteed during this session, and a clear design direction was set long before actual design began at the next meeting.

After my lecture defining the criteria for a good work environment, there was unanimous agreement on a number of issues of particular concern to lighting and energy design. Those issues included:

☐ use of a moderate level of high-quality ambient light (no more than one watt per square foot) supplemented by local task lighting where desired;

☐ maximum utilization of daylight in combination with good passive solar practice (as long as the benefits were not offset by HVAC penalty);

☐ taking advantage of building orientation, fixed architectural elements such as lightshelves, and high ceilings achieved through integrated building systems;

☐ use of dynamic controls to supplement fixed design and optimize energy performance.

At this time I was asked to investigate a recently published idea for beaming sunlight with mirrored venetian blinds and to report my findings at the next session.

USE DAYLIGHT COMBINED WITH PASSIVE SOLAR WHEN POSSIBLE WITHOUT NEGATIVE TRADE-OFF IN LOAD ON HVAC

USE 10-30 F.C. TO PROVIDE HIGH QUALITY LOW GLARE ILLUMINATION FOR PSYCHOLOGICAL NEED AND FOR GENERAL TASK THROUGH OUT THE SPACE DESIGN LOAD 1/WSP

PERIMETER AND TOP FLOOR SHOULD BE PREDOMINENTLY DAYLIT WITH WINDOWS, CLEAR STORIES AND SKYLIGHTS.

SUPPLEMENT WITH LOCALLY SWITCHED *TASK LIGHTING*, ONLY WHEN NECESSARY AT THE WORK STATION IMPACT ON SYSTEM .1W/SF BASED ON 50% OF OCCUPANTS AND A UTILIZATION RATE OF 50%

MAXIMIZE VIEWS OF SUNLIGHT TO FULLFILL PSYCHOLOGICAL NEEDS PARTICULARLY IN ATRIUMS (AVOID THE USE OF MATERIALS (LIKE REAL WALL) THAT CREATE THE FEELING OF OVERCAST CONDITIONS)

SHAPE BUILDING SYSTEMS TO INSURE HIGH EFFICIENCY AND WIDE DISTRIBUTION OF GENERAL ILLUMINATION FROM ARTIFICIAL AND DAYLIGHT SOURCES

SINCE TYPICAL DAYLIGHT LEVELS VARY FROM 500 TO 8000 F.C. USE DYNAMIC CONTROLS SUCH AS BLINDS AND SHUTTERS

B7–2. Ideas adopted using the CRS "squatters" procedure. (Courtesy of Caudill Rowlett Scott)

BEAMING SUNLIGHT—PRELIMINARY INVESTIGATION

The few days between the programming and urban design sessions was a very short amount of time in which to conduct the beam sunlighting investigation for which I was responsible. Up to this point all of my findings had been negative.

Currently available equatorial-mount heliostats, at many hundreds of dollars per square foot of sunlight redirected, seemed economically unrealistic. Having also seen a published diagram of sunlight beamed by mirrored venetian blinds and dismissed it as impractical (when first suggested and again after trying a thumbnail diagram), I had decided to experiment with the concept anyway to be fair to those who had suggested the technique.

The most convenient place to work and have immediate access to mirrored blinds was the MIT Solar 5 building, in which I could witness

B7-3. Testing mirrored louvers in a model at the MIT Solar 5 building. With normally spaced louvers, most light ''bleeds by'' at low winter sun angles, instead of being redirected deep into a space.

sunlight being beamed by mirrored blinds to thermal storage in eutectic, salt-filled, dark-colored ceiling tiles.

A 1'' scale model room with mirrored louvers was placed in the windows so that I could evaluate the beaming of sunlight for lighting purposes. As I expected, horizontal blinds in the window worked well for redirecting light to the ceiling adjacent for thermal storage, but had to be very closely spaced to redirect much light deep into rooms during the winter, when the sun is lowest and the light and heat most desirable (fig. B7-3).

I also noted that the MIT Solar 5 building designers had placed a wide window seat at the window edge so that one is less likely to be within the path from mirror blinds to ceiling and thus experience the glare. This confirmed my belief that the lower portion of a window is not a good position from which to beam sunlight for lighting.

Thus, when the subject came up again at the planning session, I reported those negative findings and recommended that we simply get as much light as possible from lightshelves and high ceilings and supplement as necessary for the deep floors desired for planning reasons.

URBAN DESIGN SESSION

The second (urban design) session, held in Chattanooga, was also very productive. Not only did it result in an urban design scheme; it also resulted in adoption of the overall building plans, sections, and integrated systems concepts.

The urban design session began with an endorsement of the urban design direction outlined by the TAC group, which had previously been assigned leadership in this area.

Their schematic investigations indicated that low buildings (rather than towers) would best fill the program requirement of being a good neighbor and avoid shading a large area of the central business district to the north. A number of low-rise buildings was also deemed desirable for a more humane lifestyle for the staff and for desired community contact (fig. B7-4).

Fewer, larger mid-rise (6–7 story) buildings were dictated by the limited site area, however. The amount of building area programmed (2 million square feet) would have required too many small (4-story) courtyard buildings. There was also insufficient spacing to adhere strictly to Knowles' solar envelope criterion that all south faces be unshaded all year long. Wise sunlighting practice dictated that the building blocks be elongated east/west for orientation to the south and north. With such building shapes, glazing east and west would be limited.

A Practical Form of Beam Sunlighting

That night, I awoke with an inspiration for beaming sunlight in very elongated atrium buildings—redirecting the sun from the roof with simplified *one-way* heliostats.

While real (two-way tracking) heliostats (which adjust on both axes) are very complex and expensive, ''one-way'' heliostats would be louvers

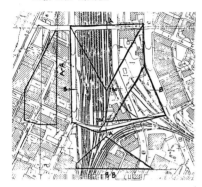

SOLAR ENVELOPE
STUDY
PARCEL B&C
9AM·3PM SUMMER
10AM·2PM WINTER

SHADOWS
DEC. 21
10AM·2PM
ALTERNATIVE
APPROACH NO.1

SHADOWS
DEC. 21
10AM·2PM
ALTERNATIVE APPROACH NO. 2

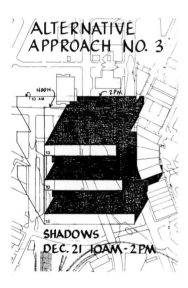

ALTERNATIVE
APPROACH NO. 3

SHADOWS
DEC. 21 10AM·2PM

SHADOWS
DEC. 21 10AM·2PM
SELECTED ALTERNATE

B7–4. Shadow studies led to the appropriate building massing. (Courtesy of Caudill Rowlett Scott)

pivoting on one axis, with flat mirrored surfaces to redirect rather than shade sunlight. Mirrors are used most efficiently when intercepting light fairly directly: therefore, a south-sloping roof would be the best configuration for redirecting low-angle winter sun (fig. B7–5). If the sunlight were redirected to be vertical, a 45-degree secondary mirror could redirect light horizontally as far into a space as desired.

I jumped out of bed, drew a quick diagram to verify the geometry, then demonstrated the phenomenon to myself with the hotel desk lamp and mirror sample from my briefcase.

With the sun out in the morning, I was able to repeat my two-dimensional demonstration with the mirror placed on my section diagram (fig. B7–6). Back at the urban design session I explained that the mirrored tracking louvers would be most effective in winter when sun angles were low and light and heat most wanted, but that they could also be set to allow diffuse light while rejecting unwanted heat in summer.

The team's response was enthusiastic. In minutes we were all drawing alternative litrium sections. I had pictured keeping the sun directly

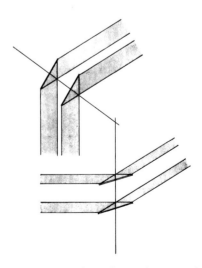

B7–5. Mirrors located on a sloping roof will intercept and beam more low-angle sunlight vertically than the same louvers located on a vertical wall will beam low-angle sunlight horizontally.

TVA Office Complex 285

B7-6. A two-dimensional demonstration of beamed sunlight made my diagram "real."

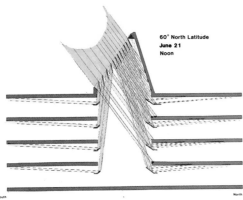

60° North Latitude
June 21
Noon

South · North

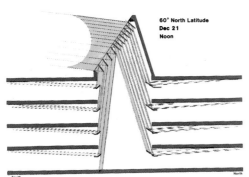

60° North Latitude
Dec 21
Noon

South · North

B7-7. If the floors are aligned vertically, the mirrors on the north can light the south side, and vice versa. This crosslighting technique is shown here for a proposed office building at 60° north latitude, a subpolar climate where beamed sunlight could be most appreciated.

overhead at all times on the north/south axis. This required that the balcony edges be stepped by the width of the mirrored lightshelves. Others suggested that the balconies could be aligned vertically if we cross-lit from the roof (fig. B7–7). This was a feasible, if somewhat more complicated solution, but most of us liked the stepped form spatially, and it was the form eventually adopted (fig. B7–8).

We all realized that tracking had to be extremely accurate because of the long distance the beams of light would travel. An error of half a degree would not be serious on the top floor, but six floors down, this error would mean that the beamed sunlight would miss the secondary louver. Achieving that degree of accuracy did not seem very formidable with high gear ratio drives and large-scale louvers located within the atria to avoid problems of wind movement.

In addition to accuracy of control, there were several other reasons for placing the mirrored louvers under rather than above the glazing:

The major benefit of an exterior location would be in the decreased cooling load (when the louvers were used in the shading mode). Outdoor access for cleaning would be easier, but it would be needed much more often than if louvers were placed indoors.

Some movement from wind seemed impossible to avoid with an exterior louver location. The brightness pattern of the sunlit ceiling would be distracting if it moved constantly and was distorted in shape. Any movement of the tracking mirrors would be multiplied because of the long "throw" distances. If located indoors and thus not subject to wind and weather, flat mirrored panels could more easily be kept free from distortion and hence be built less expensively.

Larger (and fewer) louvers were chosen for ease of maintenance and because the views reflected in large mirrors are more meaningful than those reflected in smaller ones.

Bearing-Angle Implications

By using one-way rather than two-way heliostats, these tracking louvers would be able to control the change in the sun's altitude angle but not the sweep in the sun's bearing angle. In a narrow building this could be critical, but given the width of the atria in the TVA buildings, this would not be as much of a problem. Sunlight penetration would be deepest at solar noon of each day; there would be significant penetration throughout most of the rest of the working day, however (fig. B7–9). The depth and spacing of the beams framing each floor running perpendicular to the atrium helped assure that each area would receive a similar amount of reflected light (fig. B7–10). In a narrow litrium, the changing bearing angle can be accommodated by the use of curving primary mirrors that spread the beam horizontally or by adding fixed east/west mirrors at roof level (on the sides of the beams).

Site Implications

Having designed a prototypical sunlighting system, the next step for the design team was to apply and adapt that system over the entire building complex, with adjustments for its range of programmatic requirements, urban design goals, and site constraints.

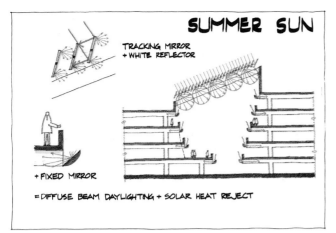

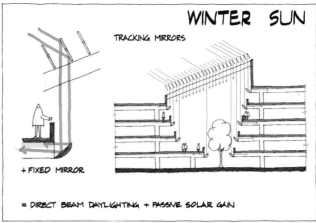

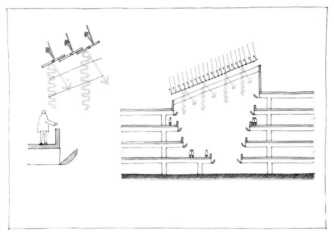

B7–8. In summer, direct sunlight is reflected onto the white side of the louver to provide diffuse sunlight with minimal heat gain. In the winter, the tracking mirrors beam sunlight onto a vertical path, which is intercepted by a fixed mirror at each floor and reflected to the ceiling. On winter nights, the louvers may be fully closed to help prevent heat loss.

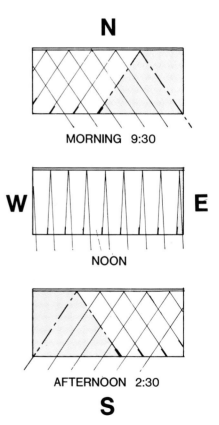

B7–9. The proportion of the atrium length to width is critical in successfully beaming oblique sunlight.

The need for accurate control of the mirror angles also had an effect at the urban design scale. We had planned to curve the buildings to align with the curving street edging the site on the south (see fig. B7–4). But a curved building would have meant that each louver in a bay would have to be different in length to fit between radial structures and, more important, that at any given moment the louvers of every bay in the buildings would have to be at a different angle because of each bay's unique orientation. With computer controls that would not have been an insurmountable problem; nevertheless, we deemed it an avoidable complexity. The buildings were kept straight and similarly aligned (figs. B7–11, B7–12).

The sunlighting system of creating vertical beams of sunlight with a mirrored louver system would provide maximum illumination within the buildings, with equal light on north and south sides. However, we decided to sacrifice some of the potential illumination and to alternate litriums with open courtyards between the buildings. We felt that giving the occupants both litria and the outdoor world to view and walk through would make the vast complex seem less formidable.

Testing the Beam Sunlighting Design

With the usual short period between meetings, the concept had to be tested very quickly so that the design development could continue. We built a 1/2″ scale model of a 60-foot section of atrium with louvers

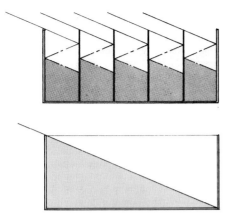

B7–10. Deep beams at wide spacing will help ensure that each bay will receive a similar amount of reflected light.

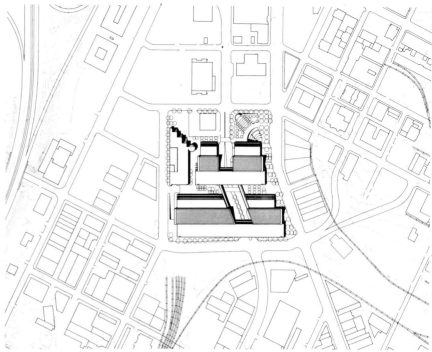

B7–11. The final site plan. (Courtesy of TAC)

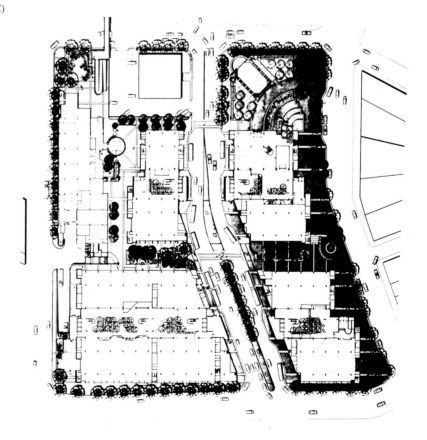

B7–12. A site model showing the alternating open and glazed courts. (Courtesy of CRS)

that could be white or mirrored. We measured the illumination in typical office bays (60 feet deep) inserted on both the north and south sides of the atrium (figs. B7–13, B7–14).

The tests showed the tracking mirrors to be so effective (measurements of more than 200 footcandles 60 feet from the window) that a second model with office bays 120 feet deep followed. Although crude in appearance because of the tight timetable, the models were accurate enough to demonstrate that the principle was sound and that the effect would be delightful as well as energy conserving (figs. B7–15, B7–16).

I had been impressed by the performance of mirrored lightshelves in the litrium and wanted to evaluate a variation for the north walls. I tried a vertical facade but found that a stepped section was marginally better quantitatively and aesthetically. These mirrors had to be set at a flatter angle than those in the atrium since they were to reflect the brightest area of overcast sky generally overhead rather than precise parallel beams of sunlight (fig. B7–17). A third model was tested later (fig. B7-18).

B7–13. The first model. (Courtesy of TAC)

B7–14. The second model.

B7–15. Data from the first model clearly indicated the value of the secondary mirror for increasing illumination far from the litrium.

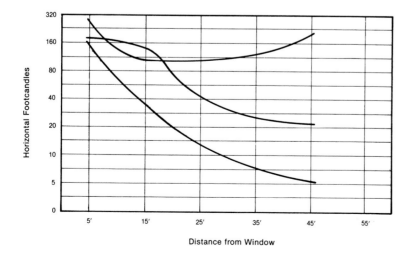

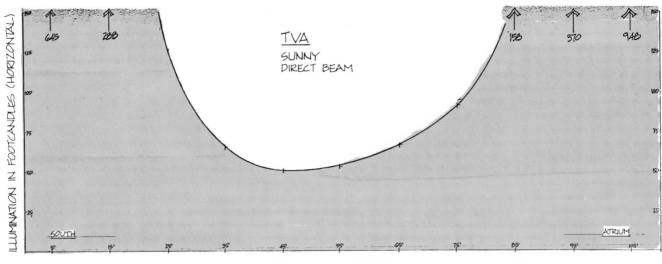

TVA
SUNNY
DIRECT BEAM

ILLUMINATION IN FOOTCANDLES (HORIZONTAL)

DISTANCE FROM WINDOW

7–16. Data from the second model show how illumination by the double mirror system would appear (with sunlight on the ceiling at midpoint).

SCHEMATIC DESIGN

The test results were sufficiently convincing that design development continued unimpeded.

At the start of the third meeting, our planning concepts and building systems were designed around atria with beam sunlighting. The concept having been verified by model testing, the design team went on to develop the full floor plans and work out the details of the construction systems for the atria and office blocks.

The building system we selected recognized the need to achieve high ceilings for distributing reflected sunlight effectively at a minimum construction cost and building volume.

We agreed on the desirability of an articulated building system with beams perpendicular to the windows and as far apart as practical, given the needs for integration of supplementary lighting and for occasional partitioning. Beam spacing was set at about 30 feet. Because of the wide beam spacing and building depth, I proposed four-foot-deep beams so that the lightshelves and beam flanges containing indirect fluorescent lighting would be maximally distant from the ceiling. Despite some initial reservations by the team, they were adopted and later found to be structurally desirable as well, for the long spans and cantilevers.

Service cores and small rooms with less need for daylighting and high ceilings (such as toilets) were located at the east and west ends of the building blocks (fig. B7–19). The net-to-gross ceiling height could have been improved with a central service spine located between paired col-

B7–17. Litrium of the second model.

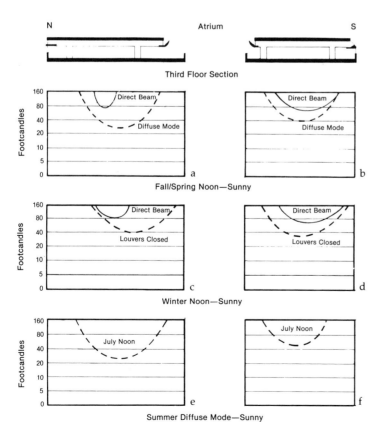

B7–18. Data from the third model was consistent with earlier series. It verified the advantage of the direct beam mode (solid lines) over the diffuse mode on clear days (doubling the illumination at the lowest point: a,b,c,d). On clear days, illumination on the atrium side would be higher than on the north exterior (b,d); the clear day illumination would be lowest in summer when the tracking louvers would operate in a diffuse mode; the north block would be better illuminated than the wider south block at the third-floor level modeled (e,f).

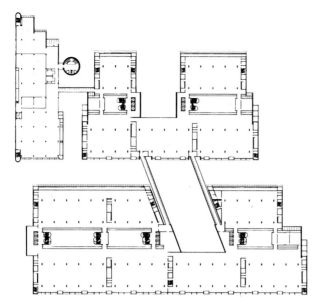

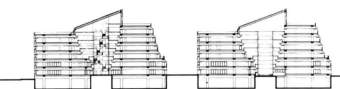

B7–19. The final plan and section.

umns (as I had designed for the Quebec Government Center[1]). Because of the very wide floors, however, there was no "natural" location in the plan for such a fixed corridor to carry services. Instead, we selected a channeled floor structure located above the major beams to carry cross services. This technique requires more overall building height, but provides maximum flexibility for corridor locations and efficient service distribution.

The structure selected for the litria roofs was affected by qualitative aspects of the tracking mirror louver scheme. The structural consultant, Bill LeMessurier, first responded to the problem with a system of open trusses. This was changed to a system of solid beams to minimize visual noise when juxtaposed with the tracking mirrored louvers. Solid beams would also control the "light leaks" from the inevitable bleed-by of light between the ends of the louvers. While such light leaks would not have been important in a hotel lobby, they would result in glare in the office spaces as they would sometimes be redirected by the fixed mirrors at the wrong angles.

DESIGN DEVELOPMENT AND ENERGY ANALYSIS

Design Model Testing

At the end of the schematic design phase, a third, more realistic model was built to collect new data, to reconfirm the generic model data in an accurate model of the proposed design, and to see what the building

1. Lam, Perception and Lighting as Formgivers for Architecture, *pp. 285–92.*

would look like (fig. B7–20). This was executed in California by the energy consultants, Van der Ryn/Calthope.

In this model, office landscape furnishings were simulated, a "tail" was added to the sloping mirrored lightshelf to control stray reflections, and the litrium roof was built with the proposed combination of beams and small-scale tracking louvers.

Illumination data confirmed that the tracking mirror system could more than double illumination levels in the middle of the building and that the target ambient illumination would be attainable even in midsummer with the mirrors acting in the heat reject-diffuse mode. Naturally, winter-fall-spring levels would be more than twice as high as summer levels.

Mock-up

The entire consulting team, being experienced professionals, had agreed on the absolute necessity of a full-scale mock-up to further verify design concepts and develop the details. Though we had faith in the quantitative data generated by the models, we wanted to evaluate how the spaces would "feel"—the effect of alternative mirror materials and construction, ceiling materials, and so on. We wanted to see the practical problems of wind movement and maintenance if the louvers were placed outside, and the effect on the view and thermal effects on the glass and energy performance if placed inside.

After my contract had expired, I and a small part of the team attended a meeting with a TVA group to clarify the requirements for a mock-up (size, materials, etc.) and test program. Over my objections, the group decided to build the mock-up with exterior mirrors because of the slightly better cooling load that would result, and for some other reasons that I felt were invalid:

☐ Easier maintenance because the area below need not be roped off for public safety. Whatever the public safety rules, I know that I would not want to be standing under workmen whether they were above or below a glass roof.

☐ More convenient maintenance because access catwalks could be provided more easily and high pressure hoses could be used. To me, the proposed catwalks would have been conspicuous and ugly, and the need for washing and repair of the mirrors much more frequent outdoors than in a protected location indoors.

☐ The major glass manufacturers were unwilling to guarantee the roof system with louvers within because of questions of heat build-up. I was advised by the director of research of one of the major glass manufacturers that he was sure the best skylight fabricators would guarantee the system with the louvers indoors. He saw little difference between the proposed louvers and other commonly used blinds and awnings in greenhouse spaces. Off the record, he said that glass manufacturers are reluctant to guarantee *anything*. They maintain that the fabricator responsible for the details should be the guarantor.

B7–20. Litrium and illumination data from the third model.
(Courtesy of Van Der Ryn/Calthorpe)

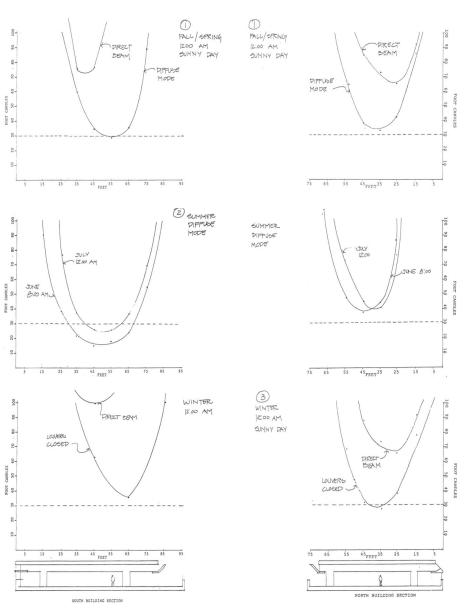

My principal disagreement however, was that if the louvers were located externally, they would not serve their principal purpose for beam sunlighting. To me, the problems of distracting light patterns from wind movement seemed unavoidable at an affordable cost.

I was not concerned as long as they built the mock-up and tested the alternatives. I knew that the test results would yield the right answers. I was also pleased that they planned to go ahead with the mock-up, because it would result in realistic bids for building and installing the system.

Instead of building the simplest, most economical mock-up to help develop and confirm the details, the plans somehow became very ambitious: I heard of a proposal to build it on a raft so that it could be moved along the river to Knoxville for the Energy Expo at the 1982 World's Fair. In the end (at least in part because of the high cost), no mock-up was built, and the information it would have provided was lost.

In retrospect, the problem was that nobody was really in charge at this stage. Since the design team's contract did not extend beyond design development, nobody with a real commitment to the concept was involved long enough to ensure that a mock-up would be built. TVA's failure to follow through on this critical step (despite many requests by design team members over an extended period) was probably the critical reason why this building failed to "advance the state of the art." Without the continuation of the design team, the tracking mirror concept was conceived but never developed.

Change in Design Team

A change in project personnel at TVA, along with the assignment of the contract documentation phase to local architectural firms, left no one who had been involved with formulation of the design concepts or who had a strong commitment to see the details fully developed—to resist eliminating beam sunlighting as a cost-saving measure. The situation might have been different if the original design team had been retained throughout the project, or at least through completion of construction documents.

Another likely cause for the lack of follow-through on the mirror system was the fact that it was not included in the original building contracts—it was to be bid separately at a later date.

The new management brought a total change in priorities. Their focus seemed to be primarily on short-term effectiveness rather than on investment in the future. TVA's willingness "to help commercialize new energy saving design concepts" was no longer evident. Also gone was the commitment to the team process. When our input was solicited at that stage, it was one at a time and by telephone.

THE COMPUTER BUILDING

The computer building was scheduled far ahead of the others and completed in 1982 (figs. B7–21 to B7–23). Although it lacks a litrium, this was the first test of the integrated building system and the north window wall.

B7–21. The computer building: north view.

B7–22. The computer building: southwest view.

B7–23. The computer building: northwest view.

A variation of the south wall (without the lower view windows and, unintentionally, with mirror-glass clerestories) was not representative of the rest of the project to be completed.

This first completed phase *did* confirm that the luminous environment created by the integrated building system with its supplementary indirect fluorescent lighting and deep beams would be as pleasant as expected. In this building, however, there was no way to confirm the sunlighting concept of the project.

THE OFFICE OF POWER BUILDING

When I visited the building in the spring of 1985, the general construction was complete except for the reflecting surfaces of lightshelves and holes in the ceiling awaiting installation of additional supplementary lighting fixtures. One could begin to evaluate the building's exterior as urban design and architecture and determine how its interior environment might be perceived by its future occupants (a small area had been furnished for demonstration).

Urban Design

There is no doubt that the complex will be a significant presence in Chattanooga. It is a large project whether seen from a distance or up close. Its formal elements are not dramatically different, but their combination in one project is certainly distinctive: large greenhouse roofs, terraced skylight forms on the north, blank walls on east and west, heavily sculptured facade to the south, and consistently oriented blocks with courtyards open to the streets (fig. B7–24). The expanse of the building's south facade with its large opening creates a distinctive gateway to the city from the south, which will become a more attractive approach when the boulevard is upgraded. The courtyards at the entrance plaza and between building blocks should be enjoyed by the public and staff.

Atria

The many linked atria should provide pleasant circulation and relaxation for the staff throughout the year, regardless of the weather (figs. B7–25, B7–26). Sunlight, although reduced 90 percent by the change to mirror glass, will be visible from many locations. The architectural colors and details created in response to sunlighting requirements have turned out to be beautiful; the curving forms of the lightshelves relate well to those of the stairs (figs. B7–27, B7–28). Unlike that of a typical hotel atrium, the view here is of softly curving white lightshelves—a pleasant contrast to the limited numbers of plants and trees dictated by the original sunlighting design.

The stepped forms (larger on the main circulation level) produce a distinctly different spatial experience at each level. It is also different in each of the several atria because of the variations in dimensions forced by conformance with the diagonal street penetration.

a.

b.

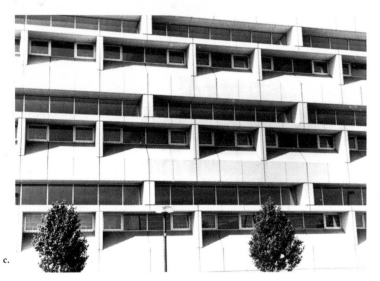

c.

d.

B7–24. The Office of Power building: (a) distant view from southwest; (b) south gateway to Chattanooga; (c) detail of a well-shaded south facade incorporating lightshelves; (d) northwest side.

B7–25. Typical courtyard.

a.

c.

B7–26. Atrium appears quite different at different levels: (a) upper level; (b) midlevel; (c) ground level.

b.

B7–28. Unusual junctions of elements make some interesting details.

B7–27. Lightshelves and stairs as sculpture.

a.

b.

Working Environment

Within the office "trays," one can appreciate the spaciousness of high ceilings glowing with indirect reflected sunlight and blending with that from fluorescent coves. The effect is attractive, even though the daylight contribution without any reflecting surface on lightshelves is less than it should be (fig. B7–29). The deep concrete beams and rounded glass reinforced plaster light coves are sculpturally beautiful and of a piece with the curving forms of the lightshelves and stair towers.

Additional ambient lighting in the form of individual indirect fluorescent fixtures makes the lighting more uniform than the designed beam-mounted cove lighting alone, though at the expense of adding a bit of visual clutter. Furniture-mounted uplighting (as at Johnson Controls, case study B2) would have been less obtrusive and allowed the amount and type of supplementary lighting to vary according to partition layout and space function. (The supplementary task lighting approach has apparently been abandoned.)

While the office landscaping in the original computer building enhanced the space, the sample layouts at the Office of Power building had many different heights and more high partitions located without much effect in relating to the structure (fig. B7–30). Hopefully, such cluttered arrangements will not be the norm. The view windows seem a bit confining, particularly from small perimeter rooms. The four-foot sill was designed to minimize air-conditioning load and with the expectation of open office landscaping with circulation along the edges, so that the views would be from a walking rather than a sitting position (fig. B7–31). In retrospect, they should have been lower; delight should have been given greater emphasis than absolute energy performance. The forms created to accommodate sloping mirrors produced beautiful forms viewed from the atrium side but ended up appearing a bit confining when viewed from the offices. Because there are no mirrors at the roof to beam sunlight

a.

b.

c.

B7–29. Typical spaces in south block: (a) at window edge; (b) at middle; (c) at litrium edge.

B7–30. Uncoordinated, high partitions.

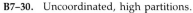

a.

b.

B7–31. When perimeter work spaces have partitions, clerestories are most appreciated: (a) south edge; (b) north edge.

down, the secondary sloping mirrors will not be installed as designed (fig. B7–32). As a result, instead of seeing reflections of the greenhouse-style roof and sky in the mirrors, one will see only the material of the sloping lightshelf itself. This view constriction will be less attractive than that of the flat lightshelves at Carrier (case study B2) or Blue Cross/Blue Shield (case study B1).

What Might Have Been

Despite the compromises, users and visitors will enjoy the planning, architectural forms, and details created to achieve optimum sunlighting; they will enjoy the courtyards, the atria, and the bright, cheerful, high-ceilinged spaces largely daylit at the perimeters. Only those who know what should have been (i.e., that the atria should in fact have been litria) will miss such features as:

☐ the delight of seeing direct sunlight spilling onto the litrium floor regardless of the sun's actual location in the sky;

☐ the delight of seeing and feeling direct sunlight in full intensity;

☐ the delight of seeing slowly changing patterns of sun on the ceiling deep in the space, throughout every sunny day;

☐ litria that would be ten times brighter on overcast days than the present atria (which are glazed with low-transmission glass). These litria would be the focal points of the building and would be brighter than, rather than a fraction as bright as, the external scene;

☐ ambient illumination of very deep spaces provided entirely by natural light on sunny days;

☐ healthier sunlit trees with no ''grow lights'' needed.

B7–32. View to atrium. Sloping lightshelf seems too heavy and confining without mirror to reflect greenhouse roof and sky.

SUMMARY

Although this building complex is not the demonstration of the luminous effects and energy–saving potential of beam sunlighting that the designers had hoped to see, it remains a major accomplishment. It is a very large demonstration of sunlighting from south and north facades, of a humane environment, and of a responsible relationship to the surrounding city. It demonstrates the possibilities for innovative design by team process when challenged to advance the state of the art.

Conversely, it demonstrates the problems of changing objectives and design teams midway through the process.

Fortunately, it is not too late to complete the demonstration or to improve the project. Having built a very substantial group of buildings, including almost everything but the critical hardware, it would be simple and not very costly to renovate a section of one building by finishing the existing lightshelf with mirror, replacing a few sheets of mirror glass with clear glass at the roof, and installing an area of available packaged louver system. An appropriate louver system is presently being manufactured and is beginning to be used in other types of buildings. For example, they are presently being installed at Park West, Dallas—(see case studies G1 and G2.)

Given TVA's role in research and its self-defined responsibility for community leadership, it would seem to be a very small commitment to public welfare "to provide a model for future development in the Valley and the nation." Doing so would give others the opportunity to evaluate for themselves the lighting potential of this highly publicized concept of beam sunlighting in other climates and in areas or periods of high electrical costs or shortages. An ideal application would be at very high latitudes (e.g. Alaska or Finland) where the low-angle winter sunlight is difficult to utilize without glare and where every ray of sunlight is appreciated.

GROUP C Schools

THE OPPORTUNITIES

As a group, schools are not as statistically important a sunlighting opportunity as are offices because the total area occupied by school buildings is not as great. Wasted energy from overlighting is not as prevalent in schools, perhaps because the lighting industry did not work as hard to influence this smaller market; school committees and boards have probably been harder to "sell" than building developers, who can pass costs on to their large corporate clients. In some states, illumination levels in schools have been as low as one-third to one-fifth of those in typical new office buildings.

Individually, schools may derive greater benefits from sunlighting, both economically and qualitatively, than do office buildings. By good utilization of the sun, schools should be able to be more self-sufficient in a number of ways. Most schools throughout the world depend on daylight as the primary source of illumination, with the exception of those schools built in the U.S. in recent decades. Even here, there was great interest in daylight in the '50s.

While power must sometimes be provided for artifical lighting at night, there is little excuse for most schools to be using much electric energy power for artifical lighting during the day. Operating hours for most schools coincide with the hours of maximum daylight availability. During the high proportion of unoccupied hours, many schools can benefit from the storage of excess solar heat.

The seasonal schedules of schools are advantageous. Most schools are closed during the hottest months, when excess sunlight can increase cooling cost.

Most schools are distant enough from adjacent structures to have good access to sunlight.

The limited depth of classrooms (often determined by class size), established to use daylight in earlier times when abundant artificial light was not available, has not changed much in recent years (as has the size of offices).

Nevertheless, I have seen few school buildings that use sunlight to produce delightful visual environments and optimum energy performance. Too often there is a dependence on blinds, shades, and other types of hardware that appear unsightly due to poor maintenance and the rough wear one would expect in a school environment.

Few schools take advantage of orientation as much as they could given the freedom offered by the generous sites they usually occupy.

Skylights and unshaded windows used in many older, un-air-conditioned schools ceased to be economical when buildings became sealed and the excess heat was being cooled rather than ventilated away.

In very hot climates, most schools have been properly designed with shading to defend against the sun as an obvious source of thermal discomfort. Very few, however, have been designed to optimize the qualitative and quantitative aspects of sunlighting.

In cold and temperate climates, relatively few schools have been designed to optimize the benefits of passive solar heating as a by-product of lighting.

As long as the option of efficient artificial lighting did not exist, daylight design could be crude and considered acceptable. Today, if the daylight design is not good, daylight is likely to be shut out and artificial lighting used instead.

C1 Soddy Daisy High School Soddy Daisy, Tennessee

Latitude: 35.4°N; climate: 3,500 degree days

117,000 square feet @ $52/sq. ft.

Architect: Franklin Group Associates (Jim Franklin, Partner in Charge; Ed Palmer, Project Architect)

Consultants: George S. Campbell & Associates, Inc.—mechanical and electrical; William Lam Associates —lighting; George Arnold, TVA Energy Group— energy analysis; Robert Pratt, Solar Resources—solar

Construction completed: 1983

CONTEXT

The architects had been exposed to sunlighting concepts during their association with the TVA Chattanooga Project (case study B7). (Their job had been to translate the design developed by the multidisciplinary design team into contract documents.) I was pleased when they asked me to help incorporate a "low-tech" version of sunlighting into a small, low-budget high school they were about to design in Soddy Daisy, a town near Chattanooga (fig. C1–1).

I suggested that a concentrated team-concept design session was the way to maximize results given the limited design budget. The overall design and construction concepts were created during an efficient, intense 2½-day session that began with only a space program. Further development, including daylight testing and energy analysis of the final design by the TVA solar group/design branch, produced only minor changes from the initial design.

LIGHTING OBJECTIVES IN CLASSROOMS

The activities most common in classrooms can benefit from the type of lighting most easily provided by sunlighting. These rooms tend to be open rather than subdivided, and the tasks performed tend to be those that can benefit from diffused sidelight, as long as the predominant direction of fixed seating is not toward the windows. Typical tasks and activities include looking at the teacher, the chalkboard, displays, classmates, three-dimensional laboratory equipment, and the like. However, classrooms today should be flexible enough to be comfortable over a wide range of seating arrangements. At present, avoiding excessive reflections on VDTs is increasing in importance in schools as it is in offices, though this problem is likely to become less severe with advances in the technology of video terminals.

Relatively few difficult and continuous horizontal tasks are performed in classrooms. Drafting and extended periods of difficult desktop work are the exception rather than the rule. The creation of pleasant, comfortable visual environments for the less critical visual activities listed

C1–1. South facade.

above will automatically provide sufficient illumination for "casual" reading. Task lighting can be provided for drafting if necessary.

The best classroom environments provide indirect light from surfaces that are enjoyable to look at—windows and room surfaces, particularly those vertical surfaces that are natural focal points (e.g., chalkboards). Thus, the key to the sunlighting of classrooms, even more than offices, is to distribute as much light as possible to all of these surfaces and minimize the sources of visual noise. Distracting signals such as direct sunlight in the eyes, too much view in the wrong place, disorderly blinds, and conspicuous light fixtures are the all-too-common causes of poor environments for concentrated study. While these environmental criteria may sometimes be difficult to quantify, the spontaneous judgments of users can be the best gauge of success or failure.

The challenge is to design schools that provide delightful, comfortable environments, both visually and thermally, using fixed architectural elements that require a minimum of adjustment or special maintenance. Adjustable elements for special uses such as film projection must also be provided, of course, and should be integrated into the overall design.

DESIGN PROCESS

After revising the space program to reflect a budget change, and following a site visit, the design process began with an introductory lecture (by me) and a discussion of the objectives, principles, concepts, and techniques of sunlighting. Taking the time to get the entire team on the same "wavelength" regarding the design objectives and principles is even more important on small, low-budget projects than on large ones, where some backtracking and inefficiency can be afforded. The first discussion session ended with the rough diagramming of some possible plans and sections for the given program.

On the second morning, different designers were assigned to the two most promising schemes, with continuous input from the consultants, including my educated guesses on the lighting impact and comments and rough calculations of the solar-thermal impacts from Robert Pratt. By afternoon, the assembled team selected a litrium scheme (over a more conventional double-loaded scheme). By midnight, part of the group had developed the floor plan; others had developed the construction and service systems and estimated the solar impact by hand calculations (figs. C1–2 to C1–6).

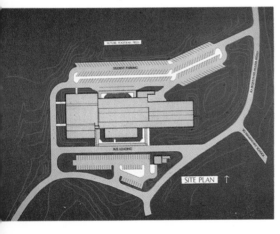

C1–2. Site plan. (Courtesy of Franklin Group)

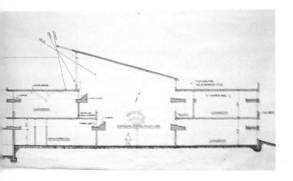

C1–3. Schematic section. (Courtesy of Franklin Group)

C1–4. Final section showing the lightshelf construction and very efficient use of building volume (12' ceiling height from 12' 8" total floor-to-floor height). (Courtesy of Franklin Group)

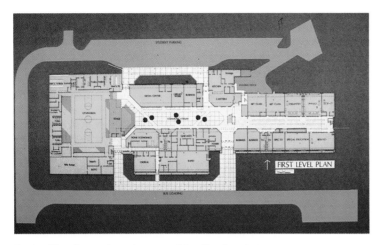

C1–5. First floor: plan. (Courtesy of Franklin Group)

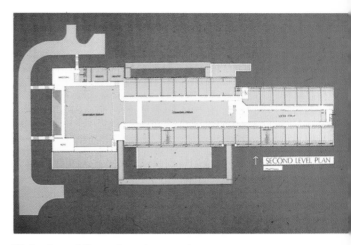

C1–6. Second floor: plan. (Courtesy of Franklin Group)

SUNLIGHTING CONCEPTS

Litrium

The litrium separating two east/west classroom blocks was considered a very important public space that could be central to casual activities as well as to circulation (fig. C1-7). This litrium will be heavily used for such purposes as lockers, eating, studying, and informal theater (or more formal theater when the double-sided stage house—common to the gym—is open).

Since no static work positions were to be located in the litrium, its comfort range could be wider than that of the office space at the Blue Cross/Blue Shield building (case study B1). Direct sunlight was considered welcome everywhere, though it was kept out in summer to optimize thermal comfort. Initially planned as a tempered buffer space, the litrium was conditioned at the client's request.

The wider section of the litrium (to the west) is illuminated by a south-facing sunscoop made more effective by an adjacent white roof. The roof slope and the height of the sunscoop glass were first set arbitrarily to allow direct sunlight to reach all of the rooms on the north side of the litrium at midwinter. Calculations indicated that the dimensions of the south-facing glazing were reasonable for supplying the needed winter heat gain, and with the overhang, not excessive in summer.

At the narrower, less efficient litrium to the east, an additional narrow band of north clerestories was added to provide additional light for the adjacent rooms on overcast days. This was not really needed, since its incremental benefit was minimal, and in retrospect, should have been omitted.

C1–7. The litrium

Classroom Blocks

All classroom blocks were bilaterally illuminated (fig. C1-8). Having previously tested models with a similar window section for the TVA project, I had no doubt that the classrooms on the south side could be quite well illuminated from the south windows alone. However, recognizing

C1–8. Typical classroom. (Photograph courtesy of John Lam)

the desirability of illumination from all directions (particularly in classrooms), I recommended redirecting as much light from the litrium as could be easily borrowed. With such small rooms, there was no need for the complex type of tracking mirror system used in the TVA project.

The potential benefit from the litrium light was increased by our initial decision to make the standard 20′ x 30′ classrooms narrow and deep. This was done to minimize both the overall length of the already long building and the span between girders, to allow the use of an inexpensive Flexicore concrete plank.

The need for bilateral lighting was even greater in the deeper (37′) lower-level rooms and in those rooms on the north side of the litrium whose shaded north exposure would receive direct sunlight only during summer holidays. Those rooms would welcome the direct sunlight received on their lightshelves from the litrium for the delightful feeling of the presence of sunlight as well as for the balanced illumination and brightness distribution gained. Because we expected to receive sufficient light from the clerestory windows, heat loss was minimized by limiting the lower ''view'' windows to those flanking the columns and illuminating the transverse walls. Such windows provide sufficient orientation for classrooms and leave useful ''teaching wall'' space.

Orientation

Instead of a true south orientation, the building was adjusted 15 degrees to the east to get the solar heat one hour earlier for the morning start-up (when heat could be used even in spring and fall). Since schools are relatively inactive at the end of the day, this orientation also provides sunlighting benefits for the longest time during the school day.

Gymnasium

The usual problem of using natural light in gyms is the inadvertent creation of glare and visual noise. Busy patterns of skylights or clerestories (or fluorescent lighting) often compete with the restful visual background that is pleasant for many gym activities, such as calisthenics and dancing, and essential for those involving overhead viewing, such as basketball and badminton.

Such problems can be eliminated by illuminating large surfaces such as the walls from sources concealed from normal view (fig. C1–9). This was accomplished here with sunscoops and lightscoops facing the north and south walls (fig. C1–10).

Both the visual environment and energy conservation could have been even better, however, if a suncatcher baffle (a technique learned from later projects) had been added to reflect sunlight into the north-facing clerestory and a similar arrangement had been carried around a third or even a fourth side (though this would have conflicted with the use of the stage). The combination of sunscoops and suncatcher baffles would have kept the lighting of the various walls quite well balanced throughout the day (fig. C1–11).

The large sloping suncatcher/lightcatcher roofs not only added interest and more human scale to the exterior forms, but also reduced the overall volume of the gym. The height of a flat roof shape would have been set by clearance over the mezzanine wrestling areas.

C1–9. The gym: (a) interior; (b) exterior.
(Photographs courtesy of John Lam)

a.

b.

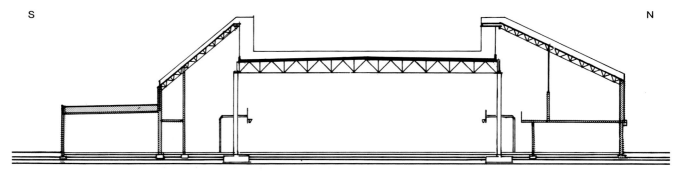

C1–10. Section through gym.

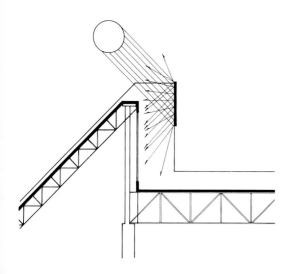

C1–11. The addition of suncatcher baffles could increase light input into the north-facing clerestories. For even better illumination, they could be used in combination with additional east- and west-facing clerestories to ensure more uniform illumination throughout the day.

MODEL TESTING

Data indicated that illumination would always be higher in the south block, which would need little supplementary lighting during daylight hours. On sunny winter days, when heat and light from the sun would be most welcome, the classrooms would be brightest. On sunny summer days, light levels would be lower, similar to typical cloudy or overcast day levels. Although levels would be far lower in the north block, those classrooms would also need little supplementary light on sunny or bright overcast days. Unlike the south block classrooms, where the levels would always be highest near the exterior window wall, the north block rooms would be brightest on the litrium side on sunny days and brightest on the exterior walls on overcast days (fig. C1–12). Testing also indicated that the contribution from the litrium would be higher if sloped mirrored lightshelves were used.

The benefits of qualitative observation of the model should not be forgotten. In the north block, it had been decided to increase the wall area for display and reduce heat loss by using a solid wall punctured for occasional windows instead of continuous view windows underneath the lightshelves. The lighting this would produce was never evaluated by diagramming. Viewing the model showed that the exterior wall would be in shadow. Looking at the model made it apparent that the lightshelves should be floated away from the wall to "leak" light to the walls below (figs. C1–13, C1–14).

BUILDING SYSTEMS

The budget for this job was very modest—equal to that of a recently completed elementary school next door built of concrete block, bar joist, and Tektum.

The system used to achieve the sunlighting objectives therefore had to be very economical. Concrete frames with beams three feet deep (in order to achieve the desired distance from the lightshelves and indirect fluorescent supplementary lighting) were spaced 22 feet o.c. Some team members suggested eliminating the beams in favor of load-bearing walls. That scheme would have worked for most of the classrooms, but not for those more than one module wide, and (without a single, uniform structural system) would have made for great inflexibility.

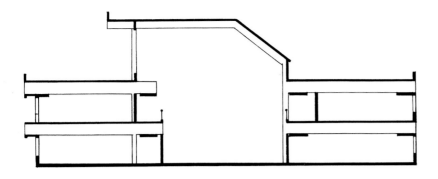

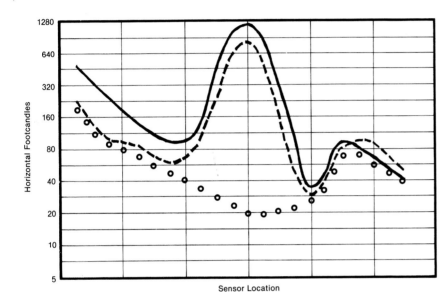

C1–12. Model testing data for December noon (solid line), March noon (dashed line), and overcast conditions (dotted line) at the lower level of the wide atrium. (Courtesy of Franklin Group)

C1–13. Model photographs showed the "teaching wall" to be in the shadow of the lightshelf.

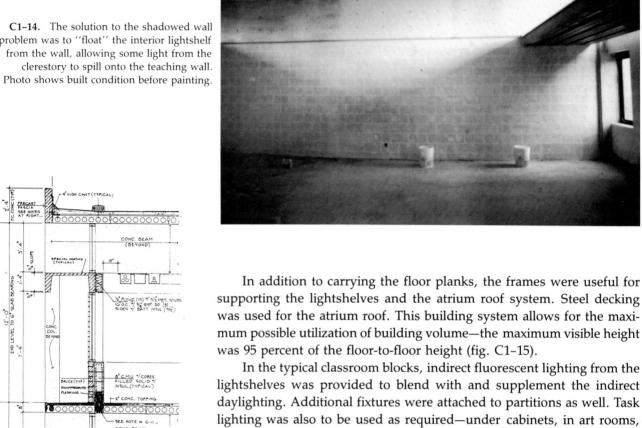

C1–14. The solution to the shadowed wall problem was to "float" the interior lightshelf from the wall, allowing some light from the clerestory to spill onto the teaching wall. Photo shows built condition before painting.

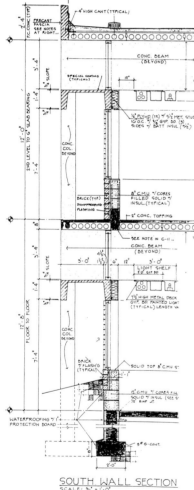

SOUTH WALL SECTION
SCALE: ¾" = 1'-0"

C1–15. South wall: section. (Courtesy of Franklin Group)

In addition to carrying the floor planks, the frames were useful for supporting the lightshelves and the atrium roof system. Steel decking was used for the atrium roof. This building system allows for the maximum possible utilization of building volume—the maximum visible height was 95 percent of the floor-to-floor height (fig. C1–15).

In the typical classroom blocks, indirect fluorescent lighting from the lightshelves was provided to blend with and supplement the indirect daylighting. Additional fixtures were attached to partitions as well. Task lighting was also to be used as required—under cabinets, in art rooms, and so forth.

Because of budget limitations (and the fact that the appropriate systems were still in the early stage of development), a limited photocell control system was installed to switch off the lighting power in various areas when natural lighting was more than sufficient. A more sophisticated system should probably be installed when funds permit, or the staff should be educated to turn off unneeded lights. A scheduled monitoring program by the TVA solar group should indicate whether or not this additional effort would be worthwhile.

CHANGES

The original duct/lightshelf design was later modified when the clients elected to change from the more efficient central ducted air system to a minimum first-cost system with inefficient through-the-wall units fed by hot and cold water pipes. In making this change, the architects found a very economical way to build the interior lightshelves: they used long-span steel decking turned upside down so that the open cells on top could enclose the HVAC pipes and supplementary fluorescent fixtures. The other open cells were covered with painted sheetrock for efficient light reflection.

Mounting the wall air-conditioning equipment also caused a reduction of the south "view" windows. Since the clerestory lightshelves already provided more than sufficient light, however, it was acceptable to reduce the cooling load and gain wall space, except in those rooms and on those occasions when the sweeping view of the landscape will be missed.

Other compromises to minimize first cost were the use of single glazing throughout and minimal roof insulation.

TVA SOLAR GROUP REPORT

In their design development, the architects received analytical help from the Solar Technology Outreach Program of the TVA before making final any of the energy-related design details. Data from the final TVA report projected excellent energy performance, exceeding both the original energy goals of the project and BEPS (DOE Building Energy Performance Standards) (fig. C1–16). The improvement is even greater in energy cost, because heat is less expensive than electricity.

It should be noted that this excellent performance was predicted *in spite of* the cost-saving compromises mentioned above—an inefficient air-conditioning system, a minimal level of roof insulation, and, most important, the single glazing throughout. These compromises had not been viewed as cost effective by the architects.

Had I known of the report and the intended compromises, I would have recommended eliminating the optional north-facing atrium clerestories, investing the savings in double glazing, and trying to get the funds for better insulation. An already energy-efficient design could have been made more so very easily, with no visible difference or added design complexity.

One source of heat loss that I would have continued to ignore in this relatively mild climate (because it would be difficult to eradicate without very different detailing) was thermal transfer through the uninsulated exposed structure.

SUMMARY

The building turned out as expected: it is a simple building with modest materials, but its forms are interesting, both inside and out. Many details could have been improved with a larger design and construction budget.

It creates a delightful educational environment, as a quick visit back-to-back with the more conventional schools nearby will demonstrate. Even though optimum energy cost savings and efficiency were compromised, the basic concepts of sunlighting and integrated building systems more than made up for these compromises. They serve to create a building more economical in cost and operations than more conventional buildings that depend on efficient hardware rather than use of the sun. More im-

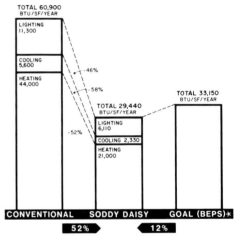

Comparative Annual Energy Consumption
*Goal based on Building Energy Performance Standards

C1–16. TVA energy evaluation. (Courtesy of TVA)

C1–17. South elevation.

portant, this building provides these economies with delight rather than gloom (figs. C1–17, C1–18).

The architects report interest by Tennessee school officials in building other schools like it and have already received a commission to duplicate the gym.

POST OCCUPANCY EVALUATION BY TVA

As a research and public service program, TVA has been monitoring the building's performance.

Qualitative Evaluation

A questionnaire completed in May 1984, during the first year of use, showed that '' . . . overall, users of the high school were generally satisfied with it, with a few exceptions. There was surprising uniformity of answers between teachers, students, and staff.'' The questionnaire also yielded the following statistics:

☐ The light level with blinds up and electric lights off on cloudy days was considered satisfactory or very good by 85 percent of respondents (76.8—satisfactory; 8.1 percent—very good);

- The light level with view-window blinds up and lights off on sunny days was considered satisfactory by 91.7 percent (38 percent—satisfactory; 53.7 percent—very good). There are no blinds at the clerestory windows;

- A total of 83.8 percent of respondents indicated no glare at their desks;

- The light level and glare at desks with view-window blinds down and electric lights on was considered comfortable by 95.5 percent of those surveyed;

- Lighting in classrooms was rated comfortable by 95.7 percent of those surveyed; that in common areas was rated comfortable by 97.8 percent. The environment was rated pleasant in classrooms by 87.1 percent and in common areas by 88.9 percent;

- The size of the windows was considered adequate by 77.5 percent of those replying;

- Windows were considered well positioned by 79.1 percent;

- Direct sunlight in the rooms was considered pleasant by 85.2 percent of respondents.

Quantitative Evaluation

It is difficult to judge how much energy could be saved by sunlighting since the photoelectric control system has not been working most of the time.

Initial surveys indicated that with lighting controlled by local switches and user action, the monthly use of electric lights varied from 33 to 80 percent of possible use during the daylight hours in the first year. The survey group has observed that in recent periods, users have been more responsible in keeping the necessary lights off and that new surveys should show better results. TVA intends to upgrade the control system to better exploit the energy-saving potential.

C1–18. South facade: detail.

C2 Canfield Hall, U.S. Coast Guard Reserve Training Center Yorktown, Virginia

CONTEXT

Latitude: 37°N; climate: 3,500 degree days

56,000 square feet

Architect: U.S. Coast Guard Headquarters, Civil Engineering Division, Facilities Branch

Consultants: Northeast Solar Energy Center of Northern Energy Corporation—energy; Wayne Place of Lawrence Berkeley Laboratories—energy analysis; William Lam Associates—lighting

Construction completed: May 1984

My involvement in this project began as a consultant to the Northeast Solar Energy Center (of Northern Energy Corp.) in their energy survey of existing USCG facilities at Yorktown. Having pointed out the missed opportunities for using daylight as well as the wasteful and unpleasant artificial lighting, I was asked to help the energy consulting team demonstrate what could be done in the design of a new classroom building (fig. C2–1).

The design process of this building began in a very unusual way. The two-day "squatters" session was led by the team of energy consultants, who effectively produced the schematic design that was later modified and developed by the USCG architects and engineers (who were present at the original design session, but, unintentionally, more as audience than participants).

In retrospect, the relatively inactive role of the USCG design staff during the concept design process is understandable. Because the team and the design process itself had been orchestrated entirely by the training center commander at Yorktown, the Washington contingent had arrived at the design session unaware of the program and completely unprepared (without drawings or even paper).

With nothing besides a space programming report and a site map, and with a vacuum in design leadership, the consultants, who had considerably more architectural and engineering experience than the USCG group, quite naturally assumed the leadership role.

THE DESIGN CONCEPT

The two-day charette resulted in a fairly detailed design of a double-loaded corridor building with classrooms shallow enough to be illuminated from one side by easily controlled sunlight from the south.

The programmed requirement to optimize conditions for the frequent use of audio-visual presentations in every classroom proved to be a dominant formgiver. The facade treatment was shaped by this requirement, which suggested placement of the projection rooms at the exterior walls.

C2–1. Rendering of building: northeast side. (Photograph courtesy of U.S. Coast Guard)

With this placement, window views can be available during moments of relaxation but totally out of sight when students are focused inward toward podium and screen. There should be no glare or distraction from windows in this position, and the amount of daylight admitted can be controlled precisely by electrically operated blackout window shades. When maximum illumination is desirable, the wide diffusion of sky light and reflected sunlight from the wall-to-wall lightshelves/clerestories should not cast noticeable shadows on desktops or chalkboards. Any sunlight admitted in the winter, when the heat will be desirable, is unlikely to cause glare with such room orientation. Whereas more continuous windows might be expected in office buildings, the limited view windows between projection rooms should be more than adequate in classrooms.

Since Wayne Place from LBL (who was later to do the detailed computer energy analysis) was also a registered structural engineer, the energy consulting team was able to suggest the construction system. Our educated guess was that the cost of the proposed building system should be very reasonable.

Schematic sections and elevations of the integrated building system and elevations were drawn by Place and myself (figs. C2–2, C2–3).

SITE CONFLICTS

From the outset, I was aware of the "conflict" between the principal north/south orientation desired for good passive solar and sunlighting design and the already established street grid, oriented 45 degrees from

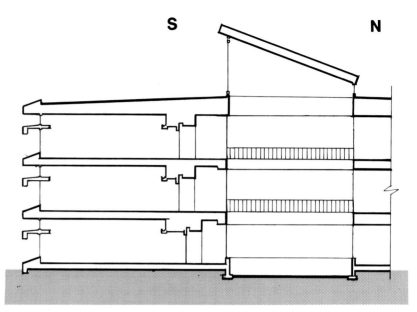

C2–2. Section.

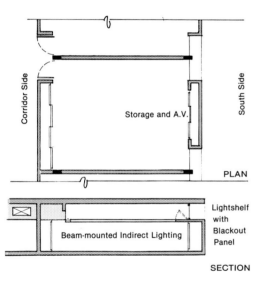

C2–3. Classroom module showing structural systems integration.

that axis. While I felt that it was not too late to establish a new axis for the major building blocks of the campus, I did want to acknowledge the street pattern at grade if possible.

An opportunity to make this transition was in the placement of a workshop-display room for a patrol boat mock-up. This room was aligned with the street in a separate block that would also enclose and define an entrance plaza. The greater plan and height dimensions needed for this room and the desirability of a high-traffic location for display were fortuitous. The low block was offset from the corner to save a large tree (fig. C2–4).

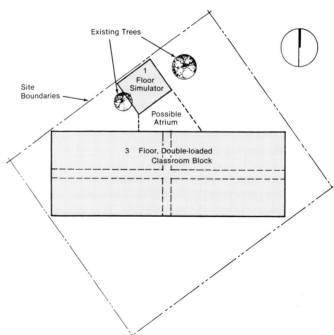

C2–4. Original site schematic.

DESIGN DEVELOPMENT

In their design development, the USCG team decided to move the mock-up boat lab to the corner of the site and to modify the double-loaded scheme to make the building-to-street transition at the upper levels as well as at grade. The northern classroom block was extended and deployed as bridges to the mock-up boat block now forming the corner. A central atrium was thus created (figs. C2–5, C2–6, C2–7).

In reviewing the revised scheme, prior to adjusting my suggested details accordingly, I was concerned that the northeast/northwest orientation of the classrooms might present glare and summer cooling problems not inherent to the original north-facing scheme. Model testing, however, indicated that the combination of the room-seating orientation and the vertical baffling provided by the "outboard" location of projection rooms helped alleviate the potential disadvantages of the changed facade orientation.

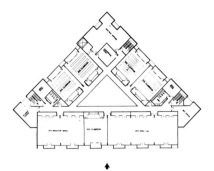

C2–5. Second floor: plan. (Courtesy of U.S. Coast Guard)

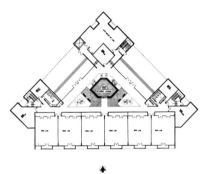

C2–6. Ground floor: plan. (Courtesy of U.S. Coast Guard)

C2–7. Final site plan. (Courtesy of U.S. Coast Guard)

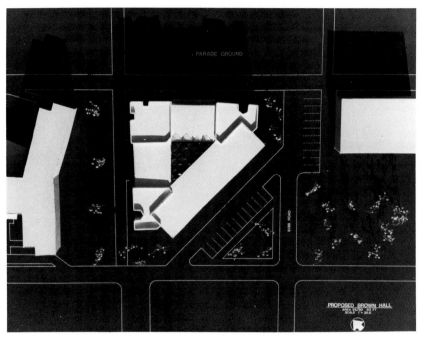

Model photos indicated that a very small amount of direct sun would be admitted on the northwest side, but only for a short time and after normal classroom hours during the summer (when the sun will reach those facades at an angle too low to control with lightshelves). However, any direct sunlight penetrating past the fixed shading elements would fall on the side walls toward the back of the room or the backs (rather than the faces) of students (figs. C2–8, C2–9).

Similarly, penetration of early morning summer sun on the northeast face would take place before classroom hours. Even without using the always available blackout shades, the total effect of sunlight penetration on air-conditioning load should be minimal.

Model measurements were made by the Northern Energy staff with

C2–8. Qualitative model testing: northwest wall, June, 4 P.M. Sunlight is now on this wall. The small band of uncontrolled sunlight is not a problem for glare control or local overheating. To reduce the cooling load, the upper blackout shade might be lowered to reduce illumination to minimum desired level (at least by 2/3) without sacrificing the view from the lower window. When the last class is over, the shades should be fully closed against the late afternoon sun, a step not necessary with the original scheme (north and south window exposures only).

C2–9. Qualitative model testing: south wall, June, noon. South wall receives minimum illumination in June: at noon it is less than half of that in December, when maximum light and heat are welcome.

my instrumentation and instructions. They began on the roof of their building facing the Boston harbor, but had to move to a less windy area after part of the model was blown away.

While the atrium, introduced in the revised plan, allowed the possibility for bilateral lighting of the classrooms (as at Soddy Daisy High School, case study C1) in this case we preferred not to use borrowed light from the atrium to minimize cost as it would create visual competition from clerestory windows adjacent to the principal teaching surfaces (projection screens and chalkboards). For the relatively shallow, wide rooms, unilateral sunlighting alone should be sufficient.

The data for the south-side laboratories showed that illumination levels should be adequate during almost all daylight hours without supplementary lighting, except for illumination of tables near the inner walls at the beginning and end of clear winter days (fig. C2–10a), and on overcast days (fig. C2–10c). The lowest noontime levels on clear days will be in June (fig. C2–10b).

As one might expect, the lowest illumination levels projected were in the northeast and northwest lecture classrooms at the beginning and end of December days, when the sun is too far south to reach these facades and too low to illuminate the ground outside very brightly (fig. C2–11). Even then, the ambient daylight will provide about half of the light needed and be sufficient to maintain operations during brownouts.

When I reviewed the USCG team's final floor plans with the model tests in mind, I realized how cleverly the designers had integrated the sunlighting system with the programmatic needs of the various spaces.

They had placed those functions that could most benefit from the highest illumination levels and most expansive views (laboratories) in the south-facing block, which would receive the most and steadiest light, and where the wide view windows are sufficiently shaded to require no supplementary shading.

They placed almost all of the lecture rooms with lower and more

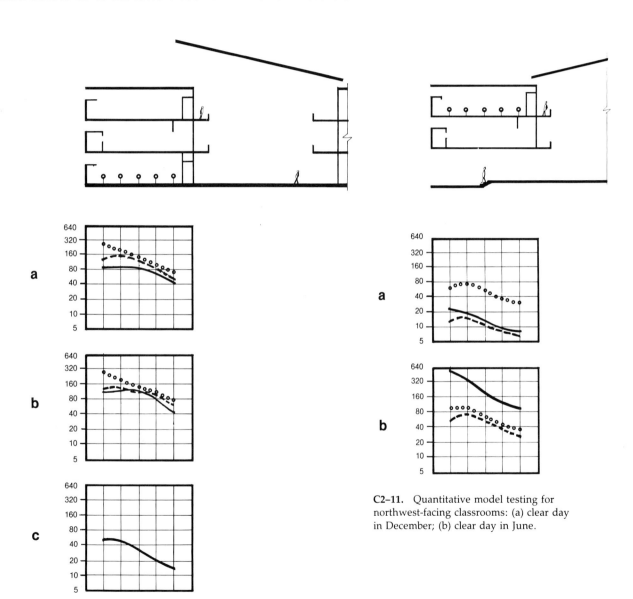

C2–10. Quantitative model testing for south-facing laboratories: (a) clear day in December; noon (dotted line), 8 A.M. (dashed line), 4 P.M. (solid line); (b) clear day in June; (c) overcast day.

C2–11. Quantitative model testing for northwest-facing classrooms: (a) clear day in December; (b) clear day in June.

variable lighting and view requirements on the northeast/northwest blocks. Here they provided enlarged audio-visual projection rooms and narrowed the view windows to increase protection from low-angle late afternoon summer sunlight, minimizing the need for using the blackout shades.

I was pleased to see that they had used the recessed pockets the building system had created for projection rooms and podia for well-placed laboratory storage and that they found good use for the irregular corners for student lounges and offices.

POST OCCUPANCY EVALUATION

Canfield Hall, completed in May 1984, turned out much as expected. It is enjoyed by staff and students for its bright, spacious, south-facing sun-lit laboratories, which have little need for artificial lighting during the day (fig. C2–12). The inward-facing lecture rooms are pleasant and free from the visual noise of bright fluorescent lighting fixtures or direct sunlight. Clerestories and view windows are out of sight during lectures, but there to enjoy during breaks, unless the room is blacked out for film projection (fig. C2–13). Daylight illumination level and distribution can be adjusted by separate blackout shades for upper and lower windows.

C2–12. South-facing laboratory on sunny day in September.

C2–13. Northeast classroom: facing the windows during breaks.

One installed detail I did not foresee during the short concept session was the use of glossy white writing surfaces, instead of chalkboards (to eliminate the possibility of chalk dust on blue uniforms). Reflection of the facing window wall and adjacent ceiling on the glossy surface is not bad for most of the classrooms (located on the northeast and northwest sides) but veiling reflections do occur when shades are fully open in the few classrooms that face south (where the skies and illuminated ceilings are brightest). If high-gloss writing surfaces are used, the reflections can be reduced by tilting the panels forward to reflect the darker lower room surfaces. Alternatively, writing surfaces should be located on the side walls. Clearly, standard blackboards or other matte surfaces are best for teaching walls facing the windows. Newsprint pads are being used successfully.

As urban design, the triangular shape of Canfield Hall fits the diagonal grid of the campus (fig. C2–14) without sacrificing the advantages of south orientation for the major facade (fig. C2–15). The entrances around the demonstration room (now scheduled to be converted to a library) are grand. The clerestory-lit atrium (fig. C2–16) is a pleasant approach to classrooms; large shaded south-facing and smaller northeast/northwest-facing clerestories admit visible bands of sunlight much of the time with net heat gain in winter and minimum impact on cooling in summer.

SUMMARY

This red brick and concrete building does not look like the energy efficient building that it is. It differs little in appearance from some of the other brick buildings that surround it, except for the strong statement of the fenestration (dictated by positive use of the sun for laboratories) and the external placement of projection rooms for effective and delightful audio-visual classrooms (fig. C2–17).

C2–14. Entrance from the northwest.

C2–15. South facade.

C2–16. The atrium.

Prototype Classrooms for a University in the Middle East Saudi Arabia

Latitude: 20°N

Architect: Campus Consortium Consultants Ltd./The Webb Zerafa Menkes Housden Partnership/Arthur Erickson Associates—joint venture architects

Consultants: William Lam Associates—lighting

THE CHALLENGE

Because I was retained toward the end of schematic design, my lighting master plan report for the entire university was primarily focused on artificial lighting. However, I also suggested a direction for design development of the fenestration and its integration with interior building systems and supplementary electric lighting, particularly for the mixture of labs, classrooms, and offices in the various faculties.

The architects' models and sketches of the urban/site design scale (see case study A2) indicated a "wall architecture" of stuccoed masses with deeply recessed horizontal and vertical windows (fig. C3–1). All larger openings were completely covered with the traditional wood screen (*moucharaby*) of the area.

My challenge was to apply the concepts of lightshelves and shaded framed views that I had been exploring in North American projects in the context of "wall architecture" and a hot climate with more continuous sunshine than anywhere else in the world. I had to develop a prototypical solution that could be applied by others to the wide variety of faculty buildings that were to be developed in detail and built. I hoped to achieve the stringent goals of high-quality interior environments that I provide for the classrooms and offices of my North American practice, without compromising the architects' desire for architectural forms indigenous to the Middle East.

PROPOSAL—MINIMUM FENESTRATION

Fortunately, the high ceilings I favor have always been traditional in this country. Thus, I proposed keeping major ductwork in corridors, in order to ensure such high ceilings in the perimeter classrooms and offices (fig. C3–2). Since the rooms were seldom deeper than twenty feet, horizontal windows about two feet high could capture and redirect sufficient sunlight when oriented to the south. While such narrow bands could be almost totally shaded within the thickness of the load-bearing masonry walls, with thinner wall sections, it was necessary to project inward or outward in a monolithic manner to achieve our sunlighting goals.

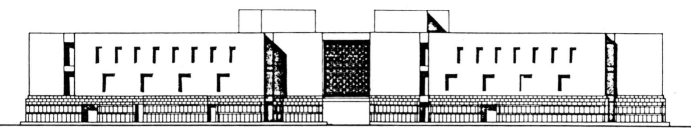

SOUTH ELEVATION

C3-1. Typical elevation of "wall architecture" with deeply recessed openings. (Courtesy of Campus Consortium)

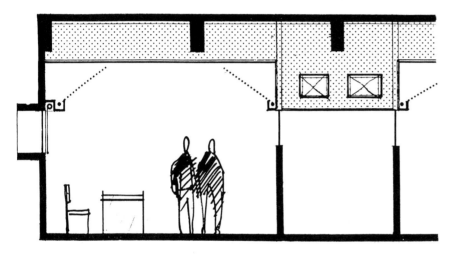

C3-2. Major HVAC systems were relegated to corridors to allow high ceilings in work spaces.

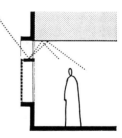

C3-3. White-painted sills were located to be above seated eye level.

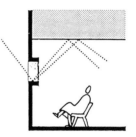

C3-4. Clerestory windows were located above the *moucharabies*.

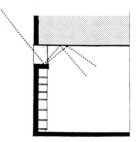

C3-5. Clerestories integrated with bookshelves.

I felt that placing the white-painted sills of those windows above eye level from the seated position, but just below eye level at a standing position, would give the best combination of optimum reflection of light to the ceiling, minimum glare, and reasonable view (fig. C3–3). Narrow vertical slits angled to control direct sunlight penetration were provided for additional views in offices and classrooms and to illuminate adjacent walls.

Because the schematic design documents had indicated that all larger windows were to be totally covered with wood screens, I placed narrow horizontal clerestory/lightshelf windows above the screened lower windows in order to get adequate light into those rooms even when the screens are closed (fig C3–4) or the same line of narrow clerestories integrated with bookshelves or display surfaces below (fig. C3–5).

Although the short time provided for the lighting concept report did not allow any testing, previous generic data generated in my office left little doubt that the design was sound for the south-facing open courts with access to dependable sources of sunlight, as indicated in the master plan (see fig. A2–4). The design should also be valid for the lower levels of eastern and western exposures, where low-angle sun is controlled by the narrow street layout. Suncatcher baffles should take care of the upper levels or else supplementary dynamic shading will have to be provided (fig. C3–6). Windows facing east and west onto courtyards will have suncatcher trellises for low-angle sun control (fig. C3–7) as was used at GSIS (case study B3).

The minimum area of fenestration proposed throughout this project should provide a reasonable amount of glare-free light without introducing excessive heat load. It is better to turn on lights when there is no sunlight than to "overfenestrate" for such conditions in hot climates and suffer from overheating when sunlight is present.

NEW INDIGENOUS FORMS

Concern about producing sunlighting forms consistent with the traditions of the indigenous "wall architecture" is reflected in fenestration facade studies by my associate, David Lafitte (fig. C3–8). I believe the windows will have an indigenous character but be sufficiently different in detail to give optimum sunlighting performance. To accomplish this goal, sun control devices such as lightshelves have been internalized whenever possible, and their presence has been minimized by their alignment with valances, wall trim, transoms, and the like (fig. C3–9).

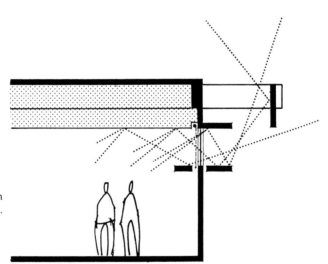

C3–6. Suncatcher baffles will be used on east/west exposures on upper levels.

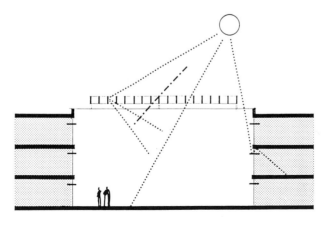

C3–7. Suncatcher trellises will be used to control low-angle east/west sun in courtyards.

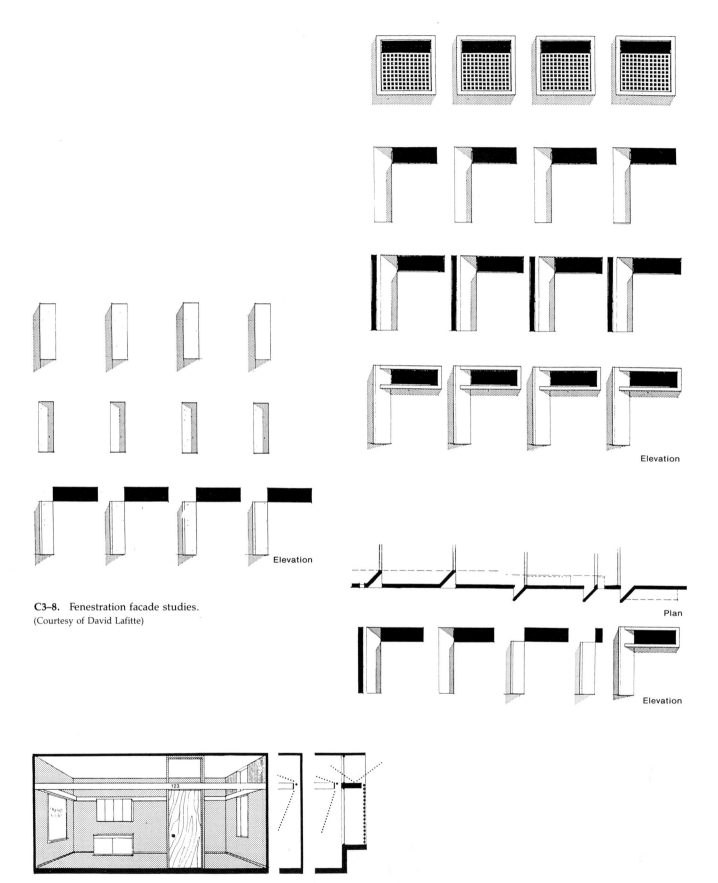

Elevation

Plan

Elevation

Elevation

C3–8. Fenestration facade studies.
(Courtesy of David Lafitte)

C3–9. Valance is used as an organizing line for sun-control devices.

GROUP D MUSEUMS

Museums, unlike offices, benefit more from the qualitative aspects than the quantitative (economic) aspects of sunlighting.

In public circulation areas, the principal objective of the luminous environment is satisfaction of biological information needs. Sunlighting can be valuable for orientation and visual relief, particularly in very large institutions, where the visitors' experience will be much more enjoyable and less tiring if they do not feel lost in an endless maze of rooms. Sunlight can emphasize important or beautiful architectural forms; beautiful sunlit surfaces will add a quiet sparkle to the spaces.

While good passive solar design practices can be economically beneficial, sunlight should be employed in museums as much for the interest created as for the "free" light received. Even more than in other types of buildings, there is no excuse for the apparent sources of light not to be those surfaces one enjoys looking at.

Circulation areas—courtyards, atria and sunlit rooms—can provide for a change in focus from concentrated viewing to a more relaxed awareness of architectural spaces and nature. These spaces are often a display of architectural virtuosity, and designers often use sunlight effectively and dramatically. Yet the range of artwork that can be displayed here is often limited; "exciting" architecture can overpower more sedate artwork. I.M. Pei's atrium at the East wing of the National Gallery in Washington is beautifully crafted and vital, but the ceiling's silhouette is strong competition even for Calder's kinetic sculpture. By contrast, the pattern of skylights at his West wing of the Boston Museum of Fine Arts is much simpler, and the space is thus a more versatile display area (figs. DI-1, DI-2). Personally, I believe that museum atria are *not* identical to hotel atria; they should be designed to display art as well as people.

Designers have often succeeded in sunlighting the nongallery spaces of museums, as these spaces differ little from similar spaces in other types of buildings, such as offices or hotels. In the galleries, the display and viewing of the artwork *is* the most important activity. The visual ordering and lighting of these spaces is more demanding and the solutions have been much less satisfactory. Doesn't failure here defeat the purpose of museums?

DI–1. The complex atrium canopy competes with a clear view of the Calder mobile at the east wing of the National Gallery (I. M. Pei, Architect).

DI–3. Philip Johnson's private gallery is the classic example of a space designed to display itself. (Photograph courtesy of Philip Johnson)

DI–2. Pei's atrium skylight at the Boston Museum of Fine Arts is much more restrained.

SUNLIGHTING IN GALLERIES— THE REAL CHALLENGE

Despite the desires of both the public and of museum donors, the use of natural light as the principal light source in galleries has often been questioned and eliminated in recent years. The reasons have generally not been economic, but rather reflect concerns about effective display and conservation of the displayed art objects. The development of such negative attitudes toward natural light that has caused this trend was inevitable, given the poor daylight design in many new museums and the changed context from that of the museums of past periods.

What is wrong with the daylight design of many contemporary museums? Too often, the display conditions are less than ideal visually, as well as being potentially damaging (physically) to the collection. Many architects apparently ignored the potential damage from excessive light, including that from extreme levels of direct sunlight, apparently more concerned about architectural form than about optimum display and conservation, or operating costs. Indeed, some galleries seems to be designed to display the architecture of the building itself rather than anything placed within it (fig. DI–3).

Why can't we follow the design concepts of museums designed exclusively around daylight before there was the choice to do otherwise? The museums created in recycled palaces and public buildings (e.g., the Isabella Stewart Gardner Museum, Boston) may be beautiful "natural" settings for work created for similar surroundings in which social functions were primary, but as conversions, these buildings were obviously not designed for optimum display or conservation. A window provided for view and light cannot but compete with display, both directly and via veiling reflection.

What about those buildings that were designed as museums: the classic nineteenth-century museums of Europe, such as the Louvre, the Prado, and the Rijksmuseum, and similar structures in the U.S., such as the Metropolitan Museum in New York, the Museum of Fine Arts in Boston, the Fogg Museum at Harvard University, the Art Gallery of Ontario, Toronto, and almost all others built during that period?

Classic Toplighted Galleries

While the minor galleries and those on the lower floors of such museums suffer from the inherent problems of sidelighting from windows (as do those in recycled palaces), the principal galleries on the upper floors of these buildings are very effectively toplit. The diffusing glass ceiling panels are generally located high enough to be out of normal view and to avoid casting reflections on wall-hung paintings from unfavorable angles (fig. DI–4). Because of intervening cornice moldings or vaulted, chamfered, or domed ceiling coffers, there is usually a good brightness transition from the luminous ceiling area to the display walls (fig. DI–5).

Sunlight and sky light are captured by the extensive areas of skylights that follow the roof slopes and help create the museums' exterior characters. The quantity of light reaching the diffusing glass ceilings is controlled by an attic full of operable louvers. The light admitted by the extensive areas of these greenhouse-type roofs is often very inefficiently utilized, since the ceiling openings are quite small relative to the roof apertures (figs. DI–6, DI–7). However, since the attics are separate thermal buffer spaces and are easily ventilated in summer (independently from the galleries), these greenhouse roofs are not a thermal liability and can afford to use light as inefficiently as necessary as a trade-off for adequate solar control. Contemporary museums that appear similar to nineteenth-century museums on the exterior are often very different on the interior, both as display environments and in the economics of their operation.

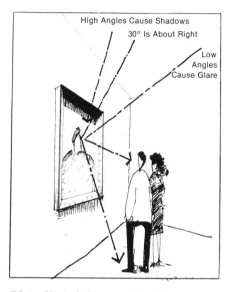

DI–4. Vertical objects are best lit at approximately 30 degrees from the vertical. At lower angles, reflected glare may be a problem; at higher angles, frames may shadow art.

DI–5. The height of the luminous ceiling at the Rijksmuseum, Amsterdam ensures a good brightness transition to the artwork.

DI-7. The attic of the Metropolitan Museum. Only a very small portion of the light admitted by the extensive area of glazing enters the occulus to the lobby domes below.

DI-6. The lobby of the Metropolitan Museum of Art in New York City. Note how the small ceiling apertures are baffled by the vaulted form.

DI-8. At the Art Gallery of Ontario, the extensive areas of skylights were painted out in favor of more controllable electric light.

For display, the nineteenth-century toplighted gallery format was a logical design, because room proportions kept the translucent ceiling surfaces of most galleries high enough to minimize the distraction of direct glare and the distortions of veiling reflections. What was logical then, however, is less logical today; several factors have changed that make the older museum format less satisfactory. These factors, listed below, must be recognized by contemporary designers:

☐ Increased knowledge about the deleterious effects of excessive light and heat on art objects and the concomitant concern for their preservation make control of overlighting more critical today. Since ambient interior light levels over 10–30 footcandles are generally unnecessary for display and undesirable for conservation reasons, glazing 50 percent of the roof is obviously excessive even under dark, overcast conditions (approximately 500 footcandles). Under several thousand footcandles (10,000 at summer noon), an attic full of adjustable louvers should be almost completely closed.

☐ The availability of efficient, highly controllable artificial light sources provides an attractive alternative to the display functions of natural light, especially if the negative aspects of daylight are not well controlled. If daylight control devices do not work easily and reliably, museum conservators are likely to eliminate daylight altogether and rely exclusively on the artificial lighting already provided for nighttime use (fig. DI-8).

☐ In most of the world, including all of the United States, the climate is sunnier than that of the original northern European prototypes.

☐ The use of air conditioning and total climate control, instead of ventilation alone, makes wise energy design practices more important economically.

☐ Lower and/or wider rooms are prevalent today. Translucent ceilings, acceptable in high spaces, become a major part of one's visual field in low rooms and thus become sources of overwhelming visual noise and veiling reflections. At the Jewett Art Center (fig. DI–9) wood louvers are effective for visually baffling the luminous ceiling in only one direction. In renovating the Clark Museum in Williamstown, Massachussetts, I blocked off most of the glass ceiling panels for the same reason (fig. DI–10). Many gallery ceiling designs, such as that at the Tate Gallery, London, are also awkward and "busy" (fig. DI–11).

Even in older museums, translucent ceilings produced excessive visual noise along the long axis of the largest rooms unless baffled by coffers or bulkheads (fig. DI–12). To reduce this problem, a panel was suspended at the Prado, Madrid (fig. DI–13).

DI–10. The luminous ceiling at the Clark Art Institute (top) dominates the art; renovation of the Institute (bottom) by blocking off most of the luminous ceiling improved the visual emphasis.

DI–9. Jewett Art Center, Wellesley College. Before renovation (top): poor thermal performance, excessive daylight, and visual noise when viewing along the louvers. Following renovation (bottom): glazing was replaced with insulated panels, eliminating all daylight.

DI–11. The visually "busy" ceiling at the Tate Gallery in London. (Photograph courtesy of Donald Watson)

DI–12. At the Louvre in Paris, the ceiling dominates when the gallery is viewed along its long axis.

DI–13. The luminous ceiling at the Prado was baffled with a large panel.

Making Preservation and Conservation of Artwork a Priority

Designers must use sunlighting well or give in to conservators' preference for black-box galleries. It is necessary to control the HVAC impact, total amount, and spectral characteristics of sunlight. Modern preservation relies on HVAC to control temperature and humidity in the galleries. This means that it is important not to admit more sunlight into the building than is necessary. Reducing glazing areas is a better approach than controlling excessive sunlight with internal louvers.

The absolute preservation of artwork would dictate that it be kept in the dark, deterioration being directly proportional to the length and intensity of exposure. However, there are recommended levels of illumination for display that minimize the damage (DI–14) but provide sufficient amounts of light if effectively used. Display conditions must be carefully designed to provide maximum visibility for the artwork. Because of the time-related effects of exposure, illuminate art only when necessary. Exclude light when the museum is closed.

The spectral characteristics of light have an important influence on preservation. Most damage comes from the ultraviolet end of the spectrum. Because accurate color rendition is important for viewing art, it is better to use a full-spectrum source such as sunlight and "filter out" the ultraviolet light. (Tungsten lamps may have little UV but they are weak in the blue portion of the visible spectrum; a combination of reflected daylighting and highlighting of some exhibits with incandescent light is ideal.) UV may be filtered directly by using Plexiglas sheet in windows and ceilings (or sleeves around fluorescent tubes). But bouncing light off of white painted surfaces will also reduce the UV component. While paint reflects only 5–10 percent of the UV, tests using a double bounce reduced the UV-to-visible-light ratio of sunlight to below that of incandescent sources (fig. DI–15). Another benefit is that sunlit building surfaces are more beautiful to look at than luminous ceilings or translucent fluorescent fixtures.

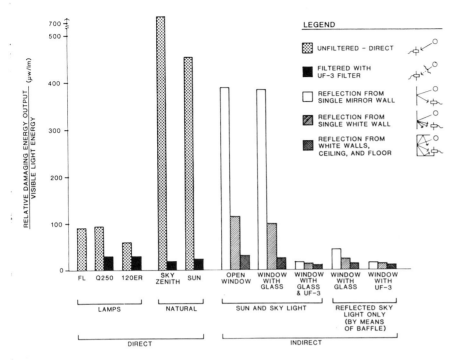

30 footcandles
metal, stone, glass, ceramics, stained glass, jewelry, enamel

15 footcandles
oil and tempera paintings, un-dyed leather, horn, bone, ivory, wood, lacquer

5 footcandles
textiles, watercolors, tapestries, prints and drawings, manu-scripts, miniatures, paintings in distemper, wallpapers, gouache, dyed leather

DI–14. Recommended maximum light levels for the display of museum objects, based on the British I.E.S. standards.

DI–15. The ultraviolet-to-visible-light ratio of various light sources; multiple reflections of light are shown to be as effective as ultraviolet filtering. (Results of William Lam Associates testing in April 1981.)

Modifying the Classic Toplighted Gallery for Today's Changed Conditions

Before the advent of electric lighting, there was reason to design around the minimum daylight condition—the dark, overcast day. Other-wise, it would have been very difficult to get sufficient light on such days, which comprise a large percentage of the year in the largely overcast, smoggy climate of northern Europe. Glazing 30–50 percent of the roof provided sufficient light even under these minimal conditions; under sunny conditions, the louvers were probably adjusted conscientiously, if only to maintain thermal and visual comfort. Without automatic controls, the adjustment of the louvers was probably not accurate enough for pro-tection of the art objects, however, at least by today's standards.

Today, considering all of these factors, it seems more reasonable to underlight than overlight. Architects should design around sunny and average overcast conditions and plan to supplement with electric lighting on dark days, when the light from overcast skies appears gloomy even if the quantity is sufficient. Much less glazing area is necessary in today's museums, compared to those of the nineteenth century.

In today's context, there is no reason to have high percent-ages of glazing, except to satisfy architects' preconceptions of how the exterior of a museum "should" look. This is particularly true if the glazed

DI-16. The Lehman Wing of the Metropolitan Museum. How much glazing is enough?

DI-17. Lehman Wing: even using low-transmission mirrored glass, shades must be drawn to prevent direct sunlight from entering the galleries at the perimeter of this atrium space.

DI-18. Lehman Wing: black louvers protect the art from the excess light (by turning it into excess heat).

volume is that of the gallery itself, rather than a thermally isolated attic space. A prominent example of such overglazing is found in the Lehman Wing of the Metropolitan Museum of Art in New York City, where the glazed area is approximately 120 percent of the floor area (figs. DI–16, DI–17, DI–18). No doubt because the designer realized that the glazing area provided would admit too much light and heat, reflecting mirror glass is used to reject most of the light. In addition, the mirror glass is lined with closely spaced black louvers to further reduce the illumination levels to a more reasonable range by converting most of the light admitted into heat. Without the traditional attic buffer zone, the penalty for heating and cooling this space must be astronomical. A small fraction of the glazed area, efficiently used, would seem more logical in every respect.

Control of overlighting must be ensured. If the fixed architectural forms must be supplemented by dynamic controls, these controls should be automatic. If manually operated, their proper use should be ensured by high visibility. When louvers are concealed above a translucent ceiling, as in the old "classic" museums, it is difficult to see if they are correctly adjusted. Light-control devices (draperies or louvers) that are more easily noticed by a passing curator are more likely to be adjusted, though the aesthetic effect can be chaotic (fig. DI–19).

The advent of fluorescent lighting and the resulting engineering of lighting design have caused some natural lighting systems to be built to resemble recessed fluorescent light fixtures (fig. DI–20); they appear almost as unsatisfactory. Anyone really "seeing" one of these installations will not be aware of the spectral composition of sunlight but may notice other factors that indicate the presence of sunlight. To most museum visitors, the perception of natural light for orientation is more appreciated than the truer rendering of colors; only real art "experts" are likely to know what the colors should be. The manner in which daylight is introduced should make its identification clear. A mere streak of sunlight or speck of blue sky will do.

DI–19. Pompidou Museum, Paris (Piano and Rogers, Architect). Much-needed sun-control devices at the excessive expanse of windows are very conspicuous. Hence, they are often correctly adjusted though with visually chaotic results.

DI–20. Van Gogh Museum, Amsterdam. (Top): pyramidal skylights, (bottom): on the interior, the skylights appear little different from fluorescent fixtures.

DI–21. Model view of Safdie's design for the National Gallery of Canada. Lightwell illuminates main gallery on lower floor. Note how sidelighting of the ceilings effectively creates toplighting of galleries in upper left and lower right of picture.

DI–22. Model view of a sidelit/toplit gallery from Safdie's National Gallery of Canada design. (Courtesy of Moshe Safdie)

Good design as well as energy efficiency should dictate that sunlight be admitted via small areas of clear glazing and bounced off of white surfaces. The surfaces lit by reflected sunlight, as compared to translucent, backlit surfaces, are perceived as signal rather than noise. Illuminated coffers are preferable to luminous ceilings. Visually simpler lit coffers are also better than louver-dominated ceilings or other complicated baffling, which is required when excessive amounts of sunlight is admitted into the building envelope.

Toplighting is the best sunlight form for museums. The classic gallery forms can be modified easily for energy efficiency and to produce controlled illumination levels for the conservation of displayed objects. Toplighting is also the best form for effective display, as it provides maximum display area, minimum visual competition of light source with displays, and reduced problems of veiling reflections on paintings and glass-enclosed displays.

While toplighting is achieved most naturally and easily on the top floors of buildings, it is sometimes worthwhile to go through considerable effort to achieve it at lower floors. Lightwells can be used much as they were in some older museums. The mirrored lightwells in Moshe Safdie's design for the National Gallery of Canada are a good example (fig. DI–21). But even sidelighting forms—windows—can be converted to provide effective ''toplighting,'' as Safdie has also done at the National Gallery (fig. DI–22).

Sidelighting in Museums

It is difficult but not impossible to use windows effectively in galleries. The traditional use of windows in museum galleries has some inherent conflicts. If a window is both a source of view *and* light, as it is in our homes and in any room designed for living and converted to gallery use, such a window must inevitably compete for display space and be a dominant source of visual competition with nearby objects, particularly those on the same wall. Any windows located at eye level will be potential sources of veiling reflections on facing walls parallel to them. Designing sidelit galleries must always involve some compromises. To minimize these compromises, the functions of a window as view and as light source for display are best separated.

For lighting of displays, sidelighting is best coverted to toplighting. Windows should be kept out of normal sight and used as an indirect source of toplighting. Sunlight should be introduced into baffled clerestory windows and bounced to reflecting surfaces that are out of sight to viewers but in favorable positions for illuminating the walls, without creating excessive shadows. The ''effective'' light source can be the ceiling, as in Safdie's design for the new National Gallery of Canada. Alternately, beams or baffles can be used to reflect light from windows to display walls, as Alvar Aalto has frequently done (fig. DI–23). It is important that neither the public nor the artwork ''sees'' the window directly, in order to avoid glare and minimize damage from ultraviolet light on the artwork. Frank Lloyd Wright's Guggenheim Museum in New York fails on both counts. The walls are sloped to ''see'' the sky, and the sloping translucent windows are visible and compete with the artwork. These prob-

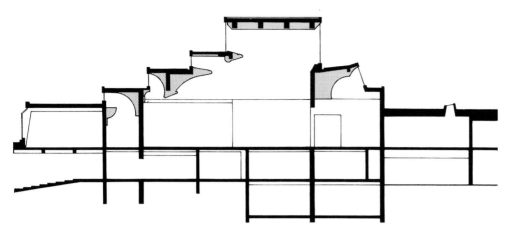

DI-23. Section of Aalto's Alborg Museum.

lems are compounded because the pictures are hung in front of the wall instead of on the sloping wall as Wright had intended; the source of daylight is in back of instead of in front of pictures displayed on the exterior wall.

Windows for both view and lighting must compromise display. Their negative impact can be minimized, however, by limiting their number and placing them carefully. A single large window in a gallery is better than several smaller ones. Fewer displays will be directly adjacent to a single window, and fewer displays will suffer from its reflections. A single window is best placed in a corner so that it illuminates the adjacent wall and makes that wall an extended low-brightness light source for the room. Single windows were placed in corners at the Clark Art Institute (TAC architects) but were designed to be used in combination with incandescent lighting (fig. DI–24). A corner placement also minimizes reflections at the middle of facing walls, where the most important works are most likely to be placed.

DI–24. Clark Art Institute, Williamstown Massachusetts (The Architects Collaborative, Architect). A view window provides both view and some general ambient illumination.

DI–25. Kimbell Museum, Fort Worth Texas (Louis I. Kahn, Architect). The daylight reference of the narrow strip windows on the end wall beneath the vault is successful. Unfortunately, the skylight/baffle system is relatively ineffective. (a): general view of galleries; (b): close-up of strip window.

a.

b.

Placement of a window as high as possible will also minimize direct competition with and veiling reflections on displays. A small high window can be very effective in providing view for orientation. The most noticeable benefits of daylighting in the Kimbell Art Museum galleries in Fort Worth, Texas (Louis Kahn, architect) come from the very narrow strip of sky seen at the end windows and the reflections of sunlight on the ceiling through those openings. The much publicized skylight baffle system, although a good concept, produces very little illumination (on one occasion I measured 1–2 footcandles on the walls on a clear, sunny, 10,000-footcandle day) because of the combined impact of glazing transmission, reflectances, and placement of baffles (fig. DI–25). Artificial lighting is used at all times. I expect that some simple changes could make the skylight system much more effective for display lighting.

View Windows

View windows are best when they are designed exclusively for view and used as an adjunct to toplighted (from clerestories or skylights) or artificially lighted galleries. When view is the only objective the windows should be:

☐ oriented or baffled by large-scale architectural elements so that no additional shading is needed to control *direct sunlight* at the window plane;

☐ transparent—maximum brightness should be limited by using tinted or mirrored glass;

☐ located to face a shaded scene so that brightness is limited. (Alternatively, the brightness should be adjusted with movable dark-colored, fine-textured screens to minimize perceptual interference of the view.)

Such a view window can be used as a "work of art" and placed in the middle of a major display wall without excessive compromise of the display function of a gallery.

ARCHITECTURE

All design involves value judgments. We seek simplicity in forms and concepts not at the expense of avoiding problems but to solve them in an aesthetically satisfying and cost-effective manner. Overly complex solutions usually come from overemphasis on one of the many variables or overthinking of the solution.

For instance, the very complex design of the recent additions to the Tate Gallery in London (fig. DI–26) appears to be based on the most extreme overcast conditions—as though artificial lighting was not available. The roof area is 100 percent glazed—a greater percent of glazing than is found in most of the classic nineteenth-century galleries.

The two sets of automatically controlled louvers (one adjusted monthly according to the solar path, the other adjusted continuously to control illumination levels) should provide total control. I suspect, however, that tests would show the very simple, clean shape of the Canadian National Gallery design (case study D1) to be much more efficient in utilizing minimum available daylight than the Tate's combination of very large areas of skylight under two layers of louvers, which can only reduce the percentage of light utilized and increase the maintenance needs.

The Tate design is effective in distributing light to display surfaces, and the deep coffers provide attractive and effective baffling. The louver system is not beautiful to look at, however (though it is more interesting than translucent glass). Worse, when supplementary ambient lighting is desired, the visually noisy lensed fluorescent fixtures, located in the most conspicuous position possible, dominate the space and destroy its character. Had freedom from visual noise been given a higher priority, all supplementary lighting could easily have been concealed in the daylight coffers. The galleries work best if the central fluorescent fixtures are never turned on, except for cleaning (DI–27). The Tate Gallery has been described as "a machine for sun control." A sunlit building, whether viewed from within or without, should be first and foremost good architecture, not a machine.

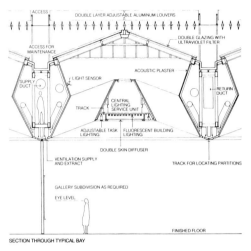

DI–26. Tate Gallery, London. Section shows double layer of exterior louvers. (Reprinted, by permission, from *Progressive Architecture*)

DI–27. Tate Gallery: gallery interior, looking up at skylight coffer—(left): center fluorescent fixtures are on; (right): daylight only. (Photographs courtesy of Donald Watson)

CASE STUDIES

The following case studies represent some recent attempts to apply sunlighting principles in today's context of conservation of art objects and energy, but with equal emphasis on good display and the overall quality of the visual environment.

They represent both completed and proposed projects located over a range of climate zones, from sultry Beaumont, Texas, and southern China to frigid Ottawa. Toplit and sidelit galleries are discussed, with both fixed architectural forms and those supplemented by dynamic controls. Several of the studies begin with the development of an individual, integrated gallery module; one details the adjusting of an already established architectural form, which dictated some unique and rich geometries in the details.

Unlike museums in which daylight is used primarily for orientation and makes only a small contribution to the ambient lighting even on the sunniest days (such as the Kimbell and Clark museums), the museums presented in the following case studies attempt to use daylight as the principal display lighting as well.

In consideration of all of the qualitative factors that make up the overall visual environment, I have tried to minimize visual noise in these museums at all levels. Most supplementary electric lighting is visually and structurally integrated—concealed in the shadows of the natural lighting—rather than highlighted by it (as in many museums) (fig. DI–28). The beauty of sunlight is never concealed by translucent ceilings (as at the Boston Museum of Fine Arts). The skylight coffers will give views of the sky and sunlit surfaces.

As much as possible, the display walls in these museums "see" reflected sunlight rather than direct light through diffusing glass or plastic. By "bouncing" the light in this manner, the spectral characteristics of sunlight are altered: almost all of the potentially damaging ultraviolet is removed. It is interesting to note that, for whatever reasons, indirect sunlighting was Aalto's usual approach to museum design.

The lighting objectives common to all the museum gallery projects are summarized in our report for the National Gallery of Canada competition, which is included in Appendix C.

DI–28. Mellon Center for British Studies, New Haven, Connecticut (Louis I. Kahn, Architect). Integration of artificial light leaves something to be desired.

D1 National Gallery of Canada— 1977 Competition Ottawa, Canada

Latitude: 45.5° N; climate: 8,735 degree days

808,550 square feet

Architect: The Webb Zerafa Menkes Housden Partnership (Boris Zerafa and Brian Brooks, Principals)/ARCOP Associates and Jodoin, Lamare, Pratte (A.B. Nichols, Partner in Charge)

Consultants: William Lam Associates—lighting

CONTEXT

In 1977, the Department of Public Works held a two-stage design competition for a new National Gallery of Canada. From a list of hundreds of qualified teams, each including the full complement of specialists necessary to design and supervise construction of such a project, they selected six teams to produce schematic designs for a site next to the Parliament.

The thick program document included extremely detailed technical requirements, particularly for the galleries. For the permanent American and European collections, it called for a number of specific room proportions and ceiling heights and specified that they be windowless but illuminated primarily by natural light (an average of no more than 30 footcandles).

Because I was the lighting consultant on two of the six competing teams, I decided to limit my participation to discussing objectives and principles with the two groups, and to designing a standard gallery module that could be adapted by each of them and integrated into their overall designs. The gallery module concept I developed had to be adaptable dimensionally to make up the various required gallery sizes and provide the controlled quantities of daylighting with minimum ultraviolet light and glare.

I was pleased to see that the lighting criteria outlined by the museum staff included more than the usual simplistic footcandle criteria. My office developed a lighting program statement, which incorporated the competition criteria with other requirements that I considered important in museums. Because this document is an important example of the design process, it is included in the Appendix.

Because of the tight timetable and in recognition of the limited input I felt to be appropriate as a member of two competing teams, I went to the initial session with each team prepared to discuss both the program (and my suggested additions) and the sunlighting design implications as I saw them. I was rather surprised that both groups accepted my initial designs for both the daylit permanent European and North American Galleries and for the windowless temporary flexible galleries.

343

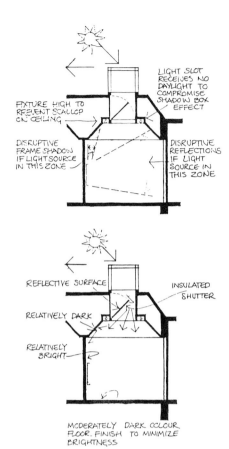

D1–1. Diagrammatic section of sunlighting module.

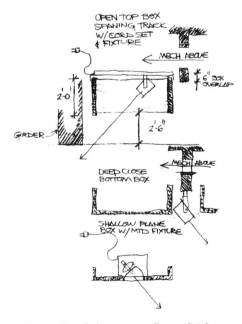

D1–2. Detail showing smaller artificial lighting module.

THE GALLERY MODULE

For the daylit galleries (which had to be toplit and windowless) I had proposed a ceiling module of 20′ × 20′ pyramids truncated at the top with clear skylights in deep wells that incorporated dynamic controls to meet the stringent lighting criteria (fig. D1–1). These daylight-control ceiling modules were assumed to be nonstructural (i.e., drywall or a molded construction of some kind) in order to be insertable at roof level into whatever structural frame was developed. Of course, a structural construction was not ruled out if dictated by the overall design that evolved.

For the flexible temporary galleries, I had proposed an assemblage of open boxes on a much smaller module (5 to 6 feet). Lighting fixtures could be placed between solid-bottomed boxes within baffle/boxes without bottoms (fig. D1–2). This system would not only allow very flexible lighting and aid in the centering of display panels, but would facilitate and invite imaginative sculpturing of the ceiling. Thus, any module could be positioned independently at whatever height would provide the best integration with the displays (fig. D1–3). I had first conceived of such a system for a project with ARCOP over ten years earlier (for the merchandise mart levels at Place Bonaventure, Montreal) and had recommended it for other museums since.

While the small-scale box system needed no testing, the daylit pyramid modules had to be tested to confirm the skylight size, configuration, and control strategy that had been proposed and tentatively accepted. The testing was carried out by my staff in Cambridge. Visual evaluation and photometric measurements of the module verified my expectations that the light patterns on the display walls and other room surfaces would be excellent. Because of the possibility that sufficient height might not be available everywhere for the pyramid-shaped ceiling (e.g., under a plaza), we also tested the same skylight in a flat ceiling for comparison (fig. D1–4). The resulting shadows on the walls were no surprise to me, having experienced this years earlier in a study for the Henry Moore Gallery at the Art Gallery of Ontario. (One can see the shadow effect where the display wall is bordered by a flat band in some of the galleries at Louis Kahn's Kimbell Museum, Fort Worth, and at I.M. Pei's Portland Museum.) Comparison of the pyramid ceiling with the lower flat ceiling also demonstrates the advantage of keeping the light source high and far displaced from the viewer's normal line of sight. (The skylight would not even appear in the model photograph without the use of a very wide angle lens, in this case turned to an unusual vertical position.)

The initial tests also revealed that the nine-cell or four-cell skylight configurations that I initially proposed were larger than needed to deliver sufficient light under most conditions. We decided that a single cell would be both more satisfying visually and less expensive to build and maintain. Further tests confirmed that the single-cell design would produce the correct quantity and quality of light (fig. D1–5).

I had initially contemplated electrically operated blackout window shades for blocking direct sunlight from the wall displays and for maintaining the 30-footcandle (average) limit. Model testing allowed me to verify the qualitative advantages of using a single panel hinged from the bottom of the skylight well instead. Such a panel would appear as an

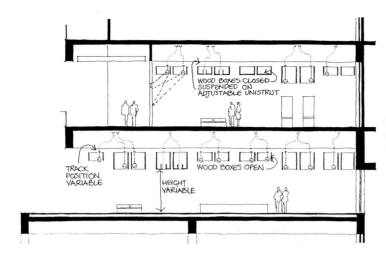

D1–3. WZMH team interpretation of my artificial light-box concept. (Courtesy of WZMH)

D1–4. Model photo shows the advantage of raised, chamfered coffer versus a flat ceiling.

D1–5. Nine-cell skylight design on left, single-cell design on right. Note the resultant difference in ceiling shape and simplicity of the scene.

integral part of the well; when it was adjusted, the apparent shape of the well would change. Anyone looking at the model could imagine how much less pleasant a view past shades or blinds would be in comparison to the uncluttered view of blue sky beautifully framed by sunlit skylight well surfaces. A similarly large-scale electrically operated panel, which I had designed for the council chamber at the Santa Clara Civic Center in San Jose, California (Caudill, Rowlett & Scott, architects) had been installed, so I knew that simple and effective motorized control systems were available.

The panels were hinged from the south side so that sunlight (usually coming from the south) would almost always be intercepted by the skylight well, rather than penetrating to the gallery wall. Testing showed that only a small open gap was needed to get the maximum allowable light on sunny summer days. Illumination of the vertical well surfaces by sunlight favors light distribution to the vertical gallery walls rather than the horizontal plane of the floor below. Whether totally open, partially open, or closed to eliminate all daylight or for optimum insulation at night, the insulated flap looks like a permanent part of the architecture rather than a temporary hardware element.

The model also enabled us to confirm and illustrate to others the value of placing the artificial accent lighting in shadowed pockets to minimize visual noise (fig. D1–6). Although more difficult to illustrate with photographs than to view in person, the model demonstrates how much more pleasant it is to look at the three-dimensional opaque well surfaces glowing with diffuse sky light or changing patterns of sunlight than at translucent lined skylights with their constant and dull appearance, day or night.

THE PROJECT REPORT

My final recommendations were incorporated in a project report and sent to the two teams. This report, summarized below, consisted of a concept statement supplemented with sunlighting diagrams and model photographs:

Daylighting System Concept

The essence of the design solution rests in the shape of the skylight wells, the method of controlling daylight intensity, and the location of these wells with respect to the display walls.

Although the clear glazing permits an unobstructed sky view when the control flap is fully open, the depth of the skylight well forces all light that illuminates the display walls to have been reflected off the vertical well surfaces. These white walls will absorb a great deal of the incident ultraviolet radiation before reflecting the visible light into the gallery spaces.

These vertical surfaces become, in effect, the principal light sources for the gallery space on both cloudy and sunny days. With the use of a single control flap, sunlight can be restricted to the upper zone so that when modulated by reflections from the deep well, all gallery walls are evenly illuminated.

Natural light will reach the sloping ceiling at steep grazing angles that will render this surface less bright than the vertical walls below. Because the lower wall portions have more direct exposure to the skylight well than their upper zone, there will be good uniformity of illumination despite the wall's great height. A moderately dark finish material will cause the floors to remain subdued relative to the vertical display surfaces.

The well's central location within the high coffer permits the introduction of useful quantities of daylight without visual competition with the displays: they are unobtrusively located, well above the normal field of view. From this point, reflections from specular materials and frame shadows are minimized.

Use of the single large flap for daylight intensity control is fundamental to the appearance and effectiveness of the installation. No matter what its position, from fully open to fully closed, the lightwell presents a neat, intentional appearance that is in scale with the space below. Unlike traditional gallery daylight controls, this design does not obscure the sky with a dirty, deteriorating film on the glass or with a clutter of louver members; natural light is collected with maximum efficiency. The flap's intermediate operating positions restrict sunlight to the upper well walls. It is possible to retain awareness of the sun's presence without permitting its unwanted intrusion into the space.

It is preferable that the daylight be monitored automatically and the controls adjusted, perhaps on an hourly basis. But if less exact control is acceptable, the flaps can also be adjusted manually on a seasonal basis or fixed in any position.

Sunlighting Diagrams

The sunlighting diagrams show the position of the light-controlling flap under various conditions, in order to attain the programmed 30-footcandle maximum (fig. D1–7).

Model Photographs

Model photographs illustrated the appearance of the gallery under various conditions: sunny days (fig. D1–6), dark overcast days when natural light is blended with supplementary incandescent illumination (fig. D1–8), and at night, with artificial lighting alone (fig. D1–9). The model photographs also showed a rectangular 20' × 30' version and the effect of a large open room with several modules (fig. D1–10).

SUMMARY

Judging from my observation of the displayed and published results of design competitions and from my experience as a juror for student designs, it is rare for a museum to be designed around a gallery concept whose performance in controlling sunlight and acting as an effective background for display was actually tested. More often, the designs are based on conjecture rather than knowledge that could have been easily acquired from model studies. In published presentations for this com-

D1–6. Final version of single-cell skylight/well. Note the slot at bottom of well for lighting fixtures.

HIGH SUMMER SUN

- MIRRORED INSULATED HATCH PARTIALLY OPEN
- REFLECTED SUNLIGHT + MINIMUM SOLAR GAIN

WHITE PAINTED SURFACES

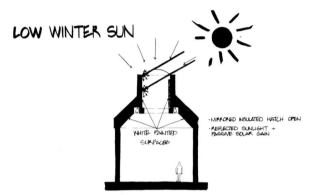

LOW WINTER SUN

- MIRRORED INSULATED HATCH OPEN
- REFLECTED SUNLIGHT + PASSIVE SOLAR GAIN

WHITE PAINTED SURFACES

NIGHT

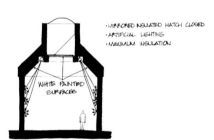

- MIRRORED INSULATED HATCH CLOSED
- ARTIFICIAL LIGHTING
- MAXIMUM INSULATION

WHITE PAINTED SURFACES

OVERCAST SKY

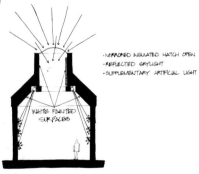

- MIRRORED INSULATED HATCH OPEN
- REFLECTED SKYLIGHT
- SUPPLEMENTARY ARTIFICIAL LIGHT

WHITE PAINTED SURFACES

D1–7. Sunlighting diagrams show flap adjusted properly for various conditions.

D1–8. Overcast condition shows sky light from the well blended with artificial light.

D1–9. Nighttime, with artificial lighting only.

348　**Museums**

petition, for example, our model photographs of gallery interiors were the only ones shown.

By using sunlight efficiently, only small areas of fenestration were required to achieve both the required interior illumination levels of 30 footcandles on clear days (with more than 8,000 footcandles outdoors) and lower but very effective lighting on dark overcast days. The pyramidal ceiling of the 20' × 20' gallery adopted by both teams was penetrated by a glazed area of less than 10 percent of the floor area. This is a small fraction of the glazing used in classic nineteenth-century galleries, many of which have glazed areas of up to 50 percent, or the new Lehman wing of the Metropolitan Museum, with glazing equal to 120 percent of floor area.

Our model studies indicated that the pyramidal module should be appropriate for both individual rooms and larger spaces. Its small skylight opening (about 40 square feet) made the deployment of the module relatively easy to integrate with structure. A rectangular variation, 20' × 30' rooms, was also developed.

Detailed accounts of how the ARCOP and WZMH teams integrated the standard gallery module into their museum designs follow.

THE ARCOP DESIGN

The ARCOP team designed a "tartan-grid" concrete frame system that would not only accept the gallery module but would naturally frame the skylight well at the top of the chamfered 20′ × 20′ ceiling (fig. D1–11).

The concrete frame could also accommodate the insertion of the box system I proposed for the flexible temporary exhibit galleries, where daylight was to be excluded. Thus, the same framing could be used at all floor levels within the exhibit blocks, separated by circulation service bands.

In developing the two types of gallery modules—large pyramids for daylighting and the smaller-scale one for artificial lighting of the flexible temporary galleries—I expected that they would always be on different floors. I was surprised to see the two types used interchangeably in adjacent spaces. The concrete tartan grid structure apparently accommodated such an arrangement easily, as is indicated by the diagrammatic section-perspective sketch in the ARCOP presentation.

That the ARCOP team, working in the material for which the firm is noted—concrete—was able to integrate the two types of gallery systems into their expressive concrete forms successfully, bore testimony to their skill and to the suitability of the modules.

The WZMH Design

The WZMH team, known for their sculpturing of smooth overall building forms, was easily able to accommodate the gallery modules in their structurally neutral building (fig. D1–12).

Since no structure was to be exposed, the ceiling shapes were clearly derived from the two gallery lighting systems I had developed. The neutral structure gave the designers the freedom to raise or lower small or

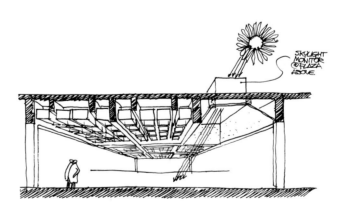

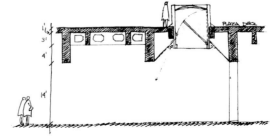

D1–11. ARCOP "tartan" grid.
(Courtesy of ARCOP Associates)

D1–12. Model photo of exterior elevation of WZMH scheme. (Courtesy of WZMH)

large areas of the temporary flexible ceiling system at will, as indicated in their building section (see fig. D1–3). Any mechanical engineer looking at the section would appreciate the flexibility for mechanical services provided by the voids in both systems (fig. D1–13).

WZMH expressed the gallery module by allowing the tops of the pyramidal skylight wells to penetrate the roofline. They chose to cap the skylights with glass cubes that would express the module and its purpose (as Aalto occasionally did with his skylight enclosures, such as those on the National Pensions Institute in Helsinki). This would also help prevent the skylights from being totally covered with snow. A flat, clear, inner lining at the top of the well could separate this excess volume and surface area and make that volume into a thermal buffer zone. This would minimize heat loss during the day, when the light-controlling insulated louver would be open.

POSTSCRIPT

I was satisfied with the module developed for the toplighted galleries. Since neither team won the competition, however, I have never actually

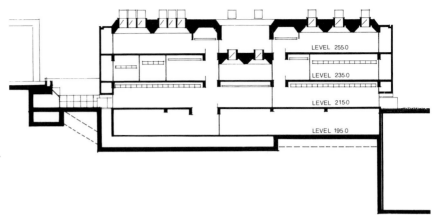

D1–13. Section of WZMH scheme. Note rectangular 20′ × 30′ module on left side. (Courtesy of WZMH)

seen the module in use. (The winning design has not been built either. After a second competition, another design by Moshe Safdie was commissioned and is presently under construction. His excellent design is presented in chapter 10.)

Nevertheless, my observations of the models at the time and subsequent reflection on those observations (after years of seeing and thinking about museums) has convinced me of the module's excellence. I had not known of Louis Kahn's Mellon Center for British Studies at Yale until after the competition. Seeing it confirmed for me the suitability of the pyramid module for the National Gallery program though I believe my design is simpler, more efficient in energy use, and more effective for the conservation of artwork, as well as being delightful to look at. I have recently designed a variation for a warmer climate (in Shenzhen, China, case study D6).

Of course, there are many other good gallery design solutions that might have evolved with different interpretations of the programming for flexibility and gallery sizes. Safdie's excellent design certainly reflects a very different program than that around which the WZMH and ARCOP designs were based—one that was doubtless modified as a result of the type of communication between architect and client that is not possible under competition conditions.

D2 Tarble Arts Center, Eastern Illinois University Charleston, Illinois

CONTEXT

Latitude: 39.5°N; climate: 5,225 degree days

Architect: E. Verner Johnson & Associates Inc.

Consultants: Souza & True—structural; Lottero and Mason—electrical; Helden Associates—mechanical; William Lam Associates—lighting

Construction completed: 1983

This university museum came very close to being the first application of the National Gallery module. I began consultation on this project in 1978, soon after the 1977 Canadian competition and thus suggested it as a possibility. The concept was well received by Verner Johnson, an architect who has become a specialist in museums and who has always placed the greatest emphasis on museum *functions* rather than on exterior building *forms*. The module apparently worked well for the program and resulted in interesting architectural forms as well (figs. D2-1, D2-2).

Working within the very small scale of the project (20,000 square feet) and its modest construction budget, the design team was able to develop the necessary construction details for a skylight well with a single large dynamic shutter (fig. D2-3). The project's cost was estimated to be within the budget. The feasibility and simple, attractive appearance of a single large louver had been demonstrated by a previous project (fig. D2-4). Unfortunately, construction had to be delayed until funding was secured.

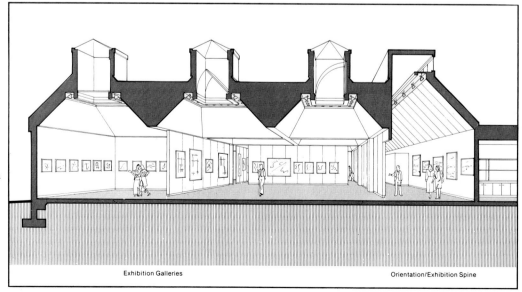

D2-1. Original section. (Courtesy of Verner Johnson Associates)

Exhibition Galleries

Orientation/Exhibition Spine

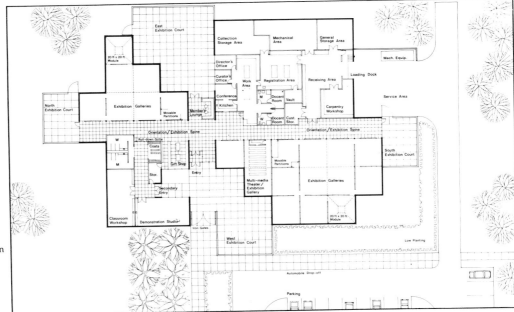

D2–2. Original plan. (Courtesy of Verner Johnson Associates)

D2–3. Original shutter design. (Shop drawing from Overly Manufacturing Co., Greensburg, PA)

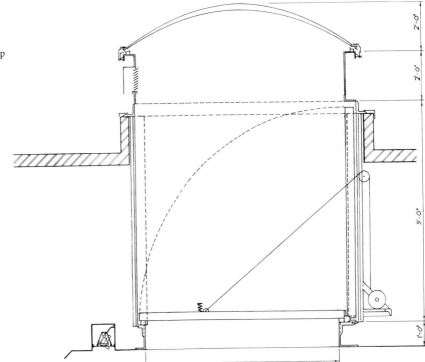

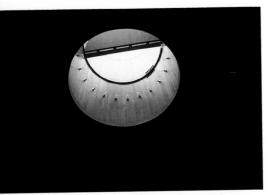

D2–4. Santa Clara County Civic Center (Caudill Rowlett Scott, Architect). The city council chamber has a cylindrical skylight well. The shutter, which folds up like a clamshell, consists of two semicircular panels hinged in the middle.

THE REVISED DESIGN

Years later, the building had to be redesigned for a different site with a greatly reduced budget. The programmed size was reduced, and a less expensive building system was developed to meet the more stringent cost requirements (fig. D2–5).

An exellent low-tech building system was developed. Long-span, tri-

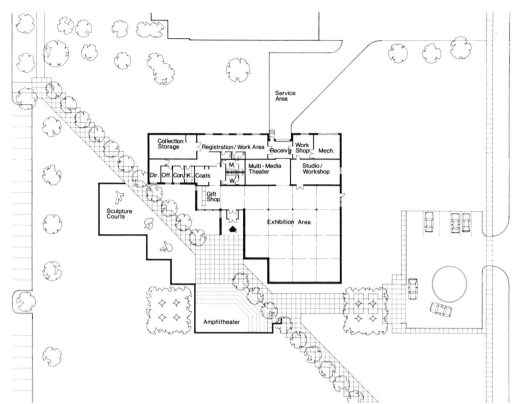

D2–5. Revised plan.
(Courtesy of Verner Johnson Associates)

angular steel box trusses were sheathed with sheetrock and formed chamfered coffers. One-way HVAC ducting and other services were run inside the trusses (fig. D2–6). Drywall transverse fins were introduced both for better brightness control and to facilitate orientation and physical support of full-height display panels in either direction (a reasonable compromise that helped gain some of the advantages of the more non-directional National Gallery coffer). Model photographs (fig. D2–7) show the brightness relation between coffers and exhibit walls to be good (there are no shadows on the walls), but not quite as good as the original National Gallery coffer in which the display wall was always brighter than the coffer because all coffer surfaces were sloped. In this case, the vertical surface of the transverse fin is likely to be brighter than the display wall directly below.

On the other hand, the south-facing vertical glazing of the revised sunscoop design has advantages in conserving HVAC energy: the south-facing glazing naturally captures a great deal of winter sunlight and receives only reflected sunlight in summer.

With the clerestory design, control of the illumination levels for light-sensitive exhibits cannot be accomplished quite as elegantly as with the single flap of the Canadian National Gallery module. Using electrically operated shades or tilting the top surface of the lightshelf can control the absolute levels of light when desired. This degree of control is probably less important for the short-term changing exhibits at Tarble than it would be for permanent collections such as those at the National Gallery.

Consequently, the manually tiltable panels selected are only large enough to eliminate direct sunlight during those periods when it could

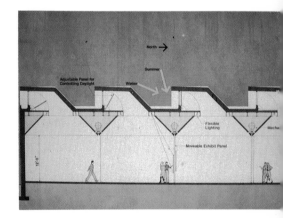

D2–6. Final section. (Courtesy of Verner Johnson Associates)

D2–7. Model photograph. Note that transverse fins are brighter than walls. (Courtesy of Verner Johnson Associates)

D2–8. Actual interior. (Courtesy of Verner Johnson Associates)

otherwise pass beyond the coffers. Other panels will be used to cover the windows for any exhibits demanding minimum lighting. In time, I expect the museum will decide to spend the money to install the recommended electrically operated blackout shades for more convenient and exact control of light levels. In any case, the control materials will be almost entirely out of sight.

As in the earlier scheme, the adjustable supplementary artificial light sources were located in shadow boxes so they would not become highlighted "visual noise" during daylight hours.

Concealed fluorescent strip fixtures were located to supplement and blend with the daylight illumination of the coffers on dark days and provide high-quality diffused ambient light at night, should it be desired.

SUMMARY

The project was completed in 1982 and appeared just as projected by the models (fig. D2–8). The architect, E. Verner Johnson, visited the building a year later and noticed that the accent lights had not been adjusted since

D2–9. South facade. (Courtesy of Verner Johnson Associates)

D2–10. West side. (Courtesy of Verner Johnson Associates)

the contractor left the job. He discovered that no one had bothered to adjust them because they had hardly been turned on. Sunlighting alone had been sufficient for the limited daytime operating schedule.

The resulting exterior architectural forms were handsome and expressive during the day and at night, aided by the sculptured architectural housings for display lighting (figs. D2–9 to D2–12).

Designed to provide sufficient but not excessive quantities of high-quality display lighting (particularly in summer when air-conditioning costs are high), the modest amount of glazing makes this building appear quite different from the greenhouse-type museums of the past.

The linear sunscoop-lit gallery system proved to be a good solution for this project, more economical to construct than, if not as universally applicable as, the original nondirectional design. It provides very attractive, well-illuminated display settings with simple control of illumination levels from elements that are located sufficiently out of sight to be almost unnoticeable. Double glazed and well insulated, it has an excellent energy performance (with minimum energy required for lighting, heating, or cooling) in the temperate climate of cold winters and warm summers for which it was designed.

The architect has been pleased enough with the Tarble concept to apply it to his design for the Virginia Beach Art Museum (fig. D2–13). Because this museum houses a permanent collection, however, automatically controlled blinds will certainly be required.

D2–11. West side at night. (Courtesy of Verner Johnson Associates)

D2–12. Overall exterior view. (Courtesy of Verner Johnson Associates)

D2–13. Johnson's Virginia Beach Museum. (Courtesy of Verner Johnson Associates)

357

D3–1. Bird's-eye view of the model. (Courtesy of Verner Johnson Associates)

D3 Beaumont Art Museum Beaumont, Texas

Latitude: 30°N; climate: 1,600 degree days
$90/sq. ft.

Architect: E. Verner Johnson & Associates, Inc.

Consultants: Souza & True—structural; Lottero & Mason—electrical; Helden Associates—mechanical; William Lam Associates—lighting

CONTEXT

The gallery form of the Beaumont Art Museum is a variation of that developed by the same design team for the Tarble Arts Center a few years earlier. The variations were influenced by the lower latitude and warmer climate that shaped the sunlighting forms and the more generous budget and larger project area that shaped the integrated building system (fig. D3–1).

SUNLIGHTING DESIGN CONCEPT

While south-facing sunscoops were appropriate for Illinois, north-facing lightscoops were selected for this hot climate, in which there is usually a need for cooling rather than heating (fig. D3–2). Without the need for overhangs and interior lightshelves for shading, the monitor profile could be simpler and admit sufficient levels of reflected sunlight and sky light on the north side.

In shaping the lightscoop profile, the short exposure to direct sun from the north was ignored since it would be thermally insignificant and never reach display walls. Blinds were recommended to keep out all daylight after museum hours and to control the sun if desired.

D3–2. Typical section. (Courtesy of Verner Johnson Associates)

North
Motorized Shade To Control Daylight
Flexible Lighting
Mechanical
Movable Exhibit Panel
Exhibit Structure
12'-0"
18'-0"
Electrical Floor Receptacles Under Removable Carpet Tiles
Courtyard

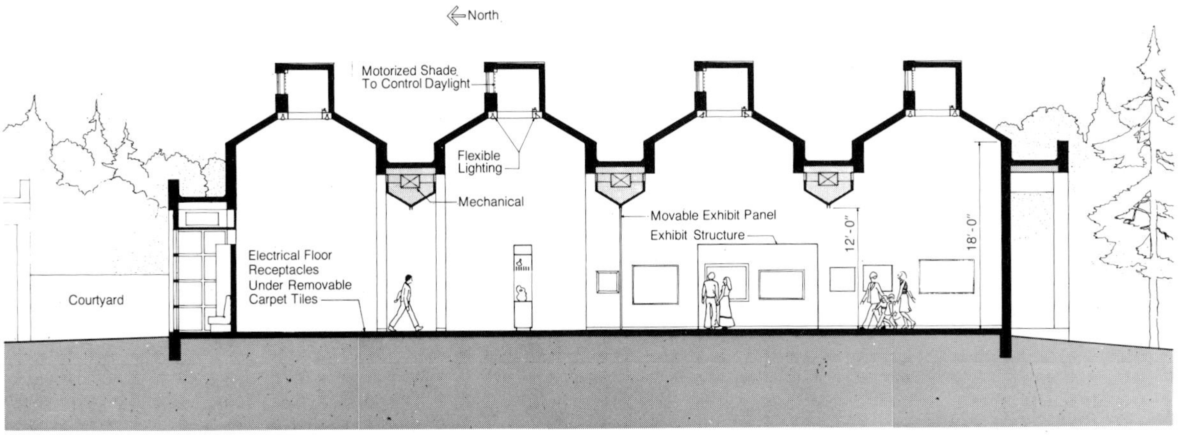

INTEGRATED BUILDING SYSTEM CONCEPT

Unlike the National Gallery of Canada, the chamfered lightwell form is here fully expressed on the exterior. As in most of the integrated building systems presented in my earlier book, *Perception and Lighting as Formgivers for Architecture*, and in some of the preceding case studies (B1 and B5 for example), the systems development began with the articulation of the HVAC systems' distribution by channel beams fed from the end walls. However, while the bottom closure of the mechanical space was flat in these office buildings (and nongallery spaces in this building), in the galleries they were sloped at the same angle as the main ceilings, in order to center partitions and minimize shadows on them.

The concrete channel beam system was an economical way to support the steel-framed gallery roofs. While the shops, lobbies, auditorium, and other nongallery spaces could have been framed differently, the basic daylit gallery system was economical enough to be applied throughout. All spaces benefit from daylight, both as a source of comfort and delight for users and for its operating economy (fig. D3–3).

The same integrated building system, without the clerestory monitor and with indirect fluorescent lighting in the coffers, was applied in the offices. The channel beams also make ideal trellis frames and gutters for the heavy rains characteristic of the area.

D3–3. Site/floor plan. (Courtesy of Verner Johnson Associates)

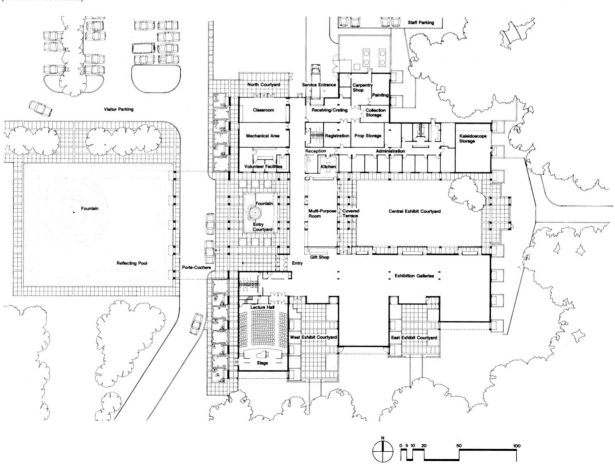

D3–4. Model photograph makes a qualitative evaluation of interior spaces possible. Note full-height partition along beam and lower-height freestanding display case perpendicular to beam.

THE ARCHITECTURE

Viewing the exterior, some may criticize this building for not clearly expressing the differences between galleries and support spaces. However, the overall application of the effective, economical integrated gallery daylight system gives the project great unity and total flexibility in its growth. Support spaces can become uncompromised galleries at any time. Even though the lightscoops are north-facing, the small area of glazing acknowledges the principle that underlighting is preferable to overlighting, recognizing the need for conserving art objects.

The interior spaces should be unified by the paired exposed concrete beams and the continuous clerestory-lit coffers (fig. D3–4). The spaciousness and the one-way expression, of course, dictate that the full-height partitions should be mounted in the same direction. Partitioning in other alignments should be lower and self-supporting, in order not to compromise the spatial character, and for display reasons. Unlike the Tarble Arts building, where the programmatic demands of a university museum with minimum staff and a range of exhibits resulted in 20' × 20' modules, here the curators wanted maximum flexibility. This can be achieved with wide (for structural stability), freestanding partitions of various heights, which can be located anywhere rather than just on the module.

POSTSCRIPT

After the completion of contract documents and during a long fund-raising period, there was a change to a downtown site. The building was modified with little difficulty, as should be the case with a good building system.

Adaptation to the new site required some compromise in the building's orientation and that of the clerestories. Fortunately, the clerestory shape prevents direct sunlight on the exhibits regardless of orientation. The increased solar exposure will require more frequent use of blinds to moderate illumination during exhibit hours and to eliminate daylight when the museum is closed. This being the case, automated controls are necessary. Construction awaits completion of the fund-raising campaign.

D4 Knight Gallery Charlotte, North Carolina

Latitude: 35.2°N; climate: 3,218 degree days

4,428 square feet

Architect: Middleton, McMillan

Consultants: M.M. Armstrong—electrical; Browning-Smith—structural; Mechanical Engineers, Inc.—mechanical; William Lam Associates—lighting

Construction completed: 1983

CONTEXT

This very small gallery illustrates the modification of a nineteenth-century industrial building to an art display space. I was hired to consult on artificial lighting on a project named *Sawtooth Gallery* and was thus surprised to note that the original daylight openings had already been roofed in because the gallery staff was concerned about the visual competition of the existing large clerestory windows.

I was able to convince all concerned that the interior roof shape could be modified to utilize natural light with minimal visual competition, in exchange for savings in energy and, more important, a more delightful space. Indeed, after seeing a sawtooth configuration on the exterior, visitors would probably be depressed to find no daylight inside (figs. D4–1, D4–2).

D4–1. Exterior.

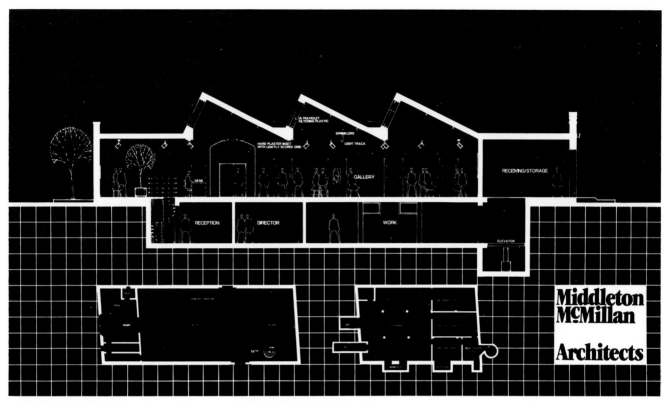

D4–2. Original section. (Courtesy of
Middleton MacMillan)

THE REVISIONS

Given the tight budget and the new unbroken roof that covered even the
sloping clerestory opening, all we could do to restore natural light to the
space was to saw through the sheathing, replacing it with an insulated,
plastic, light-transmitting material that could be installed like roofing, and
to paint the newly installed 2' × 4' joists that were left exposed. The
budget did not allow for a complete new window assembly with clear
glass, which the architect and I would have preferred.

The revised ceiling shape, related to that at the Tarble Arts Center,
minimizes the view of the crudely but economically detailed clerestory
window and distributes the light to minimize the contrast between ceilings and glazed area (fig. D4–3).

D4–3. Modified section (as built).

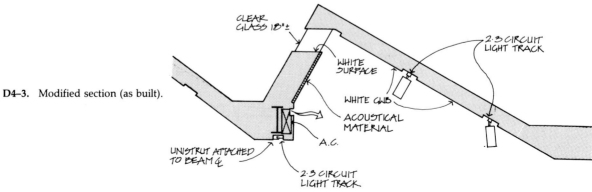

Even with the very limited glazing area of the sawtooth clerestory, the reflected sunlight and sky light eliminate the need for artificial lighting in the sawtooth area much of the time. When supplemented by the track-mounted accent lighting, the sawtooth configuration creates a richer space and provies high-quality ambient light, which is particularly valuable for sculpture (fig. D4–4).

Since part of the room has a flat ceiling and its exhibits therefore receive little daylight, I opted not to illuminate the coffered ceiling surfaces at night. The space and the exhibits thus take on a totally different night time character (fig. D4–5).

D4–4. Interior.

D4–5. Interior at night.

Musée National de la Civilisation Quebec City, Canada

Latitude: 46.5°N; climate: 9,070 degree days

200,000 square feet @ $114 (Canadian)/sq. ft.

Architect: Belzile, Brassard, Gallienne, Lavoie, Sungar Encesulu, Moshe Safdie, Desnoyers, Mercure (Moshe Safdie, Partner in Charge)

Consultants: LVLV & Associates—structural; G.B.G.M. & J.M. Lagace—mechanical and electrical; William Lam Associates—lighting

Construction completed: 1986

CONTEXT

Architectural forms dictated by existing forms of a historical neighborhood frequently make good sunlighting design difficult. As in the renovation of old buildings, however, coping with such constraints often results in unusually rich forms and details.

In his competition-winning entry, architect Moshe Safdie fitted this large museum into the neighborhood of old dormered residences by echoing their triangular ridged roofs. The ridges were alternately glazed or sheathed in copper (fig. D5–1).

I was asked to review the daylighting ramifications of the scheme after Safdie won the competition. I concluded that, although ingenious, the scheme had some flaws in terms of sunlighting. I found it difficult to reconcile the omnidirectional triangular ridge forms with effective sunlighting. Eventually, we were able to develop a scheme that retained some of the distinctive forms of the exterior, while simplifying the interior appearance and increasing the sunlighting effectiveness.

THE COMPETITION SCHEME

My first glance at the roof plan of the competition scheme showed that an excessive portion of the roof area—almost 50 percent—was to be glazed (fig. D5–2). The many small triangular "ridges," which ran perpendicular to the ridge of the roof, suggested that the ceiling inside would be visually busy, with alternating light and dark bands. This was confirmed by looking into the model.

D5–1. Competition scheme: elevation. (Courtesy of Moshe Safdie)

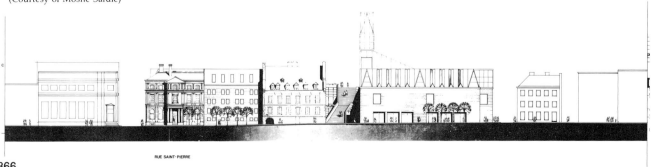

RUE SAINT-PIERRE

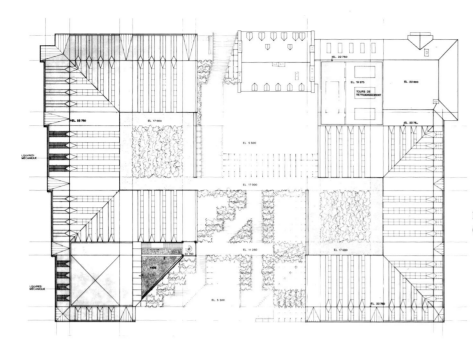

D5–2. Competition scheme: roof plan.
(Courtesy of Moshe Safdie)

Given the large area of glazing and its orientation in all directions (dictated by the plan and roof forms), the designers had done an excellent job of controlling the effects of direct sunlight. They had designed different fixed internal louver configurations for each exposure and then supplemented these quite complex louvers with blackout shades placed just below (fig. D5–3).

Testing of the competition model confirmed that the design could achieve its quantitative goals. There would be sufficient illumination to view the displays and adequate control of maximum light levels for proper conservation of artwork (fig D5–4). However, observation of the model also confirmed the design's qualitative problems. The location of the skylights made a distracting ceiling pattern that competed with the displays for attention (fig. D5–5). The omnidirectional nature of the skylights necessitated a complex pattern of louvers and shades that increased visual distraction (fig. D5–6). Like the Tate Gallery and the Lehman wing (see figs. D1–18, D1–26), the design admitted excessive amounts of sunlight and then tried to soak it up with louvers—a very inefficient approach. It was obvious that a more carefully oriented, substantially smaller glazing area could provide sufficient light with controls that were much simpler visually and mechanically.

POSSIBLE MODIFICATIONS

My experience with sunlighting other museums and office buildings suggested that the easiest solution was to reshape the roof to create a simpler, smooth roof with continuous sunscoops with suncatchers along the main ridge (fig. D5–7). This would be more efficient and provide more uniform illumination of the ceiling and the spaces below. I felt that the large triangular windows could be retained if they were baffled by a wide lightshelf. The lightshelf could be integrated with an already planned mechanical tray and be floated in the space to allow some light to spill

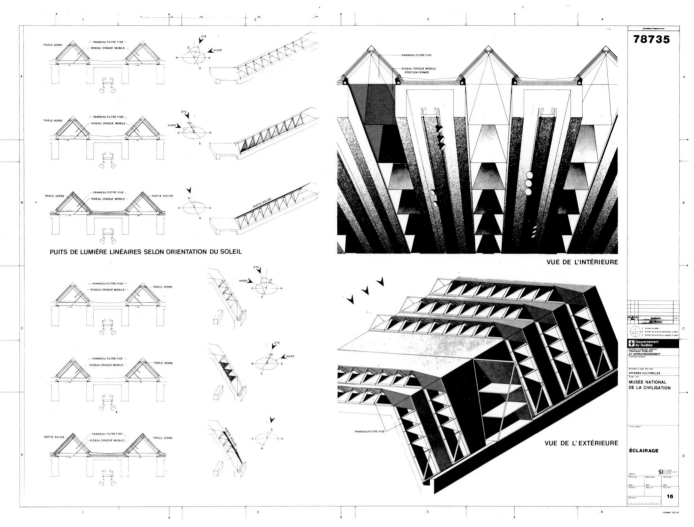

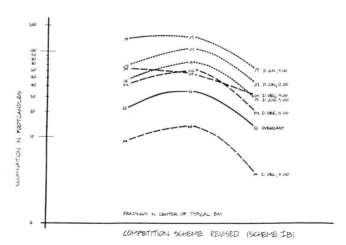

D5–3. Different triangular louvers were devised for each orientation. (Courtesy of Moshe Safdie)

D5–4. Competition model testing.

D5–5. View of competition model shows stripes.

D5–6. Diagram of inside view of triangular louvers. (Courtesy of Moshe Safdie)

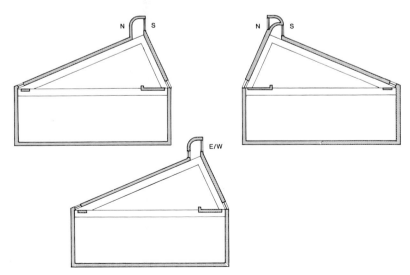

D5–7. Alternate section. (Courtesy of Moshe Safdie)

on the wall below, as I had discovered at Soddy Daisy High School (see fig. C1–13). Although my design might have been effective for lighting, it would have sacrificed the prizewinning dormer character that helped the museum blend in with its historic neighborhood.

Revised Schemes

The design team decided that the alternatives considered had to retain the characteristic features of the exterior facade: the large triangular dormer windows and the many-ridged roof. We therefore sought alternatives that combined the complexity of the multifaceted roof with the simpler more selective shapes suggested by sunlighting. The design team decided to retain the ridges running up and down the slope of the roof on the street-facing sides. It was decided to have a strip of clerestory windows running along the roof ridge with all of the light-reflecting and blocking elements within a faceted lantern form. The sunlight admitted by the lantern required an independent baffle to redirect the light against the ceiling surfaces (fig. D5–8).

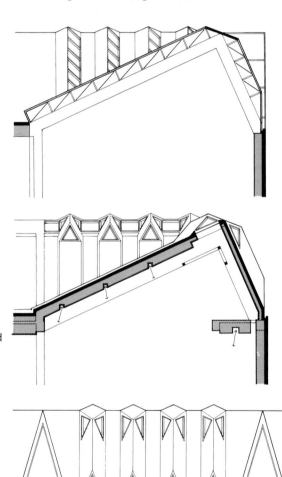

D5–8. Section-elevation of original design (top) is less interesting than that of the revised design (center) incorporating ridge lanterns with baffles below. Bottom: revised design viewed from the street.

Model testing of the revised scheme indicated that the lantern-solid baffle combination would provide sufficient and even light during sunny days. Only during very sunny summer days would a small amount of supplementary shading be required (fig. D5-9). However, it would be desirable to increase the level of illumination on overcast days and diminish the "heavy" look of the large, dark baffle overhead. For this reason it was decided that the baffle would be made of wood slats (running up and down the ceiling slope) with a translucent material on top, facing the lantern and the sky. The translucency of the baffle doubled illumination levels under overcast conditions, without the baffle appearing significantly brighter than the adjacent ceiling surfaces (figs. D5-10). Although the new baffle will require more frequent use of supplementary blinds on sunny days, the half-drawn shades will be hidden from view behind the baffle and thus will not contribute any visual noise. Because the skylight area was reduced and most of what remained is hidden by

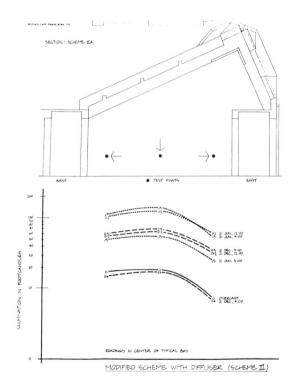

D5–9. Model testing results for the revised scheme.

the suspended baffle, the appearance of the space is simpler and less distracting. The two major planes, which define the roof shape, are washed with sunlight reflected by the baffle.

On the exterior, the complex forms of the roof have been retained, with the jewellike form of the lanterns at the roof ridge an added element. Both the large triangular "dormers" and the ends of the smaller, triangular ridges that face the street are glazed; the overhead glazing of these elements has been eliminated. The difference between the original and the revised scheme is apparent if you compare the two roof plans (fig. D5-11 vs. fig. D5-2). Since the roof forms and the vertical glazing facing the street have been retained, the difference between the two schemes' elevations is less radical.

D5–10. Interior of revised model shows less visual noise.

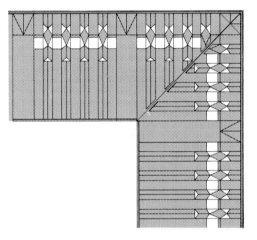

D5–11. New scheme: roof plan. (Courtesy of Moshe Safdie)

From the inside, the large lightshelf/mechanical tray blocks most view from the smaller windows, and the larger windows are only visible from a distance. Some direct light spills through the gap between the lightshelf and the exterior wall onto the wall and floor below; most of the light is reflected by the top surface of the lightshelf to the sloped ceilings above.

SUMMARY

While both schemes provide the illumination desired, the revised scheme provides a *qualitatively* superior interior environment. Without substantially changing the shape of the multifaceted roof or the building's omnidirectional orientation, we were able to achieve the quantitative illumination goals with a two-thirds reduction in glazed area.

The substantially reduced glazing area, less extensive and simpler light-controlling elements, and far simpler roof construction detailing reduced both construction and operating (cooling, heating, and maintenance) costs substantially.

Ironically, in presenting the proposed design revisions, we needed to convince the clients that our goal had been to produce a better museum, rather than a less expensive one. It is always difficult to convince the client of qualitative benefits in a design in aspects about which he is unaware. In this case, sketches, model testing data, and slides from the model were not enough. Only by viewing the models under real-sky conditions, and after I had given a lecture to explain sunlighting principles, was the client convinced that this was better architecture, rather than a cheaper design.

As exterior architecture, the reduced glazing may not look sufficiently ''museumlike'' to some designers, but I think others will delight in the jewellike lantern forms we created as both functional and elegant variations on the dormer forms of the surrounding historic neighborhood.

D6 Shenzhen Museum Shenzhen, China

Latitude: 22.2°N

Architect: Canton Institute (architects, engineers, builders)/ Palmer and Turner, Consulting Architect (James Kinoshita, Partner in Charge; Peter Pun, Project Manager)

Consultants: William Lam Associates—lighting; E. Verner Johnson—museum architecture

Construction completed: 1986

This museum for Shenzhen, an area designated as a special economic zone just north of Hong Kong, is the first museum being built in the People's Republic of China. With little museum experience to draw on, Shenzhen officials sought outside design input to review and complete the design and hired a team headed by the Hong Kong architects, Palmer and Turner. E. Verner Johnson, a Boston-based architect, and I were a part of the Palmer and Turner team. Although the structure was largely completed and the museum scheduled to be opened in a few months, no museum interiors had yet been conceived.

ARCHITECTURAL CONTEXT

The museum building, which was under construction when I first viewed it, is located in a clearing between apartment buildings. It is four stories high with an 80-square-meter central atrium that is to exhibit large objects, such as a dinosaur skeleton. The surrounding galleries, intended for a range of exhibits from large paintings to unearthed artifacts, are a series of almost square rooms (fig. D6–1). These galleries are arranged as stepped ramps—a more formal version of the Guggenheim scheme. The museum is angular instead of round in plan, stepped at each of the four sides instead of continuously ramped, and has individual rooms instead of spaces fully open to the central space. With the roof at one level, the stepping format results in top-floor ceiling heights varying from 4 to 9 meters (fig. D6–2).

At the time of my initial site visit, the atrium roof was to be fully glazed. Galleries were designed with chamfered corners on all sides, glazed with full-height windows at the exterior corners. No glazing materials or light control devices had yet been selected. No interior construction (ceilings, lighting, etc.) had been documented. The poured-in-place concrete structural system consisted of a grid of major beams connecting the columns at the chamfered corners of the galleries, with two additional secondary beams in each central coffer. The column forms for the third floor were being completed.

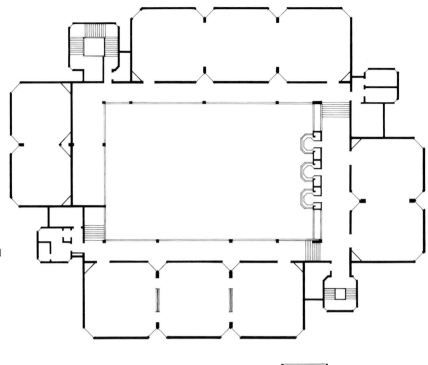

D6–1. Typical gallery floor plan: second floor.

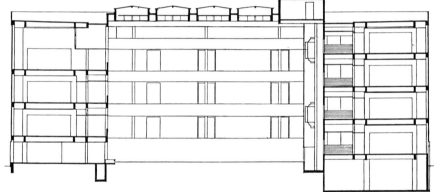

D6–2. Original east/west section with horizontal skylights between beams and solid-flat roof over top-floor galleries. (Courtesy of Palmer and Turner, Architects)

DESIGN RECOMMENDATIONS—GALLERY DETAILS AND SUNLIGHTING REVISIONS

Because of the advanced stage of construction and the time constraints for the project completion, I realized that realistic proposals should be low-tech and require minimum change of the existing design. My first proposals included designs that could be fit into the original structural design with no changes and alternate designs that needed only minor revisions in wall detailing and secondary roof structure, neither of which should cause much delay.

Atrium

The amount of horizontal glazing appeared excessive for the low lighting levels suitable for a museum. Maximum lighting and heat at mid-day in summer (characteristic of horizontal skylights) did not seem logical in a hot climate at 22 degrees latitude. In addition, transparent glazing between the concrete beams would cast disruptive shadows on any display. With translucent glazing, the ceiling would produce excessive visual noise.

I recommended merely replacing the horizontal glazing with a series of continuous vaults capped with east/west-facing monitors on top of the north/south beams (fig. D6–3). Having previously tested such a configuration for a proposed office building in Memphis, Tennessee, I knew that it would deliver a fairly constant level of illumination (and heat) throughout sunny days throughout the year and on cloudy and bright overcast days. I suggested retaining the paired beams that had been included in the original design (probably to aid skylight maintenance). The paired beams could support enclosed catwalks for aiming and maintaining lighting and provide convenient support of suspended displays. The additional depth of these catwalk enclosures would be useful for blocking all but a sliver of direct sunlight from reaching the ground floor and the exhibits, while allowing direct sunlight to be visible on the monitor and the surface of the balcony railings.

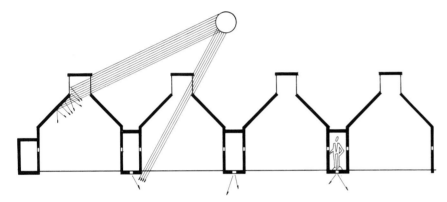

D6–3. Revised east/west section detail of east/west-facing monitors and service-enclosed catwalk.

Perimeter Galleries

If galleries are to be illuminated by visible windows, the chamfered corner location of the original design is best. However, the unavoidable conflict between windows and display always makes it desirable for the windows to be the secondary rather than primary source of light in a gallery. They should ideally be there for view alone.

Top-floor Galleries

The top-floor galleries were easily improved by providing toplighting and retaining the windows only where the view is particularly advantageous. The repetitive, almost square module suggested a variation on the pyramidal ceiling/skylight system I had proposed years before for the National Gallery of Canada, revised for Shenzhen's warmer climate and more equatorial location (with nearly overhead solar paths that are to the north at midsummer). I also wanted to avoid any moving parts during normal operation, to minimize maintenance problems and avoid complex construction details.

On two sides of the atrium, there was sufficient ceiling height avail-

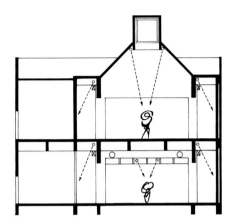

D6-4. Diagrammatic section of revised galleries: revised top-floor gallery with pyramidal roof and monitor system (looking north) and original lower gallery completed with box lighting-display system within perimeter false beam. Note removal of secondary beams at upper gallery.

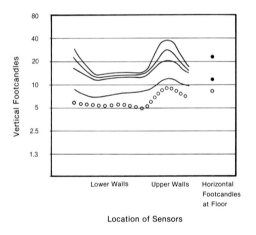

D6-5. Model testing data.

D6-6. Detailed section through revised top-floor gallery, looking west.

able to insert nonstructural pyramidal coffers and skylights as at the National Gallery (case study D1), without any change in structure beyond the removal of a square of roof slab. Because of insufficient height elsewhere, however, we proposed a minor structural change—replacing the roof structure with thin-wall concrete pyramids in place of the secondary beams and slabs (fig. D6-4). For the total system, this should be more economical and attractive than separate ceiling and roof systems. For sunlighting in a climate that has little need for heat any time and to minimize the need for dynamic control, I proposed monitors glazed to the south and north so that the sunlight could be controlled by fixed shading and lightshelves, rather than the National Gallery combination of clear skylights and adjustable internal baffling.

The design was then refined with model testing. The monitor was enlarged to get enough fenestration. Shading of both small rectangular south and square north windows was provided within an external cube monitor form for architectural reasons (so that they would be as symmetrical as possible when seen from different directions, capping a series of square galleries). Measurements of illumination on the walls verified the expected importance of white roofs as well as white sills (lightshelves) to reflect light into windows on the shady side (D6-5). As an optional feature, we also recommended small half-round windows on the east and west sides of the monitors to boost illumination early and late in the day, when the sun does not reach the north or south sides (D6-6). This combination of openings should be very effective in providing a steady 10–30 footcandles of natural light on clear days. On cloudy and bright overcast days, the five footcandles of glareless ambient illumination would be supplemented by highlighting of the displays. Fluorescent lighting in the monitors for ambient lighting would only be used on the darkest days and at night. These should be excellent galleries for displaying any type of artifact without causing visual competition but with a view of sky and sunlight for orientation (fig. D6-7). The large-scale coffers seem right for the very high spaces and the larger artifacts that will be displayed (fig. D6-8).

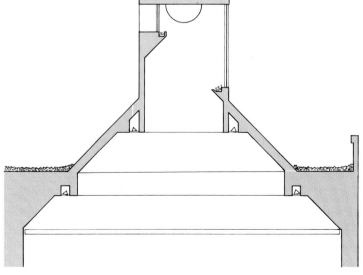

D6–7. Top-floor gallery model.

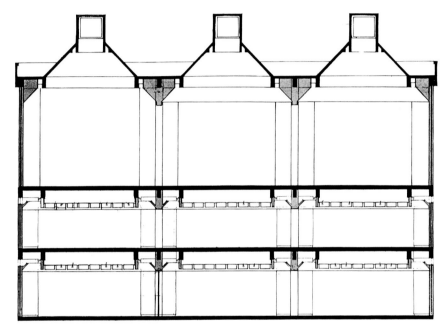

D6–8. Section through galleries illustrates appropriate scale of coffers for the tall spaces on the top floor and the definition of "rooms" by perimeter coffers in lower galleries (thus allowing walls to be inserted only when desired). (Courtesy of E. Verner Johnson)

The Lower-level Galleries

To provide for ultimate flexibility for integrated and lighting displays, we proposed a box system (similar to that recommended for the Canadian National Gallery and used at the Tennessee State Museum in Nashville) for the center of the galleries. For most displays, the boxes would be best as darker colored objects, painted, or of natural wood.

The structure and the chamfered room shapes suggested that the box ceiling should stop short of the perimeter walls and be edged by perimeter baffles, extensions of the main beams (fig. D6–9). In this way the light is kept out of the central ceiling cavity above the boxes, and perimeter track lighting is baffled. At the corners of window walls, the baffle (painted white on the outside) redirects some of the light from the window to the adjacent walls, thereby reducing the contrast between window and window wall (fig. D6–10). While this is a help, the window wall

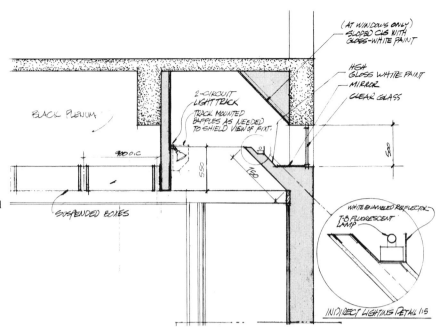

Labels in drawing:
(AT WINDOWS ONLY) SLOPED CLG WITH GLOSS-WHITE PAINT

HIGH GLOSS WHITE PAINT
MIRROR
CLEAR GLASS

2-CIRCUIT LIGHT TRACK
TRACK MOUNTED BAFFLES AS NEEDED TO SHIELD VIEW OF FIXT.

BLACK PLENUM

900 O.C.

550

180

500

SUSPENDED BOXES

WHITE ENAMELLED REFLECTOR
T-8 FLUORESCENT LAMP

INDIRECT LIGHTING DETAIL 1:5

D6–9. Detailed section through revised sidelighted gallery showing baffled clerestory in addition to box ceiling.

still remains much darker than the interior walls, which ''see'' more of the window.

To further reduce this lighting imbalance, we proposed the addition of a narrow band of clerestory windows, completely baffled from view within the galleries. Having introduced another better source of gallery lighting, I proposed that the light from the view window be reduced by using tinted (40 percent transmission) glass and that additional shades or blinds be lowered for sun control when necessary. Model testing showed that with this technique, the window wall could become the brightest wall (fig. D6–11).

We also evaluated such a window arrangement without any view windows as a prototype for other applications and found the results very promising for providing the desired levels for gallery illumination without visual noise (D6–12). (Using them alone and with a different structure, I would make them larger.)

D6–10. Sidelighted gallery: corner windows for view and light.

378   **Museums**

D6–11. Sidelighted gallery: corner windows for view, baffled clerestory for light.

D6–12. Sidelighted gallery: baffled clerestory for light, no view windows.

PROJECT STATUS

At our first team site visit and presentation, all of our concepts were well received by the user group, the Shenzhen city officials, and the regional government design and construction group (The Canton Bureau). They were all excited by the concept models that the Palmer and Turner staff had produced overnight. They had previously been briefed via a slide lecture by myself and Boston Museum architect E. Verner Johnson, whom I had recruited for the team, with simultaneous translation and additional input by Peter Pun. The design team was authorized to continue development of the design for construction.

In the end, the construction group, which had the final authority, decided that because of time constraints they would follow through only on our atrium redesign and our artificial lighting-display system, which they will apply throughout. Ironically, subsequent administrative delays have halted the project completely. Today, although the scheduled completion date is long past, the construction has progressed little since my first site visit.

Though disappointed that not all of our design solutions are being used in this project, I am nevertheless pleased to have had the opportunity to develop and test solutions to some very generic problems:

☐ toplighting of square galleries in a hot climate;

☐ sidelighting of galleries for both view and light;

☐ sidelighting of low gallery ceilings by illumination of the perimeter walls from concealed clerestory windows oriented in any direction.

D7 Musée d'Art Contemporain de Montreal (Montreal Museum of Contemporary Art) Place des Arts, Montreal, Canada

Latitude: 45.3°N; climate: 8,000 degree days

110,000 square feet @ $135 (Canadian)/sq. ft.

Architect: Jodoin Lamarre Pratte (Gabriel Charbonneau, Partner in Charge)

Consultants: Carmel Fyen & Jaques—structural; Caron, Racine, St. Denis—electrical and mechanical; Lam and Edwards — lighting

Construction completion scheduled: 1987

CONTEXT

This museum of contemporary art was the subject of an architectural competition held by the province of Quebec early in 1984. The site includes a large concert hall, a theater complex, and a park. The museum program requirements of 10,000 square meters of space indicated a long narrow building, with its long facades oriented to the northeast and to the southwest (following the downtown Montreal street alignment) (fig. D7–1).

In its comments on the winning competition entry of Jodoin Lamarre Pratte, the jury report remarked on the proposed natural lighting as being appropriate for the main circulation spaces and most of the galleries but observed an excessive use of glazing on the southwest side (fig. D7–2). The architects attempted to correct this in their final preliminary design, which was given approval in February, 1985 (fig. D7–3). In addition to a somewhat reduced glazing area, the revised design had fixed two-way louvers instead of the operable louvers indicated in the competition drawings.

It was at this point that Lam and Edwards were asked to review the natural lighting design concept and to propose alternatives if they seemed appropriate. The HVAC engineers, concerned about the total amount of skylights, asked the architects to consider the use of mirror or heat-absorbing glass.

Although we were unable to modify the building orientation, we set out to achieve steady, appropriate illumination levels throughout the day for all seasons for the galleries exposed both to the northeast and the southwest. Understanding the "grand style" (to use the architect's words) of the architectural concept, with its classic roof shapes and formal characteristics, we were able to accomplish our sunlighting objectives without obscuring the intentions of Jodoin Lamarre Pratte.

THE COMPETITION SCHEME

The winning competition entry was based on the extensive use of large areas of skylights, much as in the late nineteenth-century greenhouse-like museum roof.

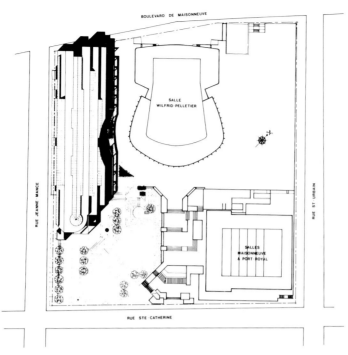

D7–1. Site plan: competition. (Courtesy of
Jodoin, Lamarre, Pratte)

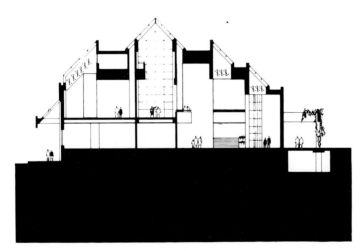

D7–2. Architects' competition section.
(Courtesy of Jodoin, Lamarre, Pratte)

D7–3. Architects' final preliminary section.
(Courtesy of Jodoin, Lamarre, Pratte)

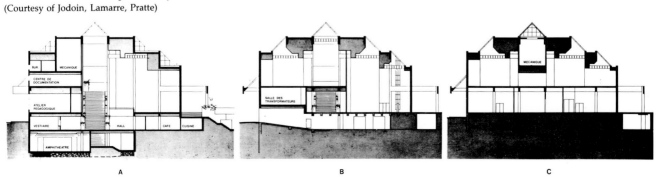

COUPES TRANSVERSALES

Our review of the drawings, before actually testing the design with models, convinced us that because of their orientation, the skylights could not possibly create steady illumination levels. Also, in spite of a deep, two-way baffle configuration, the sketches suggested that the amount of glazing would require an operable louver system as well, in order to control direct sunlight and reduce unacceptably high lighting levels. Under most sunny conditions, it would be necessary to close the skylight partially.

The drawings also revealed that the complex shapes between the ceiling grid and the glazing plane would produce a wide variation in louver brightness, with some elements actually in shadow. Building a model of a typical gallery space illustrated the dramatic sun penetration and distracting patterns created on the walls (fig. D7–4). The location of the louvers at the ceiling plane produced shadows on walls and resulted in poor brightness transition from ceiling to wall.

The two-way baffling of a linear skylight did not use the light very effectively. It was clear that a smaller area of better-oriented glazing could provide the desired illumination with fewer and less complex baffling devices.

Six vertical and one horizontal light sensors were placed in the model and were tested with both clear glass and diffusing glass for both northeast and southwest exposures for the twenty-first of December, March, and June at various times of the day.

The results of the testing showed that with clear glass on December 21, the average lighting level on the walls varied between 1 and 7 footcandles throughout the day in the northeast galleries and between 14 and 41 footcandles on the southwest; in June, these lighting levels were 6 and 93 on the northeast, 38 and 165 on the southwest. At one o'clock on March 21, the average level was 13 footcandles in the northeast galleries as compared with 98 in the southwest galleries. It could be expected that heating and air conditioning requirements for the original scheme were greater than necessary.

D7–4. Model photo of architects' revised scheme.

THE NEW DESIGN

Optimizing the performance of toplighting implies using the light indirectly: incoming sunlight must be baffled and redirected in order to avoid glare and provide the desired light distribution. In the proposed modifications, the skylight opening was fitted with large, square one-way adjustable louvers to prevent direct sunlight from reaching displays and to control illumination levels (figs. D7–5, D7–6, D7–7). It was also reduced to 1.5 meters in width. The ceiling was chamfered so that all the walls would "see" the reflected sunlight on the sides of the well. Vertical fins on column center lines express the structural system and visually subdivide the long galleries.

On examining the model, it became clear why a chamfered ceiling is preferable to a direct connection of horizontal ceiling surface with wall, as was recognized in the classic galleries with their effectively chamfered cornice moldings. Equally obvious is the advantage of keeping the light source higher and less conspicuous, thereby minimizing the contrast be-

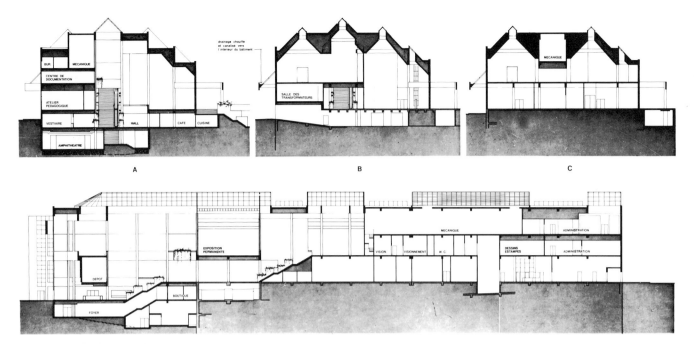

D7–5. Top: final section; bottom: longitudinal section.

tween aperture and wall and ceiling surfaces. Photographs taken under real sky conditions illustrate the pleasure of seeing walls that look evenly lit, even though illuminated by sunlight that is dynamic rather than static, while being able to have a simultaneous view of blue sky and small changing patterns of sunlight on the baffles and skylight walls.

More uniform illumination of all the galleries throughout the day was achieved by sloping most of the skylight glazing in two directions. On the extreme northeast, without changing the roof configuration dramatically, a two-sided skylight might have created snow problems; therefore, the original glazing form was retained but reduced in size. From inside the gallery, this skylight slot appears the same as all the others. In all galleries, the skylight wells were extended to the end walls defining the spaces, which was not the case in the competition entry.

After initial model testing was completed, diamond-shaped deflectors, or suncatchers, were added to the tops of the skylights to catch the low-angle sun and to reflect additional light into the galleries under those conditions. Reducing the light admitted when the sun is aligned with the axis of the skylights also helps make the amount of sunlight admitted more even throughout the day.

This design has the advantage of allowing the daylight to be used more efficiently, producing better thermal performance and requiring less adjustment of light-control elements. On the whole, this scheme is easier to build and to maintain, largely because there is less glazing and the baffling is less complicated.

Model testing indicated that the average lighting levels would be fairly steady for both sides of the museum, throughout both the day and the seasons, and approximate the optimum level of 30 footcandles. For example, the printout of the testing of the new design throughout the day on June 21 shows average vertical illumination levels of 26, 32, 26,

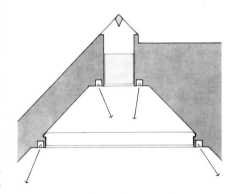

D7–6. Section detail shows slot for light fixtures, operable square louvers, optional one-way baffles, and diamond-shaped suncatcher/deflector at areas of glazing.

D7–7. Model photo of Lam/Edwards design.

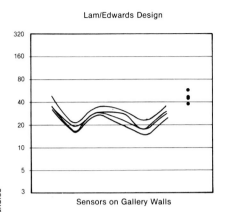

Lam/Edwards Design

Vertical Footcandles

320
160
80
40
20
10
5
3

Sensors on Gallery Walls

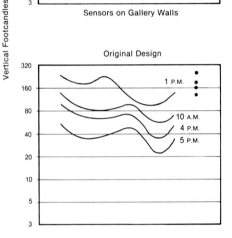

Original Design

320
160
80
40
20
10
5
3

1 P.M.
10 A.M.
4 P.M.
5 P.M.

D7–8. Top: new model performance throughout the day in June; bottom: original model performance throughout the day in June. (Dots represent horizontal footcandle readings.)

and 22 footcandles for 10:00 h, 13:00 h, 16:00 h, and 17:00 h. The corresponding results for the modified competition design are 87, 165, 64, and 38 (fig. D7–8).

With the glazing area minimized by the efficient utilization of sunlight, the available daylight under overcast conditions will also be reduced. However, the spaces will appear comparatively well illuminated because of the controlled brightness ratios and good brightness transition from sloped ceiling to wall. On dark overcast days, even if sufficient daylighting could be achieved by more extensive glazing, the gloomy color is best corrected by highlighting the artwork with warmer incandescent light. The artificial illumination is integrated inconspicuously with the architectural elements, concealed in the shadows of the natural lighting, rather than highlighted by it. If required for a particular exhibition, lighting tracks perpendicular to the concealed lighting slots can be suspended and powered from them.

CONCLUSION

All parties involved with the museum project were pleased with our proposed revisions for its lighting, thermal, and conservation implications. Some liked the more soaring spatial qualities indicated by the model photographs; others missed the more intimate character of the louvered ceiling plane. Although no additional louvering is functionally necessary, we have suggested that either effect could be had at will; individual one-way baffles can be inserted very simply if needed for particualr exhibits, at whatever spacing is desired. Such members, which span the width of the one-way coffers, can also be useful for stabilizing partitions or supporting additional lighting.

As foundation work has commenced, the architects have begun to modify their building section to reflect our new sunlighting design. When completed, the architectural forms of the Contemporary Arts Museum will appear no less ''museumlike'' in the Montreal Arts complex than intended, but perhaps more elegant on the exterior as well as more delightful within.

GROUP E Industrial Buildings

The main benefit of sunlighting in large industrial buildings is the improvement in the quality of the work environment and the resultant effects on the comfort, morale, and productivity of employees.

In large industrial buildings, most of the work spaces are likely to be distant from the building perimeter. Functional needs often require a visually complex jumble of equipment and a complicated maze of circulation paths. Sunlighting can help human adaptation to this difficult environment. Its presence can supply important biological information about the presence of the outside world, time of day and weather, and so on. Sunlighting can highlight circulation paths and clarify the physical organization of the building. Crisp, sunlit wall surfaces can be pleasant substitutes for exterior views, providing "visual rest centers" from interior clutter.

Sunlighting industrial buildings may save electrical energy for lighting, but proportionally less than in other commercial buildings, especially when plants operate two or three shifts. Savings from electrical demand charges and the potential benefits of brownout protection may be greater. The benefits of passive solar heating or the penalties for solar loads are often negligible in industrial buildings because the heat generated or the ventilation requirements of the manufacturing process tend to dominate the energy picture.

E1 Consolidated Diesel (Case/Cummins) Engine Plant Rocky Mount, North Carolina

Latitude: 35.2°N; climate: 3,218 heating degree days

Architect: Caudill Rowlett Scott/Giffels Associates—joint venture architects (Paul Kennon, C.R.S. Partner in Charge; Doss Mabe, John Cryer, and Ed Broadhaus, Project Architects)

Consultants: Caudill Rowlett Scott—engineering; Lyle Verges—acoustical; William Lam Associates—lighting

Construction completed: 1983

CONTEXT

The design of this megascale plant is an excellent example of sunlighting, specifically toplighting, as a formgiver. The lightscoops are integral to the ordering of the building and provide a quality of light superior to traditional skylights or sawtooth roofs.

DAYLIGHTING AT CUMMINS ENGINE— A REVIEW

Before discussing the design of this plant, it may be instructive to review my observations of daylighting at earlier Cummins Engine (the principal joint-venture member) facilities, beginning with my first contact with the company in 1964, when I began consultation on the Engineering Building of the Cummins Research and Engineering Center in Columbus, Indiana (Harry Weese, architect).

At that time I had observed the overwhelming visual noise and gloom of plant areas with unlit ceilings and no daylight (fig. E1–1) and the advantages of those existing spaces that had overhead diffuse skylights. These skylights beneficially illuminated the ceiling structure and allowed some light to bounce off the top of ducts and trusses accidentally

E1–1. Typical industrial building—gloomy interior environment.

E1–2. Skylights make space brighter but reveal chaos overhead.

(fig. E1–2). However, these skylights also imposed some visually noisy patterns on the complex maze of elements overhead.

Some of the older Cummins facilities were full of visual noise and glare from the large expanses of windows and the accompanying clutter: painted-out glass, improvised plywood baffles, broken blinds, and the like—not unlike many other older factories.

I integrated these observations into my consultation for the new engineering building. The strategy here was to provide a "clean," clearly structured ceiling, indirectly lit, and to emphasize the perimeter walls of the 250' × 250' space with skylights (figs. E1–3, E1–4, E1–5). Enclosed cubicles within the space were given greenhouse windows so that their occupants could have maximum views of the surrounding visual environment—the man-made "sky and horizon" (fig. E1–6). A narrow horizontal band of view windows was provided at eye level around the overall perimeter to provide interest for those circulating or located along the edge. Elsewhere, the view from lower windows was limited by partitions, storage racks, or machinery.

The building was quite successful. Thus, Cummins' facilities planners were sympathetic when, eight years later, I proposed a similar emphasis on illuminated walls, even if we had to create walls for that purpose. When I recommended using clerestory windows, however, there was initial resistance due to the high cost of cleaning the glass and the low utility value of the windows in one of their recently completed plants in Walesboro, Indiana.

I guessed that the ineffective windows cited were east- and west-facing clerestories, whose shading requirements had been tackled with venetian blinds. A plant visit confirmed that assumption: the clerestories were now permanently shaded by broken-down black venetian blinds whose automatic controls had "retired" (fig. E1–7). In that condition they provided no benefit, only visual noise and maintenance problems. On the other hand, the south-facing clerestories, shaded only by an overhang, were left uncovered and were valued for their illumination and view, as were north walls illuminated by a south-sloping diffused skylight (similar in structure to the Columbus facility described above).

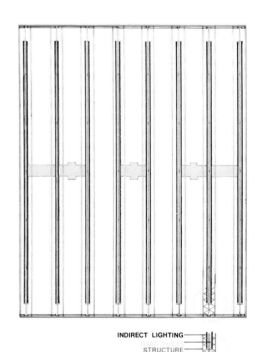

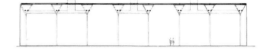

E1–3. Plan and section of Cummins Engineering building. Note perimeter skylights on two end walls.

E1–4. Integrated systems produce a visually clean ceiling.

E1–5. Skylit walls provide horizon. Note greenhouse glazing of office spaces seen here from the "exterior" corridor.

E1–6. Interior of office space with greenhouse overhead glazing.

E1–7. Broken-down blinds control glare at east and west clerestories of Cummins Walesboro plant.

CONSOLIDATED DIESEL—CONTEXT

The Consolidated Diesel plant was a joint venture of the Case Company and the Cummins Engine Company. The design goals of this manufacturing facility, the first automated diesel engine production line in the U.S., were strongly influenced by the top executive of Cummins, Irwin Miller, who has a long fostered design quality in Cummins facilities (as well as in the city of Columbus, Indiana). The primary design goal was to humanize the work environment in this urban-scale, continuous interior space (equivalent to nine city blocks in ground coverage) whose staff would probably spend its entire work day without stepping outside its doors. The method for "humanizing" this large-scale environment was suggested by the planned organizational staffing structure and the initial plan layout, which reflected that structure.

THE STAFF: ORGANIZATION AND PLAN

The production area of this "megaplant" was first divided into two halves: the automated engine block manufacturing area and the final engine assembly area. The central facilities common to the entire plant (cafeteria, administration, supplies, etc.) were located in between these halves (fig. E1–8).

Two "main streets" run along either side of the central facilities block, and each was further subdivided into a series of separate competing "businesses" (groups of production lines), each with its own "street" and back-up administration, engineering, lockers, lounges, and so forth.

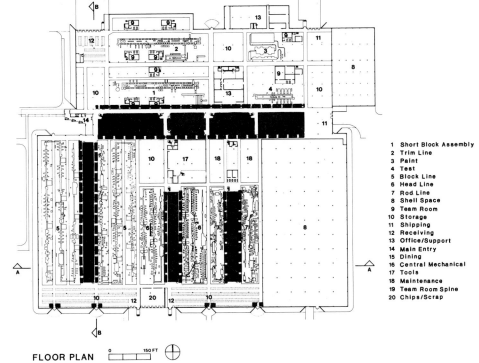

1	Short Block Assembly
2	Trim Line
3	Paint
4	Test
5	Block Line
6	Head Line
7	Rod Line
8	Shell Space
9	Team Room
10	Storage
11	Shipping
12	Receiving
13	Office/Support
14	Main Entry
15	Dining
16	Central Mechanical
17	Tools
18	Maintenance
19	Team Room Spine
20	Chips/Scrap

E1–8. Plan with central facilities block and team-block service spines shaded. Dashed line indicates location of clerestory glazing.

FLOOR PLAN   0 ____ 150 FT

THE TEAM BLOCKS

The design concept strove to reinforce the perception of these areas as separate businesses and maintain their relationship to the main street, by creating physically separate "team blocks."

Looking at the first schematic design, I noticed that the "team blocks," which appeared definitive in the plans, would be too low in section to be perceivable above the machinery and service catwalks, and therefore do little to organize the vast spaces visually (fig. E1–9).

The lighting design was conceived to reinforce the architectural concept of separate businesses. Even though the functional needs generally did not demand more than one floor of normal height space, I recommended extending the walls of the blocks through the roof and using these walls as large, light-reflecting surfaces (figs. E1–10, E1–11). With clerestories directly illuminating these walls, no other sun control would be needed regardless of orientation (hence, no broken-down blinds) and, with clear glass, the sunlight from east and west would be evident but not a source of direct glare (fig. E1–12). Changing patterns of shadows cast onto these walls should be much more interesting than the more constant glow from the translucent skylights of the earlier Columbus engineering facility.

E1–9. Section of team block as originally proposed. (Courtesy of Caudill Rowlett Scott)

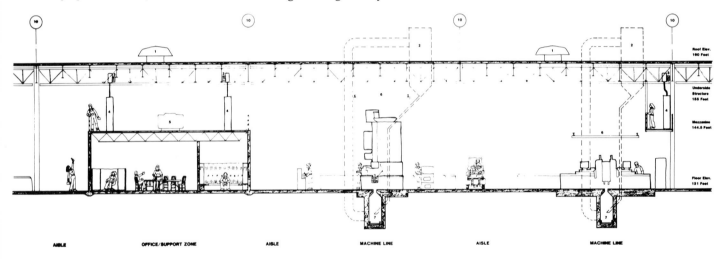

E1–10. Recommended section of team block with walls of support spine extended to the ceiling and lit by sunscoop. (Courtesy of Caudill Rowlett Scott)

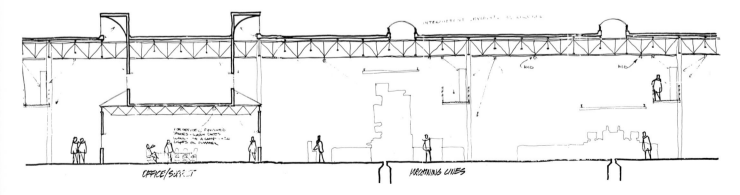

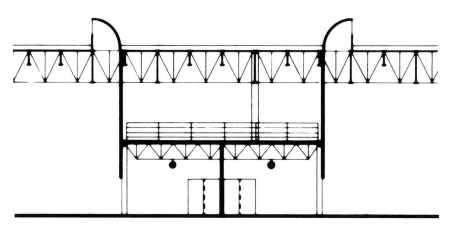

E1–11. Detail of support spine, as built.
(Courtesy of Caudill Rowlett Scott)

E1–12. Sunlit wall of team block.

This case illustrates the importance of a shared sense of values between the client and design team. Many groups would have responded, "Double the height of the walls just to reflect light? That is too expensive, we can't afford it." . . . end of idea. In this case, because both parties appreciated the difference between cost and value, the design team went on to develop the details and discovered that the concept was not only beneficial but also less costly. We realized that there would be two useful by-products: sound control and smoke control.

Sound Control

It was necessary to introduce sound absorption to reduce the effect of machine-generated noise. Acoustic materials applied under the roof deck would have been "shadowed" by the myriad ducts, pipes, structure, and equipment. The cleaning of material overhead (necessary in an environment expected to be saturated with oil vapor) would have been difficult and would also have interfered with the production below.

Incorporating sound absorption into the light-reflecting wall provided an acoustically unshadowed surface, located further from the sources of contamination and more easily accessible for cleaning (fig. E1–13).

PERFORATED
METAL WALL

E1–13. Section shows that perforated metal walls for light reflection and sound absorption will acoustically "see" machinery without shading from ducts.

Smoke Control

The clerestory windows were designed to open for cleaning from the roof. It proved much more economical to provide the means to open them automatically for smoke venting than to provide equivalent exhaust fans.

Combined with the reduced need for artificial lighting, the economics of the sunlit wall system illustrated that it is possible to be both *better* and *less expensive*.

Clerestory Construction

A key factor in the favorable cost trade-off of the clerestory system was it economical construction. A factory-built system of metal frame and steel deck was found. Finished with drywall, it cost $25 per lineal foot (fig. E1–14).

View Windows

A limited number of view windows were provided and placed, for maximum effect, at the ends of team area-production line corridors (fig. E1–15). They provide important orientation to the outdoor scene at modest cost. Brightness contrast between the view window-exit doors area and the otherwise blank walls is reduced by short sections of sunscoops that are also effective in articulating the exterior (fig. E1–16).

There is a great difference in illumination levels between those walls in sun and those on the shady side, and this difference is useful for orientation. However, some difference could have been preserved and the shady side made brighter by the addition of suncatcher baffles, which I learned about on later projects (including the study for a Cummins plant at Madison, Indiana, discussed in chapter 7).

E1–14. Roof view of prefabricated clerestory sunlighting monitors, surrounded by *white* gravel. Glazing is easily accessible from roof for cleaning.

E1–15. View window at the end of team-block corridor.

E1–16. Small sections of clerestory adjacent to view windows reduce contrast and articulate the ends of team-blocks on the exterior.

THE CENTRAL FACILITIES BLOCK

The "exterior" walls of the two-story central facilities block define the edges of "main streets" and were similarly extended through the roof (fig. E1–17). They are illuminated by a south-facing sunscoop and a north-facing lightscoop. Moreover, within this block, the interior spaces were also given the benefit of sunlighting. Though hundreds of yards away from the building perimeter, occupants of the central offices and cafeteria will enjoy the experience of sunlight within their space as well as when moving throughout the plant. The offices have north- and south-facing clerestories (lightscoops and sunscoops) to wash their enclosing walls, which provide a restful horizon that pleasantly dominates the rather splotchy patterns of illuminated ceiling from office-landscape furniture (fig. E1–18). The cafeteria receives direct sunlight from some small, clear skylights overhead, which helps to maintain the trees within. This gives an outdoor feel to the space, which diners enjoy (rather than resenting the direct sunlight as glare).

E1–17. Recommended section of central facilities block.

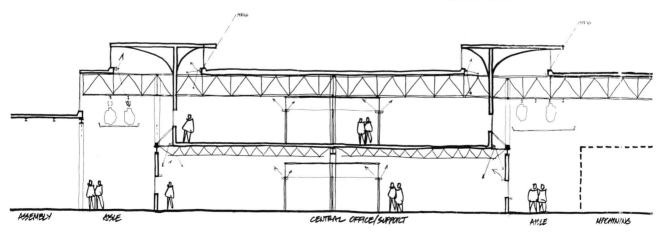

E1–18. Sunlit walls are pure visual signal and provide an "outdoor" feeling to the occupants of offices within the central facilities block, who are far from the building perimeter.

A proposed scheme would have extended some benefit to offices and lounges on the lower level of the central and team blocks. Greenhouse windows (similar to those in the engineering building) would have provided daylit walls and views of the sky within those spaces. In this case, however, the decision was for economy and sunlit walls on the upper level only.

THE DESIGN

After seeing the building in use, I expect that visitors and staff will all agree that the sunlit (daylit on the shady side) surfaces are pure visual signal, unlike the visual noise that usually accompanies daylight in industrial facilities. While even diffused sunlight/daylight (as at Cummins Engineering) satisfies many of the biological information needs, the ever-changing visible patterns of direct sunlight here give what one observer described as "the feeling of working in a series of outdoor sheds."

EFFECT OF LIGHTING DESIGN ON EXTERIOR ARCHITECTURAL FORM

The system of sunscoops and lightscoops creates an interesting roofscape that can be viewed from the air. From the ground, those few sunscoops that are close enough to the edge to be seen add attractive sculptural form to the otherwise simple, plain forms and unbroken edges of a modern, windowless industrial building. The quarter-round form of the metal sunscoops forms a sympathetic counterpoint to the rounded coping used throughout. The architects extended one of these sunscoops as the entrance canopy, thus clearly displaying the architectural lighting concept that most distinguishes this project among industrial buildings (fig. E1–19).

E1–19. Entrance canopy extends clerestory form.

GROUP F Religious Buildings

The design of natural lighting in churches has probably always been determined by aesthetic effect and religious symbolism rather than by considerations of energy or thermal comfort. This certainly seems to be true in the Gothic churches of northern Europe, where large expanses of stained-glass windows make for cold churches in winter but are effective in giving life to the dull light of overcast skies.

On the other hand, the Spanish missions of the American Southwest and the mosques of the Middle East, whether by accident or design, are good examples of passive solar design as well as good sunlighting. Both use small openings in thick walls to reflect the ever-present sunlight into the interior spaces, allowing only small beams of direct sunlight to penetrate.

In contemporary northern Europe, Jørn Utzon and Alvar Aalto have used reflected sunlight and sky light in religious buildings (figs. FI-1, FI-2, FI-3). Their churches are visually effective and beautiful, although they have much less glazing area and better energy efficiency than the traditional Gothic churches, with their expanses of visible windows. More recent and more consciously energy-efficient is the Temppeliaukio Church

FI-1. Interior of Jørn Utzon's Bagsvaerd church in Copenhagen, Denmark.

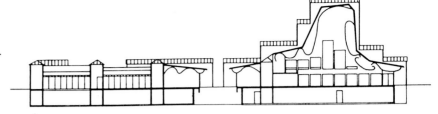

FI-2. Section through Bagsvaerd church.

FI-3. Alvar Aalto's Vuoksenniska church in Imatra, Finland (1958).

in Helsinki, designed by architects Timo and Tuomo Suomalainen. This church is buried in the top of a hill; it introduces direct sunlight onto the craggy rock walls to make the energy-efficient underground space dramatic and delightful (fig. FI-4).

The quality of lighting, both natural and artificial, in recently built religious buildings throughout the world is generally very good compared to that in other building types. In these buildings, architects have not abdicated their design responsibility to technicians and simple-minded programming. They seem to have retained common sense and to have been guided by personal experience and observations. In religious buildings, architects have been more likely to test designs by looking at physical rather than mathematical models.

Because so many good and well-known examples exist (fig. FI-5), case studies of churches are almost unnecessary. I could fill several books with examples of churches that use natural light very attractively and economically, both in construction and energy use.

Of course, there are also many churches that are visually attractive but are uneconomical or uncomfortable. Among the most notable examples is Philip Johnson's greenhouse-type church in southern California—the Crystal Cathedral (fig. FI-6). I was surprised to see it as the jacket photograph of a book on daylighting; it may be comfortable under overcast conditions but is purported by staff members to overheat in the sum-

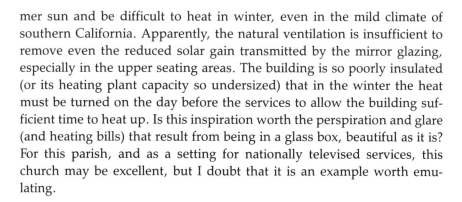

FI–4. Temppeliaukio church in Helsinki (Timo and Tumo Suomalainen, Architect). (Courtesy of Museum of Finnish Architecture)

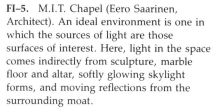

FI–5. M.I.T. Chapel (Eero Saarinen, Architect). An ideal environment is one in which the sources of light are those surfaces of interest. Here, light in the space comes indirectly from sculpture, marble floor and altar, softly glowing skylight forms, and moving reflections from the surrounding moat.

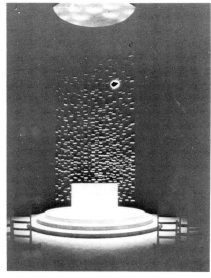

mer sun and be difficult to heat in winter, even in the mild climate of southern California. Apparently, the natural ventilation is insufficient to remove even the reduced solar gain transmitted by the mirror glazing, especially in the upper seating areas. The building is so poorly insulated (or its heating plant capacity so undersized) that in the winter the heat must be turned on the day before the services to allow the building sufficient time to heat up. Is this inspiration worth the perspiration and glare (and heating bills) that result from being in a glass box, beautiful as it is? For this parish, and as a setting for nationally televised services, this church may be excellent, but I doubt that it is an example worth emulating.

CASE STUDIES

With the economic realities of American churches today, some churches have become interested in minimizing operating costs, even with an increase in capital investment. Since only low levels of light are needed in

FI–6. The Crystal Cathedral (Philip Johnson, Architect). (Courtesy of Philip Johnson; photograph by Gordon Schenck)

churches and occupancies are of short duration, operating economies will come from the HVAC benefits of passive solar design rather than from reduced lighting costs. In churches, the objective is not to conserve lighting energy by achieving an even distribution of glare-free natural lighting for long-term occupancy, as in schools or office buildings. In fact, windowless churches that depend totally on artificial lighting may well be the most economical to operate. The sunlighting challenge here is to make buildings that were designed to minimize HVAC energy through minimal glazing (or those with minimal glazing for any other reason) more delightful and inspiring to short-term visitors.

For these reasons, the case studies presented do not represent examples of mainstream design possibilities and achievements, but rather two of the more unusual challenges I have encountered.

In a Milwaukee church (case study F1), passive solar design was the principal formgiver. Glazing was oriented to the south but limited to illuminating the chancel for heat collection. While I was able to balance the light in the otherwise windowless nave with electric lighting, I was challenged by the possibility of using mirrors to distribute direct winter sunlight more effectively from the single clerestory to the chancel itself and throughout the nave as well.

The other example is a prototype for a multidenominational chapel that could be built anywhere. Its shape and its religious symbolism suggested that a beam-sunlight, tracking mirror system be used to supplement reflected daylight.

Central United Methodist Church Milwaukee, Wisconsin

Latitude: 42.9°N; climate: 7,444 degree days

16,350 square feet @ $93.61/sq. ft.

Architect: William Wenzler & Associates

Consultants: Strass Maguire & Associates—structural; Thelen Engineering & Associates, Inc.—mechanical; Kornacki & Associates, Inc.—electrical; William Lam & Associates—lighting; Bolt, Beranek, Newman, Inc.—acoustical; Princeton Energy Group—solar energy; A. Guenther & Sons—general contractor

Construction completed: 1982

CONTEXT

While rocks and light generated the form of the Temppeliaukio church (see fig. FI-4), passive solar concepts were the initial formgivers of this Milwaukee church. Located in a cold climate, it was conceived to minimize operating costs, even at the expense of higher first cost.

The bulk of the church is earth sheltered; from three sides, all that is visible is its bell tower and entryways cut into a hillside covered with wildflowers. The form of the church is only apparent on its back (street) side. Perceptive observers will notice that its tower is glazed only on the south side and that its clerestory windows are much larger than necessary to illuminate the chancel alone (figs. F1–1, F1–2, F1–3, F1–4).

SOLAR CONCEPT

Surrounded by ancillary spaces, the nave could have been illuminated by perimeter skylights that penetrated the field of wildflowers above. However, with input from the Princeton Energy Group, architect William Wenzler created the tower and its south-facing windows to collect solar energy. A large shutter was designed to isolate the upper cavity of the tower from the rest of the church, except during those times when it would be advantageous to turn on the fans to draw warm air into the nave.

As is common with south-facing windows, maximum light and heat from the sun are received during winter, when they are most desirable. Sunlight is used to heat a dark-colored wall in the tower, except when the shutter is opened and some of the sunlight is redirected down and into the space. The possibility of an additional clerestory at the rear of the nave was rejected, as it would have been costly to build and maintain.

SUNLIGHTING CONCEPT

On joining the design team after the basic architectural design had been completed, I realized that while the chancel would always be well lighted from the clerestory window, the nave would not be. The addition of an

F1–1. The street-level entrance.

F1–2. The roof of wildflowers and the south-facing chancel aperture.

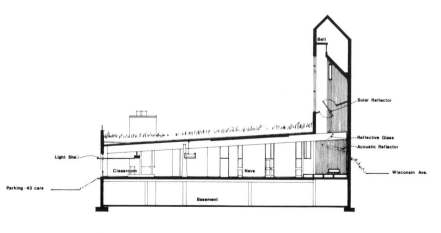

F1–3. Section. (Courtesy of William Wenzler Associates)

CENTRAL UNITED METHODIST CHURCH · SECTION   William Wenzler and Associates, Architects

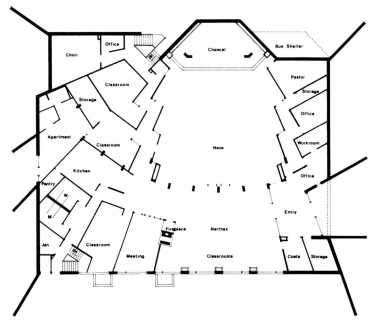

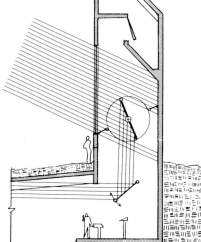

F1–4. Plan, showing radial beam pattern and location of chancel. (Courtesy of William Wenzler Associates)

WINTER

operable thermal shutter offered an inexpensive opportunity for redirecting low-angle winter sunlight down toward the floor level of the chancel and, via secondary mirrors, redirecting some of it to the ceiling of the nave, where it could be seen and enjoyed.

The concept of mirroring the shutter was easily conveyed by a thumbnail sketch, which also indicted that the mirror would have some value in rejecting high-angle summer light and heat (fig. F1–5).

Electric lighting was designed to balance the dominant daylight from the chancel, except during the limited periods when the beam sunlighting could be effective in the nave. The architects built a model to examine the visual effect of the sunlighting design and were pleased with the dramatic sunlight patterns that were achieved under the test conditons.

Construction

The thermal shutter was constructed as a glass curtain wall with an off-the-shelf, motor-driven, clerestory control mechanism. Mirror glass was used for the operable portion and clear glass for the surrounding infill.

RESULTS

As the building neared completion, everyone was pleased with the evolving appearance of the glowing chancel walls and the ability of the primary tracking mirror to redirect winter sunlight to the lower walls and floor. When the fixed secondary mirrors were finally installed, however, I received a frantic phone call from the architects. Only one beam of sunlight was being reflected across the nave ceiling, unlike the more extensive pattern of sunlight in the model studies. "Was the model tested under real sunlight as instructed," I asked, "or with an artificial light source?"

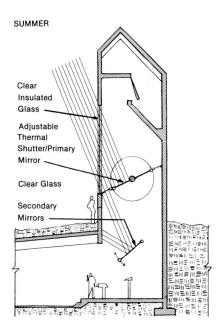

SUMMER

Clear Insulated Glass

Adjustable Thermal Shutter/Primary Mirror

Clear Glass

Secondary Mirrors

F1–5. Schematic diagrams of the lightshaft operation. In winter, large amounts of solar radiation are admitted and a portion is redirected to the ceiling. In summer, most of the light and heat are rejected, except during services.

F1–6. (a) Interior of the church with the flat primary mirror; (b) interior with the addition of the curved primary mirror, showing the sunlight streaming along the beams; (c) secondary mirrors.

It turned out that, due to time and weather restrictions, the model had been tested indoors with an overhead spotlight simulating the sun. When it hit the flat mirrors, the speading pattern from the spotlight at that distance continued to spread radially, illuminating the area between the radial beams, as was desired. Under actual conditons, however, the parallel beams of sunlight did not spread out radially, but remained parallel.

To remedy the situation, I suggested that a slight curvature in the *primary* mirrors would spread the beams of light laterally, reasoning that a wider, less intense beam would also reduce the effect of changing solar azimuth in this relatively narrow, tall mirror system. (This problem was less severe in the very wide TVA atria, due to the wide spacing of beams on the typical office floors receiving the light.) Small panels of mirrored acrylic sheet were slightly bowed and popped into place. It worked! All sections of the ceiling were sunlit simultaneously during the midday period (fig. F1–6).

Unfortunately, most church services have been scheduled for very early morning hours before the sunlight reaches the south exposure and the space can be experienced at its most dramatic. For the earlier events, a more easterly orientation would have been better so that both maximum heat and light could be experienced.

SUMMARY

The parallel rays of incoming sunlight have distinct advantages that can be utilized, but testing *must* be done with real sunlight to find out what will happen over a period of time, both daily and seasonally. Shortcuts in testing can be deceiving.

The original single, large, mirror-glass shutter seemed to be a good construction. Its durable, easy-to-clean mirrored surface had the very true surface characteristics of heavy glass, producing undistorted reflections. The shutter used standard materials and could be tuned to place the light at the exact angle desired. However, because of the need to spread the light laterally in this situation, the glass was covered with curving mirrored acrylic sheet. The one-way curvature is a good method for achieving the lateral spread. Should this be done in an office building in which maximum lighting *intensity* was more important, the curvature could be very slight (for example, to double the beam width and reduce the effect of changing azimuth).

F2 The Universel Chapel Suresnes, France

CONTEXT

Latitude: 48°N

Architect: Nader Ardalan & Associates

Consultants: Zareh Cregrian—structural; Lottero & Mason—electrical; William Lam Associates—lighting

Schematic design begun: 1982

The supercircular (squared circle) plan form of this prototype building for the International Sufi Order is symbolic of its religious concept. Designed to be built anywhere in the world, the first unit is to be built in France, followed by units in Jerusalem and the United States.

The Universel is to be "a place of all religions," their coming together represented as "four meditating figures facing the cardinal directions and fused back to back in a transcendent unity of illumination."

The design concepts are best described by excerpts from the project report:

Order of Architecture

The design of the building allows for the Universal Worship Ceremony of the Sufi Order to take place at the center, while also accommodating the correct observance and orientation of rites of each of the major faiths. Because of its purity and simplicity of form, the place can be easily transformed by the introduction of signs and symbols and rituals of any of the major faiths.

The architectural form that resulted from this program is that of a unifying central directionless space surrounded by an ambulatory with multiple niches to provide focal points when desired for the diverse religions represented. (Christian to the east, Buddhist to the north, Moslem toward Mecca, Jewish toward Jerusalem, etc.)

Order of Light

The vaulted shell and natural light from the central occulus reinforce the idea of a central unifying space. Further reinforcement of the idea of centricity is accomplished by designing the occulus lantern to automatically track and beam a shaft of direct sunlight directly below to the center of the space, when the occasion demands such an effort and the sun shines. The central point of light represents the unity of all religions (fig. F2–1).

On overcast days and at night, an artificial light source could also be redirected by the same mirror to create a similar but less intense effect. The direct lighting would be supplemented by the glowing surfaces of the light-colored vault (illuminated by the diffuse component of light from the skylight during the day and illuminated indirectly from incandescent cove lighting along its bottom edge at night).

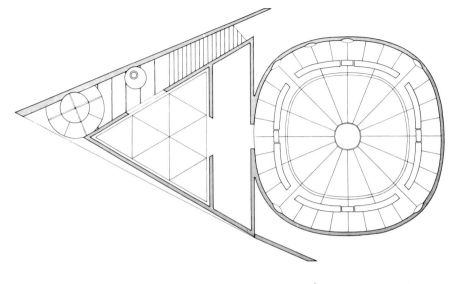

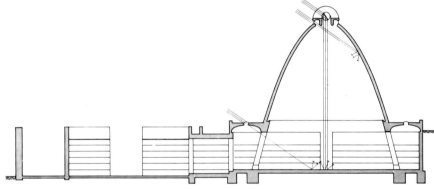

F2–2. Section. (Courtesy of Nader Ardalan & Associates)

In contrast, the ambulatory is illuminated only indirectly, by ambient daylight and incandescent sources baffled by perimeter beams (fig. F2–2). When desired, a particular niche and the accessories placed therein can be highlighted by spotlights concealed behind the same beams. The concealed lighting concept is also applied in the foyer and forecourt by illuminating the walls from incandescent lamps concealed behind benches and cabinets.

In total, the illumination should reinforce the quiet visual simplicity of the architecture and the religious concepts. Light sources are not seen, only the glowing surfaces of the architectural forms and highlighting of those selected focal points relevant to the ceremonial purposes at the time.

DESIGN CONCEPTS CONFIRMED AND REJECTED

The lighting concept was developed very quickly by the design team. The dimensions of the occulus were confirmed by visual inspection and a few hand-held illumination measurements with and without direct sunlight present. Having a minimal consulting budget, I demonstrated the beam effect with hand-held mirrors above the model of the room. By tracking

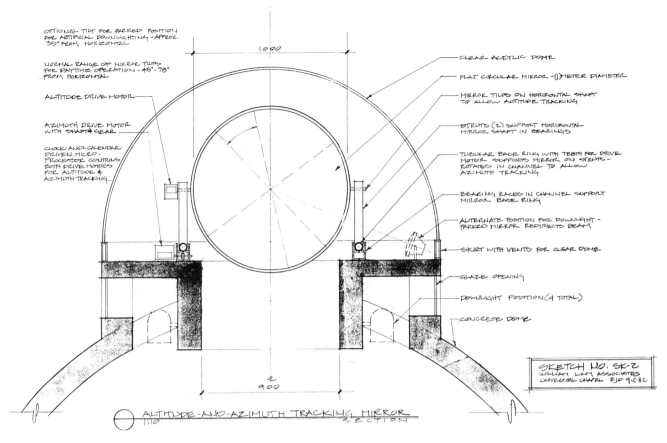

F2–3. The final heliostat design. (Courtesy of Nader Ardalan & Associates)

and redirecting the sunlight, the effect will be fairly similar anywhere in the world on sunny days. Results in different locales will vary primarily in the extent of supplementary light used under overcast conditions. The percentage of glazing is too small to have much impact on HVAC.

We experimented with methods for redirecting some of the light from the occulus upward to the upper dome. A large reflector with a central hole for the beamed sunlight was effective in lighting the dome but conflicted spatially. The idea was rejected in favor of depending on a light-colored floor to redirect light upward.

Design Details

The design challenge here was to integrate the several occulus elements to be visual jewels as well as to function properly.

The Heliostat

The most efficient, already developed design—double mirror and equatorial mount—was not considered for this particular use because its appearance would have been unsuitable.

Even though the size of the projected beam will vary with the changing solar elevation, I decided on and designed a simple single mirror system that could be considered "sculpture" instead of industrial hardware when viewed from the interior of the building (fig. F2–3). The round mirror can be rotated easily on two axes. The small amount of uncontrolled light that will "bleed by" was considered unimportant. The design was simple enough so that very reasonable price quotations were received even for the first and only unit.

The Well

A hemispheric acrylic dome will provide weather protection for the mirror. Inside, supplementary downlights will be located within a slot at the perimeter of the skylight well to minimize visual conflict with the integrity of the central feature, as well as to avoid blocking the daylight admitted, without increasing the well diameter. Alternately, supplementary lighting could also be provided via reflection from the mirror.

Current Status of Project

The design was well received by the clients and has been exhibited at La Biennale di Venezia. As of this writing, however, it has not yet been built. The Paris site is now no longer available, and another site is being sought. As intended, however, this concept should work in any location.

GROUP Ⓖ Hotel Atria

The greatest opportunity to use sunlighting in hotels is in those public spaces that are important during the daytime. These circulation and gathering spaces include enclosed swimming pools, lobbies, and, most important, the atria, onto which shops and restaurants face. The public image and economic vitality of the hotel and associated commercial space is dependent on the success of its atrium. A well designed and well populated atrium will command premium rents.

For the bulk of the hotel—its guest rooms—innovative sunlighting strategies are not required. The sun must be controlled primarily to reduce air-conditioning loads. The lighting requirements of hotel rooms are minimal and are easily met by task lighting. There will always be view windows with adjustable shades and blinds with local control. Because it can be assumed that the blinds will be adjusted by the guests or staff to get privacy, view, shading or complete black-out for sleeping, glare is never a problem. In any case, guest rooms are infrequently occupied during the daytime.

A hotel atrium is an atrium, not a litrium. As discussed in chapter 8, an atrium is designed for enjoyment, not to light adjacent spaces. An atrium can meet its qualitative goals with even a narrow shaft of direct sunlight. A small concentration of sunlight will give the drama and biological reference of the sun.

The preceding case studies include a number of litrium-type office buildings. What is the difference between good used sunlight in offices and in hotels?

Sunlit office buildings use litria to deliver light to the large openings of the surrounding offices. In contrast, hotel atria are designed primarily to provide illumination for the spaces they define—the floor level and the surrounding balconies. The corridor-facing walls of the upper floors of most hotel atria are solid. With bedrooms oriented entirely to the exterior scene, the upper atrium is generally used for circulation only; most important activities occur at the lowest levels. Optimum enjoyment of those lower activity spaces is critical to the image and financial success of hotels.

Since guests are likely to spend some time there, the atrium floor should be as delightful as a beautiful outdoor garden. Unconscious needs for orientation to the outdoor world, time of day, weather, and so on, make the presence of sunlight important to most people.

DESIGN IMPLICATIONS

In offices, optimizing illumination and the view into the litrium in a cost-effective manner requires efficient utilization of the light admitted throughout the full height of the atrium.

In hotels, on the other hand, little light is needed for circulation at the upper levels. One does not view the atrium and the outdoor scene simultaneously, or think of the atrium as a compromised substitute for the outdoor scene. Almost any atrium view is a pleasant change from the familiar, stuffy, interior hotel corridor. Brick, concrete, and other dark-colored outdoor materials can be usd in atria without negative effect, though lighter colors create a brighter effect. Definition of the space, interesting views, and focal points are important in making circulation a pleasant experience. Since views of the public activities and the landscaping elements that relate to those activities are probably of greatest interest, hotel atria should maximize the illumination low in the space. Office litria, on the other hand, should provide illumination in the spaces surrounding the central space, on both upper and lower levels.

A brightly lit, highly reflective upper atrium may provide abundant diffuse illumination to the lower atrium space. But if the materials used are dark colored and the total amount of sunlight/daylight admitted is modest, a few rays of direct sunlight will still make a big difference in giving life to a space.

Sunlighting design effort should be focused on getting as much sunlight as possible to the lowest levels. Any direct sunlight is likely to be enjoyed rather than considered glare, particularly during heating seasons in temperate climates. However, even if the intensity of the sunlight is reduced by low-transmission glass, surfaces illuminated by the precise parallel rays of sunlight will still be perceived as sunlit.

While good passive solar practice and construction economy should be kept in mind, any necessary cost in hardware or HVAC energy to create an enjoyable lobby floor is likely to be insignificant when weighed against the benefits resulting from increased patronage. Because the objective is to get a maximum amount of direct sunlight to the atrium's lower floors, horizontal skylights, rather than clerestories, may be the best solution.

LIGHT FOR TREES

The quantitative goals for sunlighting in atria are often determined by the light levels required for sustaining plant life. Most atria are landscaped with a significant amount of vegetation. In both offices and hotels, the cost for providing high natural light levels on trees can offset the cost of very high levels of artificial lighting or that of replacing trees. As in the deterioration of art materials, the effect of light on tree growth is a function of intensity and time. One hour of direct sunlight (if reduced by glazing to 6,000 footcandles) is roughly equivalent to 600 footcandles of light for ten hours. Similarly, fifteen minutes of this intensity of direct sunlight is equivalent to 150 footcandles of artificial light for ten hours.

GI-1. Renaissance Center, Detroit. (Courtesy of John Portman Associates)

CHALLENGES IN HOTEL ATRIA DESIGN

When hotel atria are wide and low and the roofs are unshaded by other buildings, sunlighting design is relatively easy: simply use clear instead of translucent glazing to achieve satisfying views of the sky and beams of direct sunlight. When the expanse of skylights is too large, creating unjustifiable HVAC loads, reduce the glazing area and adjust the orientation or the light transmission. At the Chicago O'Hare Hyatt, I persuaded the architect, John Portman, to abandon plans for a translucent ceiling illuminated by skylights above. Continuous transparent bronze tinted glazing at the perimeter creates sunlit surfaces that can be seen from the lobby floor.

Surrounding buildings may keep skylights in shade too much of the time. This is one situation in which I welcome mirror-glass curtain walls on neighboring building(s) to reflect sunlight to the shady side. For example, the Detroit Plaza Hotel benefits from reflected sunlight from the surrounding office towers at the Renaissance Center (fig. GI-1). On one visit to this hotel I had difficulty perceiving where the sun was, since the mirror-reflected sunlight was so similar in appearance to direct sunlight and was coming from several directions. This reflected sunlight was being enjoyed by an atrium full of noontime picnickers (fig. GI-2).

GI–2. Detroit Plaza Hotel atrium (John Portman, Architect).

THE CASE STUDIES

The real challenge in sunlighting design for hotel atria is to achieve the objectives outlined both in very tall, narrow atrium spaces and in those with shapes that limit the possibilities for glazing and tend to block the passage of light to important areas of the space. I was given such challenges in the two case studies that follow.

G1 Atlanta Marriott Marquis
Atlanta, Georgia

Latitude: 336°N; climate: 3,095 degree days

1,526,235 square feet

Architect: John Portman & Associates

Consultants: John Portman & Associates—structural; Newcomb & Boyd—mechanical and electrical

Construction completed: 1985

CONTEXT

This was my first serious proposal for using tracking mirrors in a hotel. I had considered the possibility in other tall Portman-designed atria in Singapore but rejected it due to Singapore's equatorial location. An overhead arc of sun movement already ensured that sunlight would reach the lower public levels at noon on every sunny day (fig. G1–3). Tracking mirrors could retain that effect throughout the day, but in that hot climate I considered it sufficient to see a play of sunlight on the balcony walls for the balance of the day. In addition, at the time of my design participation, no off-the-shelf hardware was available.

In Atlanta, both conditions were different. Even though many think of it as the heart of the sunny South, Atlanta is far enough from the equator to have cool winter days in which the warmth of direct sunlight is welcomed. The solar path at this latitude is low enough that in a fifty-story east/west atrium, direct sunlight from a thirty-foot-wide skylight (fig. G1–4) never reaches the floor. In December, direct sunlight does not even penetrate to the balcony rail of the top guest floor (fig. G1–5).

Low-angle sunlight does penetrate briefly from narrow vertical windows at the east and west ends at the beginning and end of summer days. The architects provided the means for increasing the level of diffused light in the lower atrium with a twelfth-floor concourse level that is open from the atrium to full-height windows on the exterior. However, although the diffused reflected sunlight entering the lobby is significant, particularly in winter when the sun is low, even then no direct sunlight from that level is seen from the atrium floor.

THE OPPORTUNITY

Using diagrams, we had no difficulty showing the architect that the sunlight at the fiftieth floor would hardly be perceived from the atrium floor and that without design changes, sunlight would reach the lower third of the atrium only for a short time in midsummer. Reminded of how dramatic and pleasant those brief moments of sunlight were at his Hyatt Embarcadero Hotel, San Francisco (case study G2) atrium, he was easily

G1–1. Model of fifty-story Atlanta Marriott Marquis.

G1–2. Building section. (Courtesy of John Portman Associates)

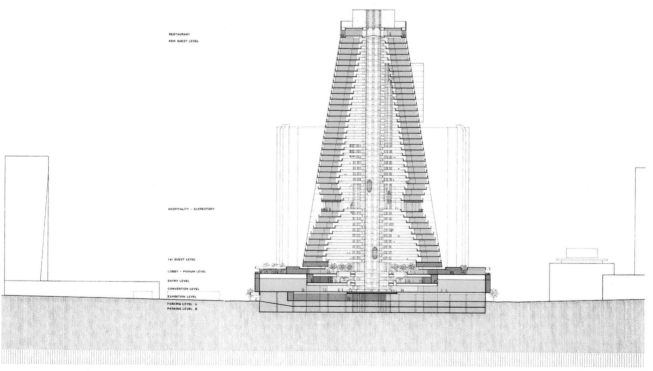

SECTION LOOKING EAST

PROPOSED ST. JOSEPH DEVELOPMENT
JUNE 12, 1979
JOHN PORTMAN & ASSOCIATES

G1–3. Getting sunlight to the atrium walls and floor for a large part of the day is easiest with the overhead sunpath at the equator. (Pavilion Intercontinental Hotel, Singapore—John Portman, Architect.)

G1–4. Thirty-foot skylight.

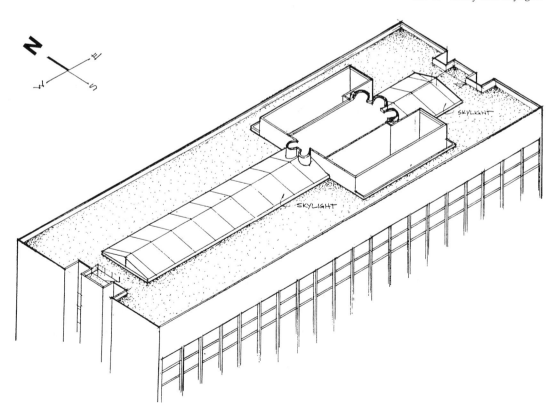

MARRIOTT ATLANTA   EXISTING

DECEMBER 21, NOON

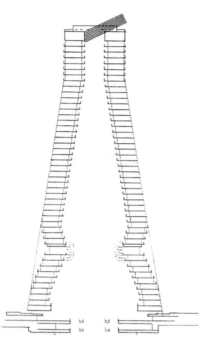

Section looking East

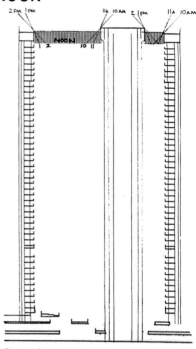

Section looking North

JUNE 21, NOON

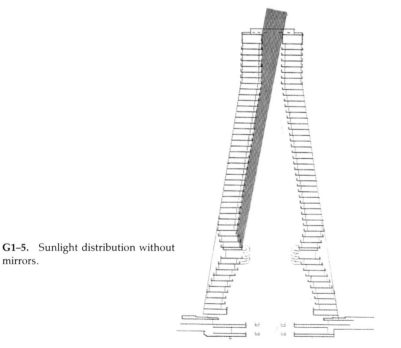

Section looking East

G1–5. Sunlight distribution without mirrors.

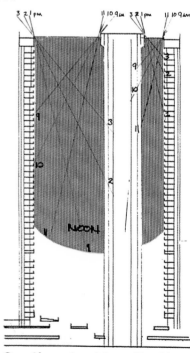

Section looking North

MARRIOTT ATLANTA   PROPOSED

DECEMBER 21, NOON

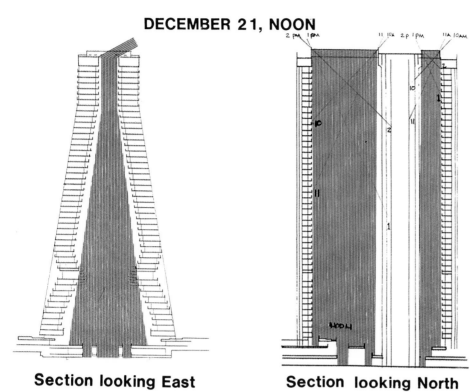

Section looking East

Section looking North

JUNE 21, NOON

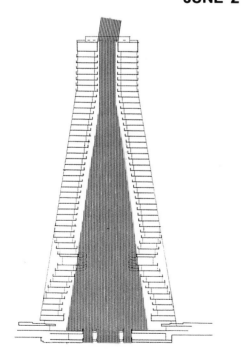

Section looking East

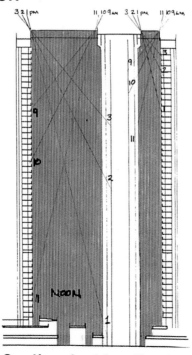

Section looking North

G1–6. Proposed sunlight distribution with tracking mirrors.

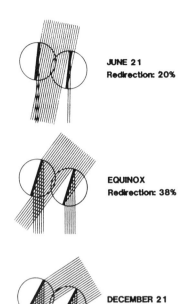

JUNE 21
Redirection: 20%

EQUINOX
Redirection: 38%

DECEMBER 21
Redirection: 75%

G1–7. Percentage of sunlight redirected.

G1–8. Atrium with supplementary artificial lighting—no visible sunlight.

G1–9. Atrium with sunlight on balconies. (Courtesy of John Portman Associates) *opposite page*

convinced of the desirability of being able to place a band of sunlight on the floor for an extended period every sunny day, particularly in winter, when even Atlanta is cold (fig. G1–6).

Fortunately, by this time (1983) we were very close to having off-the-shelf hardware available—tracking mirrors I had been helping to develop on my own time with the hopes that TVA would install a test demonstration in the otherwise compromised building nearing completion in Chattanooga (case study B7).

Detailed sunlight projections for using mirrored louvers within the atrium greenhouse roof were made. Because of the elongated east/west shape of the atrium and the wide directional tolerance of aiming for this purpose (in contrast to the TVA double mirror system, in which the light from the roof mirrors must be *exactly* vertical), louver adjustments could be made weekly or monthly.

Such results seemed unbelievable to some of the Portman staff. To be convincing, I presented photographs of a mirror demonstration we had witnessed outdoors in New Hampshire and then suggested that the newly developed mirror tracking system should be tested immediately at the existing Portman-designed San Francisco Hyatt Embarcadero Hotel.

Even though the San Francisco atrium is much lower in height, the results could be extrapolated easily, since parallel rays of sunlight do not diminish in intensity with distance (fig. G1–7). Portman asked his staff to proceed with such arrangments for a mock-up.

Meanwhile, the tracking mirror louvers were listed by the architects as a recommended change order, to be "sold" to the owners with the help of the Embarcadero demonstration. Because of unexpected administrative delays in San Francisco, the mock-up has yet to be built. Hence, the Atlanta Marriott has been completed without tracking mirrors. Fortunately, since its atrium roof is equipped with a rail-suspended window-washing rig, installation of the mirror system is still easily possible at any time.

SUMMARY

Although this particular system has not yet been built, there is no doubt in my mind that beam sunlighting by tracking mirror louvers has good potential in tall hotel atria. The technical problems are not as critical as in office buildings with double mirror requirements. It is a cost-effective way to improve the daytime environment in tall atrium greatly. Tall atrium hotels, such as the Atlanta Marriott, are the most logical places for their use because of the high economic value of happy patrons. Such positive effect seems to be difficult to prove without a full-size working demonstration or, better yet, a real installation.

Prototype tracking mirror systems have been built and are now being offered as an available product by Structures Unlimited, a division of Kalwall Corp., Nashua, New Hampshire. With my first installation actually on order for the Park West Building in Dallas, I can finally look forward confidently to more installations, as others see for themselves what I predict. The Atlanta Marriott design may yet be realized.

POSTSCRIPT

The Atlanta Marriott opened in the fall of 1984. When daylight is supplemented by artificial illumination (balcony handrail lighting, highlighting of sculpture and trees, and patterns of clear lamps) the atrium is an impressive and beautiful space (fig. G1–8). The space appears quite different during the short time each day when direct sunlight penetrates (fig. G1–9)—an effect that could be more frequent with the proposed mirror system.

G2 Hyatt Regency Embarcadero Hotel San Francisco, California

Latitude: 37.6°N; climate: 3,042 degree days

Architect: John Portman & Associates

Consultants: John Portman & Associates—structural; Morris Harrison Engineers—electrical; Britt Alderman Engineers—mechanical; William C. Lam and Associates—lighting

Construction completed: 1973

Proposed revisions: 1985

CONTEXT

John Portman once described his atrium design objective as the creation of the equivalent of the fishmarket square in a small French town—the sense of an outdoor square full of activity that can be enjoyed from the surrounding balconies and cafés.

In my opinion he usually succeeds, even when the amount of daylight is quite minimal (as it was at the Hyatt Regency Embarcadero), because of the use of outdoor materials and outdoor-type details (fig. G2–1). In contrast, the Galleria in Houston appears as an indoor space with abundant natural light because it is constructed with "indoor" materials—carpeted floors and plastered walls.

G2–1. Exterior view.

Nevertheless, after working with tracking mirrors in other projects (see case studies B7 and F1), I realized that the installation of tracking mirrors could make a major improvment in what many already considered one of the world's greatest large architectural spaces.

Unlike Portman's O'Hare Hyatt or Detroit Plaza hotels, in which at least a small splash of sunlight is visible throughout the day at all times of the year, the narrow neck of the skylight well here and its orientation (to Market Street) 45 degrees from north/south (fig. G2–2) allows direct sunlight to be visible from the center of the atrium for only a few minutes each day. At that time, the very small band of sunlight is sufficient to transform the space (figs. G2–3, G2–4, G2–5).

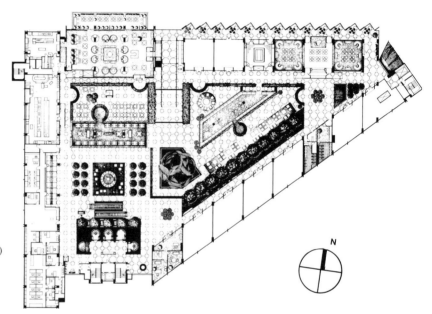

G2–2. Plan. (Courtesy of John Portman Associates)

RECOMMENDED REVISION

I realized that tracking mirrors could direct a similar band of sunlight onto the atrium floor for considerable periods on every sunny day. Using diagrams (fig. G2–6), I was able to persuade Portman and the Embarcadero management to make the change. Computer-controlled continuous tracking is necessary here because of the wide daily changes in solar elevation with the orientation (unlike the south/north louver orientation at the Atlanta project).

I had earlier proposed correcting the optics of the electrical lighting fixture to achieve much narrower light distribution and much more illumination on the trees. With directed sunlight on the trees, the changes would be unneeded, and the electric lights could be used only for visual effect, rather than for tree health.

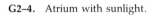

G2–3. On clear days, the club floors are blessed with a beautiful sunny garden. Unfortunately, little sunlight passes through this neck to the atrium below.

G2–4. Atrium with sunlight.

G2–5. Atrium without sunlight.

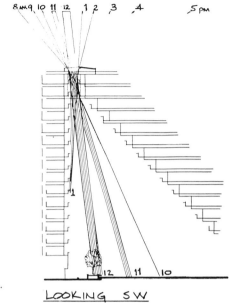

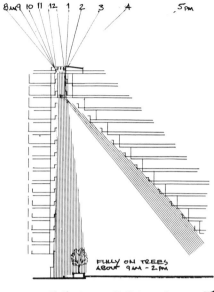

8 AM 9 10 11 12 1 2 3 4 5 PM

8 AM 9 10 11 12 1 2 3 4 5 PM

G2–6. Sunlight diagrams.

LOOKING SW

FULLY ON TREES
ABOUT 9 AM – 2 PM

HYATT EMBARCADERO
LAM ASSOCIATES 7

2 NOV. 83   PMC

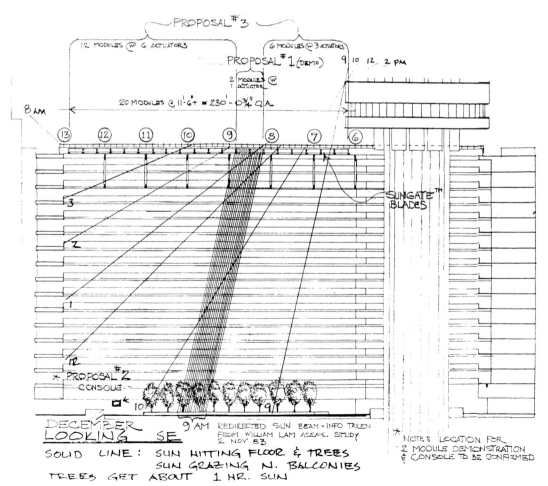

PROPOSAL #3

12 MODULES @ 6 ACTUATORS

6 MODULES @ 3 ACTUATORS

PROPOSAL #1 (DEMO)

2 MODULES W
1 ACTUATOR

9 10 12, 2 PM

20 MODULES @ 11'-6"± = 230'-0¾" O.A.

8 AM

13 12 11 10 9 8 7 6

SUNGATE™
BLADES

3

2

1

PROPOSAL #2
CONSOLE

10

9

DECEMBER
LOOKING SE

9 AM REDIRECTED SUN BEAM - INFO TAKEN
FROM WILLIAM LAM ASSOC. STUDY
2 NOV 83

NOTE: LOCATION FOR
2 MODULE DEMONSTRATION
& CONSOLE TO BE CONFIRMED

SOLID LINE: SUN HITTING FLOOR & TREES
SUN GRAZING N. BALCONIES
TREES GET ABOUT 1 HR. SUN

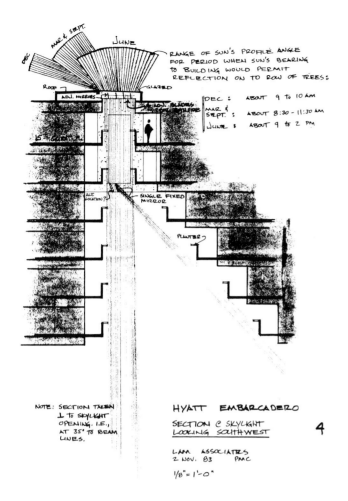

RANGE OF SUN'S PROFILE ANGLE
FOR PERIOD WHEN SUN'S BEARING
TO BUILDING WOULD PERMIT
REFLECTION ON TO ROW OF TREES:

DEC : ABOUT 9 TO 10 AM
MAR & SEPT. : ABOUT 8:30 - 11:30 AM
JUNE : ABOUT 9 to 2 PM

NOTE: SECTION TAKEN ⊥ TO SKYLIGHT OPENING. I.E., AT 35° TO BEAM LINES.

HYATT EMBARCADERO

SECTION @ SKYLIGHT LOOKING SOUTHWEST

4

LAM ASSOCIATES
2 NOV. 83   PMC
1/8" = 1'-0"

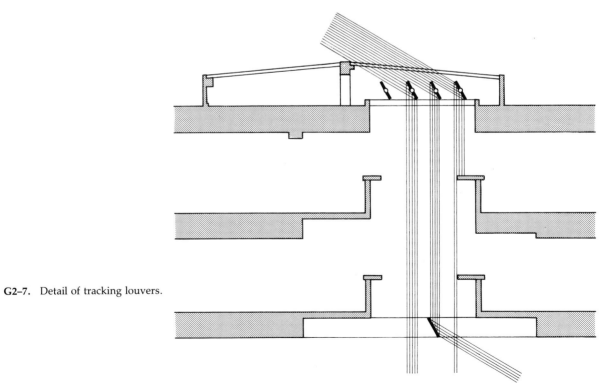

G2–7. Detail of tracking louvers.

A daily cycle of constant sunlight on the floor should not only make the space more exciting and enjoyable, but also make up for otherwise inadequate tree lighting.

Fortunately, the installation could be fairly simple. The preassembled louver assemblies could be easily dropped into place onto the edge beams (fig. G2–7). For additional effect, we recommended placement of a stationary secondary mirror spanning beams below, which could reflect a narrow band of light onto the normally shaded inward-sloping north balconies.

The cost quotation for this transformation was very modest—$42 per square foot of louver and $15,000 for the automated control system—a total of $84,000 for the preassembled system plus installation.

SUMMARY

The timing was not right when Portman recommended addition of the tracking mirror system. Financial reorganization was in process. Despite the administrative delays, beam sunlighting may yet be realized and enjoyed in the form of pleasure for the guests, improved health of trees, and operating cost savings for reduction of tree lighting.

GROUP H Libraries

When one thinks of the most enjoyable rooms in one's experience, libraries often come to mind, particularly those designed before the advent of electric lighting. I often think of the Boston Atheneum or the main reading room in the old Boston Public Library (fig. HI–1) designed by McKim, Mead and White (1885). These spaces contrast greatly with the unpleasant, ungracious spaces in the new Boston Public Library addition by Philip Johnson (1977), which recognized the arched window shape of the old library on the exterior, but retained none of the spatial or light qualities of the old interiors. In the new addition, low ceilings enclose the space, which is dominated by the visual noise of glaring lenses of fluorescent light fixtures (fig. HI–2). There is minimal daylight, no courtyard, and limited views. This contrast exemplifies the changing priorities of architects today.

As a building type, libraries offer many reasons and opportunities for making sunlighting a design priority:

☐ They are considered important public buildings, whether located in towns, cities, or universities. They are symbols of community status and repositories of knowledge.

☐ Because of their importance, libraries are usually well sited relative to open space and to other buildings, with adequate solar exposure for side- or toplighting.

☐ Libraries tend to be open and used primarily during daytime hours. Natural lighting can therefore be used during a significant percentage of their programmed operating hours.

☐ Funding is generally more scarce for operation than for construction. Costs cannot be passed on by raising prices or justified by increased productivity. Lower operating costs, civic pride, or sheer pleasure of use can often justify increased construction costs.

☐ Lighting requirements in libraries are not as stringent as those for schools and offices. There is less need for uniform illumination because of the patterns of use. Functions requiring the most light and view can be located accordingly—people are free to move about, so equal "comfort conditions" everywhere, at all times,

427

HI–1. The reading room in the old Boston Public Library (McKim, Mead and White, Architect). (Photograph courtesy of John Lam)

are unnecessary (particularly since libraries are rarely fully occupied). For all these reasons, limited areas of direct sunlight will create more enjoyment than problems as long as readers are free to seek or avoid them.

☐ Much of a typical library floor area is filled with stacks that need minimal light *levels* but good light *distribution* onto vertical surfaces. Stacks can benefit from the light of distant windows if placed perpendicular to them. In open reading rooms, bookcase walls parallel to distant windows will be well illuminated even when nearby tables need task lighting.

☐ Libraries have plenty of thermal mass to dampen fluctuations in solar load.

☐ High ceilings in reading rooms are expected, are accepted as normal, and need no justification.

☐ Balcony-lined open wells, good for distributing toplighting to more than one floor, can be used as pleasant locations for carrels, counters, and work tables as well as for circulation or stacks.

THE CLASSIC LIBRARIES

The grandeur and elegance of the sunlit, high-ceilinged spaces of the older libraries are worth emulating. However, the control of sunlight must reflect today's context. Similar to the old museums, old libraries that relied solely on daylighting for illumination are overglazed by today's standards, when supplemental artificial illumination is readily available. In former times, the human effort required to manipulate shades and blinds was taken for granted; today, we expect engineering rather than staff or user actions to "solve" these "problems."

The old reading rooms worked because the blinds, shades, or draperies were conscientiously opened and closed according to perceived needs for light and solar heat. Ventilation was accomplished through open windows, with no user expectation of perfect thermal comfort on the hottest days.

In the process of doing a study (with Harry Weese) to help preserve New York's Fifth Avenue library from being destroyed by unwarranted modernizing, I found many windows in the main reading room painted out and the draperies closed at a time when they should have been open. Apparently, the conscientious management required to open and close blinds was too difficult.

Similarly, the fifth-floor reading room at the Boston Atheneum is a beautiful room with the draperies open, but much less beautiful with all the draperies closed (as is often the case on summer days, to reduce the need for cooling). In this case, with individually occupied window work areas, occupants are likely to open the draperies when necessary.

HI–2. The new addition to the Boston Public Library (Philip Johnson, Architect). (Photograph courtesy of John Lam)

HI–3. The library at Boston University.

A CONTEMPORARY APPROACH

Recognition of today's conditions suggests that unshaded windows should be controlled automatically. Better yet, good sunlighting design should require minimum daily adjustments. The availability of efficient electric lighting and its provision for nighttime use and dark days, suggests that designing for sunny conditions is best even with the less stringent uniformity and glare criteria in libraries. As with other building types, it is better to have limited windows with glare controlled by architectural design, rather than oversized, unshaded windows permanently darkened by effectively inoperative interior shading devices or paint. Certainly, with the available sources of economical electric lighting and the high expectations of visual comfort, there is no excuse today for fiascos such as the Cambridge University History Faculty building (fig. 7–8) or Boston University's library (fig HI–3).

SOME GOOD EXAMPLES

Reasonably good sunlighting can probably be found in contemporary libraries far more often than in offices and schools but less often than in churches. As with churches, architects have been reluctant to abandon their judgment to the convenience of accepting engineers' numbers or to do merely what is easiest and cheapest because that is all the market demands.

Certain programmatic demands may also have been responsible for the relatively good fenestration design found in many contemporary libraries. The need for bookshelves probably accounts for the common use of clerestory windows above door-height, shelving-lined exterior walls. One does not expect to find libraries designed as glass boxes (such as that at Cambridge University, (fig. 7–8).

Architects have had some good contemporary library models to emulate, such as the wonderful libraries of Alvar Aalto. In both the Mt. Angel and the Seinäjoki libraries (figs. HI–4, HI–5) the combination of restricted perimeter windows and well-baffled toplighting helps these buildings achieve the necessary quantities of glare-free light in a manner that enlivens the architecture.

HI–4. Alvar Aalto's Mt. Angel library, Oregon.

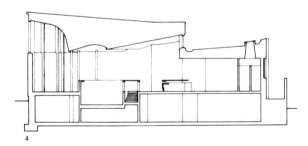

HI–5. Aalto's Seinäjoki library, Finland. South- and north-facing clerestories provide light with minimal glare from direct sunlight.

The Eaglebrook School Library in Deerfield, Massachusetts, completed in 1966 (designed by Sarah Harkness, The Architects Collaborative), has well-shaded clerestory windows above perimeter bookcases. A white soffit and an upward-sloping ceiling distribute ground-reflected sunlight evenly and efficiently. In the main reading room at the center of the space, the light is supplemented by a small area of clear skylight that provides skylight and reflected sunlight from the chamfered walls of the skylight wells, with little effect on cooling and little glare (fig. HI–6).

The Clayton Library in St. Louis, Missouri, completed in 1975 (Pearce Corporation, architects), is also illuminated by shaded clerestory windows. In this case, they separate a pyramidal roof (and white ceiling) from surrounding flat roofs (fig. HI–7).

In both Eaglebrook and Clayton the quality of natural lighting is excellent but could have been much more efficient and even more delightful if energy conservation had been given a higher priority (as it probably would have been today). A more recent library by Pearce is presented in case study H1.

Conscious attempts to optimize the use of sunlight for lighting and passive solar contributions include the recently completed town library at Mt. Airy, North Carolina, designed by Mazria Schiff, architects (fig. HI–8). With fenestration oriented mostly to the south, its energy use is a fraction of that of the neighboring municipal building, which has unshaded heat-absorbing glass concentrated on the east and west sides and is entirely dependent on artificial lighting. Lightshelves on the south facade, a small north clerestory, and sunscoops in wells or with baffles provide more than adequate quantities of glare-free illumination.

HI–6. Eaglebrook School library, Deerfield, MA (The Architect's Collaborative, Architect). The large chamfered well makes the small clear skylight (8′ × 8′) seem much larger than it is. The small projected area of direct sunlight is acceptable in a library, where readers are free to move.

HI–7. Clayton Public Library, Clayton, Montana (Pearce Corporation, Architect). The indirect metal halide chandelier blends with the clerestory sunlighting in illuminating the ceiling. Perimeter fluorescent lighting integrated with ducts provides supplementary lighting at night.

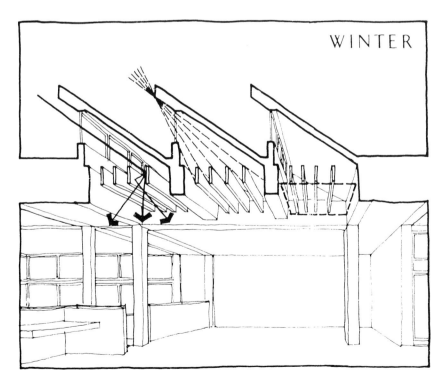

WINTER

HI–8. Mt. Airy library (Mazria/Schiff, Architect).

SUNLIGHTING

H1 University of Missouri Medical Library Columbia, Missouri

Latitude: 38.6°N; climate: 5,113 degree days

50,000 square feet @ $60/sq. ft.

Architect: Pearce Corporation (David Pearce, Partner in Charge; John Bird and Kent Turner, key staff)

Consultants: Siebold, Sydow & Elfenbaum—structural; William Tao & Associates, Inc.— mechanical and electrical; William Lam Associates— lighting and building systems; C. Rallo Construction Company— general contractor

Construction completed: 1985

CONTEXT

The Johnson Controls office/warehouse prototype (case study B4) achieved bilateral sunlighting for the single floor of offices by using a combination of a lightshelf on the south facade and a sunscoop on the north to reflect sunlight against the windowless north masonry wall separating the office from the warehouse. I recommended the same approach of reflecting sunlight from the south against a common wall to illuminate the north side of three floors of offices at the Naval Air Station, Jacksonville (fig. H1–1). In neither case was the alternative of conventional north-facing windows possible.

The Missouri Medical School library, on the other hand, was designed to get most of its light on the north side from largely blank sunlit north walls *in preference* to north-facing windows.

DESIGN OBJECTIVES AND PROCESS

The program called for the addition of 60,000 square feet of medical offices and laboratories and a 50,000-square-foot Health Sciences library to the north side of the existing School of Medicine. The budget was a moderate $60 per square foot (1984 dollars).

The most obvious and economical scheme might have been to locate the library within the existing entrance court and continue the medical offices around it. This would have been the most central location for the library. While such a concept, based on artificially illuminated windowless spaces, might have been considered by others, particularly a decade earlier, it was immediately rejected as inherently unpleasant.

The design team set out to optimize sunlighting both for energy conservation and to create a delightful working environment. Due in part to our previous work together (on the Clayton Public library), architect David Pearce had an interest in both natural lighting and articulation of integrated building systems.

With a very limited budget for consultation, I had to limit my input to the concept design phase, beginning with the schematic team design session. In this context, my judgment, based on previous experience, had

H1–1. The Naval Air Station, Jacksonville, Florida (James Rink of Kemp, Bunch, Jackson, Architect) was designed around a litrium that separates the north wall of the office building from the warehouse. (Courtesy of Pearce Corp.)

to suffice in lieu of quantified model testing. The resulting building was thus conceived almost in its entirety during this initial two-day session.

THE PLAN

Instead of filling the courtyard to achieve a spatially efficient, tightly packed complex, the additions were massed in the form of two separate parallel blocks that could best utilize sunlight with minimum sacrifice of outdoor orientation and light in the old building (figs. H1–2, H1–7). The location of the library at the northwest corner not only allowed more flexibility in its design, but also allowed it (with the School of Nursing) to frame and anchor a new and more inviting main entrance to the Medical School from the main campus to the north (fig. H1–3).

The four-story gallery connecting the library and new medical office block provides a grand entrance foyer from the parking area to the west as well as from the north.

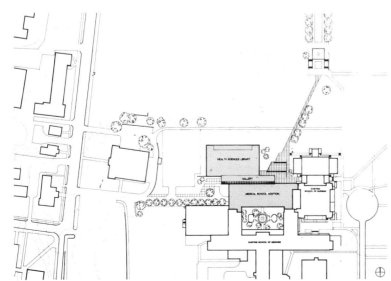

H1–2. Site plan. (Courtesy of Pearce Corp.)

H1–3. Main entrance from campus to the north, as built. (Courtesy of Pearce Corp.)

H1–4. Side entrance from the west with south window-wall of library to the left of the gallery/litrium, as built. (Courtesy of Pearce Corp.)

SUNLIGHTING CONCEPTS

The formation of the plan and the distinguishing forms of the structure designed were substantially derived from the sunlighting concepts. A favorable southern exposure for the elongated office/lab addition having been provided, the gallery was first conceived as a way to get reflected sunlight to the north facade as well as to provide a more pleasant connection to the library without excessive sacrifice of light to its south face (fig. H1–4).

The clerestoried barrel vault form of the gallery was derived from its role as a litrium, (i.e., its function of providing light to the adjacent offices

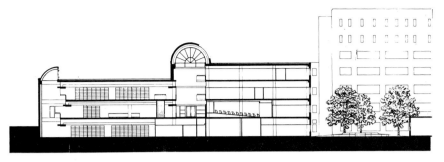

H1–5. Section showing south-facing clerestories of library (at left) and partially glazed barrel vault of gallery/litrium. (Courtesy of Pearce Corp.)

H1–6. Aperture shapes considered for gallery/litrium. (Courtesy of Pearce Corp.)

and library) (fig. H1–5). Without that purpose, the glazing area would have been reduced and sloped for reduced summer air-conditoning load. Initially designed as unshaded vertical glazing to reduce the amount of summer sunlight received (relative to that in winter) in order to minimize cooling loads, the effective slope was later changed to 60 degrees in response to the architect's desire for a barrel rather than a sawtooth shape, and to provide as much light in summer as in winter (fig. H1–6). The increased cooling cost resulting from the increased solar energy admitted was expected to be offset by savings in lighting. Such a trade-off is more acceptable in buffer spaces such as this one, with occupied spaces separated by windows and doors, than in gallery spaces that are open to adjacent spaces and fully air conditioned.

In hindsight, particularly after observation of the completed Carrier building (case study B2) in which we "oversacrificed" summer sunlight to reduce cooling load, this seems to have been the right decision.

Note that we did not glaze the entire vault but only the south-facing third. We did not need the quantity of light and the accompanying heat in summer that a totally glazed barrel vault would have provided.

Originally, the gallery was to have been longer so that the sheltered foyer would connect to the School of Nursing and provide reflected sunlight to more of the offices. It was cut back to reduce first costs and to offer a choice of either exterior or gallery views from the north office/labs (fig. H1–7).

In the office block, the attempt to optimize the utilization of reflected sunlight from the gallery and the sunlit south courtyard facade was abandoned early in the process as an economy measure and because of the difficulty in achieving consistently high ceilings with the difficult mix of small rooms, auditoria, and different major circulation paths at each level.

Instead, the decision was made to concentrate the construction funds and design time on the library and atrium spaces by using standard office practice for the office/labs. Sunlighting was used to the extent possible with lower (8') ceilings and interior blinds without the architectural-scale devices for sun and light control. Since the building came in well under budget, in retrospect we might have tried to accomplish more.

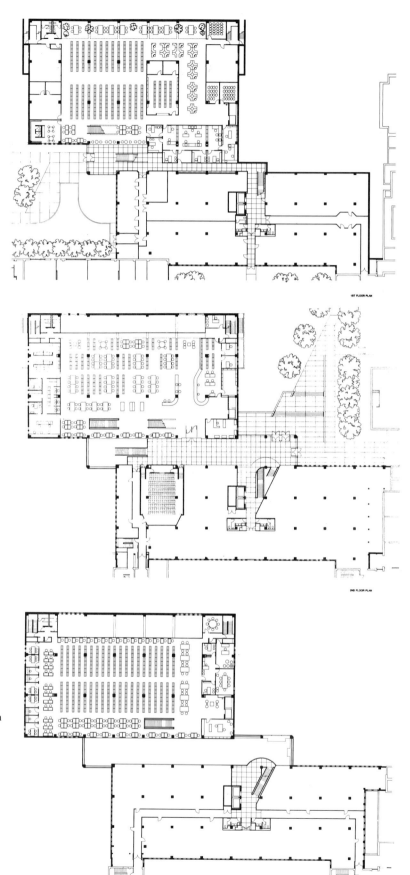

H1–7. Floor plans showing gallery-litrium separating library and faculty office-lab-auditorium block. (Courtesy of Pearce Corp.)

THE LIBRARY BLOCK

In the library block, we did achieve seasonally controlled entrance and redirection of sunlight along with high ceilings from integrated systems. Lightshelves control the sun on the south wall, both on that part exposed to the litrium and on the exterior.

Reading areas are spread throughout the floors, intermingled with stacks that are oriented north/south, perpendicular to the fenestration. Most reading areas are concentrated near the best natural light at the south wall and along the balconies facing the largely blank, but sunlit north wall. We felt that carrels along these edges of quiet, internal, open balconied spaces would be appreciated (due to the combination of spaciousness and sense of community) than those along windows to the exterior or the public gallery. Aalto's Mt. Angel Library in Oregon seemed a good model in this respect. On the other hand, we did not emulate Mt. Angel, which blocked exterior views with closed carrels along the windows.

On clear days, spaces adjacent to the internal north litrium will be illuminated by the sunlit north wall, similar to those facing north to the gallery. In this case, the vault section is a half barrel, and the band of clear glazing is vertical rather than sloped, because it encloses a fully conditioned rather than a buffer space. There is no need for glare control because of the relationship of the clerestory to the wall, thus allowing the clerestory to be unshaded. I learned from Johnson Controls not to reduce summer sunlighting levels to the point that electric lights must be used on sunny summer days. In this case, I wanted to capitalize on sunlight to save annual energy costs, reduce peak load penalties, and allow the occupants to enjoy sunlight in summer as well as in winter.

While on clear and partly cloudy days most of the light will come from the sunlit north wall, two large view windows are provided so that readers on all levels, including the lower level halfway below grade, will enjoy views of the landscape in addition to the sparkle of sunlit walls. On dark overcast days, however, when reflected light will be greatly diminished, the windows will be the dominant source of natural illumination for the nearby areas. At these times, supplementary electric illumination should blend with daylight in illuminating the north wall and the ceilings, which are otherwise illuminated by the interior lightshelves and light-colored floors and furnishings.

INTEGRATED BUILDING SYSTEM

The integrated building system used has similarities to those used in the BC/BS and Westinghouse buildings (case studies B1 and B5). Air distribution east and west (parallel to the atrium) is through interior light shelves (per Westinghouse); north/south air distribution is through drywall enclosures that extend the depth of shallow concrete beams and house the indirect fluorescent supplementary lighting (fig. H1–8). In this way, the full ceiling height between beams is available for light distribution and airy stack and reading spaces. In this manner, 92 percent of the floor-to-floor height is available for sunlighting.

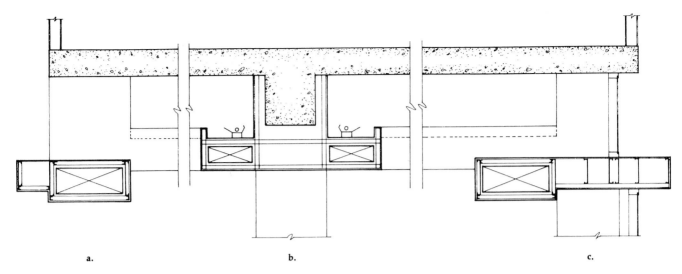

a.   b.   c.

H1–8. Detail sections showing integration of structure-HVAC-lighting-lightshelves in order to get maximum ceiling height at minimum cost: (a) north lightshelf-duct; (b) typical section through beam, duct, lightcove; (c) south lightshelf-duct.

On the east and west ends, ceilings were lowered to accommodate the largest ducts, pipes, etc. Less important and smaller rooms were located here, and minimum-size windows were provided on these exposures, where positive sun control is more difficult.

SUMMARY

The new library was occupied in October 1985 and was well received by staff and students. Sunlit north walls seem to be a good way to treat atria and internal balcony rooms with north exposure (fig. H1–9). The result can be brighter, livelier, more delightful luminous environments and more thermal comfort than with shaded interior walls seen in contrast to north-facing windows (fig. H1–10).

Although the structure built may be very economical, I would have preferred to minimize the number of beams that pass through the library litrium and interrupt views of the north wall from the lowest level. The balconies could have been supported independently of the north wall (perhaps cantilevered as at the TVA building, case study B7).

Daylight from the north litrium and south lightshelves blends with indirect fluorescent lighting on the high ceilings. The indirect fluorescent cove lighting is integrated with the structural and HVAC systems. At the south wall, the lightshelves provide good illumination and frame a pleasant view of the litrium/gallery and the exterior courtyard (fig. H1–11).

Because of the programmatic needs of this building, the relationship between HVAC and illumination was balanced to allow a greater than normal amount of summer sun and heat. In this instance, with a thermally isolated buffer litrium, the trade-off seems wise, making the Missouri Medical library a delightful sunlit building throughout the seasons (fig. H1–12).

H1–9. Library balconies face sunlit north wall of litrium.

H1–10. Carrel at bottom of north litrium with planter on top of duct-lightshelf enclosure.

H1–11. Study areas along south-wall duct-lightshelves receive direct and reflected sunlight from courtyard and gallery/litrium: (a) at third floor; (b) at first floor.

H1–12. Gallery/litrium admits direct sunlight to south side of lightshelves and light-colored walls, which reflect sunlight to north-facing windows of faculty offices and labs.

442 **Libraries**

APPENDIX A Self Education Exercises

#1: 24-HOUR LIGHTING LOG

Purpose

To increase your awareness of the various quantities and qualities of light encountered in a typical 24-hour period and your perception of those conditions.

Method

Each activity you do—walking, reading, making breakfast, shaving, looking for a book on a shelf, riding in an elevator, playing frisbee, watching television—takes place in a different luminous environment. To make detailed measurements of each would be unnecessarily tedious and time consuming for the purposes of this exercise. Instead, list each *activity* and the *space* in which it takes place and note with an ''X'' on the log graph the range of footcandles falling on a horizontal surface (maximum to minimum) at the more or less typical level, if you feel some other measurement is relevant (such as the vertical footcandles incident on a bookshelf). Put a dot at the measured value and indicate the type of measurement (horizontal, vertical, or maximum from any direction).

Next, evaluate the *quality* of the luminous environment by placing a check in the appropriate boxes—dim or bright, adequate or inadequate. Make enough measurements to fill in all the blank lines and try to test as varied a selection of environments as possible.

Afterthoughts

Was the correlation between the quantity of light and adequacy of light for a given task predictable? Why?

Did you encounter environments where low light levels seemed bright, or conversely, where high light levels appeared dim?

Any surprises?

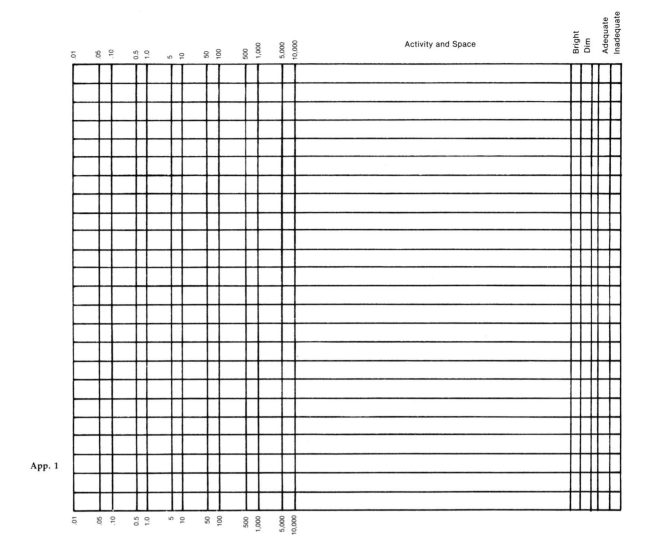

App. 1

#2: PERCEIVED BRIGHTNESS, DAYLIGHT LEVELS, AND USER NEEDS

Purpose

To assess the adequacy of daylight illumination for a task in a given room under different conditions. To understand how your *perception* of brightness relates to *quantity* of illumination.

Method

Draw a simple, schematic cross section through one daylit room with which you are familiar (¼" = 1'0" scale or ⅛" = 1'0" scale).

The section should be taken through the room such that it cuts through the centerline of the main window providing daylight. To one side of this section, draw two vertical scales extending from the floor level to the ceiling. One scale should be linear, ranging from 0 to 1,000 foot-candles. The second scale is exponential, ranging from 0 to 10,240 foot-candles. Make three copies of this drawing; label one "sunny clear sky," one "overcast sky," and one "nighttime."

Initially, without referring to a light meter, visually assess and record on a line underneath the appropriate cross section the location of the following conditions:

A. *Lighting adequate.* Ambient daylight level is sufficient for biological needs and for any normally expected task or activity. (Label "OK.")

B. *Task lighting needed.* Ambient daylight level is adequate for biological needs and casual tasks, but additional lighting is needed for some tasks or for local conditions, e.g., next to a partition. (Label "Task Required.")

C. *Ambient lighting needed.* Ambient daylight level is inadequate for either biological needs or tasks. (Label "Ambient Required.")

Still without using a light meter, estimate the relative light levels at several points across the room section, and plot.

Next, measure and record with a light meter the illumination on a horizontal surface directly at the plane of the window, 5' in from this point, at the center of the cross section, 5' from the interior wall, and at the plane of the interior wall. Plot this data both on the linear and exponential scales, using different types of dotted and dashed lines.

Your completed section should now have four types of information:

1. Line indicating the areas of lighting adequacy,

2. Estimate of lighting levels (linear scale),

3. Data on linear scale, and

4. Data graphed on the exponential scale.

Repeat this procedure for the other two lighting conditions.

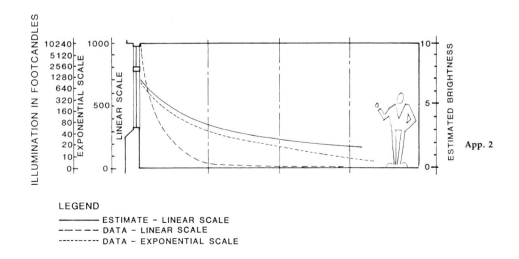

LEGEND
———————— ESTIMATE – LINEAR SCALE
– – – – – DATA – LINEAR SCALE
·········· DATA – EXPONENTIAL SCALE

Result

From your accumulated data, extrapolate findings and suggest illumination level criteria at which:

A. Lighting is totally adequate for normal office activities.

B. Task lighting only is needed.

C. Ambient lighting needs to be supplemented.

Submit

A section/graph of the room under sunny clear and fully overcast skies, and at night. (Use illumination scale similar to the example given.)

Conclusion

After comparing perceived values with illumination levels plotted on linear and exponential scales for three spaces on the blank forms above, decide which type of scale is best related to perceived brightness and thus most suitable for plotting illumination gradients in daylit rooms.

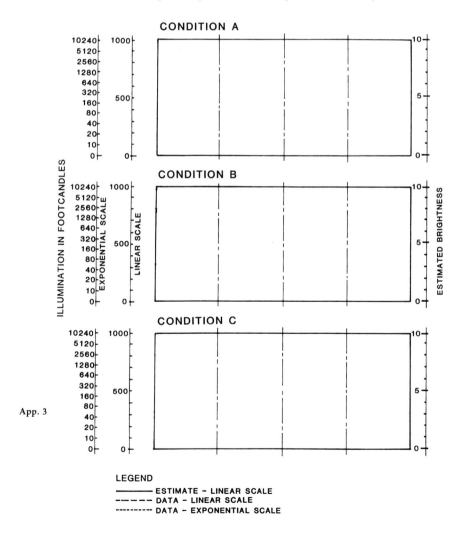

App. 3

APPENDIX B Data Normalization Procedures for Daylight Model Testing Program

To normalize *clear day* data, use the following equation:

$$A_2 = \frac{B_2 A_1}{B_1} \times MF \times T$$

Where:

A_2 = Projected illumination level (fc) in proposed building;

B_2 = Standard reference illumination (fc) normal to sun at project site (see table);

A_1 = Model illumination (fc) reading at test site;

B_1 = Reference illumination (fc) normal to sun at model test site;

MF = Glass maintenance factor for dirt, etc. (.85 suggested); and

T = Light transmission of clear glass (single pane = .85, double pane = .80).

To normalize *fully overcast* data, let B_2 = 2,000 fc.

App. 4

SOLAR ILLUMINATION ON A SURFACE PERPENDICULAR TO THE SUN'S RAYS
(lm/ft²)

Latitude	21 December			21 March/21 September			21 June		
	8 am/4 pm	10 am/2 pm	Noon	8 am/4 pm	10 am/2 pm	Noon	8 am/4 pm	10 am/2 pm	Noon
0°	7,720	9,440	9,810	8,010	9,670	10,000	7,720	9,440	9,810
30°	4,140	7,950	8,600	7,500	9,290	9,670	8,600	9,730	9,980
40°	1,450	6,680	7,600	7,010	8,940	9,360	8,670	9,660	9,910
50° (peak)	—	4,260	5,680	6,230	8,380	8,850	8,630	9,510	9,750
50° (average)	—	2,980	3,980	4,360	5,870	6,200	6,040	6,660	6,820
60° (peak)	—	600	1,990	5,130	7,500	8,010	8,480	9,260	9,480
60° (average)	—	420	1,390	3,590	5,250	5,610	5,940	6,480	6,640

* Source: Hopkinson, B.S., et al, Daylighting, Heinemann: London, 1966, Pg 35.

APPENDIX Ⓒ Programming—An Example

LIGHTING DESIGN FOR THE NATIONAL GALLERY OF CANADA

Criteria for the use of natural and artificial light in the museum fall into four broad categories:

1. Optimum display of the art.

2. Conservation of works susceptible to damage by visible and ultraviolet radiation.

3. Creation of a comfortable, attractive, and relevant visual environment for all users.

4. Economy of installation and use.

Daylighting Objectives

A. Display

    1. Daylighting should be designed to create the highest brightness on display walls, relative to other room surfaces.

    2. Daylighting should be able to provide the principal gallery illumination on all but darkest days, with relatively uniform illumination on all display walls. Light intensity on display walls should be allowed to vary within controlled limits in acknowledgment of daylight's changing intensity, color, and character.

    3. Daylight sources should not create unwanted visual competition with the objects of interest.

    4. Daylight sources should be so located as to minimize reflected glare from artworks.

    5. Daylighting should blend well with supplementary lighting.

    6. Daylighting should minimize frame shadows.

B. Conservation of works of art

1. It should be possible to control strictly the intensity and duration of natural light, because of its particular potential for damaging susceptible art materials.

2. Daylight controls should: a) have variable limits so that maximums or minimums appropriate to the works on display can be selected; b) make it possible to exclude daylight entirely when the museum is closed to the public or when its presence is not desired; c) be of simple construction and operation and be visible, so that malfunctions or inappropriate settings will be immediately evident to the staff; d) make it possible to filter or reflect out as much of the ultraviolet wavelengths as feasible.

C. Visual environment

1. Daylight should be introduced in a logical, understandable manner that will be comprehensible to the visitor. It should provide orientation clues to the weather, the time of day, and direction. Satisfaction of these basic human needs, fundamental in us all, is especially important in the often unfamiliar, closed spaces of an art museum.

2. An awareness of daylight and a view of sunlight's sparkle should be provided whenever this is possible without conflicting with conservation and display criteria.

3. The design should minimize visual noise that distracts from or competes with the purposes of the facility. Such visual noise might come from glaring windows or light-control materials (such as translucent plastic) that are in the field of view or from views of busy patterns of louvers or complicated skylight construction.

4. A sense of gloom results when contact with daylight is unnecessarily obstructed, from objects of interest being underlit relative to their surroundings, and from large glass areas prominently in view which are dim or unlit. These should be avoided.

D. Economy

1. Maximize the efficiency of light collection and transmission to the useful zones. This will minimize the area of glazing required, with attendant savings in installation, maintenance, and operating costs.

2. Controls should be simple to operate and have few moving parts. Protection from the weather is desirable.

Artificial Lighting Objectives

A. Display

1. The artificial lighting system should enable the display designer to create an appropriate visual focus on selected objects of interest by highlighting them above the level of ambient daylighting illumination.

2. It should allow flexibility of location and fixture aiming direction so that all areas of the gallery space can be used for display.

3. Reflected glare, visual competition with the objects of interest, and frame shadows should be minimized.

B. Conservation of works of art

1. The control system should allow selection of appropriate illumination intensity through use of dimmer controls and a variety of lamp types.

2. Fixtures should be selected that will accept accessories such as heat and UV filters for critical display situations.

C. Visual environment

1. Fixtures should be located so that visual clutter of the gallery space is minimized.

2. Fixtures should be located so that awareness of the lamps and their attendant glare is minimized.

3. The design should provide multiple circuits and switching flexibility for choice of operating modes.

D. Economy

1. A range of operating modes appropriate to the gallery use periods should be provided. These might include: normal daytime display lighting; nighttime display lighting; lighting appropriate to off-hours, work, or cleaning needs; all-night security lighting.

2. Easy access for adjustments and relamping should be provided.

APPENDIX Ⓓ Polar Sundial

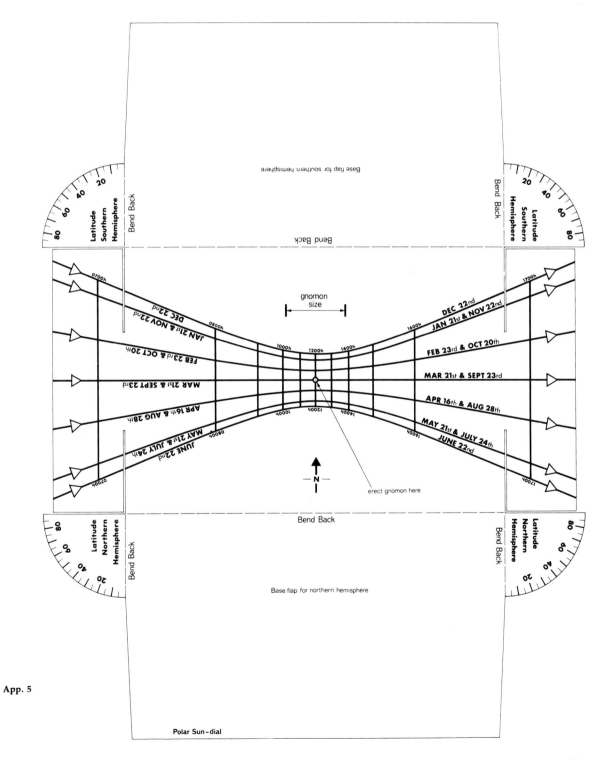

App. 5

Polar Sun-dial

451

BIBLIOGRAPHY

Allen, W. "Daylight and Town Planning." In *Proceedings of the Illuminating Engineering Society Convention.* New York: Illuminating Engineering Society of North America, 1946.

——, and Crompton, D. "A Form of Building Development in Terms of Daylighting." Journal of the Royal Institute of British Architects, August 1947.

Atkinson, William. *Orientation of Buildings or Planning for Sunlight.* New York: John Wiley & Sons, 1912.

Berry, Harry W., and Darlington, Robert P. *Daylighting for Schools in the State of Washington.* State College of Washington, 1955.

Butti, Ken, and Perlin, John. *A Golden Thread.* New York: Van Nostrand Reinhold, 1979.

Danz, Ernest. *Sun Protection.* New York: Frederick Praeger, 1967.

Department of the Environment, Welsh Office. *Sunlight and Daylight.* London; Her Majesty's Stationery Office, 1971.

Dietz, Albert, Lam, William, and Hallenback, Roger. *An Approach to the Design of the Luminous Environment.* State University Construction Fund of New York, 1976.

Duffie, John A., and Beckman, William A. *Solar Energy Thermal Processes.* New York: John Wiley & Sons, 1979.

Evans, Benjamin H. *Daylight in Architecture.* New York: McGraw-Hill, 1981.

Haas, Eileen, ed. *Natural Lighting: How to Use Daylight.* Harrisville: Solarvision Publications, 1982.

Harkness, Edward L., and Mehta, Madan L. *Solar Radiation Control in Buildings.* London: Applied Science Publishers, Ltd., 1978.

Hastings, Robert S., and Crenshaw, Richard W. *Window Design Strategies to Conserve Energy.* N.B.S. Building Science Series 104. U.S. Department of Commerce-National Bureau of Standards, June 1977.

Heydecker, Wayne D., and Goodrich, Ernest P. *Sunlight and Daylight for Urban Areas—Neighborhood and Community Planning.* Regional Plan of New York and its Environs, 1929.

Hopkinson, R. G., Petherbridge, P., and Longmore, J. *Daylighting.* London: William Heinemann Ltd., 1966.

Hopkinson, R. G., ed. "Sunlight in Buildings." In *Proceedings of the C.I.E. Intersessional Conference,* April, 1965.

Johnson, Timothy E. *Solar Architecture—The Direct Gain Approach.* New York: McGraw-Hill, 1981.

Knowles, Ralph L. *Sun Rhythm Form*. Cambridge: The MIT Press, 1981.

Kusada, Tamani, and Collins, Belinda L. *Simplified Analysis of Thermal Lighting Characteristics of Windows: Two Case Studies*. N.B.S. Building Science Series 109, February 1978.

—— and Ishii. "Hourly Solar Radiation Data for Vertical and Horizontal Surfaces on Average Days in the United States and Canada." Center for Building Technology, National Bureau of Standards, 1977.

Lam, William M. C. *Perception and Lighting as Formgivers for Architecture*. New York: McGraw-Hill, 1977.

Marcus, Thomas A. *Daylight with Insulation*. England: Baynard Press, 1960.

Meninel, Aden B., and Meninel, Marjorie P. *Applied Solar Energy—An Introduction*. Reading: Addison-Wesley Publishing Co., 1976.

Olgyay, V., and Olgyay, A. *Solar Control and Shading Devices*. Princeton: Princeton University Press, 1963.

Paul, High. *Daylight in School Classrooms:* Owens-Illinois Glass Company, 1947.

Pilkington Environmental Advisory Service. *Windows and Environment*. Newton-le-Willows: McCorquodale & Co., Ltd., 1969.

R.I.B.A. Joint Committee on the Orientation of Buildings. *The Orientation of Buildings*. London: Royal Institute of British Architects, 1933.

Rosen, James E. "Natural Daylighting and Energy Conservation: Innovative Solutions for Office Buildings." Master of Architecture Thesis, M.I.T., 1981.

Ruegg, Rosalie T., and Chapman, Robert E. *Economic Evaluation of Windows in Buildings: Methodology*. N.B.S. Building Science Series 119. U.S. Department of Commerce-National Bureau of Standards, April 1979.

S.E.R.I. Solar Conservation Study. *A New Prosperity—Building a Sustainable Energy Future*. Andover: Brick House Publishing Co., 1981.

Swarbrick, John. *Daylight: Its Nature, Therapeutic Properties, Measurement and Legal Protection*. London: Wykeham Press, 1953.

Tse, Brian. "A Study of Natural Light for Museums: The Addition to the Fogg Art Museum in Cambridge, Massachusetts." Master of Architecture Thesis, M.I.T., 1977.

Vonier, Thomas, ed. *Proceedings, International Daylighting Conference*. Washington, D.C.: American Institute of Architects Service Corporation, 1983.

Walsh, John W.T. *The Science of Daylight*. London: Pitman Publishing Corporation, 1961.

Watson, Donald, ed. *Energy Conservation Through Building Design*. New York: McGraw-Hill, 1979.

INDEX

Museum design, 148, 189, 205-7, 328, 329-42, 344, 448-50
  artwork, preservation of, 331-32, 334-35, 449-50
  Beaumont Art Museum, 358-65
  display lighting in, 335, 448-49, 450
  Guggenheim Museum, 20, 21, 338
  Knight Gallery, 363-65
  National Gallery of Canada, 343-52
  Shenzhen Museum, 373-79
  Tarble Arts Center, 143, 203, 205, 353-57

Narrow building blocks, 73
National Gallery East Wing (Washington, DC), 328, 329
National Gallery of Canada (Ottawa) design, 206-8, 337, 338, 343-52, 448-50
National Pensions Institute (Helsinki), 115
Naval Air Station (Jacksonville, FL), 434, 435
New Mexico, 61
New York, 20, 21, 111-13, 201, 207, 231, 239, 332, 336, 338, 367
New York State Education building (Albany), 169
Niemeyer, Oscar, 110
Nineteenth-century toplit galleries, 331-33, 335-37, 380, 382
Nondirectional sources, 30-31
North Carolina
  Consolidated Diesel Engine Plant, 386-94
  Knight Gallery, 363-65
  Mt. Airy Library, 147, 199, 432, 433
Northeast Solar Energy Center, 316
Northern hemisphere, 49-50, 55

Occulus lanterns, 404-7
Office buildings, xi, xii, 138-39, 183, 221-55, 409-10
  Blue Cross/Blue Shield of Connecticut, 223-28
  Denver Technological Center Prototype building, 276-79
  Johnson Controls, Inc., 258-68
  Melvin C. Holm Center, 231-38
  Tennessee Valley Authority Chattanooga Office Complex, 280-301
  Westinghouse Steam Turbine-Generator Division, 269-74
Office landscaping, 76, 299
Operable glazing, 168
Operable shading devices, 71, 200, 201
  louvers, 109-10, 111-13
Operating costs, 3, 5-7, 8, 427
Ordinances, 282

Oregon
  Mt. Angel Library, 205, 431, 439
  Portland Museum of Art, 148, 344
  Reed College Library, 116
Orientation, 58-59, 62-63, 65-67, 164, 220, 309, 435
Overbite window aperture, 80
Overcast climates, xiv, 73, 80
Overcast conditions, 13-14, 16, 40, 48, 76, 77, 79, 134, 136, 141, 348, 384
Overexposure to light, 25-26
Overglazing, 142, 155, 331-32, 335-36, 341, 367
Overhangs, 87-94, 147, 167
Overseas Chinese Bank building (Singapore), 107
Owens-Corning Energy Conservation Award, 254

Paired beams, 176-77, 271, 273
Pan joists, 175
Pantheon (Rome), 139
Park West (Dallas, TX), 163
Partitioning, 122-23, 235-36
Pavilion Intercontinental Hotel (Singapore), 88, 163, 415
Payback periods, 184, 277-79
Peak electrical demand periods, 7, 184-85, 221
Pedestrian circulation, 61-63, 207, 219, 247
Pei, I. M., 107, 148, 205, 328, 329, 330, 344
Penetration of light, 79, 123
Perception, 12-16, 22
Perception and Lighting as Formgivers for Architecture, 360
Petro Brazil Headquarters (Rio de Janeiro), 110
Photaria, 23-24
Photoelectric controls, 92, 183-85, 237, 248
Photographing models, 191-92, 272, 347, 349, 351, 355, 361, 382, 383
Piped sunlight, 36
Plans, 241, 270, 354, 355
Planters as shading devices, 88
Plants, 26, 162, 163, 168
Plazas, 66
Pods, 247
Point sources, 29-30
Pompidou Museum (Paris), 337
Portland Museum of Art, 148, 344
Portman, John, 36, 88, 116, 411, 412, 415, 421-26
Post-occupancy evaluation, 196-97, 322-23
Prado (Madrid), 333, 334
Precast concrete, 100, 180-81, 277, 278

Smoke control, 391, 392
Snow, 82
Soddy Daisy High School (Tennessee), 166, 305–15
Solar access, 59–67, 188
Solar altitude, 45–46, 48, 50–51, 84, 85, 87–90
Solar angle, 42, 58, 67–68, 69, 115–18, 188, 286
Solar courts, 66, 281
Solar energy, 27, 260, 399
Solar heat gain, 71, 98–99, 147, 201, 240
Solar envelope concept, 62, 81, 276
Solar path diagrams, 84–85
Solar Pathfinder, 188
Solaria, 23–24
Solex glass, 246
Sound absorption, 204, 391
Sources of light, 29–31, 40–55
Southern hemisphere, 55
Soviet Union, 23–24
Spain, 330, 334
Spandrel panels, 277
Spanish grid, 62
Spanish missions, 395
Sparkle, 13–14
Spectral characteristics of light, 50–51, 334
Specular reflection, 31–32, 36, 86, 99, 115
Speed of light, 28–29
Spread reflection, 32, 34
Squatters concept, 186, 283
Stained glass, xiv, 73, 119
Standard Charter Bank (Zurich), 110
State Trade School (Zurich), 104
Steel structural systems, 177, 180, 223
St. Elizabeth's College Primary School, 108
Street orientation, 61–62, 65
Structural system integration, 174–75, 270. *See also* Building system integration
Structure as shading, 172, 204
Subpolar climate, 286
Summer shading, 233
Suncatchers, 108, 155, 156, 167, 225, 383
    baffles, 91, 148–52, 240, 271–72, 309–10, 325–26
    trellises, 165, 240, 256–57, 326
Sunlight, 22, 27, 40–41, 43, 53–55
Sunlighting, ix, 3–8, 40–55
    diagrams, 347, 424–25
    module, 344
    tools, 187–96
Sunlit walls, 391, 394
Sunny climates, xv, 73–74

Sunny conditions, 136
Sunscoops
    design of, 68–70, 167, 180
    performance of, 265, 267, 268, 355, 394
    with suncatchers, 149, 367
Sunshine recorders, 51
Suomalainen, Tuomo and Timo, 395–96, 397
Supplementary dynamic shading, 119–23
Supplementary lighting, 181–84, 203, 205, 226, 237, 247–48, 299, 342, 433. *See also* Artificial lighting
Surface reflectance, 5, 31–34, 43–44, 48–50, 76, 77, 86, 99, 126, 143, 393
Switching and dimming systems, 184
Switzerland, 104, 110
Synergetics, Inc., 108

TVA Chattanooga Office complex, 280–301
TVA Solar Technology Outreach Program, 313–15
TWA Terminal of Kennedy Airport, 20
Tallahassee District Court of Appeals, 270
Tarble Arts Center, Eastern Illinois University (Charleston), 147, 203, 205, 353–57
Tartan grid, 350
Task lighting, 12, 182, 240
Tate Gallery (London), 333, 334, 341, 367
Team blocks in industrial buildings, 390–92
Team design process, 186–87, 305
Temperate climates, 98, 142, 144, 146
Temppeliaukio Church (Helsinki), 395–96, 397, 399
Tennessee, 280–301, 305–15
Terrestrial sunlight, 44
Test conditions, 190–94
Texas, 140, 163, 200, 340, 344, 358–62
Textural scale, 201
Thermal breaks, 102, 103, 278
Thermal comfort, 27, 71–72, 245
Thermal mass, 88
Thermal shutters, 399–401
Time, orientation to, 20–25, 338, 385
Tinted glazings, 15, 36
Toplighting, 66, 68–70, 138–49, 152–56, 206
    building system integration for, 174–75
    of galleries, 207, 331–33, 375, 382–84
    geometry of, 140–44
    historical precedents for, 139–40
    in industrial buildings, 386–94
    of shared central spaces, 157–69
    structural systems for, 179–81